ADVANCES IN FAMILY INTERVENTION, ASSESSMENT AND THEORY

Volume 1 • 1980

ADVANCES IN FAMILY INTERVENTION, ASSESSMENT AND THEORY

A Research Annual

Editor: JOHN P. VINCENT
Department of Psychology
University of Houston

VOLUME 1 • 1980

JAI PRESS INC.
Greenwich, Connecticut

165 West Putnam Avenue
Greenwich, Connecticut 06830

ISBN: 0-89232-137-7

Manufactured in the United States of America

CONTENTS

PREFACE

In the past decade, we have witnessed a proliferation of clinical research in an area of marriage and family. Even though the family has always represented an intuitively appealing focus of study, largely because it provided a natural context in which to study social phenomena of many varieties, the bulk of research has reflected a low level of methodological and conceptual sophistication. Recently, however, we have seen the emergence of a new breed of clinical-family researcher—a breed that has fostered rapid acceleration in the development of new theoretical models and innovative approaches to assessment and intervention. While family researchers perhaps have always been enamored with the intricacies of family life, this new breed is unified on other grounds as well—a commitment to empiricism in theory and clinical development. The intention of this series is to provide an arena for these clinical-family researchers to share their work.

The impetus for the series was provided by Robert L. Sprague. Bob approached me with the idea of an annual compilation of research in an area for which there was no clear publication outlet. After some deliberation, we settled on the title, *Advances in Family Intervention, Assessment, and Theory*. I then approached some clinical researchers I consider to be leaders in this area and was gratified when they agreed to contribute their work to the first volume. The chapters reflect a mix of empirical studies on family intervention and assessment, as well as theory-directed papers which are intended to serve as catalysts for further empirical research and clinical innovation.

In Volume I, I have tried to sample work that spans two major populations: married couples where the focus is dissatisfaction within their relationships, and families, where the focus is usually on some problem exhibited by a child. While such a distinction is admittedly arbitrary, it reflects the way the field has evolved, and mirrors to some extent the two most common ways that troubled families present themselves for help.

Some ideological bias may exist in this first volume. In most instances, the contributions are loosely tied to a social learning or behavioral systems framework. This choice was a conscious one, at least for this first volume, and reflects, in part, my own theoretical preferences. As will be seen upon reading the chapters, however, this apparent ideological emphasis vanishes quickly, since most of the authors who align themselves with the social learning position have presented work which addresses why behavioral approaches do not work and what can be done to remedy the situation. Their novel suggestions for change reflect strong pressure from within the field to expand theoretical and technical boundaries. There is no smug complacency among this group. The intent of this series, however, is not to restrict the contents to any particular theoretical persuasion. The overriding goal is to provide a vehicle through which the best family clinical researchers can present their work and grapple with the complicated issues involved in conceptualizing, assessing, and intervening with problem families.

My own Chapter one involves a detailed discussion of the social learning theory perspective on families. I attempt to trace the historical development of the approach along with what I believe are its distinguishing features. Through a discussion of "coercion" in families and "reciprocity" in couples, the major thrust of the chapter involves illustrations of how theory development, empirical research, and clinical application have worked hand-in-hand in shaping, modifying, and embellishing the approach. As a point of departure, social learning theory provides an excellent model for how clinically relevant family research derived from other theoretical models can, and perhaps should, evolve.

Chapter two by Robert G. Wahler deals with the identification of family characteristics that are associated with treatment failures. He presents some recent work on two interrelated concepts: social insularity and multiple entrapment, both of which seem to be associated with troubled families for whom standard treatments do not work. Wahler's beginning attempts to incorporate these variables into a family intervention program provide a good example of the technical and conceptual ingenuity of Wahler's work with the families of oppositional children.

Chapter three by James F. Alexander and Cole Barton describes a series of studies involved in the development of an intervention program for families with delinquent children. The sequence of steps in program development illustrates well how clinical research questions are sharpened. Initial broad-based questions about whether "it works" are followed by more pointed concerns in determining treatment factors which will help with a subset of "hard core" families who respond poorly to standard behavior training programs. This line of inquiry led Alexander and his associates at the University of Utah to (a) incorporate nonbehavioral therapeutic strategies in their program, and (b) identify those therapist characteristics which augment the effectiveness of their particular family intervention program. In a final section, Alexander and Cole wrestle with a knotty methodological-statistical issue—the nonindependence of behavior among family members. They propose a nested-interactant analysis of variance model to deal with the statistical dependence problems in clinical-family research, and they suggest that these phenomena may rest squarely in the middle of the very processes which we are trying to understand.

Chapter four by Edwin P. Willems and Dennis Stuart represents a first attempt to apply some of the concepts from behavioral ecology to study of the family. Willems and his associates at the Texas Institute for Rehabilitation and Research have pioneered behavioral-ecological applications to understanding the recovery process of patients with spinal cord injuries. Since behavioral ecology is a variant of systems theory, its application in helping to understand the man-environmental dynamics in family systems seems natural. Through this paper, Willems and Stuart hope to stimulate both thought and research in new ways to study the troubled family.

Chapter five by David H. Olson, Candyce S. Russell, and Douglas H. Sprenkle reviews the clinical and empirical support for a circumplex model of marital and family systems. Olson and his colleagues at the University of Minnesota have formulated a typology of family systems along two fundamental dimensions: cohesion and adaptability. Their chapter attempts to order the array of family research in this two-dimensional circumplex model. Since most family research has proceeded in a haphazard fashion, this contribution serves the very important function of integrating a variety of theoretical concepts which have been generated to explain family pathology. Olson, Russell, and Sprenkle illustrate how the circumplex model can be used to assess various kinds of marital and family problems, as well as to help the clinician articulate goals for intervention.

Chapter six by Gwendolyn Mettetal and John M. Gottman addresses two of the major concepts in the marital therapy literature: reciprocity and dominance. After reviewing the origins of these constructs from social and clinical psychology, Mettetal and Gottman describe a series of studies conducted by Gottman's group at the University of Illinois. The authors trace the development and validation of a comprehensive observational assessment system for describing both the verbal and nonverbal behavior of married couples. They then present their findings based on sequential and time series analysis techniques directed toward hypothesized patterns of reciprocity and dominance among distressed and nondistressed couples.

Chapter seven by Robert L. Weiss is an attempt to integrate two prevailing approaches to marital therapy: the strategic and behavioral. Weiss, a well known proponent of the behavioral approach, reviews several arguments about why the straightforward behavioral approach is not successful with certain types of couples and suggests how both the mindset and technical prowess of strategic therapists may be helpful with these couples. Weiss appeals to some of the recent work of Bandura to suggest a competency-based model which integrates both the strategic and behavioral approach. Using this strategic-behavioral model, Weiss reviews some of the empirical research which supports this position, and suggests how the model can be applied in assessment and intervention.

Preparation of a volume like this on family clinical research is by no means a one-man show. I am grateful to Robert L. Sprague for first suggesting the idea and supporting my efforts over the many months of preparation. I also wish to express my appreciation to David Crossley and Joanne Harrison, who helped with editing early drafts of each chapter. Finally, and most importantly, I wish to express my deep gratitude and affection to Robert L. Weiss. In many ways, my own commitment to a truly integrated clinical-research enterprise was shaped by him. When under his direction, the clinical training program at the University of Oregon epitomized this perspective. As a mentor and friend, Bob has provided an invaluable model of a truly committed, doggedly persistent scientist and clinician. He has set an impressive standard of professional excellence which I hope will help shape the destiny of our clinical-research efforts to better understand the family.

John P. Vincent

THE EMPIRICAL-CLINICAL STUDY OF FAMILIES:

SOCIAL LEARNING THEORY AS A POINT OF DEPARTURE

John P. Vincent, UNIVERSITY OF HOUSTON

This chapter is an attempt to set a stage. In the first volume of a new series, it is the editor's prerogative to share some of the premises and biases that have shaped the selection of contents for this volume and which will help to guide the direction of future volumes. After all, what *is* "empirical" study of the family, and what kinds of work are worthy of being considered "empirical?" To help answer that question, I have chosen to discuss the social learning approach to clinical-family research. Social Learning Theory (SLT) is not the only empirical approach to families, but it does represent an excellent model of how clinically-relevant family research can be conducted. In this context, the social

Advances in Family Intervention, Assessment and Theory, Volume 1, pages 1–28.

ISBN: 0-89232-137-7

learning perspective can be viewed as a point of departure, in large measure because aspects of the approach fall short of being an ideal model, but also because attempts to deal with the shortcomings of the paradigm illustrate the iterative process of clinical-empirical-theoretical evolution in action. It is precisely this self-corrective feature of empirical-clinical psychology that helps guarantee that conceptual complacency—having the "right answer"—will not replace the creativity involved in discovering "better answers." Evolution of the social learning perspective also illustrates nicely, in Kuhnian terms (1962), the process by which, over time, advocates of a particular theoretical persuasion embrace ideas from other perspectives so that "pure strains" become "hybrids." Some insist that this process is tantamount to theoretical promiscuity, but we must remember that, depending on the quality of the parent strains, and the care of the breeder, "hybrids" frequently are stronger stock.

I. BACKGROUND

It would be impossible to trace the development of social learning theory without acknowledging contributions from social psychology (Thibaut and Kelley, 1959), psychiatry (Sullivan, 1965), and experimental psychology (Skinner, 1957). Nevertheless, social learning theory probably emerged as a somewhat distinct theoretical entity through the work of Bandura and his associates (e.g., Bandura and Walters, 1963). At that time, distinctions between operant conditioning (Skinner, 1963), behavior modification (Ullmann and Krasner, 1965), and behavior therapy (Wolpe, 1958) were admittedly blurry, although some differences did exist, even in the early sixties. Social learning theory meant, quite literally, "learning from others"; it encompassed processes that were frequently described as "modeling" or "vicarious learning." The focus of this approach was on basic phenomena within the normal range of human experience. Thus, most research efforts focused on theory-directed experiments grouped around such topics and social development in children (Bandura, 1969a), human aggression (Bandura, Ross, and Ross, 1963), and moral development (Bandura, 1969b). Children were prominent research subjects, and cartoon characters, bobo dolls, marbles, and M & M's were typically used as experimental apparati.

Social learning theory went "clinical" when Patterson and his associates began to look at children who evidenced problematic courses of development (Patterson and Brodsky, 1966) or who exhibited clinically elevated levels of activity (Patterson, 1965). Because problem children frequently originate in social environments (families) in which the learning contingencies may have somehow gone awry, social learning theory very quickly became focused on family theory and family therapy. Once a problem focus had been defined, the momentum of development grew exponentially. Briefly, social learning theorists launched a multifrontal assault on family pathology involving development of naturalistic and behavioral approaches to assessment (Jones, Reid, and Patterson, 1975), embellishment and refinement of theoretical and conceptual bases (Patterson and Reid, 1970), expanded inquiry into other aspects of family functionings such as marital discord (Stuart, 1969; Weiss, Hops, and Patterson, 1973), experimental theory-directed research (Patterson, 1974), development and validation of family intervention procedures (Patterson, 1974c), and theoretical inquiry into mechanisms of change in social systems such as maintenance of effects and generalization of nontreated phenomena (Johnson, Bolstad, and Lobitz, 1974). A relatively organized body of theoretical concepts, research findings, assessment devices, and intervention procedures have established the social learning approach as an important contender for the title of, if not the best example of, a clinical research perspective on the family.

II. ESSENTIAL FEATURES OF SOCIAL LEARNING THEORIES

Theoretical Eclecticism

Social learning theory is not a unified, original statement of propositions; instead, the "theory" is an assemblage of several models, the most prominent of which are operant learning (Skinner, 1963), and social exchange theories (Thibaut and Kelley, 1959), with recent smatterings of "general systems" theory (Alexander and Barton, 1976) and attribution theory (Margolin and Weiss, 1978). Operant concepts have been applied as descriptive metaphors to aid in understanding the behavior-altering properties of social contingencies (Patterson and Reid, 1970), antecedent (setting) control over behavior (Patterson, 1974a; 1974b; Jacobson, 1978a), and the interplay of antecedents and consequences in shaping the learning curve of both maladaptive and normal behaviors. Social exchange theory provided a quasi-economic language to help describe the regularities in interactional sequences—such as reciprocity and coercion—in which the affective valence of behavior (positive or aversive) is the coin of the realm (Weiss, Hops, and Patterson, 1973; Patterson and Reid, 1970). The contribution of general systems theory has been to supplement microbehavioral analyses of family interaction with somewhat more abstract theoretical constructs (Alexander et al., 1976). Particularly when one works clinically with families, focus on the small detail of family interaction may obscure certain system-like processes, such as an alcoholic wife's providing ample opportunity for her insecure husband to gratify his "needs" for rescue and nurturance. The incorporation of attribution theory has helped social learning theorists to understand how the personal interpretation that family members place on each other's behavior alters the reinforcing or punishing effect of that behavior (Gottman et al., 1976).

Systems Focus

Like most behavioral theories, social learning approaches assume that persons and settings are inextricably bound together to form social environmental systems. In this context, the term "system" means simply that the whole, in this case the social environment, is not equal to the sum of its parts, persons, and settings. Rather, it means that elements of social environmental systems interact reciprocally, each simultaneously exerting influence on and reacting to the influences of every other element. A child's tantrum occasions a reprimand from its mother, which in turn increases the intensity and resilience of the tantrum behavior. A husband's affectionate whisper in his wife's ear results in a passionate kiss from her, which elicits from him an invitation for sex. Each member of a family system both affects and is affected by every other member.

States Versus Traits

Following Mischel (1968), social learning theory assumes that variance in behavior is more dependent upon properties of the setting (states) than on dispositional consistencies in personality (traits). This assumption has led to some interesting questions. Do problem children exhibit inappropriate behaviors in both home and school settings? Some children do (Patterson, 1975), but many do not (Wahler, 1973). Does treatment of problem behaviors in one setting (home versus school) generalize to nontreated settings? Some behavioral improvements appear to generalize (Walker, Hops, and Johnson, 1975), but most treatment gains are place-dependent, unless explicit attempts are made to program generalization (Johnson, Bolstad, and Lobitz, 1974). The complexity of such behavior-setting relationships is further underscored by findings that positive changes in treatment settings are sometimes accompanied by negative changes in nontreatment settings (Johnson, Bolstad, and Lobitz, 1974; Wahler, 1974). Do discorded interactions between married partners represent consistencies in behavioral style that each partner carries from relationship to relationship? Apparently not, at least when comparisons between spouses' interactions with their partners versus those with strangers yield different behavior profiles (Vincent, Weiss, and Birchler, 1975; Birchler, Weiss, and Vincent, 1975).

Naturalistic Emphasis

Social learning theorists study family behavior in real-life settings. In many ways, this bias has led to research that is perhaps more descriptive than manipulative, in that the interactions between persons and settings are observed and recorded with a minimum of intrusion by the experimenter. The data base for therapy development has thus been a descriptive account of natural behavior (c.f. Patterson, 1977). When quasi-experiments have been designed by social learning theorists, the laboratory has generally been a home, school, or some other "natural setting." In studies where interactional phenomena have been examined in formal laboratory settings, ecological validity is accentuated by selecting readily transportable phenomena, those that are elicited by social setting variables (e.g., problem-solving behavior) rather than by physical setting variables (e.g., Vincent, Birchler, and Weiss, 1975).

The emphasis on natural environments has prompted social learning theorists to use observational assessment methods (Patterson et al., 1969; Hops et al., 1971). The psychometric properties of observation methods have become legitimate targets of study in their own right, and the number of investigations have proliferated (Johnson and Bolstad, 1973). These studies have examined factors affecting interobserver reliability, such as the knowledge and timing of reliability checks (Kass and O'Leary, 1970; Kent, 1972), stability of observations over time (Jones, Reid, and Patterson, 1975), representativeness of reliability estimates (Reid and DeMaster, 1972), and the appropriateness of various computational formulae (Hawkins and Dotson, 1975; Hartmann, 1977). Likewise, investigators have addressed issues of validity, such as the reactive effects of an observer's presence (Patterson and Harris, 1968; White, 1972), and the impact of demand characteristics (Lobitz and Johnson, 1975; Pollack, 1978; Vincent et al., 1979). Recently, social learning theorists and behavioral ecologists have begun to study the dimensional structure of observational coding systems in the hope of eliminating redundancies and providing data concerning the topographical structure of behavior (Alexander, 1978; Wahler, 1975).

Clinical Applicability

After branching off from the social developmental thrust of Bandura and his associates, social learning theorists have tended to be clinical in focus. Target populations have been the families of children who exhibit problem behaviors ranging from hyperactivity (Patterson, 1965) to aggressive conduct disorders (Alexander et al., 1976), and married couples who express dissatisfaction with their relationships (Jacobson, 1977a). In both cases, the goal of social learning theory has been to formulate workable conceptual models to explain both the etiology and the maintenance of these problems, valid and reliable procedures for assessment, and effective programs of intervention. As with all empirically-based strategies of intervention, much emphasis has been placed on methodological issues in clinical research, such as the reactive effects of assessment, comparability of treatment groups, design of appropriate control conditions, and durability of effects over time (Jacobson and Baucom, 1977; O'Leary and Turkewitz, 1978). Social learning applications to treatment have been among the best examples of methodologically sound, family therapy outcome research (Gurman and Kniskern, 1978).

Behavioral Specificity

Since much of the approach is based on operant learning principles, it is quite obvious that social learning theory is directed primarily toward observable behavior. Even though recent "cognitive" developments have expanded the scope of inquiry, behavior is the bottom line. Thus, it is not sufficient to show that the father of a delinquent girl has "reformulated" her misbehavior to mean that the mother now has a "*raison d'être*"; the social learning theorist must demonstrate that the "reformulation" has had some impact on the father's behavior toward his daughter. Social learning theory is not only behavioral, it is also fairly specific in its level of analysis. For example, a macrobehavioral description such as "childhood misbehavior" would be broken down into microunits involving the actual frequency of specific behavioral events—"hit baby brother with fist four times, called mother a 'bitch' two times, urinated in closet once during an eight-minute period." Good behavioral accounts provide a blow-by-blow description of what actually happens.

Interplay of Data, Theory, and Clinical Application

An attractive feature of social learning theory is the reciprocal relationship that exists between data, theory, and application. Theoretical concepts are operationalized in behavioral terms and examined in relation to hypothesized forms and functions. Inconsistencies in result, unexpected findings, and other serendipitous events lead to theoretical refinements and further empirical study. The clinical arena then becomes a testing ground for theory-derived techniques.

III. EVOLUTION OF THE SOCIAL LEARNING POSITION

Ignoring momentarily the practical significance of findings emerging from SLT, the process by which the approach has evolved is in itself interesting. It is SLT's commitment to a "scientific" process that establishes it as a model for clinical-family research and it is that process which will be discussed here. To illustrate this evolution, we will examine aspects of two general areas—clinical innovation and theory development—with emphasis as much on *how* knowledge has been generated as on *what* findings have actually emerged.

Clinical Innovation

Most empirically-minded clinicians tend to revere the contribution of data in the developmental course of a particular framework, while at the same time downplaying the contribution of clinical experience. The role of clinical experience in scientific progress is difficult to document; still, at least in the case of the social learning perspective, it provides important grist for the empirical and theoretical mill. Intuitive facility and good ideas both precede well-designed research and help shape the interpretation of results that derive from such research. While these uniquely human activities are often invisible in the tangible products of science, we must recognize their vital contribution to the scientific process.

Early Work. First approximations to a program of clinical intervention were essentially technological and educational in nature. Through a series of structured exercises, family members (usually parents) were taught alternative behavior-change strategies based on the principles of learning. In treatment of family (child) problems, intervention consisted of: (1) initial assessment using home observation, self-report, and interview methods, and (2) teaching parents a simplified version of the principles of behavior. Through use of programmed reading material, such as *Living with Children* (Patterson and Gullion, 1968), and *Families* (Patterson, 1971), parents were familiarized with concepts such as shaping, positive reinforcement, time out, etc. (3) Parents' skills in making behavioral discriminations were also sharpened through exercises in pinpointing problem behaviors in specific terms, observing the antecedents and consequences of problem behaviors, and tracking the actual frequencies of target behaviors. Parenthetically, exercises in behavioral tracking were assumed to impact the parents' cognitive system by mollifying their pernicious attitudes toward their children. (4) Parents were also taught to implement various operant-based techniques for behavior change, such as shaping and positive reinforcement to increase prosocial behaviors, and extinction, time out, and response cost to reduce noxious behaviors. (5) Readministration of the assessment battery at post-treatment sessions and follow-up provided measures of outcome effectiveness.

Social learning therapy with couples involved a similar educational technology. (1) A preassessment battery incorporated observational measures of couple interaction in the laboratory, self-report measures of marital satisfaction (adjustment), and behavioral interviews. (2) Teaching couples about marriage was accomplished by assigned reading in *Mirages of Marriage* (Lederer and Jackson, 1968), as well as through the use of other materials. (3) Behavioral discrimination exercises involved pinpointing target behaviors to be changed, constructing utility matrices and reinforcement menus, and behavior tracking using instruments such as the Spouse Observation Checklist (Weiss, Hops, and Patterson, 1973). Behavior-change training focused on communication skills, problem solving, contracting, and promoting positive behaviors ("love days"). (5) Post-treatment and follow-up administrations of the assessment battery provided data for outcome evaluation.

Empirical Support. The course of investigation involved in empirically validating the effectiveness of social learning therapy provides a good example of Paul's (1969) suggested "tactical use of different levels of research." Early investigations involving case studies and single group designs were followed by later research using treatment analogues, factorial designs with controls for no treatment and nonspecific effects, and comparative outcome studies with groups receiving alternative treatments. Recent reviews of this work are available elsewhere and therefore will not be included as part of this chapter. The interested reader should consult Jacobson (in press), Jacobson and Martin (1976), Weiss (1978), Gurman and Kniskern (1978a), and Gurman and Kniskern (1978b). In general, the results of empirical studies of social learning therapy can be summarized as follows: with populations of problem children and their families, uncontrolled investigations have shown that social learning therapy generally produces significant improvement over baseline in target behaviors (Thomas and Walter, 1973). Controlled investigations have shown that these changes are generally superior to those associated with no treatment or wait list control conditions (Wiltz and Patterson, 1974), as well as with nonspecific and alternative treatment conditions (Walter and Gilmore, 1973; Parsons and Alexander, 1973), although positive treatment effects tend to diminish at follow-up. There is also some question as to whether or not changes in the target child are associated with more fundamental changes in the family system, particularly in patterns of positive and negative consequation (Taplin, 1974). Furthermore, methodological flaws have been identified with these studies (Kent, 1976), and these flaws may restrict the generalizability of the findings. Analogue treatment studies have generally shown that SLT is superior to control conditions (Martin, 1975) but, as with any analogue treatment study, generalization of results to clinical populations or standard treatment methods is questionable. Although the few studies published to date that directly compare SLT with other methods have shown superior effects with SLT, "box score" comparisons with other forms of family therapy suggest that the approach may be no more effective. In a somewhat disturbing note, Gurman and Kniskern (1978b) suggest that deterioration effects associated with SLT may be greater than those associated with other forms of family therapy. It must be emphasized, however, that such statements of comparative effectiveness between SLT and nonbehavioral approaches to family therapy are suggestive at best, since a variety of between-study confounding variables may account in large part for any differences in result.

A similar pattern of results has been found in outcome studies of SLT with couples. Uncontrolled investigations demonstrated a variety of changes in couple behavior over baseline (Stuart, 1969; Patterson, Hops, and Weiss, 1975; Azrin, Naster, and Jones, 1973). Controlled investigations and analogue treatment studies also have shown that SLT is, in most cases, superior to no treatment, nonspecific treatment, and alternative treatment, the degree of which varies across studies (Roberts, 1975; Wieman, 1973; Harrell and Guerney, 1976; Liberman et al., 1976; Jacobson, 1977a, 1978b; Turkewitz and O'Leary, 1976). As in the case of SLT with families, caution is necessary in generalizing findings from analogue treatment studies. There is no study which has established definitively the efficacy of SLT with severely distressed couples. Jacobson (1977b), however, had shown the approach to be effective with severely distressed couples in an uncontrolled single group design. "Box score" comparisons indicate that SLT may be no more effective than nonbehavioral approaches to couples therapy, the effectiveness of both hovering around the 66% figure (Gurman & Kniskern, 1978b). For SLT with both couples and families (child-focused), no one yet has identified the essential ingredients of effective therapy. The few investigations that have compared the effectiveness of component modules (e.g. type of contracting) have not demonstrated that any single module is significantly better than any other module (Jacobson, 1978b)—a common finding in clinical research studies on behavioral therapies.

Seeds for Refinement of Clinical Techniques. It is tempting to rewrite history so that social learning theorists are seen busily poring over their data to find clues to revamp their intervention procedures. While it is no doubt true that some clinical innovation is data-based, such as attempts to account for the variance in treatment effectiveness, many of the developments within the SLT approach either have preceded or have occurred concurrently with the accumulation of data on outcome effectiveness. The details of how this occurred are at best sketchy, but no doubt some of the following sources have provided the seeds for change. Inherently, reductionistic approaches to clinical work are appealing as metaphors for behavioral processes, but their simplicity can be somewhat unsatisfying intellectually, even to social learning theorists. Certain problems in translation also developed, contributed in part by "novice" family therapists who chose to believe that all one had to do is to teach family members how to write behavioral contracts, and in part by SLT practitioners themselves, who somehow forgot or dismissed the importance of the clinical "lubrication" necessary to implement an effective technology of behavior change. For example, Ferber, Keeley, and Shemberg (1974) tried to replicate the SLT program developed by Patterson and his associates, based on published reports alone. Only three of seven families responded successfully, and after one year, only one family had maintained treatment gains. The "simple-minded," "mechanistic," "naive" critiques of SLT undoubtedly served as additional stimuli for exposition of the clinical model. SLT clinicians also encountered a variety of "resistant" clients who either would not accept the rationale behind the approach ("I am not going to use bribery to get my kid to shape up!"), would not comply with treatment ("Gee, Doctor, I was too busy this week to get to the exercise"), or otherwise would sabotage the course of treatment ("All this reinforcement stuff is great, but the problem is that my wife has an inferiority complex"). Perhaps worst of all were the clients who successfully went through all aspects of treatment and whose data indicated substantial improvement, but who complained at termination that "they didn't feel any better." This was reflected, in part, by a high rate of attrition, even for families who had responded successfully to treatment (Weathers and Liberman, 1975).

In response to these and perhaps other sources of input, SLT clinicians began to refine the approach and integrate it with other clinical strategies outside the traditional behavioral domain. The following is a sampling of the various ways that clinical researchers embarked upon this evolutionary process.

Explicate the Clinical Nuance. In response to criticisms that the treatment model was "over technological," SLT clinicians have published several papers detailing how the approach is implemented in practice (Margolin, Christensen, and Weiss, 1975; Patterson et al., 1975; Jacobson, 1977c, 1977d). In so doing, they had hoped to eradicate the false impression that SLT is simply a formula for clinical work—titrate a little reinforcement, add some extinction reagent, and bang, you have a cure! SLT is neither simple nor surefire. If anything, effective implementation of this approach is, perhaps, just as difficult, and requires as much clinical "chutzpah," as any other approach to marriage and family therapy.

Consider Therapist Characteristics. In attempting to identify unaccounted-for sources of variance in their outcome data, Alexander and his associates examined characteristics of the therapists (see Chapter 3 of this volume for a more complete discussion). Based upon post hoc groupings, two dimensions of therapist skill were identified: structuring skills, consisting of attributes such as directness and self-confidence; and relationship skills, consisting of qualities such as affect-behavior integration, warmth, and humor. Interestingly, relationship skills alone accounted for roughly 45% and structuring skills accounted for about 36% of the variance in the outcome measures. When combined as a single composite index, "therapist characteristics" accounted for almost 60% of the variance in treatment effectiveness. What is perhaps most interesting in this regard is that "relationship" skills are precisely those attributes that tend to be neglected in discussions of the SLT programs. This data would support Gurman and Kniskern's (1978b) recommendation that more attention needs to be directed toward training neophyte family therapists to be more adept at the "soft" aspects of clinical work.

Therapy First, Education Second. Another refinement has come from the Alexander group at the University of Utah, which, incidently, has won the dubious honor in Gurman and Kniskern's (1978b) recent review of being considered a somewhat "nonbehavioral" family therapy program. This notion suggests that although education is the ultimate goal of the SLT approach, a certain amount of groundwork must first be laid. For many families, the level of emotional turmoil at the outset of treatment is so high that family members are unable to respond to the slower-paced, more cognitively directed aspects of SLT. Consequently, therapeutic first-aid must be applied so that family members can experience some degree of symptom relief. After the chaos has subsided, therapy then shifts to a "retraining" focus along the lines of standard SLT programs. While there is as yet no data evaluating the efficacy of a two-staged program of family therapy, it is certainly appealing at an intuitive level. A recent paper by Jacobson (1977b) has demonstrated the effectiveness of a similar approach when applied to severely distressed couples. By loosening the adherence to a standard clinical package, it was possible to "intervene according to the requirements of the clinical situation" (Jacobson, in press). It is unfortunate that existing group designs for outcome research tend to "punish" the investigator for such lack of standardization across couples. It is entirely possible, however, that slavish worship of factorial group designs may in fact forestall rather than facilitate the design of consistently effective treatment procedures.

Identify Variables Which Compete With Treatment. Findings that favorable treatment effects of SLT with families often do not maintain well at follow-up have prompted several investigators to search for possible explanations. Presence of significant marital problems between parents may be one factor in the failure of child management programs (Reisinger, Frangia, and Hoffman, 1976). Wahler has suggested that social insularity, "the gradual reduction of reinforcement values" between parties, may also help to account for the phenomenon (see Chapter 2 in this volume for complete discussion of the concept). This analysis suggests that certain consumers of family therapy, especially those from low socio-economic backgrounds, may be multiply entrapped in coercive, unrewarding interaction networks. Consequently, favorable change in one aspect of family life, namely the child's behavior, may be "water off a duck's back" and therefore insufficient to compensate for the generalized aversiveness that pervades virtually all aspects of life. An expanded focus for SLT programs to deal with interactions involving the larger social network of family, kinship, and community appears to be an important implication of this analysis.

According to Patterson (1975), "for about a third of the families, it is sufficient to adopt the *simplest* possible strategy, e.g. *teach the parent the specific skills for changing child behaviors.* Another third seem to require more than this, including the teaching of negotiation skills, resolution of marital conflict, and depression being the most common, . . . If these problems are not dealt with, we believe the long-term follow-up will show the treatment to have been ineffective. The remaining third fail in spite of our best efforts" (p. 29).

Incorporate New Clinical Techniques. Since SLT tends to be theoretically eclectic, why not so clinically? This line of reasoning has prompted several SLT clinicians, and behavior therapists more generally, to consider alternative treatment strategies to augment their clinical armamentarium. "Go cognitive" has been one example of this development. Ample evidence exists to suggest that cognitive (attributional) processes reside at the core of many of the disturbing phenomena we observe clinically. For example, Gottman et al. (1976) demonstrated that good intentions on the part of one distressed spouse tend to be viewed more negatively than intended by the other spouse. Similarly, as Gurman and Kniskern (1978b) noted, findings that the problem children studied by Arnold, Levine, and Patterson (1975) often engaged in aversive behavior at the same rate as their non-referred siblings suggest that much of disordered child behavior is in the eye (cognition) of the beholder (parent). Similar difficulties in differentiating hyperactive children from normal children have been reported by Williams, Vincent, and Elrod (1977), based on objective classroom observations, even though teachers reported that the children differed markedly. As Karoly and Rosenthal (1977) suggested, perhaps clinicians should concentrate on changing parental perceptions rather than child behavior.

Cognitive restructuring techniques designed to change negative attributions have recently been incorporated into SLT programs. In a recent analogue treatment study by Margolin and Weiss (1978), couples participated in a cognitive-behavioral, behavioral, or nondirective treatment condition. Based on both self-report and observational measures of marital adjustment, couples in the cognitive-behavioral treatment improved significantly more than couples in either of the other two conditions. In a similar vein, Weiss (see Chapter 7 this volume) has suggested that principles from strategic systems therapy (Watzlavick, Weakland, and Fisch, 1974) can be incorporated into the SLT program. The rationale for this is that SLT provides a good model of "what" should be done to remediate family/couple problems, but it does not necessarily tell us *how* best to accomplish this clinically. Use of "paradoxical" behavioral prescriptions, such as encouraging resistance, sabotaging treatment exercises, and problem reframing, may be quite effective in dealing with certain kinds of client resistance. Interestingly, the strategic intervention of "reframing" is not unlike "cognitive restructuring" even though both techniques derive from treatment paradigms that are conceptually quite different.

Back to the Theoretical Drawing Board. Information from the clinical arena has also encouraged the development and refinement of the theoretical model behind the social learning approach. Phenomena such as generalization and maintenance of effects, once thought to be simply facets of clinical-outcome research, are now considered valid topics for study in their own right. Furthermore, shortcomings in the results of clinical studies have encouraged the pursuit of entirely new lines of theory-directed research into questions such as the structural properties of disordered interaction (Patterson, 1975; Wahler, 1975). Further examples of theoretical development will be considered in the discussion of "reciprocity" and "coercion," two major concepts that underlie much of the SLT position.

Theoretical Development

The concepts of reciprocity and coercion have long been prominent in social learning formulations of family interaction. The concepts as applied to SLT were first articulated in a classic paper by Patterson and Reid (1970), which reviewed the origins of the constructs from operant learning theory (Skinner, 1957) and social exchange theory (Homans, 1961; Thibaut and Kelley, 1959). According to Patterson and Reid, "reciprocity describes dyadic interaction in which the persons A and B reinforce each other, at an equitable rate. In this interaction, positive reinforcers maintain the behavior of both persons. 'Coercion,' on the other hand, refers to interaction in which aversive stimuli control the behavior of one person and positive reinforcers maintain the behavior of the other" (p. 133). A description of the evolution of these concepts during the last ten years provides another glimpse of the main thrust of this chapter, that "theory building is a continuous but empirically oriented boot-strapping operation" (Patterson, 1977). This material is most easily discussed within the context of the populations studied, coercion in problem children and their families, and reciprocity in married couples.

Coercion in Problem Children and Their Families. Early support for SLT formulations of family interaction came from studies that demonstrated correlations between family members for certain classes of behavior. For example, Reid (1967) found that exchange rates for aversive behaviors correlated .65 between members of problem families. Likewise, Arnold, Levine, and Patterson (1975) found that the correlation for deviant behavior was .74 between problem children and their older siblings, .76 between problem children and their fathers, and .16 between problem children and their mothers. Except for the failure to find significant correlations between mothers and problem children in this data, the findings replicated those of Johnson et al. (1973). Johnson et al. also found that problem children engaged in significantly less prosocial behavior than their normal counterparts. Patterson and his associates (Patterson, 1975) observed that target children, their older siblings, and fathers engaged in significantly more deviant behavior than the same members in normal families. Mothers and younger siblings were not different in the two samples. In several studies based on the sample collected by the Oregon Research Institute, parents were shown to positively consequate between 19% and 31% of behaviors of their problem children (Shaw, 1971; Sallows, 1972; Taplin, 1974). In the Taplin study, positive parent consequences for child behaviors were shown to be quite stable (r = .56) over several months. Although these findings provide suggestive evidence to support the "coercion" hypothesis, they tell us little about the acquisition process of such interactions, nor whether patterns of antecedents and consequences in the social environment provide the necessary maintenance conditions for coercive interaction.

To examine these questions, two strategies have been employed: (1) laboratory analogue studies in which child behavior was measured as parental social contingencies were manipulated, and (2) sequential analyses of naturalistic observations. Using the first strategy, Atkinson (1971) studied the effect of "mothers' presence but non-availability" on the aversive behaviors of their children. This manipulation produced significant increases for four out of seven a priori defined classes of child deviant behavior. A study by Devine (1971) replicated the effect and provided additional evidence for the coercion hypothesis by showing that when the discriminative stimulus was removed (mother became available again), the child's deviant behavior quickly stopped.

The sequential analyses strategy has been much more prominent than laboratory analogues in studying family coercion. The intent here is not to review the current status of the theory, since good summaries of this work are available elsewhere (e.g., Patterson, 1975, 1977, in press). Rather, the intent is to illustrate ways in which the theory has evolved, based on additional data and further examination of the construct.

The goal of sequential analyses has been to search for behaviors among family members which serve one of four types of "stimulus function" for coercive behaviors: antecedents that precede coercive behaviors and are associated with increases in conditional probability (F^s—facilitating stimuli) or with decreases in conditional probability (I^s—inhibiting stimuli), and consequences that follow coercive behaviors and increase the probability of occurrence (Acc^s—accelerating stimuli) or decrease the probability of occurrence (Dc^s—decelerating stimuli). In an example of this strategy, Patterson (1977) reported an intensive analysis of one subject and his family based upon seventy-two hours of home observation chunked into blocks of approximately six seconds duration. Using "hostile behavior," a response class comprised of three different behaviors (whine, yell, and disapproval) as the dependent variable, Patterson found that father's disapproval and "talk" for all family members functioned as facilitative stimuli. Inhibitory stimuli included attending from father or sister, command from father or mother, disapproval from mother, and negative command from father. While similar networks of accelerating and decelerating stimuli were also found, Patterson identified a curious phenomenon in the pattern of mother consequences following the target child's hostile behavior. According to the sequential analyses, both mother "talk and ignore" functioned as accelerating stimuli. This pattern, which Patterson labeled a coercion "trap," illustrates that mother is between the proverbial rock and a hard spot. "If the consequence she gave was 'talk,' the probability was .446 that the child would continue to be hostile in the next time frame. If, on the other hand, she chose to follow the typical advice of some child management experts and 'ignored' it, the probability was .56 that the child would repeat! Either reaction exceeded the value p (Ho_2/Ho_1) of .3657" (Patterson, 1977, p. 21). Analyses of longer time spans (eighteen seconds) indicated that with some of the extended interactional chains, "four fold increments (were produced) . . . in the conditional probability values for the boy's behavior. . . ." Unfortunately, study of even longer behavior chains (up to twenty minutes) using multiple regression techniques was not feasible due to serial dependence problems in the data. Nevertheless, this approach demonstrates the dogged persistence with which at least one investigator and his colleagues have searched through a veritable mountain of data for evidence that helps to articulate a "performance theory" of disordered family interaction.

Lest we be trapped in the minutia of six-second time blocks of family interaction, it may prove useful to discuss just how this data has helped to shape the theory of "coercion" for problem children and their families. As first articulated, "coercion" defined interactions wherein one person's behavior was governed by positive reinforcement and the other person's behavior was controlled by aversive stimuli. According to later versions of the construct, Patterson conceded that "in natural settings, variations in reinforcing contingencies account directly for only a small proportion of the variance . . . rather, . . . social behaviors vary primarily as a function of covariations in the densities of stimuli which control the initiations and maintenance of . . . (these) . . . behaviors" (1977, p. 2). Note that here the emphasis is away from a single pattern of contingencies to acknowledgment of, perhaps, many patterns involving both antecedents to and consequences of behavior. A second shift concerns the nature of reinforcing consequences that maintain the victimizer's behavior. Initially, it was believed that such consequences were primarily positive. That is, the obnoxious child who whines for an ice cream cone at the grocery store is positively reinforced for such behavior because he gets what he wants. However, close inspection of field observation data has shown that such an explanation is not sufficient, since in many "coercive interactions," the victimizer is "punished" for his "manding" behavior (Patterson, 1975). It is interesting, however, that such "punishment" serves to accelerate coercive behaviors in problem families, while in normal families, similar behaviors suppress such responses (Patterson and Cobb, 1971; Kopfstein, 1972). This effect, referred to as the "punishment paradox" or punishment acceleration effect, suggests that the consequences maintaining coercive behaviors may be more complicated than originally supposed. Ardent supporters of operant theory may argue, of course, that the so-called punishment "acceleration" is not a paradox at all, but rather an illustration of the distinction between "punishment" defined on an a priori basis versus punishment defined empirically or on a functional basis. Technically, consequences that increase the probability of behavior function as positive reinforcers, no matter how "punitive" they may appear to the outside observer. On the other hand, some social learning theorists argue that the simplified "operant" explanation of coercive behavior is inadequate to capture the full flavor of the reciprocal, mutual causality that appears to be operating when one examines long chains of family interaction. Perhaps this is another example of how naturalistic data is seldom "explained" by constructing simple theoretical models; rather it forces us constantly to remodel our theoretical structures.

Another interesting revision of the coercion theory addresses the question of initiation of maladaptive interactions. While the paradigm asserted that once initiated both parties play a role in sustaining the duration of these episodes, more often than not it had been assumed that the "deviant child" started the ball rolling. Recent data suggests that this may not always be the case. In some instances, child coercive behaviors are initiated *in response* to negative provocations from other family members, a pattern Patterson (1977, 1979) labels "counterattack." These findings suggest that "coercion" may be more a characteristic of the entire family system than of the "deviant" child.

The evolution of the "coercion paradigm" as a theoretical explanation for certain maladaptive family interactions is by no means complete. To underscore again the thesis of this chapter, the natural history of the concept illustrates the great power, and sometimes monumental frustration of a clinically derived and empirically validated approach to theory building. When the data base for this effort is a set of natural observations obtained in the real world, the approach is both conservative and self-correcting, at least over long time spans. Since real world phenomena are precisely what empirically-oriented clinicians wish to describe, compelling arguments can be made for advocating this strategy.

Reciprocity in Couples. Early applications of SLT to couples rested heavily on concepts of reinforcement and reciprocity to explain the etiology and maintenance of marital problems (Azrin et al., 1973; Rappaport and Harrell, 1972; Stuart, 1969). These concepts, used side by side, demonstrate the interesting blend of language from the operant and social exchange theories that characterize the SLT position. These formulations have used concepts of both "rate" and "parity" to explain marital distress. That is, unhappily married couples are assumed to emit lower rates of positive reinforcers (higher rates of negative behaviors), and these reinforcers are assumed to be exchanged in a less reciprocal manner (more reciprocal for negative behaviors). The concept of positive reinforcement implies temporal or at least functional contingency. Support for the SLT formulation of marriage came from studies by Birchler, Weiss, and Vincent (1975); Vincent, Weiss, and Birchler (1975); Wills, Weiss, and Patterson (1974); and Patterson, Hops, and Weiss (1975). In the Birchler et al. studies, distressed married couples were shown to exhibit higher rates of negative and lower rates of positive reinforcers (Birchler et al., 1975) and more aversive and less positive problem-solving behavior (Vincent et al., 1975). In an earlier analysis of this data, Birchler (1972) showed that these behaviors were exchanged reciprocally. The respective husband-wife correlations for nondistressed and distressed couples were .97 and .74 for positive behaviors, and .26 and .54 for negative behaviors. Wills et al. (1974) used a repeated measures, within-subjects analysis to study covariations in marital behaviors across time. They found correlations of .29 between husband and wife exchanges of positive behaviors and .59 for negative behaviors. Rank order correlations across the seven couples in the study were 1.00 for positive behaviors and .61 for negative behaviors. Patterson et al. (1975) reported data on couples seen in treatment. Rank order correlations demonstrated equity in exchange rates of pleasing behaviors at both the beginning and end of treatment (Rho = .82, $p < .01$, and .75, $p < .05$, respectively), but exchange rates of displeasing behaviors were reciprocal only at the end of treatment (Rho = .35 n.s., Rho = .67, $p < .05$, respectively). Discussion of reciprocity has generally been specified according to the type of behavior that is exchanged. Positive reciprocity deals with the interpersonal niceties in marriage; negative reciprocity involves the mutual irritations. In some discussions, the notions of negative reciprocity and coercion have been used interchangeably (Patterson and Hops, 1972), even though recent definitions of "coercion" may not completely overlap with negative reciprocity.

Evaluation of the Reciprocity in Couples. Recent investigations have called into question several facets of the literature on reciprocity. Gottman et al. (1976) argued that response class definitions, such as social reinforcement (Birchler et al., 1975), have not been derived empirically. For one to define an a priori-determined set of behaviors as "reinforcers," it would be necessary to determine empirically that their contingent application increases the probability of a target event (positive reinforcers), or decreases its probability (for aversive stimuli). Similar arguments could be directed toward the Vincent et al. (1975) definition of "problem-solving" behavior, since no independent evidence was presented to demonstrate that particular behaviors either facilitated resolution of a problem (positive behaviors) or impeded its resolution (negative behaviors). The appropriate construct validation studies for empirically defining either "social reinforcement" or "problem-solving" behavior have not been conducted as yet.

Gottman et al. (1976) and Gottman, Markman, and Notarius (1977) also questioned the evidence for "reciprocity." They argued that while correlational data may support a "bank account" model of marital interaction, such data does not establish evidence of "temporal reciprocity." High correlations may be an artifact of high rates of positive behaviors in nondistressed couples. In order to examine patterns of reciprocity, one must examine the conditional probabilities of "if husband does X/wife does Y" against the unconditional probability of Husband X and Wife Y. If the conditional probability of the sequence HX/WY exceeds the unconditional probability of WY, evidence would exist for temporal reciprocity. Observe here the parallel lines of research between family studies of coercion and couple studies of reciprocity. Gottman et al.'s analyses of lag sequential patterns among distressed and nondistressed couples provided partial support for a reciprocity hypothesis. "Controlling for base rate, clinic couples were more likely to reciprocate positive affect at early lags, while nonclinic couples were somewhat more likely than clinic couples to reciprocate positive affect at later lags. Both groups of couples were more likely at all lags to reciprocate negative affect than positive affect, with clinic couples showing a greater tendency to reciprocate negative affect" (Gottman, Markman, and Notarius, 1977, p. 177). Similar analyses of a sample of distressed couples (n = 27) was conducted by Margolin (1977). She found evidence for "an overall parity" in husband-wife exchanges of verbal negatives in laboratory-based interactions. Margolin also found evidence for reciprocity in problem-solving and nonverbal positive behaviors, but not for nonverbal negative or verbal positive behaviors. Furthermore, she argued that Gottman's previous critique of reciprocity findings based on "base rate" did not hold in her sample of verbal negative behaviors. It accounted for only 9% of the couples' total output of behavior.

Questions have also been raised concerning reciprocity at an "objective" level versus a "functional" level. In this case, Gottman et al. (1976) argued that what observers might count as evidence of reciprocity may indeed be quite different from that which the spouses themselves perceive. To circumvent this definitional problem, Gottman et al. asked spouses to interact under conditions of high and low conflict at a "talk table," a laboratory device that allows spouses to indicate the "intent" and "impact" of each message. Using a first order Markov analysis of this data, Gottman et al. found minimal support for "the view that distressed marriage is characterized by less positive and more negative (functional) reciprocity than nondistressed marriage" (1976, p. 14). These findings led the investigators to speculate on whether or not it is the "lack" of reciprocity that characterizes interaction in nondistressed couples.

As in the case of research on coercion in families, theory-directed studies of reciprocity in couples have served a "desimplifying" function. In the reciprocity studies, two related issues continue to emerge, and, as yet, they remain unresolved. The first concerns how one defines the coin of the relationship realm. SLT concepts of marriage, and social exchange theories in general, assume that behaviors exchanged within the marriage have some value—either as benefits or costs. Reciprocity is a descriptive metaphor for the rules by which these relationship resources are allocated. One major problem is determining whose frame of reference to adopt in defining the value of behaviors, the investigators' or the couple's. Let us assume, as Gottman et al. do, that we use the couple's definition. How do we deduce the "scale" on which value is to be measured? It is reasonable to assume that the unit value is variable. In other words, the same behavior for different spouses on different occasions would fluctuate in value in the cost-benefit dimension. As in the international monetary sphere, value is arbitrary, a problem that plagues both clinical researchers and consumers in foreign markets. These "subjective" value definitions are problematic in other ways. For example, as Gurman and Knudson (1978) questioned, how can reciprocity theory explain the transactions in traditional marriages? The answer is simple, but problematic from the standpoint of empirical research. Traditional spouses may reciprocally trade behaviors which on the surface look very different (apples for oranges), yet at a functional level are actually quite similar (fruit). Husband's employment outside the home may be reciprocated by wife's meal planning, laundry, and childcare. Across couples, such patterns may be quite idiosyncratic at the content level, yet similar at a functional level. The issue is further complicated by the fact that acts of "omission" frequently can play an important role in reciprocal interaction. Consider the common example of a wife's withholding affection to reciprocate for her husband's lack of attention to her. Given these problems, we now question how much variance in marital economics can be accounted for by fixed-category systems of describing marital behaviors either at home or in the laboratory.

The second issue concerns the dimension of time. As Weiss (1978) pointed out, marital reciprocity need not function on a "tit for tat" basis. In fact, as Gottman et al. (1977) found, evidence for such patterns of immediate, temporal reciprocity is rather weak. But questions still remain about the time dimensions across which reciprocity operates. Some interactions may be characterized by a rapid-fire form of reciprocity, as in the coercive "bursts" noted by Patterson (1975). But such bursts are episodic, and there are long time spans between them, during which a different kind of reciprocity is probably involved. Lag sequential analyses beyond the first order are helpful in sorting out the longer span patterns of reciprocity, but even the longest lag analyses capture only perhaps thirty seconds of interaction. What about those reciprocal interactions that occur at time intervals longer than half a minute? Reciprocity of marital behaviors is actually cast within a multilayered temporal domain. It includes moment-for-moment exchanges ("You bitch, how dare you call me inconsiderate!"), day-by-day exchanges ("It's your turn to do the dishes tonight"), to much longer reciprocal exchanges ("You went to law school for the last three years, now it's my turn to study art"). The variable time problem makes it very difficult for us to study any but the shortest length exchanges, but these may not be of greatest interest, either clinically or theoretically. If we can find appropriate analytic models to study reciprocity over very long time periods, we may be able to recast the problem to aid understanding of how exchange media operate across different kinds of relationships. As data from Jacobson, Waldron and Moore (1979) suggested, distressed and nondistressed couples may differ in important ways as to how they react to various temporal contingencies. The interactions of distressed couples may be characterized by relatively short-term reciprocal contingencies, whereas those of nondistressed couples may be governed by relatively long-term contingencies. In one sense, such amorphous concepts as "trust" may be operationalized as reciprocity patterns over very long time periods.

New Directions

Many of the developments are both clinically and theoretically still very much underway. As the SLT approach to family research continues to mold itself to the accumulation of clinical and empirical information, we can expect further iterations of this developmental process. In addition to the changes already in progress, there are at least two other arenas in which the social learning approach is destined for exposure. The first involves a kind of cross-fertilization of the social learning approach with behavioral ecology (Willems, 1974, Alexander, Dreher, and Willems, 1976; Chapter 4 of this volume by Willems and Stuart). Like SLT, behavioral ecology focuses on man-environment systems, placing more emphasis perhaps on the effects of setting, both social and physical, on behavior. In contrast to SLT, at least in its early forms, behavioral ecologists view such man-environment systems as highly complex, the exact nature of which can be deduced only after extended observations of the multiple facets (levels) of each system. In a brilliant critique of behavioral approach to intervention, Willems (1974) cautioned against the usual tendency of behavioral clinicians to intervene in such systems before having full appreciation of the many intricacies involved. Willems's arguments have been bolstered by several studies which indicate that such intervention often can trigger a variety of unintended effects, both disagreeable and sometimes catastrophic (Alkire and Brunse, 1974). Similar concerns have been voiced by ecologists who study the delicate balance of natural habitats involving man as well as nonhuman species (Dubos, 1965, 1968). As Willems and others have suggested, behavioral ecology may provide a useful perspective for family clinicians by highlighting other facets of systems to study, suggesting more encompassing targets for outcome evaluation, and providing further theoretical input for understanding processes, like homeostasis (resistance) and synergy, that have much to do with how family systems respond to change. Furthermore, such dialogue may help uncover new and powerful strategies for intervention that capitalize on the delicate interplay among elements of ongoing social systems.

The second arena involves a new domain of application. Until recently, SLT has focused primarily on oppositional children and their families and unhappily married couples. In both cases, the focus has been decidedly on the mental health aspects of family systems. Recently, however, investigators have begun to expand the social learning perspective to include application to physical health problems. Vincent and Friedman (1978) used a social learning assessment procedure to examine the covariation of spouse behaviors, anxiety and psychosomatic symptoms in pregnant women and their husbands. This study, which was modeled after that reported by Wills, Weiss, and Patterson (1974), found that considerable variance in reports of physical symptoms was accounted for by positive and negative behaviors exchanged between spouses on a daily basis. The potential contribution of marital variables in "risk"-enhancing symptoms is suggested by these preliminary findings.

In another "health" application of the SLT approach, Baer and his associates at Baylor College of Medicine (Baer et al., 1979) examined family interactions during conflict resolution tasks among normal families and those with a hypertensive father. Unlike traditional research on family aggregation of high blood pressure, which assumes that cross-generation incidences of "hypertension" is based on a genetic transmission process, this research examined whether vicarious learning of particular affect management styles may account in part for such findings. Thus far, one study has compared sixteen families with hypertensive fathers to fifteen normal families. Of interest here was the finding that, while fathers in the two samples did not differ in their behavior, mothers and male children in the hypertensive families engaged in significantly more "not tracking," a behavior category presumed to indicate some form of conflict avoidance. Furthermore, it was interesting to note that the male children's systolic blood pressure in hypertensive families was significantly correlated with parental nonverbal behavior ($r = .52$). While only suggestive, these findings illustrate the potential promise of SLT in understanding the etiology of certain chronic health problems. While these "new" directions are in their earliest stages, optimism for some important new developments seems warranted. The growth of these new applications illustrates again the great power of integrating theoretical development, empirical research, and clinical application under the same rubric. To borrow a somewhat hackneyed concept from the circles of government, each element within the three-pronged clinical research approach provides certain checks and balances for the other elements. Theory development alone frequently leads to unbridled armchair speculation. Theory and research are teammates in the arena of verification, yet their products can easily err on the side of being scientifically valid yet clinically meaningless. When theoretical development, empirical verification, and clinical application are welded together, we have the possibility of generating good ideas that can pass muster in both clinical and scientific arenas. It is precisely those qualities that have catapulted the social learning approach to the forefront of clinical research with families. In a mere fifteen years, great strides have been made in both our clinical and empirical expertise. It is the commitment to a process of theory, development, research, and application that helps to ensure that our vision in the future can only become clearer.

REFERENCES

Alexander, J. F., & Barton, C. Behavioral systems therapy with delinquent families. In D. H. L. Olson (Ed.), *Treating relationships*. Lake Mills, Iowa: Graphic Publishing, 1976.

Alexander, J. F., Barton, C., Schiavo, R., & Parsons, B. Systems-behavioral intervention with families of delinquents: Therapist characteristics, family behavior, and outcome. *Journal of Consulting and Clinical Psychology*, 1976, *44*, 656–664.

Alexander, J. L. Performance assessment in spinal cord injury. Unpublished doctoral dissertation, University of Houston, 1978.

Alexander, J. L., Dreher, G. F., & Willems, E. P. Behavioral ecology and humanistic and behaviorist approaches to change. In A. Wandersman, P. Poppen & D. Ricks (Eds.), *Humanism and behaviorism: Dialogue and growth*. Elmsford, N. Y.: Pergamon Press, 1976.

Alkire, A. A., & Brunse, A. J. Impact and possible casualty from videotape feedback in marital therapy. *Journal of Consulting and Clinical Psychology*, 1974, *42*, 203–210.

Arnold, J. E., Levine, A. G., & Patterson, G. R. Changes in sibling behavior following family intervention. *Journal of Consulting and Clinical Psychology*, 1975, *43*, 683–688.

Atkinson, J. A. Nonavailability of mother-attention as an antecedent event for coercive mands in the preschool child. Unpublished master's thesis, University of Oregon, 1971.

Azrin, N. H., Naster, B. J., & Jones, R. Reciprocity counseling: A rapid learning-based procedure for marital counseling. *Behavior Research and Therapy*, 1973, *11*, 365–382.

Baer, P. B., Vincent, J. P., Williams, B. J., Bourianoff, G. G., & Bartlett, P. Conflict resolution among normal families and those with a hypertension father. Paper presented to American Psychosomatic Society, March 1979.

Bandura, A. Social learning theory of identificatory processes. In D. A. Goslin (Ed.), *Handbook of socialization theory and research*. Chicago: Rand McNally, 1969. (a)

——— Social learning of moral judgements. *Journal of Personality and Social Psychology*, 1969, *11*, 275–279. (b)

Bandura, A., Ross, D., & Ross, S. Imitation of film mediated aggressive models. *Journal of Abnormal and Social Psychology*, 1963, *66*, 3–11.

Bandura, A., & Walters, R. H. *Social learning and personality development*. New York: Holt, Rinehart and Winston, 1963.

Birchler, G. R. Differential patterns of instrumental affiliative behavior as a function of degree of marital distress and level of intimacy. Unpublished doctoral dissertation, University of Oregon, 1972.

Birchler, G. R., Weiss, R. L., & Vincent, J. P. Multimethod analysis of social reinforcement exchange between maritally distressed and nondistressed spouse and stranger dyads. *Journal of Personality and Social Psychology*, 1975, *31*, 349–360.

Devine, V. T. The coercion process: A laboratory analogue. Unpublished doctoral dissertation, State University of New York at Stony Brook, 1971.

Dubos, R. *Man adapting*. New Haven, Conn.: Yale University Press, 1965.

——— *So human an animal*. New York: Charles Scribner & Sons, 1968.

Ferber, H., Keeley, S., & Shemberg, K. Training parents in behavior modification: Outcome of and problems encountered after Patterson's work. *Behavior Therapy,* 1974, *5,* 415–419.

Gottman, J., Markman, H., & Notarius, C. The topography of marital conflict: A sequential analysis of verbal and nonverbal behavior. *Journal of Marriage and the Family,* 1977, *39,* 461–477.

Gottman, J., Notarius, C., Markman, H., Bank, S., Yoppi, B., & Rubin, M. E. Behavior exchange theory and marital decision making. *Journal of Personality and Social Psychology,* 1976, *34,* 14–231.

Gurman, A. S., & Kniskern, D. P. Behavioral marriage therapy: II. Empirical perspective. *Family Process,* 1978, *17,* 139–148. (a)

——— Research on marital and family therapy: Progress, perspective and prospect. In S. L. Garfield & A. E. Bergin (Eds.), *Handbook of psychotherapy and behavior change: An empirical analysis.* Second edition. New York: Wiley, 1978. (b)

Gurman, A. S., & Knudson, R. M. Behavior marriage therapy: I. A psychodynamic-systems analysis and critique. *Family Process,* 1978, *17.*

Harrell, J., & Guerney, B. Training married couples in conflict negotiation skills. In D. H. L. Olson (Ed.), *Treating relationships.* Lake Mills, Iowa: Graphic Publishing, 1976.

Hartman, D. P. Considerations in the choice of interobserver reliability estimates. *Journal of Applied Behavior Analysis,* 1977, *10,* 103–116.

Hawkins, R. P., & Dotson, V. A. Reliability scores that delude: An Alice in Wonderland trip through the misleading characteristics of interobserver agreement scores in interval recording. In E. Ramp & A. Semb (Eds.), *Behavior analysis: Areas of research and application.* Englewood Cliffs, N.J.: Prentice Hall, 1975.

Homans, G. C. *Social behavior: Its elementary forms.* New York: Harcourt, Brace and World, Inc., 1961.

Hops, H., Wills, T., Patterson, G. R., & Weiss, R. L. Marital interaction coding system. Unpublished manuscript, University of Oregon, 1971.

Jacobson, N. S. Behavioral treatments for marital discord: A critical appraisal. In M. Hersen, R. M. Eisler, & P. M. Miller (Eds.), *Progress in behavior modification.* New York: Academic Press. In press.

——— Problem solving and contingency contracting in the treatment of marital discord. *Journal of Consulting and Clinical Psychology,* 1977, *45,* 92–100. (a)

——— The role of problem solving in behavioral marital therapy. Paper presented at the meeting of Association for Advancement of Behavior Therapy, Atlanta, December, 1977. (b)

——— Training couples to solve their marital problems: A behavioral approach to relationship discord. Part I: Problem solving skills. *International Journal of Family Counseling,* 1977, *5,* 22–31. (c)

——— Training couples to solve their marital problems. A behavioral approach to relationship discord. Part II: Intervention strategies. *International Journal of Family Counseling,* 1977, *5,* 20–28. (d)

——— A stimulus control model of change in behavioral marital therapy: Implications for contingency contracting. *Journal of Marriage and Family Counseling,* 1978, *4,* 29–35. (a)

——— Specific and nonspecific factors in the effectiveness of a behavioral approach to the treatment of marital discord. *Journal of Consulting and Clinical Psychology,* 1978, *46,* 442–452. (b)

Jacobson, N. S., & Baucom, D. Design and assessment of nonspecific control groups in behavior modification research. *Behavior Therapy,* 1977, *8,* 709–719.

Jacobson, N. S., & Martin, B. Behavioral marriage therapy: Current status. *Psychological Bulletin,* 1976, *83,* 540–566.

Jacobson, N. S., Waldron, H., & Moore, D. Toward a behavioral profile of marital distress. Unpublished manuscript, University of Iowa, 1979.

Jacobson, N., & Weiss, R. L. Behavioral marriage therapy. III. The contents of Gurman et al. may be hazardous to our health. *Family Process,* 1978, *17,* 149–160.

Johnson, S. M., & Bolstad, O. D. Methodological issues in naturalistic observation: Some problems and solutions for field research. In L. A. Hamerlynck, L. C. Handy & E. J. Mash (Eds.), *Behavior change: Methodology, concepts and practice.* Champaign, Ill.: Research Press, 1973.

Johnson, S. M., Bolstad, O. D., & Lobitz, G. K. Generalization and contrast phenomena in behavior modification with children. In L. A. Hamerlynck, L. D. Handy & E. J. Mash (Eds.), *Parenting: Directions, change and maintenance of healthy family behavior.* Champaign, Ill.: Research Press, 1974.

Johnson, S. M., Wahl, G., Martin, S., & Johansson, S. How deviant is the normal child? A behavioral analysis of the preschool child and his family. In R. D. Rubin, J. P. Brady & J. D. Henderson (Eds.), *Advances in behavior therapy,* volume 4. New York: Academic Press, 1973.

Jones, R. R., Reid, J. B., & Patterson, G. R. Naturalistic observation in clinical assessment. In P. McReynolds (Ed.), *Advances in psychological assessment,* volume 3. San Francisco: Jossey-Bass, Inc., 1975.

Karoly, P., & Rosenthal, M. Training parents in behavior modification: Effects on perceptions of family interactions and deviant child behavior. *Behavior Therapy.* In press.

Kass, R. E., & O'Leary, K. D. The effects of observer bias in field-experimental settings. Paper presented at a symposium entitled "Behavior Analysis in Education", University of Kansas, Lawrence, April, 1970.

Kent, R. The human observer: An imperfect cumulative recorder. Paper presented at the Fourth Banff Conference on Behavior Modification, Banff, Alberta, Canada, March, 1972.

——— A methodological critique of "interventions for boys with conduct problems". *Journal of Consulting and Clinical Psychology,* 1976, *44,* 297–298.

Kopfstein, D. The effects of accelerating and decelerating consequences on the social behavior of trainable retarded children. *Child Development,* 1972, *43,* 800–809.

Kuhn, T. S. *The structure of scientific revolutions.* Chicago: The University of Chicago Press, 1962.

Lederer, W. S., & Jackson, D. D. *The mirages of marriage.* New York: Norton, 1968.

Liberman, R. P., Levine, J., Wheeler, E., Sanders, N., & Wallace, C. Experimental evaluation of marital group therapy: Behavioral vs. interaction-insight formats. *Acta Psychiatry Scandinavia,* Supplement, 1976.

Lobitz, W. C., & Johnson, S. M. Parental manipulation of the behavior of normal and deviant children. *Child Development,* 1975, *46,* 719–726.

Margolin, G. A sequential analysis of dyadic communication. Paper presented at the Association for the Advancement of Behavior Therapy, Atlanta, December, 1977.

Margolin, G., Christensen, A., & Weiss, R. L. Contracts, cognition, and change: A behavioral approach to marital therapy. *The Counseling Psychologist,* 1975, *5,* 115–125.

Margolin, G., & Weiss, R. L. Comparative evaluation of therapeutic components associated with behavioral marital treatments. *Journal of Consulting and Clinical Psychology,* 1978, *46,* 1476–1486.

Martin, B. Brief family intervention: Effectiveness and the importance of including father. Paper presented at the Conference on Social Learning in the Family, Eugene, Oregon, 1975.

Mischel, W. *Personality and assessment.* New York: Wiley, 1968.

O'Leary, K. D., & Turkewitz, H. Methodological errors in marital and child treatment research. *Journal of Consulting and Clinical Psychology,* 1978, *46,* 747–758.

Parsons, B. V., & Alexander, J. F. Short term family intervention: A therapy outcome study. *Journal of Consulting and Clinical Psychology,* 1972, *41,* 195–201.

Patterson, G. G. An application of conditioning techniques to the control of a hyperactive child. In L. P. Ullmann & L. Krasner (Eds.), *Case studies in behavior modification.* New York: Holt, Rinehart and Winston, 1965.

——— *Families: Application of social learning in family life.* Champaign, Ill.: Research Press, 1971.

——— A basis for identifying stimuli which control behaviors in natural settings. *Child Development,* 1974, *45,* 900–911. (a)

——— Stimulus control in natural settings. Paper prepared for conference, "Determinants and Origins of Aggressive Behavior", sponsored by Scientific Affairs Division, NATO, J. DeWit & W. Hartup (Eds.). The Hague, Netherlands: Mouton Press, 1974. (b)

——— Interventions for boys with conduct problems: Multiple settings, treatments, and criteria. *Journal of Consulting and Clinical Psychology,* 1974, *42,* 471–481. (c)

——— The aggressive child: Victim and architect of a coercive system. In L. A. Hamerlynck, E. J. Mash & L. C. Handy (Eds.), *Behavior modification and families: I. Theory and research. II. Applications and developments.* New York: Brunner/Mazel, 1975.

——— A three stage functional analysis for children's coercive behaviors: A tactic for developing a performance theory. In D. Baer, B. C. Etzel & J. M. LeBlanc (Eds.), *New developments in behavioral research: Theory, methods, and applications. In honor of Sidney W. Bijou.* Lawrence, Kansas: Lawrence Erlbaum Associates, Inc., 1977.

——— Mothers: The unacknowledged victims. Unpublished manuscript, Oregon Social Learning Center, Eugene, Oregon, 1979.

——— A performance theory for coercive family interaction. In R. Cairns (Ed.), *Social interaction: Methods, analysis, and evaluation.* In press.

Patterson, G. R., & Brodsky, G. D. A behavior modification programme for a child with multiple problem behaviors. *Journal of Experimental Psychology and Psychiatry,* 1966, *7,* 277–295.

Patterson, G. R., & Cobb, J. A. A dyadic analysis of "aggressive" behaviors. In J. P. Hill (Ed.), *Minnesota symposia on child psychology,* volume 5. Minneapolis: University of Minnesota Press, 1971.

Patterson, G. R., & Gullion, M. E. *Living with children: New methods for parents and teachers.* Champaign, Ill.: Research Press, 1968.

Patterson, G. R., & Harris, A. Some methodological considerations for observation procedures. Paper presented at the meeting of the American Psychological Association, San Francisco, September, 1968.

Patterson, G. R., & Hops, H. Coercion, a game for two: Intervention techniques for marital conflict. In R. E. Ulrich & P. Mountjoy (Eds.), *The experimental analysis of social behavior.* New York: Appleton-Century-Crofts, 1972.

Patterson, G. R., Hops, H., & Weiss, R. L. Interpersonal skills training for couples in early stages of conflict. *Journal of Marriage and the Family,* 1975, *37,* 295–302.

Patterson, G. R., Ray, R. S., Shaw, D. A., & Cobb, J. A. Manual for coding of family interactions. 1969 revision. Document #01234. New York: ASIS/NAPS, Microfiche publications, 1969.

Patterson, G. R., & Reid, J. B. Reciprocity and coercion: Two facets of social systems. In C. Neuringer & J. D. Michael (Eds.), *Behavior modification in clinical psychology.* New York: Appleton-Century-Crofts, 1970.

Patterson, G. R., Reid, J. B., Jones, R. R., & Conger, R. E. *A social learning approach to family intervention.* Eugene, Oregon: Castalia Press, 1975.

Paul, G. L. Behavior modification research: Design and tactics. In C. M. Franks (Ed.), *Behavior therapy: Appraisal and status.* New York: McGraw-Hill, 1969.

Pollack, S. Reactivity to classroom observation with hyperactive and normal children. Unpublished doctoral dissertation, University of Houston, 1978.

Rappaport, A. F., & Harrell, J. A behavioral exchange model for marital counseling. *Family Coordinator,* 1972, *22,* 203–212.

Reid, J. B. Reciprocity and family interaction. Unpublished doctoral dissertation, University of Oregon, 1967.

Reid, J. B., & DeMaster, B. The efficacy of the spot-check procedure in maintaining the reliability of data collected by observers in quasi-natural settings: Two pilot studies. *Oregon Research Institute Research Bulletin,* 1972, *12(8).*

Reisinger, J. J., Frangia, G. W., & Hoffman, E. H. Toddler management training: Generalization and marital status. *Journal of Behavior Therapy and Experimental Psychiatry,* 1976, *7,* 335–340.

Roberts, P. V. The effects on marital satisfaction of brief training in behavioral exchange negotiation mediated by differentially experienced trainers. Doctoral dissertation, Fuller Theological Seminary, 1974. *Dissertation Abstracts International,* 1975, *36,* 457B.

Sallows, G. Comparative responsiveness of normal and deviant children to naturally occurring consequences. Unpublished doctoral dissertation, University of Oregon, 1972.

Shaw, D. Family maintenance schedules for deviant behaviors. Unpublished doctoral dissertation, University of Oregon, 1971.

Skinner, B. F. Operant behavior. *American Psychologist,* 1963, *18,* 503–515.

——— *Verbal behavior.* New York: Appleton-Century-Crofts, 1975.

Stuart, R. B. Operant-interpersonal treatment for marital discord. *Journal of Consulting and Clinical Psychology,* 1969, *33,* 675–682.

Sullivan, H. S. *Collected works.* New York: Basic Books, 1965.

Taplin, P. Changes in parental consequation as a function of intervention. Unpublished doctoral dissertation, University of Wisconsin, 1974.

Thibaut, J. W., & Kelley, H. H. *The social psychology of groups.* New York: John Wiley and Sons, 1959.

Thomas, E. J., & Walter, C. L. Guidelines for behavioral practice in the open community agency: Procedure and evaluation. *Behavior Research and Therapy,* 1973, *11,* 193–205.

Turkewitz, H., & O'Leary, K. D. Communication and behavioral marital therapy: An outcome study. Paper read at the meeting of the Association for the Advancement of Behavior Therapy, New York, December, 1976.

Ullmann, L. P., & Krasner, L. *Case studies in behavior modifications.* New York: Holt, Rinehart and Winston, 1965.

Vincent, J. P., & Friedman, L. C. Interpersonal factors which accompany psychosomatic reactions to pregnancy: A pilot study. Technical report submitted to the Hogg Foundation for Mental Health, 1978.

Vincent, J. P., Friedman, L. C., Nugent, J., & Messerly, L. Demand characteristics in observations of marital interaction. *Journal of Consulting and Clinical Psychology,* 1979, *47,* 557–566.

Vincent, J. P., Weiss, R. L., & Birchler, G. R. A behavioral analysis of problem solving in distressed and nondistressed married and stranger dyads. *Behavior Therapy,* 1975, *6,* 475–487.

Wahler, R. G. Deviant child behavior in home and school settings: Some categories for comprehensive discription. Part I of progress report on NIMH Research Grant MH18516–01A1, University of Tennessee, 1973.

——— Some structural aspects of deviant child behavior. *Journal of Applied Behavioral Analysis,* 1975, *8,* 27–42.

Walker, H. M., Hops, H., & Johnson, S. M. Generalization and maintenance of classroom treatment effects. *Behavior Therapy,* 1975, *6,* 188–200.

Walter, H. I., & Gilmore, S. K. Placebo versus social learning effects in parent training procedures designed to alter the behavior of aggressive boys. *Behavior Therapy,* 1973, *4,* 361–377.

Watzlavick, P., Weakland, J., & Fisch, R. *Change: Principles of problem formulation and problem resolution.* New York: W. W. Norton, 1974.

Weathers, L., & Liberman, R. Contingency contracting with families of delinquent adolescents. *Behavior Therapy,* 1975, *6,* 356–366.

Weiss, R. L. The conceptualization of marriage from a behavioral perspective. In T. J. Paolino & B. S. McCrady (Eds.), *Marriage and marital therapy.* New York: Brunner/Mazel, 1978.

Weiss, R. L., Hops, H., & Patterson, G. R. A framework for conceptualizing marital conflict. In L. A. Hamerlynck, L. C. Handy & E. J. Mash (Eds.), *Behavior change: Methodology, concepts, and practice.* Champaign, Ill.: Research Press, 1973.

White, G. The effects of observer presence on mother and child behavior. Unpublished doctoral dissertation, University of Oregon, 1972.

Wieman, R. J. Conjugal relationship modification and reciprocal reinforcement: A comparison of treatments for marital discord. Unpublished doctoral dissertation, Pennsylvania State University, 1973.

Willems, E. P. Behavioral technology and behavioral ecology. *Journal of Applied Behavior Analysis,* 1974, *7,* 151–165.

Williams, B. J., Vincent, J. P., & Elrod, J. J. The behavioral components of hyperactivity. Paper presented at the annual meeting of the American Psychological Association, San Francisco, 1977.

Wills, T. A., Weiss, R. L., & Patterson, G. R. A behavioral analysis of the determinants of marital satisfaction. *Journal of Consulting and Clinical Psychology,* 1974, *42,* 802–811.

Wiltz, W. A., & Patterson, G. R. An evaluation of parent training procedures designed to alter inappropriate aggressive behavior of boys. *Behavior Therapy,* 1974, *5,* 215–221.

Wolpe, J. *Psychotherapy by reciprocal inhibition.* Stanford: Stanford University Press, 1958.

THE MULTIPLY ENTRAPPED PARENT:
OBSTACLES TO CHANGE IN PARENT-CHILD PROBLEMS[1]

Robert G. Wahler, THE UNIVERSITY OF TENNESSEE

The focal point of this paper entails therapeutic change in children referred to helping agencies for psychological problems. More specifically, the nature of these problems concerns a pattern of child behavior called *opposition*, or the pronounced tendency of a child to violate rule systems by which a community (such as family, peer group, or school) operates. Some of these rule violations may be passive (e.g., non-compliance with adult instructions) and others may be aggressive (e.g., fighting with peers). This type of childhood problem is a common referral complaint

Advances in Family Intervention, Assessment and Theory, Volume 1, pages 29-520.

ISBN: 0-89232-137-7

and worry of parents and teachers, and there is reason to believe that the pattern is not one that the child will readily outgrow (Robins, 1966).

A helping agency's efforts to work therapeutically with a referred child are usually focused on social contingencies between the child and his or her natural community of adults and peers. Of course, the degree of direct involvement expected of members of this community varies with different theoretical approaches to therapy. Some approaches (i.e., psychodynamic) may expect little; others (i.e., social learning) may require a great deal. Regardless, all approaches aim their intervention strategies at the child's current relationships with certain significant people.

When the referred child is in the pre-teen years, people who constitute these significant others will certainly include those in his or her family. Other groups, such as those centered in the school, may also present important contingencies for the child, but most developmental and clinical theorists see the family as the single most likely source of factors in the young child's behavioral adjustment. The author's look at treatment strategies for oppositional children also takes this perspective.

Social learning theory is the chosen set of hypotheses guiding the above perspective. It is argued here that children develop a good many of their interpersonal characteristics through instrumental learning. The bits and pieces making up a child's overall style of relating to people seems reasonably viewed as a shaping process, a process in which parents selectively reinforce certain behaviors in their child's repertoire. Thus, if some of these selectively reinforced behaviors are considered by others to be signs of maladjustment, it follows that both child and parents would be targeted for therapeutic intervention. Of course, an ample literature on the effectiveness of parent-child re-education already speaks to the utility of this social learning strategy (e.g., Forehand and Atkeson, 1977).

The present study, set within the above guidelines, represents an empirical and conceptual expansion of these guidelines. As is true of any effort to expand or change theoretical and procedural strategies, inadequacies of the strategies are the usual bases for the proposed change. In the case of social learning approaches to family treatment, such inadequacies have emerged in recent years. We turn now to a review of these problems.

MAINTAINING THERAPEUTIC CHANGE: SOME FOLLOW-UP PROBLEMS

Earlier in this chapter, reference was made to longitudinal studies of oppositional children referred for psychological help. The often-quoted Robins (1966) assessment of such children indicated that these sorts of childhood problems were unlikely to change over a thirty-year time span. In a more recent longitudinal study of chronic oppositional problems,

McCord's (1978) analysis of treated and untreated samples of these childhood disorders revealed a similar stability of problem tendencies. In fact, the psychologically treated group produced significantly *more* behavior problems as adults than did the control group. All in all, one must come away with a certain respect for the durability of childhood opposition when the pattern represents enough of a problem to warrant psychological intervention.

The stability of a child's oppositional tendencies makes sense when viewed within some known facets of family interchange. When objective observers sample home-based interactions between a parent and a referred child, some predictable sequences usually occur. Both parent and child react to each other in verbal and nonverbal ways that observers can agree are either aversive (e.g., whine, yell) or non-aversive (e.g., smile, talk quietly). However, given that one of the parties produces an aversive behavior (e.g., child whine), the probability that such behavior will be immediately followed by some response from the other party is suddenly increased. As Patterson and his co-workers showed, a child's aversive behavior significantly increases the likelihood that a parent will then produce both aversive and non-aversive reactions to the child (Patterson and Moore, in press; Patterson, in press). If, in fact, parental social responses do function as reinforcers for the child, it would seem reasonable to conclude that the child's aversive-oppositional actions are highly efficient ways of obtaining these reinforcers. Even more impressive evidence on this potency of child aversive behavior is seen when these sequential analyses are contrasted for referred and non-referred children. Data from Patterson (1976) and Snyder (1977) showed marked differences in the immediate outcome of parental aversive behaviors when used in response to the aversive approaches of their children. In non-problem children, these parent consequences significantly reduced the likelihood of ongoing child aversive behaviors. However, for the problem children, these consequences actually *increased* the probability of subsequent aversive behaviors. As Patterson and Moore (in press) discovered in their single case analysis, these increased bursts of child aggression are likely to continue until the harassed parent reacts non-aversively (gives in?).

When oppositional children are referred for psychological help, it is usually after years of the above sort of coercive interchanges within their families. Given such extensive "practice" by all family members, it is surprising that *any* form of psychological intervention could dent the family structure. But, as the data indicate, it is possible to do so through the relatively simple strategy of parent re-education (Patterson and Fleischmann, in press). Parents *can* alter the coercive process supporting a child's oppositional actions through a systematic application of reinforcement and punishment contingencies. If the parent is taught to understand the molecular sequences defining coercion, and if the parent obtains supervised practice in altering these sequences, stable and desirable shifts will occur in the parent-child relationship. In addition, there is clear evidence that such competently re-educated parents can maintain these shifts for at least one year (Patterson and Fleischmann, in press).

Even in light of these highly promising follow-up findings, the population of families in which parent re-education "works" remains unclear. Patterson (1974) reported that a portion of families treated in his program required an average of 1.9 hours of additional treatment time in follow-up. In this same program, further studies by Reid and Patterson (1976) and Reid and Hinjosa (1977) showed that some of the families dropped out of the program during or prior to follow-up. Just why these families quit the program is puzzling, since their decisions to leave had nothing to do with their success or failure in applying program techniques with their children. For those families remaining in the program through follow-up, roughly 75% of them showed clear evidence of sustaining treatment gains.

This mixed evidence of maintenance must also be considered in light of treatment difficulties reported by other social learning researchers. Johnson and Christensen (1977) and Ferber, Keeley, and Shembert (1974) found *no* evidence of treatment success in their family samples. Of course, the poor follow-up picture would be expected in these studies. Along with these treatment failure reports, Wahler and Moore (1975) brought family characteristics into the success-failure picture. These researchers found quite different treatment outcomes in two socioeconomic groupings of families. The middle-class group of six families showed marked and sustained improvement in child problems over a one-year follow-up period. However, the low-income group of eight families showed only minimal evidence of treatment gains and no evidence of improvement in follow-up. Finally, Wahler (1978) replicated part of this outcome with a sample of eighteen families characterized by very low socioeconomic features. Although the parent-child dyads under observation showed significant improvement during treatment, these gains were lost during a one-year follow-up phase. This study provided the first clear evidence that maintenance problems may occur even when treatment success is obtained.

SOCIAL INSULARITY: A BYPRODUCT OF COERCION TRAPS

Sometimes parent training produces substantial and durable changes in child problem behavior and sometimes it does not. Recent data from social learning research projects would suggest that some hypotheses can now be offered to make tentative sense of these discrepancies. One such hypothesis, representing a major thrust of this paper, is that of *social insularity*—in essence, a narrowing of family interaction style. A description of this hypothesis might best start by outlining another more widely known hypothesis called the *coercion trap* (Patterson, 1978).

Coercion, as described by Patterson, is an operant explanation of one very common style of interchange between parents and their children. The style amounts to a "trap" if it becomes the characteristic relationship manner of that dyad. The coercion operation starts with child behaviors that fit Skinner's (1954) functional concept, *mand.* A mand is essentially an instructional behavior; a behavior specifying or "demanding" some act of compliance on the part of some other person or persons. Thus, child actions such as whining, nagging, screaming, hitting, and so forth are mands in the functional sense that their likely reinforcers would become apparent over repeated interchanges with another party. Nagging, for example, may be reinforced *only* by a certain act of parental compliance—perhaps permitting the child to have a parent's undivided attention when siblings are in the vicinity. The actual compliance action serving as a reinforcer will be idiosyncratic to each child-parent dyad and may be specific to each environmental setting making up the child's day. Each of these parents, however, can soon predict the relevant reinforcer when a child mand is presented.

The next obvious step in a coercion operation occurs when a parent provides that relevant reinforcer. When this happens, the child then presumably completes the third and final step by terminating his or her manding behavior. In the process, both parties are reinforced for their particular behavioral actions. The child is *positively* reinforced by parental presentation of the compliance outcome and the parent is *negatively* reinforced by child termination of the undoubtedly aversive manding behavior.

There seems little doubt that coercion operations are common episodes in all families. Observational studies of "normal" families with preschool children show that the mother-child dyads are likely to engage in some aspects of coercive interchanges every few minutes (Minton, Kagan, and Levine, 1971; Forehand et al., 1975). But, for some unknown reasons, these interchanges may become "traps" for some dyads and not for others. The interchanges become traps in the sense that all three steps of the operation are completed and this complete operation becomes a characteristic feature of the dyad.

Now, when parents seek help because of coercion traps, there are commonly seen "secondary" features of parental behavior that are important to note. Presumably, the key functional features of an entrapped parent's behavior center on eventual compliance with the entrapped child's manding behavior. When such apparent positive reinforcement occurs on a predictable basis (see Patterson and Moore, 1978), the child's stable manding behavior makes good sense. But, it is also well known that these parents return the child's aversive manding with high rates of equally aversive behavior (Burgess and Conger, 1978; Taplin and Reid, 1977). In other words, the aversive-aversive exchanges in the dyad are just as apparent as those making up the aversive-positive exchanges. While the oppositional child's manding behavior *does* increase the likelihood of parent-positive actions (presumably compliance with child mands), these outcomes typically occur within a context of parent retaliation.

The point to be made in describing these secondary features is that *both* child and parent receive mutually aversive consequences by engaging in coercion traps. Apparently, the periodic positive and negative reinforcement is sufficient to keep this dyad operating along the specific steps of coercion. However, one would also expect that the mutual punishment will eventually have impact on some other interpersonal characteristics of that dyad. In this author's view, the anticipated characteristics ought to involve a gradual reduction of reinforcement values between the two parties—social insularity, if you will. In other words, the overall power of parent behaviors as reinforcers for the child should diminish, and vice versa. Approval, quiet talk, eye contact, touching, and other common social reinforcers will not have much of a reinforcement function when offered within the dyad. Another way of looking at this hypothesized drop in reinforcement value is in terms of the sheer number of functional connections describing social exchanges in the dyad. Dyads with low mutual values would be expected to manifest fewer social exchange options; other than coercive interchanges, one would not anticipate many additional child-parent lines of communication. In a sense, the coercion-oriented dyad ought to be more predictable in day-to-day operations than those less fraught with turmoil.

Empirical support for these insularity speculations is modest. It seems clear that coercion-entrapped mothers engage in fewer positive exchanges with their oppositional children (Patterson, 1978; Burgess and Conger, 1978). And Wahler (1969) offered a direct test of mother reinforcement value in two such dyads. His analysis demonstrated that mother approval had little reinforcement value for the children until the coercive problems were altered. These studies suggest a sparse network of positive interchanges in which the child, and probably the parent, are relatively unaffected by their mutual noncoercive exchanges. Along the lines of interaction predictability, Berland's (1977) observational analyses of problem and nonproblem families revealed the expected patterns: there were more significant intercorrelations among problem family members than in the comparison nonproblem families. Thus, not only did problem family members produce the previously documented higher rates of aversive interchange, but their overall interaction styles were more predictable.

If social insularity is a by-product of parent-child coercion traps, what implications does this byproduct hold for the previously discussed treatment maintenance problems? One would expect that a resolution of coercion problems *without* a broadening of the social reinforcement network could only lead to a poor prognosis. Fortunately, the data show that interrupting the coercion process may also lead to insularity reduction within the dyad. Wahler's (1969) analysis clearly showed marked increments in mother reinforcement values following a successful use of time out. The children not only engaged in more cooperative activity with their mothers, they also worked harder for their mothers' approval in a game situation. Likewise, Patterson and Reid (1973) reported data to show the other side of this important change. When the mothers in this study altered their children's coercive actions, these parents also reported more positive feelings toward the children—an indirect measure of child reinforcement value for the mothers. These studies suggest that a systematic means of interrupting the coercion process might actually broaden the affectional base of interchange for both members of the dyad. Thus, a maintenance of therapeutic change would be more likely.

GENERALIZED INSULARITY: SOME EXPECTED EFFECTS OF MULTIPLE COERCION TRAPS

If coercion traps are developed in parent-child dyads, it would seem reasonable to expect that this sort of entrapment might also occur in other dyadic interchanges involving these people. Additional traps involving the parent member of this dyad would be of particular importance to consider because of that adult's necessary cooperative role in social learning treatment. Trap possibilities for a parent would seem feasible both inside and outside that adult's home setting. In addition to the already discussed coercive interchanges with children, similar problems are possible with a spouse, relatives, friends, and formal community representatives such as social welfare officials.

The likelihood of such multiple coercion traps is illustrated by self-report studies of a variety of nontroubled and troubled parents. In reference to parent-parent coercion, Birchler, Weiss, and Vincent (1975) found an average parent report of at least one aversive interchange per week. Even more frequent problems were noted by Wills, Weiss, and Patterson (1974) when mothers were asked to provide wife-husband reports on a daily basis. Aversive interchanges in this case were found to occur more than twice a day. Some suggestive connections between these parent-parent problems and parent-child aversiveness is also found in this self-report literature. In the Johnson and Lobitz (1974) sample of referred problem children, 85% of the parents reported marital dissatisfaction severe enough to warrant help. Russell (1974) likewise reported lower ratings of parent-parent relational satisfaction if their child was judged "irritable" by the couple. And, in line with both of these studies, Feldman's (1971) evaluation of child day-to-day problem behavior indicated some parent-reported effects on the marriage. Across the board, partners without children were *happier* than those who were parents. Obviously, the marital dissatisfaction problems could have been precursors of the child-management problems as well as the other way around. The important point to be made is that the two sets of interpersonal problems seem to cluster together. Given that parents are faced with a child's coercive interactions, they may also experience significant coercive interchanges with each other.

The elaboration of coercion problems into relationships outside the immediate family is also indicated through parent self-report studies. Sociological survey studies clearly suggest that parents who abuse their children tend to have minimal contact with people in the surrounding community (Parke and Collmer, 1975; Garbarino, 1977). Further, the notion that such isolation may reflect coercion interchanges outside the family is supported by day-to-day parent reports analyzed by Wahler, Leske, and Rogers (in press) and Wahler (in press). These investigators discovered that parents of troubled children who had minimal community contact also described some of their outside interchanges as coercive. In contrast, the Wahler, Leske, and Rogers sample of troubled parents who reported higher rates of daily community contact seldom regarded their contacts as coercive. It is of interest to note that the isolated parents reported most of their coercive contacts to be with kinfolk and helping agency representatives.

Recent findings by the author show correlational ties between these parent extra-family coercive interchanges and the same parents' coercive interchanges with their children (Wahler, 1978). This study replicated the Wahler, Leske, and Rogers (in press) portrayal of isolated, child-troubled parents as people who report coercive contacts with their kinfolk and helping agency representatives. On the other hand, their contacts with friends were seldom rated as coercive. The correlational ties were shown in a comparison of mother-child coercive interactions during two sets of days: one set was selected through mother reports of community contacts primarily with friends; in the second set, mother reports were marked by high proportions of the aversive kinfolk and helping agent interchanges. Results showed highly significant differences in the rate of mother-child coercion during the two sets of days. These parent-child problems were worse during days in which the mother was faced primarily by her kinfolk and helpers. In fact, the evidence suggested that mother success in using some recommended child contingency management procedures was indirectly affected by such extra-family contacts. Thus, a parent's social exchanges in the community may affect that parent's childrearing efforts in much the same fashion as do marital problems. More importantly, these two indirect sources of parent coercion could also play significant roles in the maintenance success of child-oriented family treatment. Once again, we turn to that by-product of coercion traps—social insularity.

Given that a parent is entrapped in multiple coercion exchanges, one would suspect that the insularity phenomenon described earlier might become a pervasive feature of that parent's interpersonal style. In other words, might such a multiply entrapped parent find little reinforcement value in *most* day-to-day social contacts? And, as argued earlier, the absence of a positive reinforcement network is related to poor treatment maintenance. The persistence of such *generalized insularity* means that child change could be accomplished coercively (e.g., by therapist manding of parent) but not through a reciprocal exchange of positive reinforcers. Once the therapist departs (and stops manding), the indirect source of change is terminated; without change in parent-parent and parent-community coercion traps, the only positive source of maintenance is the improved child. This source might well be outweighed by the still existing aversive input to the parent—if this input does in fact have indirect and undesirable effects on the parent-child relationship.

Evidence that multiply entrapped parents do not maintain such therapeutic gains in child behavior has been offered by the author (Wahler, 1978). The eighteen mothers in this study were shown to experience persistent coercive relationships with at least one of their children and at least one adult in their communities (usually kinfolk). Following parent contingency management training, these mothers produced demonstrable improvements in their children's coercive behaviors. However, a one-year follow-up showed that the parent-child problems had returned to baseline levels of severity. Since no efforts were made to deal with the mothers' community problems, these mother-reported coercive contacts remained unchanged throughout the study. Conceivably, this source of extra-family coercion was responsible for the maintenance failure. While this finding is directly in line with insularity predictions, the field has yet to generate additional outcome studies of multiply entrapped parents.

Despite this dearth of follow-up studies, there are sociological data reflecting the issue of therapeutic change in these sorts of troubled families. In an overall inspection of these data, it becomes apparent that multiply coerced parents tend also to suffer hardships associated with poor education and poverty. In particular, this relationship appears to be the case when one of the coercion traps involves people living outside the troubled family. The previously cited Wahler, Leske, and Rogers (in press) analysis of troubled families indicated marked socioeconomic differences in those parents reporting extra-family aversive interactions. The low-income parents reported themselves to be more isolated in their communities—primarily because of infrequent contacts with *friends*. These parents reported fewer than three contacts per day outside their families and most of these were made up of unsolicited, sometimes aversive approaches by their kinfolk and helping agency representatives. While parent reports indicated that friend contacts were regarded very positively, such contacts simply did not occur in the large proportions reported by the higher-income troubled families. The largely isolated low-income parents clearly viewed their community settings as unfriendly places in which it "seemed best to mind your own business."

Now, this sort of isolated entrapment, often reported by low-income troubled parents, seems likely to perpetuate within-family problems. Sociological surveys by Giovannoni and Billingsley (1970) and Giovannoni (1971) indicate that poverty level parents have little knowledge of, or working contact with, those "community support" services designed to help troubled families (e.g., medical and mental health facilities). Interestingly enough, most of these families with serious child-related problems were "known" by services such as the public welfare department, the public health system, and the juvenile probation department. Thus, in line with the parent reports seen in Wahler, Leske, and Rogers (in press), these helping agencies did keep contact with the families. However, these same contacting agencies could provide little information to show their knowledge of the child problem and how the parents were attempting to deal with it. In other words, the agencies had little working knowledge of parent-child problems and the parents had equally sparse information on what the agencies were supposed to do. As Giovannoni (1971) argues, social contacts between the families and these helping agencies cannot be taken as an index of ongoing therapeutic change.

Apparently then, there is good reason for at least some of the aversive ratings provided by multiply entrapped parents with regard to their potential "helpers." It might well be that the typical change agents available to such parents actually function as another pole of the coercion process. Giovannoni (1971) cites an interesting set of data on predictors of appointments kept by mothers seeking help for their babies. This investigator found that the referral source (public health department) did not permit these mothers to choose the place of care even though two options were available. The mothers could have gone to the well-baby clinic at the hospital where birth occurred or they could have sought help at their district neighborhood clinic. However, the public health department "manded" the referrals on a geographic basis—to the closer of the two clinics. As the appointment data revealed, significantly more appointments were kept with the hospital clinic as compared to the neighborhood clinic. The supposedly logical choice of the helping agency may not have been the mothers' choice.

SUMMARY REPORTS BY INSULAR PARENTS: SOME PERSONAL VIEWS OF ENTRAPMENT

Multiply entrapped parents seem to have few positive social exchange options available to them within and outside their families. Whether the ultimate causes are poverty, ignorance, or more specific unfortunate learning experiences, it is probably true that therapeutic changes in their troubled children will be hard to come by. As we argued in the case of the more singular, within-family coercion traps, a systematic breaking of these traps ought to expand the positive reinforcement network for the entrapped members of the family. But the task of breaking these traps when they are multiple is evidently a good deal more difficult than the same task for singularly entrapped families. In a final look at the degree of difficulty, we turn now to a view of this dilemma from the parents' perspective: in essence, the insular parents' summary reports on multiple entrapment.

There is an extensive correlational literature depicting relationships between parental self-reports and these parents' interpersonal problems. In this literature, the self-reports will be described as "summary reports" in the sense that the content is expressed in abstract form—a summary of more specific information. The tradition of measuring interpersonal problems in summary self-report form stems partly from psychodynamic conceptions of "personality" as the basis of such problems. But it is also obvious that people who are socially entrapped do have their own summary views on causality. Since the popular tendency is to offer these views as summary reports, a complete description of entrapment must include these reports as well as the more specific components making up the process.

Parents who seek help because of coercive interchanges with their children are prone to describe themselves in negative terms (Patterson, 1976). Compared to parents who are not experiencing such problems, these adults are more apt to describe themselves as depressed, angry, and low in self-esteem. Not surprisingly, similar reports of personal dissatisfaction are likely to be endorsed by parents who seek help for coercive exchanges between themselves (Raush et al., 1974). The negative evaluations are not only self-directed, however. Entrapped parents are also likely to assign aversive qualities to the other parent involved in the trap relationship (Murphy and Mendelson, 1973). Along with the negative descriptions, there is a tendency to offer these reports in such abstract summary fashion as to virtually prevent identification of specific behaviors (Olsen, 1972; Raush et al., 1974). In other words, a description of the other partner's role in the trap may be so vague that neither partner could readily identify key behaviors in the coercive interchange. For example, consider the following complaint by a wife: "He just thinks he's God Almighty. I got to do just as he says or he lets me know in a hurry what he thinks of me." While it seems evident that this mother is referring to some pattern of coercion in her husband's behavior, it is not at all clear what he does to harass her. Just as is true in parent-child coercive problems, greater clarity of these summary reports is an obvious prerequisite to change.

The summary reports of multiply entrapped parents were recently presented by the author (Wahler, in press). Much as described in the parent-parent coercion studies, these parents were also likely to offer negative and abstract evaluations of the extra-family member involved. The Wahler parent sample could generate at least four targets for such evaluative reports: themselves, their children, their spouses, and community members such as kinfolk and helping agency representatives. In addition to the abstract and negative nature of these parents' evaluations, there was another feature that made these reports similar to the overt actions described earlier in relation to coercion traps. That is, the reports usually described a manding interchange with someone else. The multiply entrapped parent usually outlined how another party (e.g., kinfolk, spouse, child) approached with the intent to force that parent's compliance with certain vaguely specified mands.

A review of Table 1 indicates that most of the mands emanate from the other party. It also appears that the entrapped parent views herself as sometimes countermanding. The overall picture as presented by these parents is remarkably consistent with observational data reviewed earlier in this chapter. These earlier data, taken from parent-child coercive interchanges, show that *both* parties engage in manding behaviors (e.g., Taplin and Reid, 1977). Presumably, as Patterson and Moore (1978) found, the mother is likely to comply consistently enough to sustain the coercion process. The overall picture, however, describes a parent whose day-to-day encounters within and outside the family are typically unpleasant. Once again, the sociological view of these multiply entrapped parents as isolated from positive social contact makes sense. The term "generalized insularity" seems particularly appropriate.

A final feature to notice in Table 1 concerns the reporter's evident conception of blame or causality. The author has recently shown (Wahler, 1979) that observers can reliably score a parent's blame attribution in these summary reports. When this is done, a highly consistent pattern

Table 1. Mother Summary Reports of Aversive Interactions with Adults and Children. These Other Parties Were Named as Coercion Trap Participants.

Mother's Summary Report of Her Aversive Encounters	*Other Party Involved In Report*
1. She's all the time telling me what to do.	Maternal Grandmother
2. I tell you, she's not only a snoop, she expects me to be perfect.	Welfare Worker
3. Well when he just sits there and acts depressed, I know he expects me to wait on him.	Husband
4. He'll start into teasing his brother—anything to get on my nerves.	Child
5. We didn't want him in here. We know what's wrong. He don't need to keep reminding me.	Psychologist
6. He says the house is dirty. Well, even when I've cleaned up it don't suit him.	Husband
7. I don't know if I can stand it. When he starts at me I get so mad I could kill him.	Child
8. She's really got a way of making me feel like a kid again.	Maternal Grandmother
9. He's all the time making me feel small.	Husband
10. It's pick at this and pick at that. I just wish she's stay away.	Mother's Aunt

emerges: the parent describing these manding episodes almost always attributes blame to the other party. Regardless of who is viewed as the principal mand source in the episode, the parent reporter clearly believes that she or he is not responsible for initiating the encounter. In the author's opinion, these blame attributions are important because they reveal some crucial aspects of that parent's observation style. When an observer assigns blame in offering a summary report, the observer must be attending selectively to certain components making up that report. For example, consider the following reports by a husband and wife. (Father): "Hell, if she'd spend some time cleaning up the dishes and the kitchen instead of watching the tube, we wouldn't get into these scraps." (Mother). "Oh sure! And with you drinking beer all the time, what have I got to look forward to? You don't never pay attention to me when you're drinking." In these two reports, the reporters are clearly blaming the other party involved in the reported encounter. When the father blames the mother for their "scraps," he is attending selectively to her housekeeping behavior, one setting event for these battles. On the other hand, mother's recount of such episodes shifts the blame to father—blame meaning that she attends to his drinking as a setting event. Now, if these summary reports can be taken as an index of parent observational performance, it seems apparent that these observers are incomplete scanners or trackers of social events composing their own coercion traps. In essence, a parent "sees" only one segment of the stimulus pattern making up the trap.

The selective attention hypothesis has one important implication with regard to the stability of coercion traps: if the stimulus segment attended to is fairly small, the summary report could be maintained indefinitely. That is, an entrapped parent's coercion report could remain unchanged even if the other party reduced his or her manding behavior.[2] For example, suppose that the husband in our earlier example based his marital problem report partly on his wife's housekeeping. It is conceivable that she could change her manding role in their mutual trap without altering his coercion report—if her housekeeping pattern was in fact discriminative for his report. And, if the husband still reports entrapment, it is likely that he will also continue his manding role in that particular problem relationship.

In the author's opinion, parent summary reports are primarily significant as an index of attention to social stimuli comprising the coercion process. When the parent reporter is part of the process, that parent seems quite selective in attending to the trap components. If change is to occur, this biased observer must obviously acquire better attending behavior—a capability to view his or her entrapment more objectively. Of course, such observational skill has long been recognized as a prerequisite part of parent training from the social learning perspective. However, teaching this skill, as well as the teaching of subsequent contingency contracting skills, has been aimed primarily at the singularly entrapped parent. Multiply entrapped parents must learn to use attending and contracting skills in a number of child-adult and adult-adult coercion traps. In addition, this learning process might well be devoid of the positive reinforcers typically available to the non-insular singularly entrapped parent. Thus, while the problems of treatment are reasonably clear, a means of solving them is yet uncertain.

THE MAND REVIEW PROCESS: A TREATMENT SUPPLEMENT TO PARENT TRAINING

It is possible that therapeutic strategies for multiply entrapped parents might involve a quantitative extension of those used successfully with singularly entrapped parents. If re-educating a troubled parent leads to a resolution of that parent's child-centered problems, couldn't the same re-education process be aimed at parent-parent and other parent-adult problems? This possibility seems particularly attractive in view of recent developments in the treatment of marital problems from a social learning perspective (Weiss, Birchler, and Vincent, 1974). These studies demonstrate that a combination of communication training (attending skills) and contingency contracting can lead to behavioral and self-reported improvements in distressed couples (Jacobson, 1978). However, the samples studied thus far have apparently been singularly entrapped couples, whose referral problems appear restricted to marital dissatisfaction. Nevertheless, the availability of an adult-adult intervention strategy makes it clearly plausible to add such a strategy to the parent-child approach already used with multiply entrapped parents.

While such a quantitative expansion of parent re-education procedures makes good sense, the "generalized insularity" of multiply entrapped parents will probably require something more than a training focus in treatment. Recall that many of the day-to-day social experiences of these parents are marked by coercive rather than positive exchanges. It is as if *avoidance* constitutes their prevalent mode of community adaptation. Certainly such a social style has been noted in the multiply entrapped parent's relationship with helping agency representatives. Thus, as we pointed out earlier in this chapter, potential therapeutic helpers are likely to find themselves embroiled in the coercion traps so common to these parents—traps that appear to sustain rather than change family problems. A parent training or educational focus can readily become a coercive focus. Of course, these last statements constitute a moot point: if the multiple coercion traps can be resolved, generalized insularity ought to give way to a more positive, more gregarious parent lifestyle. As such, these therapeutic changes ought to persist. We are simply voicing a pessimistic clinical guess on the effectiveness of any educational procedure as the sole means of treatment for multiply entrapped parents.

Alexander et al. (1976) have pointed to a notable gap in the empirical base of social learning treatment: the social relationship between helper and those to be helped. These investigators found that therapist characteristics such as observer-rated smiling, active listening, humor, and self disclosure were good predictors of success in family treatment. In this study, family treatment was geared to coercive interchanges between a delinquent adolescent and that youth's parents. While all family members were "taught" communication and contracting, therapist skill in this sort of teaching accounted for about 36% of the variance in treatment outcome. In contrast, the previously listed therapist "relationship" characteristics (e.g., self-disclosure, humor) accounted for almost 45% of the variance. Clearly, the beneficial change in parent and youth behavior was not a simple function of standard social learning techniques. In some unknown fashion, therapist relationship skills augmented changes in family interactions. Presumably, as Alexander et al. speculate in their introduction, therapist social skills may have added *motivation* to the treatment process—motivation for the family members to actually use the behavior change techniques.

In the author's opinion, the relationship factors studied by Alexander and his colleagues provide guidelines in approaching the insularity problems associated with multiply entrapped parents. Positive reinforcement contingencies (motivation?) are notably sparse for these parents, within and outside their family structures. If a therapeutic helper is to serve a positive reinforcement function in such a social network, it would appear that he or she must utilize a relationship strategy along the lines suggested by Alexander et al. Conceivably, the specifics of this strategy could be derived from the same source through which coercion became understandable—naturalistic study of troubled families. We turn now to the author's recent work in this direction.

The manding nature of parental coercive interactions became evident through direct observation and parent self-report on the content of interchanges with children, spouses, kinfolk, and helping agency representatives. What then is the nature and content of those few *positive* interactions experienced by multiply entrapped parents? Wahler (1978) also asked his sample of eighteen multiply coerced mothers to provide this kind of self-report data.

Table 2 provides a brief look at the pleasant side of life for the multiply entrapped parent. The mothers providing these reports judged the interactions as being unusually positive for them. When one inspects the report content, there is little evidence of stated approval, physical affection, or helping activity. Rather, the uniform characteristic of each episode is physical closeness without interdirected activity. It is impossible to tell who is directing or controlling the activity described by these mothers. These sorts of verbal episodes fit Skinner's definition of the term "tact" (Skinner, 1954). In contrast to mands, tacts do not specify acts of compliance by another party. Tacts are descriptive verbal reports in which no obvious reinforcers are cited by the reporter. Thus, the experience of interpersonal activity with no particular direction appears to be a valued, but probably infrequent, phenomenon for the multiply entrapped parent.

The incorporation of tacting interchanges within the framework of parent training has become a focal point of the author's treatment research with multiply entrapped parents. In this approach, parents are trained to use standard contingency management techniques to resolve coercion traps between themselves and their children. At the same time, it is recognized that these parents are likely to be caught in other coercion traps—including potential entrapment with the parent-training therapist. The technique of producing this recognition, including an attention-oriented means of dealing with coercion, will now be referred to as the

Table 2. Mother Summary Reports of Positive Interactions with Adults and Children.

Mother's Summary Report of Her Positive Encounters	*Other Party Involved in Report*
1. You know—we just sit on the porch and talk about nothing.	Friend
2. You'd be amazed how nice it is to have somebody just listen.	Friend
3. A lot of the time we don't even talk. I just like to have her around.	Sister-in-Law
4. Sometimes she tells me her troubles.	Friend
5. Sometimes we play cards or gossip. But, gee, I don't know what all.	Friend
6. When he's not feeling good, he'll just sit by me and do nothing.	Child
7. We have set together in the kitchen. He'll tell me about fishing while I cook.	Husband
8. We both like to go for a drive together without the kids.	Husband
9. When he gets a new toy, he'll play with it and not ask me anything.	Child
10. I like to watch him work on the car. He tells me what he's doing.	Husband

"mand review process." This supplementary treatment strategy has yet to be evaluated empirically. At present it is offered as a plausible means of motivating parents as well as helping them attend objectively to their personal coercion traps. Because the data base for mand review is so limited, we intend only to present the strategy briefly as an example of new directions in social learning treatment.

As a physical operation, the mand review process entails regular (once weekly) meetings between parents and the therapist who directs their child management efforts. It is also feasible to include other members of the parent traps whenever these people become known (e.g., children and kinfolk). The process is presented frankly as a way of enabling the parents and therapist to better understand coercion. In this framework, it is emphasized that a parent's child-rearing problems are apt to be affected by relationships with spouse, kinfolk, and the sometimes demanding therapist. Understanding is viewed as the capability to point to specific things that entrapped people do to perpetuate a trap: by talking about or "reviewing" recent manding episodes, the people involved can eventually see these specifics.

This much of the treatment process has been instructive and has already included standard child management procedures as well as feedback to the parents on how they seem to be perpetuating entrapment with the referred child. Thus far, nothing along the lines of tacting interchanges has materialized. In fact, the therapist has been largely a source of mands for the parents. However, once the therapist is satisfied that the parents are correctly using the contingency management procedures, that professional's instructive role becomes restricted to insuring that the session discussions center on personal coercion topics—topics that cover any regularly occurring manding interchanges in the parents' daily lives.

The therapist's tacting style in these mand review sessions will usually involve two central themes: first, a request for more detail in a family member's review of an episode. While these requests are instructive (questions), they do not constitute the usual training mands for parent compliance (e.g., "do this"); second, therapist review of his or her impressions of relationships among various recurring trap episodes. For example, a parent-child coercive encounter may regularly follow a coercive experience between parents or between a parent and kinfolk.

The search for detail and relationships among various traps are viewed as two means of expanding parent attention to the specific social events comprising that parent's entrapment. Both sets of information are obviously absent in parent reports of manding interchanges. Not only are the details of each report sketchy, a parent's trap episodes with different people are typically described without reference to possible connections between episodes. The importance of expanding parent attention in these directions is obvious for the detail requirement but less evident for the trap interrelationships. Obviously, one who seeks to produce behavior change must first be able to specify the behaviors to be changed. And if in fact the multiple traps involving a parent do combine to produce "generalized insularity," the parent must seek to resolve all such traps. However, if the parent does not attend to the functional class organization of these traps, there is little reason to expect parent interest in dealing with all traps. Why should a parent be interested in discussing entrapment beyond the parent-child referral problem? Before pursuing further rationale behind mand review, consider two examples of this dual search process.

Example No.1: Attention to Detail in a Parent-Parent Trap Episode

Therapist (T): Well, who does have to take care of M (child) when he acts up?

Mother (M): I do. Whenever he needs to be put in time-out or stopped from doing something, it's me who does it. Yesterday he showed out at the doctor's office, but so did some other kids.

T to Father (F):	Do you not put M in time-out?
F:	Sure.
M (laughing):	Since when? He don't never help me when I need it. I got to do it all by myself. Like yesterday when he was throwing rocks at the paper boy, it was me who had to take him into the house.
F (to no one):	My hands were all dirty with grease from the car.
M:	Well, they wasn't too dirty to pay the paper boy.
F (to no one):	If you want to go to work all day and earn the money, that's OK by me.
M to T:	I know he's tired when he comes home, but I get tired too having to watch M all day long.
T to F:	What happened when he was throwing rocks at the paper boy?
F:	I was working on the car because I can't afford to take it to nobody. When the paper boy came to collect, M started to throw rocks at him.
M to T:	And then he (F) starts yelling across the yard at me to stop M from doing it.
T to F:	What happened?
F:	I told him to quit but he don't pay attention to me.
M:	Well, you don't ever do anything about it.
T to F:	So you told M to quit. And then what?
F:	He just kept on throwing rocks.
T looks at F:	(Silence.)
F (to no one):	I told her to get him to stop.
T to F:	Why didn't you stop him?
F:	My hands was all dirty and he won't mind me anyway.
M:	If you'd just try to. . . .
F (interrupting):	If you want to go to work all day, that's fine by me.
T to M:	What were you doing when M started throwing rocks?
M:	I was mowing the lawn. I was clear across the yard when it happened and he (F) just yells at me to do something. I was

	real embarrassed. I told the paper boy I was sorry and I took M into the house.
T to F:	You couldn't make M stop?
F:	My hands were all greasy.
T:	Were you mad?
F:	Yes.
T:	Were you mad at M or at her?
M:	He was mad at me for not getting right over there.
T to F:	Were you mad at her?
F:	He (M) don't never pay attention to me, so I told her to make him stop.
T:	Were you mad at her?
F:	I guess.

Example No. 2: Attention to Trap Relationships in Parent-Parent and Parent-Child Trap Episodes

Therapist (T) to Father (F):	So when you were about to tell your friend what kind of a car you were going to buy, B (Mother) interrupted you and finished your story?
Father (F):	It's the same old story. She couldn't wait to let me finish.
Mother (M) to (F):	But you know it's because I didn't think he could understand your speech.
F to M:	You could have waited.
T to F:	What did you do when she interrupted?
F:	I started to. . . .
M to T:	He just glared at me and gave me *that* look.

(30 minutes later)

Father (F):	He (child) didn't want to come in the house.
Therapist (T) to F:	But you told him to come in.
F to T:	I can't get him to do anything.
T to F:	What did you do when he didn't mind?
F to T:	I left him alone.
T to F:	You know, that's the second time that you

gave up on (child) after you had an argument with (mother). Remember we were talking about her interrupting you when you were talking to your friend about the car? That happened on the same day that you gave up on (child).

F to T: (Nodding head) She thinks she wants to run the show—so I just let her do it.

M to F: But you're his father!

Expected outcomes of this review process center on positive parent-therapist relationships as well as expanded parent attention to events comprising their own coercion traps. While there is good reason to expect both phenomena, the matter of change in a parent's multiple coercion traps is left ambiguous. That is, is there reason to expect resolution of a parent's manding interchanges with a spouse or kinfolk without training these parties in contingency contracting? And, since contingency contracting is *always* used in handling a parent's child-centered coercion trap, why not apply this training to the other traps? At this point in the author's treatment research, these questions remain unanswered. Certainly it is quite possible that such formal training could be incorporated after a parent is objectively attending to all relevant stimuli in a coercive interchange. Given that the mand review process *does* produce a positive therapist-parent relationship, there may be little reason to anticipate later coercion problems when the therapist adds further mands to the treatment process. On the other hand, there are suggestions from the marital treatment literature that some form of attention training may produce behavioral change *without* contingency training (Jacobson, 1977).

Treatment research with multiply entrapped parents has only begun. It is far too early to even venture a guess on what will constitute an effective, durable intervention in the troubled families of these adults. The author is convinced that the relationship factors encompassed in insularity phenomena must become a focal point of treatment—particularly in terms of the therapist's relationship with a parent. In addition, it seems clear that parent-attending skills will be vital to the overall behavior change process. Social learning theory and its presently available treatment principles offer an excellent base for building in these directions.

NOTES

1. The preparation of this paper was supported by research grant MH 18516 from the National Institute of Mental Health, Crime and Delinquency Section.

2. The author's laboratory analyses of adult summary reports confirm the selective attend-

ing aspects of observer behavior. Wahler and Leske (1973) showed that adult observers' summary reports in describing child problem behavior could readily be maintained even when the child's problem behaviors were markedly reduced in frequency.

REFERENCES

Alexander, J. F., Barton, C., Schiavo, R. S., & Parsons, B. V. Systems-behavioral intervention with families of delinquents: Therapist characteristics, family behavior and outcome. *Journal of Consulting and Clinical Psychology,* 1976, *44,* 4, 565–664.

Berland, R. M. The family social system and child deviance: A comparison of deviant and non-deviant families. Unpublished dissertation, University of Tennessee, Knoxville, 1977.

Birchler, G. R., Weiss, R. L., & Vincent J. P. Multi-method analyses of social reinforcement exchange between maritally distressed and nondistressed spouse and stranger dyads. *Journal of Personality and Social Psychology,* 1975, *31,* 2, 349–360.

Burgess, R. L., & Conger, R. D. Family interaction in abusive, neglectful and normal families. Unpublished paper submitted for publication. Pennsylvania State University, 1978.

Feldman, H. The effects of children on the family. In A. Mischel (Ed.), *Family issues of employed women in Europe and America.* The Netherlands: Leiden Press, 1971.

Ferber, H., Keeley, S. M., & Shemberg, K. M. Training parents in behavior modification: Outcome of and problems encountered in a program after Patterson's work. *Behavior Therapy,* 1974, *5,* 415–419.

Forehand, R., & Atkeson, B.M. Generalization of treatment effects with parents as therapists: A review of assessment and implementation procedures. *Behavior Therapy.* In press.

Forehand, R., King, H., Peed, S., & Yoder, P. Mother-child interactions: Comparisons of a non-compliant clinic group and a non-clinic group. *Behavior Research and Therapy,* 1975, *13,* 79–84.

Garbarino, J. The price of privacy in the social dynamics of child abuse. *Child Welfare,* 1977, *56,* 565–575.

Giovannoni, J. M. Parental mistreatment: Perpetrators and victims. *Journal of Marriage and the Family,* November 1971, 649–657.

Giovannoni, J. M., & Billingsley, A. Child neglect among the poor: A study of parental adequacy in three ethnic groups. *Child Welfare,* 1970, *49,* 196–204.

Jacobson, N. S. Problem solving and contingency contracting in the treatment of marital discord. *Journal of Consulting and Clinical Psychology,* 1977, *45,* 92–100.

——— Specific and nonspecific factors in the effectiveness of a behavioral approach to the treatment of marital discord. *Journal of Consulting and Clinical Psychology,* 1978, *46,* 3, 442–452.

Johnson, S., & Christensen, A. Multiple criteria follow-up of behavior modification with families. Unpublished paper. University of Oregon, Eugene, Oregon, 1977.

Johnson, S. M., & Lobitz, G. K. The personal and marital adjustment of parents as related to observed child deviance and parenting behaviors. *Journal of Abnormal Child Psychology,* 1974, *2,* 193–208.

McCord, J. A thirty-year follow-up of treatment effects. *American Psychologist,* 1978, *33,* 284–289.

Minton, C., Kogan, J., & Levine, J. Maternal control and obedience in the two-year-old. *Child Development,* 1971, *42,* 1873–1894.

Murphy, D. C., & Mendelson, L. A. Communication and adjustment in marriage: Investigating the relationship. *Family Process,* 1973, *12,* 317–326.

Olson, D. H. Empirically unbinding the double-bind: Review of research and conceptual reformulations. *Family Process,* 1972, *11,* 69–91.

Parke, R., & Collmer, M. Child abuse: An interdisciplinary analysis. In M. Hetherington (Ed.), *Review of child development research.* Chicago: University of Chicago Press, 1975.

Patterson, G. R. The aggressive child: Victim and architect of a coercive system. In E. Mash, L. Hamerlynck & L. Handy (Eds.), *Behavior modification and families. I. Theory and research.* New York: Brunner/Mazell, 1976.

——— Intervention for boys with conduct problems: Multiple settings, treatments and criteria. *Journal of Consulting and Clinical Psychology,* 1974, *42,* 471–481.

——— A performance theory for coercive family interaction. In R. Cairns (Ed.), *Social interaction: Methods, analysis and evaluation,* 1978.

Patterson, G. R., & Fleischman, M. J. Maintenance of treatment effects: Some considerations concerning family systems and follow-up data. *Behavior Therapy.* In press.

Patterson, G. R., & Moore, D. R. Interactional patterns in dyadic units. In S. Suomi, M. Lamb & G. Stevenson (Eds.), *The study of social interaction: Methodological issues.* Madison, Wisc.: University of Wisconsin Press, 1978.

Patterson, G. R., & Reid, J. B. Intervention for families of aggressive boys: A replication study. *Behavior Research and Therapy,* 1973, *11,* 383–394.

——— Reciprocity and coercion: Two facets of social systems. In C. Neuringer & J. D. Michael (Eds.), *Behavior modification in clinical psychology.* New York: Appleton-Century-Crofts, 1970.

Raush, H. L., Barry, W. A., Hertel, R. K., & Swain, M. A. *Communication, conflict and marriage.* San Francisco: Jossey-Bass, 1974.

Reid, J. B., & Hinajosa, G. Treatment of children who steal. Unpublished paper, Oregon Social Learning Center, Eugene, Oregon, 1977.

Reid, J. B., & Patterson, G. R. Follow-up analyses of a behavioral treatment program for boys with conduct problems: A reply to Kent. *Journal of Consulting and Clinical Psychology,* 1976, *44,* 297–302.

Robins, L. N. *Deviant children grown up: A sociological study of sociopathic personality.* Baltimore: Williams and Wilkins, 1966.

Russell, C. S. Transition to parenthood: Problems and gratifications. *Journal of Marriage and the Family,* 1974, 294–301.

Skinner, B. F. *Science and human behavior.* New York: Appleton-Century-Crofts, 1954.

Snyder, J. J. A reinforcement analysis of interaction in problem and non-problem children. *Journal of Abnormal Psychology,* 1977, *86,* 5, 528–535.

Taplin, P., & Reid, J. B. Changes in parent consequation as a function of family intervention. *Journal of Consulting and Clinical Psychology,* 1977, *4,* 973–981.

Wahler, R. G. Generalization processes in child behavior change. NIMH progress report to Crime and Delinquency Section, 1979.

——— The insular mother: The problems in parent-child treatment. Unpublished paper submitted for publication. The University of Tennessee, 1978.

——— Oppositional children: A quest for parental reinforcement control. *Journal of Applied Behavior Analysis,* 1969, *2,* 159–170.

——— Parent insularity as a determinant of generalization success in family treatment. *The ecosystem of the sick kid: Implications for classification and intervention.* New York: CUNY Graduate Center. In press.

Wahler, R. G., & Leske, G. Accurate and inaccurate observer summary reports. *Journal of Nervous and Mental Disease,* 1973, *165,* 386–394.

Wahler, R. G., Leske, G., & Rogers, E. S. The insular family: A deviance support system for oppositional children. *Banff international conference on behavior modification.* In press.

Wahler, R. G., & Moore, D. M. School-home behavior change procedures for oppositional children. Paper presented at the Association for the Advancement of Behavior Theory, San Francisco, 1975.

Weiss, R. L., Birchler, G. R., & Vincent, J. P. Contractual models for negotiation training in marital dyads. *Journal of Marriage and the Family,* 1974, *36,* 321–331.

Wills, T. A., Weiss, R. L., & Patterson, G. R. A behavioral analysis of the determinants of marital satisfaction. *Journal of Consulting and Clinical Psychology,* 1974, *42,* 6, 802–811.

SYSTEMS-BEHAVIORAL INTERVENTION WITH DELINQUENT FAMILIES: CLINICAL, METHODOLOGICAL, AND CONCEPTUAL CONSIDERATIONS

James F. Alexander, UNIVERSITY OF UTAH

Cole Barton, UNIVERSITY OF UTAH

The purpose of this chapter is to describe an intervention strategy for dealing with disturbed adolescents and delinquents, particularly those whose "transgressions" are primarily social (e.g., running away, truancy, ungovernableness, substance abuse) as opposed to massively destructive to persons or property (e.g., rape, murder, major theft). This description will have three major foci: (1) a review of the development and application of the treatment program, with special emphasis on empirical evaluation; (2) a summary of several important clinical issues and still unanswered

Advances in Family Intervention, Assessment and Theory, Volume 1, pages 53–87.

ISBN: 0-89232-137-7

conceptual questions surrounding the program; and (3) a discussion of the methodological and statistical issues that have been raised in the development and evaluation of the program.

I. PROGRAM DEVELOPMENT

A. Alternatives for Treating Delinquency

During the 1960s, a number of factors created a strong national mandate for the prevention and more effective treatment of delinquent youth. One factor was sheer numbers; because of high birth rates during the previous two decades, the number of adolescents available to become delinquent had reached an all-time high (Turner and Dodd, in press). Changes in child-rearing and other social attitudes, an increasingly mobile society, rising divorce rates, and a variety of economic factors seemed to have contributed to the vast amount of delinquency and other forms of family disruption. Faced with the onslaught of new cases, the juvenile justice system first responded by trying to increase the availability for delinquent youth of traditional treatment (particularly individual psychotherapy) and, in more severe situations, institutionalization (in both mental health and criminal institutions). However, it quickly became apparent that these traditional approaches demonstrated little, if any, beneficial impact on youth (Stumphauzer, 1973), and, whether effective or not, these traditional approaches were extraordinarily costly. Additionally, these methods did not seem to have any real potential for prevention because they were designed primarily for remediation (Stumphauzer, 1973; Klein, Alexander, and Parsons, 1976).

Two of the major factors underlying the inefficiency of these traditional intervention approaches with troubled adolescents have been the basic assumptions underlying these approaches and the corresponding methods for developing therapeutic goals. The traditional personality or trait models have viewed maladaptive behavior as symptomatic, reflecting or *resulting from* aberrant intrapsychic mechanisms such as psychosexual conflict, projection, denial, low self-esteem, or confusion about identity. Because of this assumption, traditional treatment has been focused on the "abnormal" individual, utilizing techniques that are designed to modify or eliminate those hypothesized problematic mechanisms. While all clinicians realized that maladaptive environments such as the problem family were, in a sense, responsible for these aberrant intrapsychic mechanisms, it was nevertheless the individual, not the environment, upon whom treatment was lavished. As a result, even if individual adolescents experienced positive treatment effects, when thrust back into maladaptive family environments, they tended to experience a return to lower levels of functioning (The President's Commission on Law Enforcement and Administration of Justice, 1967).

Traditional personality or trait approaches have also utilized an inappropriate method for developing therapeutic goals. Specifically, these approaches have conceptualized the hypothesized intrapsychic problems as mental illness and contrasted this state with mental health, which represented the absence of hypothesized intrapsychic problems. Unfortunately, mental health as an ideal goal of therapeutic intervention may be both unrealistic and inappropriate. Most delinquents possess neither the resources nor the motivation to successfully undergo the types of intervention required to attain ideal mental health. Moreover, projects such as the Midtown Manhattan Study (Srole et al., 1962) have clearly demonstrated that very few people have ideal levels of mental health. Despite this, many people are nonetheless adaptive, "normal," and certainly more valued by society than juvenile delinquents. Thus, treatment approaches derived from the ideal mental health model may not be as reasonable or appropriate for dealing with delinquency as approaches that are derived from an "adaptive functioning" model.

In light of these two limiting factors of traditional intervention models, many clinicians, theorists, and researchers changed their focus from the individual delinquent to the natural environment (especially the family) in which the delinquent lives. As this refocusing occurred, two conceptual models came to the fore: systems theory (Buckley, 1968; Haley, 1963, 1971), and social learning (or behavioral) theory (Agras, 1972; Patterson and Reid, 1970; Tharpe and Wetzel, 1969). These models are particularly well-suited to applications within the family context because they formally and specifically contain principles that deal with the ways environments produce and maintain deviant behavior. The systems-behavioral model posits that deviant behaviors result from certain patterns of interdependent behaviors to which all family members contribute. For example, Patterson and Reid (1970) demonstrated how a child's "coercive" behavior (e.g., a tantrum) can elicit a response from mother (e.g., providing a reinforcer such as attention or a desired object), and this mother's response in turn is reinforced by the child's cessation of the coercive stimulus. With respect to delinquency, the systems-behavioral model argues that the main distinction between "adaptive" and "symptomatic" families is that when adaptive families experience stress, they engage in effective problem-solving sequences that allow them to overcome the disruptive impact of stress by developing new adaptive interaction patterns (Morton, Alexander, and Altman, 1976). Maladaptive families, on the other hand, respond to stress by developing interdependent interactions in which all family members reciprocally generate increasingly maladaptive behavior in one another (Alexander, 1973), resulting in the development of stable coercive interactions (Patterson and Reid, 1970) or such family system breakdowns as runaway, divorce, extramarital affairs, drinking, escaping for a "night out with the boys," and physical abuse.

Systems-behavioral theories have also adopted an empirical "matching-to-sample" strategy to develop therapeutic goals (Parsons and Alexander, 1973; Alexander and Barton, 1976). Rather than isolating processes that have been hypothesized to be maladaptive, the systems-behavioral approach has studied families with delinquent children and adaptive families to observe directly the difference in interaction patterns that produce and maintain maladaptive outcomes on the one hand and adaptive outcomes on the other. The patterns that are so identified then become the focus of intervention, and techniques are developed to modify these maladaptive patterns in families with delinquents.

The following sections describe the process of developing and evaluating a systems-behavioral intervention program for families with delinquent children. The stages of the program are: (1) identifying the relevant interaction patterns, (2) developing techniques to produce positive changes in these patterns, (3) evaluating the changes, and (4) evaluating overall program effectiveness.

B. The Identification Phase: Developing the Targets of Change

1. Conceptual Framework and Methodology. In order to provide a basis for the development of an intervention program, Alexander (1973) recorded on videotape twenty-two delinquent and twenty normal families as they attempted to resolve differences of opinion regarding family issues. The dependent measures chosen for the study needed to satisfy stringent research criteria, and at the same time be sufficiently relevant clinically. For example, the measures had to reflect interaction processes that were potentially modifiable and easily measured. Processes that cannot be relatively easily observed and measured (without additional complex equipment) and then modified in a therapeutic context are of little use to the clinician no matter how scientifically admirable they may be. On the other hand, the measures also had to represent reliable and nonreactive data that generate methodological confidence, and that are replicable across populations and raters. The dependent measures also had to reflect interaction-driving or -maintaining dynamic properties, reflecting interaction processes that distinguished between adaptive and maladaptive families and could produce the maladaptive outcomes represented by delinquency. Finally, the measures had to reflect an interdependency among family members that could explain how the maladaptive processes are maintained, as well as suggest how intervention into these processes could produce stable and long-term beneficial changes.

The final two criteria for the dependent measures simultaneously represent conceptual, technical, and methodological issues. These issues concern generality of the measures and the locus of control that they implicitly assume. The generality issue relates to the concern that while the measures must be sufficiently sensitive to distinguish between adaptive and maladaptive families, they must also be able to transcend the uniqueness of individual families. That is, the measures had to reflect the systems theory assumption that quite different behaviors can serve the same interpersonal *function,* and thus must be coded in the same way. For example, while in one family a "put-down" may take the form of a belittling verbal comment, in another family the *same interpersonal impact* may be felt from a condescending stare. Though topographically dissimilar, these maneuvers serve to create identical interpersonal states, and thus must be conceptualized and measured as the same type of interactive event. This issue is perhaps best exemplified in the coercion hypothesis (Patterson and Reid, 1970). The coercion hypothesis represented a single paradigm concerning a dynamic interpersonal relationship form, yet it can consist of a wide range of specific behaviors in myriad contexts (e.g., a child's tantrums in the supermarket, husband's "incompetence" at helping around the house, a wife's nagging, etc.). To identify this coercion paradigm, researchers and clinicians must be able to look beyond specific behavioral forms, and instead look for certain regularities of interaction patterns in which specific behaviors may vary greatly but in which the relational nature of the interaction is constant.

Finally, the processes that were measured had to reflect an implicit assumption regarding locus of control that is consistent with the systems-behavioral framework. Particularly in the case of adolescents, the measures could not reflect an *implicit* assumption of one-way control, that is, parent control of the child. Unlike the situation with young children in which parents are conceptualized as the "controllers" (an assumption seriously questioned by Bell, 1968), adolescents cannot reasonably be conceptualized as mere "passive" recipients of stimulus control (antecedents) and consequating events. Thus any measurement systems that identify only deviant adolescent responses and parental antecedents and consequences are doomed to extraordinary inefficiency, if not downright failure. Simply put, in adolescent families, the parents often have only slightly more control over the adolescents than the adolescents have over the parents. It can be argued, of course, that parents still maintain control over the basic reinforcers (money, food, shelter, etc.), but even these reinforcers become incredibly nonsalient in situations where teenagers simply refuse to be reinforced by them, and develop alternatives through such means as running away or developing their own sources of income (i.e., by burglary, by staying with boy friends who have jobs, etc.). Unlike younger children, adolescents can find and/or *create* more salient reinforcers outside the home than within the home. Because of this, measurement systems that view the adolescent only as a passive recipient of parental influence ignore major dynamic influences on the nature of interaction in such families. Thus the processes that are investigated must inherently contain the possibility of reciprocal or two-way control, which acknowledges and legitimizes the impact of the adolescent as much as the impact of the parents.

The measurement system available at the time of early program development that seemed to best meet the numerous criteria listed above was represented in Gibb's (1961) work with group dynamics. His conceptual scheme involved two major categories of behavior: defensiveness and supportiveness. Gibb's early work had demonstrated that adaptive problem-solving groups were characterized by high rates of supportiveness and low rates of defensiveness. Maladaptive and disintegrating groups, on the other hand, experienced the inverse—high rates of defensiveness and low rates of supportiveness. Gibb's framework also argued that defensiveness and supportiveness were inherently dynamic behaviors in that they tended to generate reciprocal behaviors among all members of a system; that is, defensiveness begets defensiveness, supportiveness begets supportiveness. These measures thus reflected a conceptual framework that could explain both the interdependency of family members' behavior, additionally explaining the production of maladaptive outcomes in the case of delinquent families, and the absence of such outcomes in normals.

2. *Results.* Table I summarizes the data from the identification study (Alexander, 1973). For purposes of this chapter, the data (average reliabilities for defensiveness, r = .85; for supportiveness, r = .94) have been highly collapsed, but nonetheless demonstrate their success in accomplishing the main goals of the study. Specifically, strong support is found for the systems theory prediction that whereas higher supportiveness is characteristic of adaptive families, a much higher rate of systems-destructive defensiveness is found in the communication patterns of maladaptive or deliquent families. This "static" level of finding is not as potentially important as is the "dynamic" finding that, whereas maladaptive families are reciprocal around defensiveness, adaptive families are reciprocal around supportiveness. Specifically, in delinquent families, when one member behaves in a defensive manner, other family

Table I. Defensiveness and Supportiveness Among Dyads in Normal and Delinquent Families

	Supportiveness		*Defensiveness*	
	Family Means	*Reciprocity (average correlation)*	*Family Means*	*Reciprocity (average correlation)*
Normal parent & child dyads	52.5*	+.63[1]	6.9[2]	−.02
Delinquent parents & child dyads	36.8*	+.12	34.8[2]	+.41[1]

* Difference between means significant at $p < .05$.
[1] Correlation significant at $p < .05$.
[2] Difference between means significant at $p < .05$.

members "reciprocate" this defensiveness at a similar level; that is, the rates are significantly positively correlated ($r = .41$). In contrast, defensiveness, when it does occur in adaptive families, is not reciprocated ($r = .02$). The converse situation occurs in the case of supportiveness (delinquent families' reciprocity of supportiveness, $r = .12$; normal families' reciprocity of supportiveness, $r = .63$). While these data provide some support for Gibb's concepts regarding the system-destructive vs. -enhancing properties of defensiveness and supportiveness, respectively, his hypotheses must be modified somewhat in the case of delinquent and normal families. That is, reciprocity does not appear to be a pervasive phenomenon; the more meaningful distinction between the two family outcomes may be the data that adaptive families restrict their reciprocity to supportiveness, whereas delinquent families restrict their reciprocity to defensiveness. The clinical issue is therefore not simply one of "stimulus control." People do not respond "in kind" to either a defensive or supportive antecedent. Rather, families that contingently respond to defensiveness ultimately experience delinquency, while families that contingently respond to supportiveness create and maintain adaptive family outcomes. These data make it imperative that an intervention program identify and modify those conditions that create adaptive reciprocity in healthy families and maladaptive reciprocity in others.

C. *Developing Therapeutic Procedures*

1. Methodology. Based on the promising empirical support provided by the identification study for the systems-behavioral conceptual framework, a program for developing an intervention program was initiated.

The first step involved investigating the degree to which the processes of defensiveness and supportiveness could be modified in a family therapy context (Alexander, 1971). In this study, forty delinquent families were randomly assigned to one of four treatment conditions: family therapy, family and individual therapy, individual therapy alone, and a no-treatment control group. The age, prior offense rate, and socioeconomic status of the families were comparable for all four groups and were also comparable to the families studied in the earlier investigation. In the two systems-behavioral family therapy conditions, families were seen for a total of eight hours (in groups of five) by therapists who were trained to teach families effective communication skills (Alexander, 1974) and procedures for contingency contracting (Stuart, 1971). In particular, therapists were trained to identify defensive and supportive communications and were taught to model, prompt, and reinforce supportive communications, at the same time ignoring or actively terminating defensive interactions. The family plus individual treatment group received, in addition to the family therapy, four one-hour individual sessions between a counselor (probation officer) and the identified delinquent. The individual therapy group received only the individual counseling sessions, and the no-treatment control received no attention beyond minimal bookkeeping required by the juvenile court. Family interactions pre- and post-treatment were recorded on audio-tape while they experienced the same resolution-of-differences tasks that were used in the matching-to-sample study. As in the earlier study, raters were trained to a reliability criteria of 90% and once again were "blind" to the condition of the families.

2. *Results.* A comparison of the pre-to-post changes in supportiveness and defensiveness in the four groups strongly suggested that these components of family interaction are quite modifiable in a family intervention context. Specifically, Figure 1 shows the changes in supportive to defensive ratios from pre to post, and indicates that whereas the individual therapy condition showed only nonsignificant gains in supportiveness and reductions in defensiveness, the groups in the two family therapy conditions demonstrated significant increases in supportiveness and decreases in defensiveness. In contrast, the no-treatment groups demonstrated a slight deterioration in family functioning (i.e., decrease in supportiveness and increase in defensiveness).

This study was, of course, far from definitive in that the design contained confounds (i.e., different amounts of time given to treated groups), plus the fact that these modifications in family functioning were not examined in light of subsequent changes in outcome (i.e., delinquency). However, the data did provide additional impetus for the continued de-

Figure 1. Pre and Post Ratios of Average Supportive-to-Defensive Communications among Family Members in Four Treatment Conditions

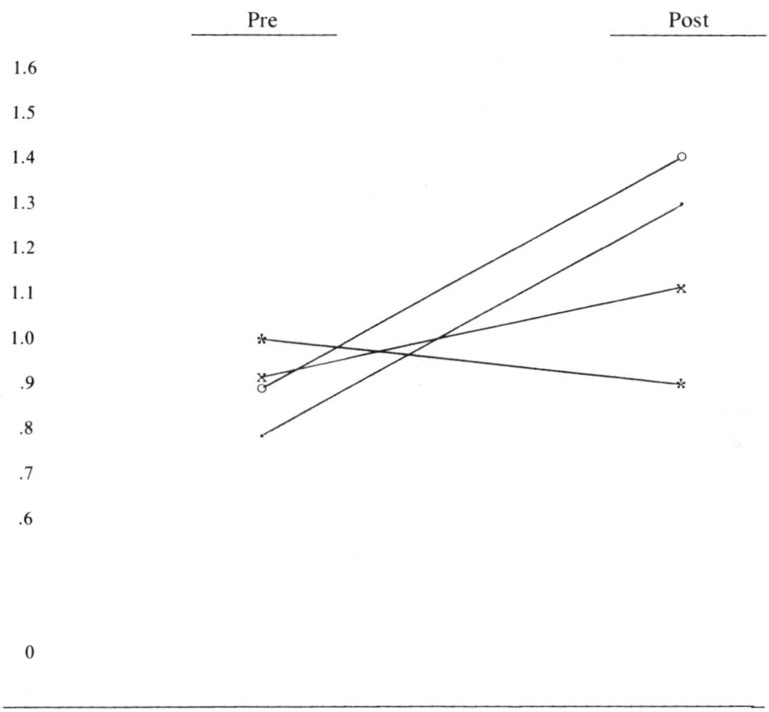

· —— · Systems-behavioral family therapy condition (increase significant at $p \leq .05$).
o —— o Systems-behavioral family therapy plus individual therapy (increase significant at $p \leq .05$).
x —— x Individual therapy alone (increase nonsignificant).
* —— * No treatment controls (decrease nonsignificant).

velopment of an intervention program that was designed to modify family interaction patterns. A major program development and evaluation project was undertaken (Alexander, 1973; Parsons and Alexander, 1973) to examine more critical and global features of family outcomes.

D. Refining and Evaluating the Program

1. Methodology and Procedures. While the previous intervention study had demonstrated an impact on family process variables, clinical experience with the treated families had made it clear that simple "training" in communication skills were not sufficient to help families develop the kind of adaptive problem-solving strategies that would be maintained over long periods of time. That is, while families demonstrated an ability to "talk together" differently, they continued to demonstrate significant resistance to long-term changes when dealing with such critical issues as teenagers' freedom, access to peers, and so forth. It therefore became apparent that in addition to a strong "educational" component of intervention, families required additional techniques to reduce their rigidity and resistance to change, to change the "malevolent" attributions they were making about one another, and to develop more enthusiasm for generalizing the styles they had learned in their home environment on a longer-term basis. Therapists were therefore trained to conceptualize intervention as a two-phase process, the first phase consisting of relabeling motivational states, removing blaming attributes from the family members, helping all family members see the interdependency of their behaviors and feelings, and helping them see that change would benefit them all. (Because a complete description of the therapeutic strategies utilized during this phase is beyond the scope of this chapter, the reader is referred to the following sources: Alexander, 1974; Alexander and Barton, 1976; Barton and Alexander, 1977; Malouf and Alexander, 1974.) Therapists were also trained to utilize a wider range of "educational" devices, including bibliotherapy, token systems, and "individualized" adjunct techniques such as relaxation training and self-control techniques (Alexander, 1974).

For this study, additional dependent measures were developed that could be "content free" and yet reflect the adaptiveness of family interaction. These measures—based on considerable earlier research that had identified them as distinguishing between adaptive and maladaptive families—included equality of talk time, silence, and the frequency and duration of interruptions. All of these measures reflect the flexibility of family communication patterns and the lability of problem-solving attempts (Alexander, 1970; Duncan, 1968; Mischler and Waxler, 1968; Stuart, 1968; Winter and Ferreira, 1969). To evaluate the impact of the intervention program on these process measures, forty families were randomly assigned to one of four conditions using a modified Solomon group design. Ten families received pre- and post-testing in addition to the systems-behavioral family intervention. A second group of ten families received the systems behavioral family intervention but were only post-tested. A third group received pre- and post-testing but no intervention whatsoever, and a fourth group received no pre-testing and an alternative form of intervention (a client-centered treatment program) prior to post-testing. Once again, demographic characteristics of all the families were comparable, both among groups and when compared to subjects studied earlier. The time interval between pre- and post-testing was comparable (approximately five weeks) for all families that received both. Data were automatically recorded on event recorders from voice-actuated microphones worn by each family member. During interaction testing, all families participated in the same type of discussion and resolution-of-differences tasks that had been utilized in earlier studies.

2. *Results.* A 2 × 2 analysis of variance indicated that pre-testing had no main or interactive effects. For purposes of simplicity, the two systems-behavioral family groups are combined in Table II. The data contained in Table III replicate the previously found beneficial impact of systems behavioral intervention on the functioning of delinquents and their families. That is, systems-behaviorally treated families at post-test demonstrated significantly less variance in talk time (reflecting greater equality, i.e., adaptiveness), less silence, and greater frequency and duration of interruptions. These changes reflect the increase in adaptive flexibility of problem-solving which approximates that found in normal

*Table II.** Process Measures: Post-Test Means on Three Interaction Variables

	Variance of Talk Time[1] *(in seconds)*	*Silence (seconds)*	*Frequency of Interruptions*	*Duration of Interruptions*
Short-term family behavioral treatment (N – 20)	1194.8	154.4	65.9	31.38
Client-centered family groups (N = 10)	1494.6	220.1	18.5	6.98
No-treatment controls (N – 6)[2]	2099.5	237.0	20.2	15.25
H value[3] (df = 2) of differences	11.19[4]	11.70[4]	13.75[4]	14.21[4]

* Reprinted from Alexander, J. F., and Barton, C., "Behavioral systems therapy for families." In D. H. Olson, *Treating Relationships* (Lake Mills, Iowa: Graphic Publishing Company, Inc., 1976).

[1] Lower score indicates more equality of speech.

[2] Four families were unavailable for testing.

[3] Rank sum test for several samples.

[4] $p < .05$.

*Table III.** Outcome by Treatment

	N	*Impact-Outcome Study: % Recidivism after 3–15 Months*	*Long-Term Effect: % Sibling Referrals after 3 Years*
No Formal Treatment			
No Treatment Controls	6	50	40
Post-Hoc Yoked Control	46	48	
Baserate for SL County	2800	51	
		Average 50%	
Alternative Treatment			
Client-Centered Family Group	19	47	59
Eclectic-Dynamic Social Services	11	73	63
		Average 57%	
Short-Term Family Systems Treatment			
1970–72 Program	46	26	20
1972–73 Replication Study	45	27	
		Average 26%	

* Reprinted from Alexander, J. F., and Barton, C., "Behavioral systems therapy for families." In D. H. Olson, *Treating Relationships* (Lake Mills, Iowa: Graphic Publishing Company, Inc., 1976).

families. The client-centered family groups were considerably less adaptive on these dimensions, and across all measures appeared not significantly different from the no-treated controls.

Though important as a replication of the direct positive impact of the program on family functioning, these data did not constitute the main focus of this phase of program development. The main emphasis in this study was to specifically demonstrate the additional link between beneficial changes in family functioning at the time of post-test and long-term positive effects on family viability as reflected in recidivism and subsequent family problems. To study these long-term effects, additional families were randomly assigned to the various groups and two additional comparison groups were added. An additional alternative treatment group that was seen in an "eclectic-dynamically" oriented, church-sponsored treatment program was evaluated, along with an additional group of no-treatment controls that were "yoked" on a post hoc basis with each of the families seen in the treatment condition (Alexander and Parsons, 1973).

3. *Evaluating Program Impact.* Two different measures of program impact were evaluated. The obvious measure of program impact was recidivism, which was measured for all groups at an average of one year after termination of the project. Juvenile court records were searched under blind conditions, and the occurrence of any offense (with the exception of minor traffic violations, e.g., overtime parking) was noted. Table III contains the recidivism data for the various control, alternative treatment, and systems-behavioral treatment groups, and clearly demonstrates the superiority of the systems-behavioral approach. The data reflect a common finding that some therapeutic treatments (in this case the client-centered group) are essentially comparable in outcome to no-treatment controls. And, even more ominous, one alternative treatment group (in this case the eclectic-dynamic church-sponsored intervention) seemed to generate a recidivism rate that was 50% higher than no-treatment controls. In contrast, the systems-behavioral family treatment program cut recidivism roughly in half, and this finding was replicated two years later (Alexander and Barton, 1976).

A second major outcome variable reflected the underlying philosophy of the systems-behavioral family approach; that is, changes occur not only around the "target" behavior of an identified individual, but more pervasive changes take place in the interaction (i.e., problem-solving) style of the entire family (Malouf and Alexander, 1974). If these hypothesized changes are both long-term and related to adaptiveness in family function, then the systems-behavioral model predicts that not only the identified patient, but also all of the siblings in the family, would be beneficially affected (Klein, Alexander, and Parsons, 1976). Therefore, on the average of three years following program termination, juvenile court computerized records were searched for the occurrence of a referral for any sibling in each of the treated families. As can also be seen in Table III, the systems-behavioral family program, as hypothesized, demonstrated a strong beneficial impact, reflecting sibling referral rates that were half those of the controls, and roughly one-third those of the alternative treatment groups. As reported by Alexander and Parsons (1973), the beneficial outcome effects of the systems-behavioral family program were directly and statistically related to the previously cited positive changes in family interaction processes (Parsons and Alexander, 1973).

II. CURRENT CLINICAL ISSUES

A. The Service Delivery System

In a way that is consistent with the old "half empty-half full" cup story, the systems-behavioral outcome data can be seen in one of two lights, either "having significantly reduced recidivism to only 25%" or as "still reflecting a 26% recidivism rate." In other words, an improved but nevertheless still uncomfortable rate of recidivism continues to exist.

One way to conceptualize this problem is in terms of estimating, or accounting for, components of "positive outcome variance." The previously cited outcome study (Alexander and Parsons, 1973) replicated numerous other studies that have demonstrated that even in the absence of specific clinical intervention, a significant proportion of families (50%) seem to improve, that is, experience no additional referrals to the juvenile court. The systems-behavioral program, in contrast to two alternative programs, was shown to produce an additional—roughly 25%—positive outcome variance, and now the question centers on how to positively influence the remaining 25% outcome variance.

Clinical programs have traditionally adopted one of three strategies to deal with this problem: improve the technical components of the program, identify and deal with the family (or client) characteristics that contribute to negative outcomes, or identify and modify the characteristics of the service delivery system (in this case the therapist) that differentially influence outcome.

In the systems-behavioral family program, three attempts (i.e., replications) were made to improve the technology of the program. New training tapes were produced, additional manuals written, and additional expertise, developed through experience, was passed on to therapists. Unfortunately, it appears that systems-behavioral family therapy technology had gone as far as possible; the assumed improvements in technology did not produce any further reductions in recidivism, dropout rates, or adaptive changes in family process (Alexander and Barton, 1976; Alexander et al., 1976).

The second alternative, that of trying to identify family characteristics that predicted poor outcome, was overtly rejected. Though certainly an important clinical and research issue, the systems-behavioral program was determined to avoid the result that often accrues when typologies of families or clients are used to "explain" failure, or avoid providing service (e.g., the family has excessively rigid boundaries, the patient didn't possess sufficient ego strength, the family wasn't sufficiently motivated, etc.). The issue of family characteristics, then, remains a legitimate and unanswered question, and must be investigated more thoroughly before a complete intervention program can be developed.

However, at this time, the third strategy for improving program effectiveness appears to be sufficiently important to constitute the major focus. This strategy consists of identifying the dimensions of therapist behavior that differentially affect treatment outcome, either independently or in interaction with the treatment program. Whereas the "traditional" psychotherapy literature has placed a great deal of emphasis on the therapist, both the systems and behavioral literature have seemingly ignored the therapist, apparently falling back into the "therapist uniformity myth" identified long ago by Kiesler (1966). In fact, both the systems and behavioral literature seem to imply that if one possesses the appropriate technical skills, as well as the appropriate conceptual framework, positive impact is assured. Believing that this sort of assumption was inappropriate, the systems-behavioral program, after demonstrating overall therapeutic impact, turned its attention to the service delivery system.

1. Methodology. Alexander et al. (1976) initiated an essentially exploratory study that was designed to determine which, if any, dimensions of therapist behavior or "characteristics" had a significant impact on therapeutic outcome in the context of the systems-behavioral family intervention model with delinquents.

To obtain information about therapists, twenty-two trainees were instructed in the use of the intervention program in ways comparable to therapist training in the previous studies, which included role-playing and group discussion. At the end of training, the two primary trainers independently rated "characteristic" styles based on trainees' performance in role-play along eight interpersonal dimensions. These dimensions, which were behaviorally-based, were derived from already existing literature (particularly the one-to-one psychotherapy literature—see Truax and Carkhuff, 1967) as well as "intuition" regarding what could be gleaned from the systems and behavioral literature. The final list included the following behavioral categories: affect-behavior integration (e.g., relating feelings to behavior), non-blaming (prevents and avoids the use of pejorative or negative labels concerning behavior or motives), warmth, humor, self-disclosure, directiveness, self-confidence, and clarity.

These ratings, performed prior to any direct contact with families, were then simply put aside until one year after that group of therapists had terminated the families they were seeing in the project. These families, with only a few exceptions (the sample included two overtly psychotic families), were comparable to families seen in the numerous previous projects. The number of sessions was also comparable, ranging from one to fourteen sessions. The "outcome" of therapeutic intervention was jointly determined by the therapist and supervisor at the time of termination. Outcomes were sorted into four groups: *Outcome Group 1*—This group terminated against therapeutic advice after only one session (this group consisted, obviously, of immediate dropouts). *Outcome Group 2*—These families maintained therapeutic contact for more than one session and demonstrated small to moderate degrees of improvement in response to intervention but failed to maintain this improvement and subsequently dropped out of the program against therapeutic advice. *Outcome Group 3*—This group remained in therapy and demonstrated steady (but slow) improvement on the kinds of "process" criterion utilized in previous studies (the quantity of talk time, spontaneity—i.e., less silence, greater lability in communication and problem-solving patterns, a decrease in defensiveness and increase in supportiveness, etc.). They also reported improvements in their behavior at home. However, these families did not seem to be able to attain totally adaptive functioning independent of direct continued therapist intervention and were terminated by the project at the end of the ten-week period that was imposed because of the university course structure in which the project operates. These families demonstrated considerable improvement, but not completely satisfactory results. *Outcome Group 4*—These families represented a jointly determined termination between themselves and the therapist. They demonstrated the independent and spontaneous ability to communicate according to the adaptive criteria of family functioning described above, and in addition reported a cessation of problems in the home.

2. *Results.* In order to independently validate the clinically defined outcome designations, supportive-to-defensive (S/D) ratios were derived from global ratings by independent (and blind) ratings of first and last therapy session audio-taped recordings. These ratios were subjected to an unequal N analysis of variance with repeated measures. Table IV demonstrates that while the independently defined good outcome groups experienced a dramatic improvement in S/D ratios, the poor outcome groups experienced a deterioration. To provide additional validation for the outcome groupings, one year after termination, juvenile court and community mental health records were searched, as in prior studies, for re-referral or other forms of recidivism subsequent to therapeutic termination. As can be seen in Table IV, the total recidivism rate for the group was 24%, comparable to previous studies and replications. However, when the total sample was broken into the independently (clinically)

Table IV. Family Process (Defensive/Supportive Communication) and Family Outcome (Re-Referrals) for Four Clinically-Defined Outcome Groups

Clinically-Defined Outcome Groups	*Average Supportive-* to-Defensive Ratios*		*Re-Referrals*[1]	
	First Session	*Last Session*	*N*	*%*
1 & 2 (poor outcome) N = 9	.84	.64	5	55
3 & 4 (good outcome) N = 12	.71	1.25	0	0

* Outcome groups effect $F(2,18) = 5.25$, $p < .05$. Session effect $F(2,36) = 7.79$, $p < .01$. Groups X sessions $F(4,36) = 5.12$, $p < .01$.

[1] Re-referral rate for entire sample = 24%.

defined poor and good outcome groups, significant differences in recidivism rates were apparent. Specifically, Outcome Groups 3 and 4 reflected no recidivism or re-referral, whereas Outcome Groups 1 and 2, which were determined as "poor" outcome based on "clinical" criteria, demonstrated very high recidivism rates (55%).

Thus the independently derived outcome criteria of re-referral and family process measures converged, providing support for the therapeutically derived outcome designations utilized in the study. Because of this convergence, it was felt that the good versus poor outcome designations represented reasonable dependent measures upon which we could regress the impact of the various therapist characteristic variables that had been measured prior to the therapy phase itself. Of the eight dimensions, five predicted outcome (correlations ranged from $r = .57$ to $r = .65$), and these five fell into two independent groupings within which the dimensions were highly intercorrelated. These groupings were defined, post hoc, as "structuring skills" (directiveness and self-confidence) and "relationship skills" (affect-behavior integration, warmth, and humor). Because the dimensions within each of the two major classes were so highly intercorrelated, it was decided to use simply a composite score for each dimension. Table V reflects the relationship between these composite scores and therapeutic outcome. Specifically, relationship skills alone accounted for 44.6% of outcome variance, whereas structuring skills accounted for 35.8% of outcome variance. Taken together, these aspects of therapist behavior accounted for a total of 60% of outcome variance. Multiple regression analyses of the therapist skill classes on the basis of good versus poor outcome verified these effects.

Table V. Correlation and Regression Relationships between Therapist Behavior Characteristics and Family Treatment Outcome

Therapist Skill Category	*Independent Correlation with Outcome**	*Multiple Regression Significance Test*
Structuring Skills (Composite of directiveness and self-confidence)	r = .594[1]	F (1,17) = 11.84[1]
Relationship Skills (Composite of affect-behavior integration, warmth, & humor)	r = .661[1]	F (1,17) = 7.92[1]

* Jointly, relationship and structuring skills accounted for 59.65% of the variance in outcome [$F(2,18) = 26.61$, $p < .01$].
[1] $p < .05$.

This study has numerous conceptual and methodological weaknesses, not the least of which is the fact that therapist behavior was not *directly* related to therapeutic outcome; instead, the measures reflected "characteristic therapist style" prior to the therapy itself. Nevertheless, the fact that such a major portion of outcome variance within the systems-behavioral program could be accounted for by variations on these therapist dimensions suggests that the lack of attention that has been given to therapist characteristics in the systems-behavioral literature represents an unfortunate oversight, if not a critical omission. Subsequent research must be performed that will more directly examine the relationship between *in vivo* therapist behavior and family changes in process and outcome. However, considerably more attention must also be paid to the conceptual implications of these findings. On the one hand, the therapist could be looked at as "mere technician" and we in the field could continue to interpret data such as these as representing a simple technical issue of the "best" way to intervene. However, it could well be that these data have implications for our conceptual model. The therapist skills, particularly "relationship" behaviors, strongly suggest that intervention and change in families is considerably more than a "technical" or "educational" process. It is, in addition, a relationship process involving the family and the therapist. Since the data demonstrate that it is not sufficient to simply "train therapists" in the process of modeling, communication, etc., it may be that the same situation exists with families. That is, we cannot simply think of them as people we "train" in these skills; they must be treated in terms of their *relationships* as well.

B. Family Attributions

This issue brings us to a second major clinical phenomenon that has been inadequately examined in the systems-behavioral literature with delinquent families. This issue concerns the relationship between the families' interaction styles, the "problems" experienced by the families as an outgrowth of their interaction styles, the "sets" or attributional frameworks under which the families operate, and the way programs conceptualize the intervention process with these families. Stated in oversimplified terms, families of delinquents in the systems-behavioral literature are often seen as ignorant, as not possessing adequate knowledge or communication skills, contingency management skills, and so forth, which would enable them to interact in more adaptive ways. As a result, the literature often implies that the main goal of intervention is to simply educate these families in terms of more adaptive or effective means for control and communication. However, all therapists who work with delinquent families recognize that this conceptualization represents a gross oversimplification. In fact, a significant amount of time and energy put into intervention by therapists surrounds the processes of "getting cooperation," "motivating family members," "generating reinforcers," and the like. Unfortunately, because this process has not been incorporated into our conceptual frameworks regarding clinical intervention, this phase of intervention has often been left to luck, folklore, and less than programmatic approaches to training new therapists. Also, the profession has not developed an adequate framework or category system for understanding these attributional variables and how they operate nor how they can be modified most efficiently in the therapeutic context.

Data relevant to this issue are provided in a project in progress by Barton and Alexander. In this study, sixteen delinquent and sixteen normal families, again comparable to each other and to families investigated in previous studies, were randomly assigned to one of two conditions: a "competitive" attitudinal set, in which only one family member could benefit in a family interaction setting (playing a modified game of Scrabble), and a "cooperative" set in which the total score for all family members was added together and the entire family could benefit from the performance of each family member. Of major interest in this study was evaluation of the assumptions made in the family interaction literature that "pathological" families demonstrate, essentially, a "trait-like" form of maladaptive interaction. However, data from the Barton and Alexander study raise serious questions about this interpretation of family interaction (see Figure 2). Specifically, though delinquent families demonstrate a significant main effect (i.e., generate considerably higher rates of defensiveness and lower rates of supportiveness than do normals), this effect is almost completely generated by delinquent families in the com-

Figure 2. Sums of Defensiveness of Control and Delinquent Families in Competitive and Cooperative Conditions

	Competitive	Cooperative
Delinquent Families	$\bar{x} = 22.396$ $\sigma = 8.448$	$\bar{x} = 11.729$ $\sigma = 6.875$
Control Families	$\bar{x} = 11.5$ $\sigma = 6.311$	$\bar{x} = 11.715$ $\sigma = 8.014$

petitive condition. That is, under "cooperating" conditions, the interaction of delinquent families is almost indistinguishable from that of normal families, particularly in their rates of defensiveness.

These data suggest tremendous implications for intervention programs. It appears that given the appropriate "set" or attributional context, delinquent families seem to be capable of behaving in ways roughly comparable to adaptive families. It thus appears at best inefficient, if not grossly inappropriate, to conceptualize delinquent families as "ignorant." Instead, a considerable component of their maladaptive behavior styles may be the result of attributional sets under which they operate. This conclusion is particularly meaningful in light of the fact that the bulk of systems-behavioral intervention programs do not formally contain propositions about and techniques for changing attributional sets. Historically, the focus has been instead on interaction styles, control techniques such as contingency management, and the techniques of "good communication."

Of course, the data do not imply that the problem with maladaptive families is totally cognitive. That is, though they do approximate normals in cooperative situations, delinquent families are considerably more maladaptive than normals in competitive situations. Stated differently, the competitive situation does produce greater amounts of defensiveness and less supportiveness in adaptive families but not nearly at the magnitude demonstrated in delinquent families. Since all families experience situations of value differences, conflict over resources, and other situations that could be conceptualized as "competitive," it does appear that delinquent families do require considerable attention aimed toward changing their interactions in this context. Once again, however, our change programs historically may have adopted an inefficient approach in assuming that delinquent families "are" maladaptive, whereas adaptive families "are not." Based on these findings, perhaps one major focus for the early stages of intervention with delinquent families would be to develop, expand, investigate, and disseminate technologies that are designed to impact the motivational or attributional sets under which families characteristically operate when they enter therapy. If, for example, delinquent families can be helped to adopt a cooperative set, the Barton and Alexander study suggests they will automatically experience positive changes in their interactive behaviors. In this context of positive change, it will be much easier for therapists to generate and shape additional adaptive changes in their interaction styles, develop new adaptive interaction norms, and then program the generalization of these changes to situations where the context is, in fact, competitive.

III. MEASUREMENT ISSUES: CONCEPTUAL AND METHODOLOGICAL CONSIDERATIONS

In the course of developing and evaluating the systems-behavioral family intervention program, a number of conceptual and methodological issues have emerged, ranging from the mechanics of reliability estimates to problems of insuring that the independent variable (i.e., treatment), was in fact being administered in a consistent manner to families. As the program has attempted to resolve these myriad issues, however, two overriding measurement problems have continued to emerge, and because they represent such pervasive issues with both methodological and conceptual implications, they will receive particular attention in the present section. These issues can be put in the form of two sets of related questions: (1) what is the appropriate unit of assessment (e.g., the deviant individual's behavior, the immediately antecedent and consequent events, longer interactive chains, etc.), and how can we measure family interaction to best understand the evaluation and maintenance of maladaptive behavior; and (2) how can we conceptualize and statistically treat the dependencies that exist among the respective behaviors of individual family members?

A. The Unit of Measurement

The unit of measurement problem is basically one of scope: what should be included in the measurement process, and for what length of time? At first glance, this issue seems to be a minor one, as clinicians and researchers have already developed elegant methodological and statistical models for studying such maladaptive interactions as a mother-daughter argument that produces a runaway. The interaction of these two family members can be relatively easily measured, and the way in which the interaction escalates into an unacceptable outcome is obvious. Consider the following simple example:

Mother: "It's about time you got home. Where have you been?" (Said in a belligerent way.)
Daughter: "At school." (Similarly belligerent.)

Mother:	"Oh, sure! 'Til 4:30?"
Daughter:	"I couldn't get a ride home." (Starts to walk toward room.)
Mother:	"Hold it, kiddo, we're not through."
Daughter:	"I gotta change."
Mother:	"Change! Change for what?"
Daughter:	"To go to Susan's."
Mother:	"Uh-uh. You're going nowhere. Your room is a mess, and I'm tired of picking up your crap all over the place."
Daughter:	"Then don't." (Turns again toward room.)
Mother:	"I said hold it." (Grabs daughter's arm.)
Daughter:	"I'm not a kid any more." (Pulls mother's hand off.)
Mother:	"You are as long as you're in this house." (Mother is now yelling and appearing very angry. Grabs daughter again.)
Daughter:	"I said buzz off." (Pulls away mother's hand.)
Mother:	"Dammit!" (Slaps daughter.)
Daughter:	(Glares at mother, then grabs coat and purse and literally runs out the door.)

In some families, this incident may produce a runaway for several hours. In others, the runaway episode may be of much longer duration. In any event, the clinician and researcher have "an interaction" which is obviously problematic, and which could be relatively easily subjected to one of a number of static (e.g., frequency of aversive events) or sequential analyses. And, in a matching-to-sample sense, the spiraling maladaptive nature of the interaction could be descriptively contrasted with the kind of adaptive resolution that is found in normal families (e.g., clarifying expectations, negotiating regarding "going to Susan's," etc.). This has unfortunately been the level of analysis primarily used by interaction researchers and clinicians. It is reliable, predictive—and at many levels very confusing. Why would a daughter characteristically engage in an interaction that resulted in her being demeaned and slapped? Why would a mother characteristically engage in an interaction that would leave her alone, angry, frustrated, and sobbing? The level and unit of analysis presented above cannot provide the researcher and clinician these answers, and it becomes descriptively accurate but dynamically useless.

However, broadening the scope of the assessment can make the answers to these "why's" considerably more clear and, in a sense, reasonable. Consider the scene one and a half hours later, when daughter is with Tom (not Susan!), sharing her tale of malevolent mothering and receiving a great deal of nurturance, including offers to live with him, a promise of no hassles, etc. In other words, daughter has, *as a result of the interaction sequence,* created a very reinforcing interpersonal context with her peer, and at the same time legitimized her independence from the family (Morton, Alexander, and Altman, 1976). The situation has also changed for mother. Upon returning home from work, father's response to the tear-stained face is also nurturance and other forms of support, including such comments as "I'll not have her treating you like that!" In families where father does not characteristically emit high rates of "noncontingent" nurturance, it can be seen that the interaction with daughter has allowed mother to create a reinforcing relationship context with father.

The "moral of the story" concerns the conceptual jump that has been made from the immediate sequential analysis of the problematic interaction *per se* to the larger set of relational "payoffs" or functions that drive these problematic interactions. To make sense out of the interaction, the researcher and clinician have had to expand the scope of assessment to include more people and a longer time frame. In other words, the meaning and motivational-reinforcing properties of many sequences are not inherently contained in the sequences themselves, but in longer-term interpersonal contexts they create. Additional examples include: the husband who continues to create distance in his marriage (e.g., initiates a sexual sequence in a way that produces wife's refusal) in order to maintain an extramarital affair; a wife whose "family problems" allow her to continue a dependent relationship with others (e.g., her parents, the minister, etc.); the child whose "fears" allow him to continue a close relationship with a parent, and so on.

Viewed in this way, the issue of the meaning and dynamic interactions become more than a question of how large a scope to include in the measurement. It becomes also a conceptual issue involving the locus of cause and effect. Are individuals (such as the mother and daughter) merely passive recipients of stimulus control? Did mother's belligerence "cause" daughter's belligerence, and did daughter's belligerence in turn "cause" mother's slapping behavior? Or, as the systems-behavioral model suggests, did mother and daughter *both* create an interactive sequence that later on resulted in a highly reinforcing set of relational contexts? If so, the traditional concepts of the stimulus must be expanded from the event that causes (sets the occasion for) behavior, to an event that is produced or influenced by people in order to set in motion certain interaction trajectories. Looked at in this light, the understanding of sequences must involve more than the measurement of sequential behaviors that constitute them. To this point, the systems-behavioral program has a considerably better clinical, rather than experimental, grasp on this process. That is, the "decision rule" regarding the scope of analysis remains at the *post hoc* level, wherein the appropriate unit of analysis is determined by the question: "What is the impact of a problematic interaction (such as the mother-daughter argument) on the relationships between all members of the system?" If, as above, the end result of the problematic interaction is mother-father contact (especially nurturance), daughter-boyfriend contact, and parent-child distance, then those three relationship "states" are part of the analysis. And if these outcomes are a reliable and regular result of the problematic interaction, it is assumed they are the "reinforcing events" that maintain such interactions. If, to offer one contrasting example, daughter and mother "make up," and in the process exclude father, then the resulting relational states are seen as mother-daughter contact and nurturance, mother-father distance, and daughter-father distance. A second contrasting example would involve mother going to her own parents' home, father going out with the boys ("to get away from all this crap!"), and daughter going to the boyfriend. In this case, we assume that each member in the family is reinforced by distance from one another, or perhaps by the extrafamilial relationships that the problematic interaction has allowed them to maintain.

As mentioned above, problematic sequences like that found in the example make little sense when examined only at a microscopic level. Unfortunately, it is difficult to deal with them in research context because we cannot meaningfully create them. Instead, at least to this point in the development of the systems-behavioral model, we can only adopt the stance of naturalistic observer and explain their regularities on a *post hoc* basis. On the other hand, to the extent that the model can better develop a conceptual framework for looking at this phenomenon, we can also begin to develop more effective research strategies.

B. *Statistical and Conceptual Implications of Dependency*

At one level, dependency in data has been a problem only to researchers. Clinicians recognize and accept the notion that the behavior of family members are interdependent. In fact, for many of the clinical approaches cited above, this interdependency of behavior constitutes the main underlying rationale for treating families or other social networks as opposed to individuals. On the other hand, for many researchers, the recognition of the potential for statistical dependence in one's data evokes strong visceral reactions and even discontinuance of certain research projects. There are two reasons for including this issue in the current chapter: (1) as the systems-behavioral program has struggled with this issue, it has become clear that the problem of statistical dependency is a problem only because interaction researchers have often made an unfortunate and erroneous set of assumptions about the nature of human behavior; (2) furthermore, it has become apparent that the process of solving the statistical dependency problem can facilitate the development of the conceptual framework used to describe interaction. Though this may represent a variant of the "methodological tail wagging the conceptual dog" problem, in this case it can be beneficial by forcing us to reconceptualize the interaction process. To place this issue in proper perspective, it is useful to briefly review the development of analysis of variance analytic models, then consider the assumptions that underly these univariate statistics in the context of their application to models of behavior.

1. Analysis of Variance: Background and Assumptions. As traditionally taught and used, univariate statistics are based on a restrictive set of independence assumptions. Basically, the analysis of variance model (ANOVA) was originated to evaluate crop yields in agriculture. Terms like "split-plot" designs serve as reminders of these origins. But it is further worthwhile to consider the implicit assumptions in the development of such a statistical model, and the implications of these assumptions for our methods. Wheat or alfalfa are passive recipients of what their environments offer to them. Their yield, height, rapidity of growth, and so forth are determined by their location, density, type of fertilizer, amount of water, and other externally provided agents. It is therefore intuitively consistent to assume that analytic models could and should be developed that describe the relatively passive effects of growth as related to independent contributions (or sources of variance) of farmers, land, rain, and so forth. The degree of control over crop growth rate can be conceptualized as *dependent* upon the contributions of a variety of elements that can be *independently* applied. Under circumstances such as these, the ANOVA allowed farmers (or agricultural researchers) to describe *main effects* for independently applied agents such as manure as contrasted with mulch, or different amounts of irrigation water. As the analysis models developed further, it was clear that farmers could additionally describe nurturing *combinations,* such as *low water–lots of manure* as contrasted with *high water–little manure* and other independent but additive combinations of the two, by *interaction effects.*

It was probably the appeal of these quantifiable, relatively empirical descriptions that led psychologists to apply these models to understanding human behavior. To be philosophically consistent, human beings must be perceived as a *tabula rasa,* their behavior influenced by the independent impact of such variables as nurturance, stimulus visibility, and rate of reinforcement. Further appeal of these models was that human idiosyncrasies could be appropriately categorized or lumped together in an error term. However, the relative properties of crops in fields and humans in their environment show some important dissimilarities. Crops *are* in fact predominantly passive recipients of their environments. The analysis of variance model fits their properties nicely, since we can reasonably assume that crops do little to influence their futures. Only if humans are completely designated in the role of a *tabula rasa* can we make similar assumptions and similarly apply the model.

Rather, all psychological theories argue that at some level people impact their environment. They are undoubtedly influenced by it, but it would be incredibly restrictive to argue that they are influenced by it in the same passive degree as a crop yield. It is more likely that people are constantly having impact on what their environment does to them: dry crops wilt, while people seek water. This view, though common in theory, has not generated commensurate innovative or updating impact on research methodology. Even when investigating the impact of people on each other, researchers have characteristically maintained the unidirectional cause-effect paradigm, *functionally* treating subjects as passive recipients. Examples include studies such as those of the effects of parental behavior on children's behavior (Hawkins et al., 1966; Wahler, 1965; Wahler et al., 1965), and the effects of leader behavior on group performance (Fiedler, 1955, 1966; Gerard, 1954; Hand, Lamontague, and Marks, 1974; Liberman, 1971).

In developing the systems-behavioral program, however, it has become apparent that such studies have not placed the study of human interaction in the proper context with respect to traditional uses of the analysis of variance. Many problems of statistical dependence that hold true when conceiving of people's behavior in the same ways we consider crop yields may in fact not be so problematic. In fact, these "problems of dependency" may be the properties of conceptual interest if considered in different statistical ways. That is, it may be possible to rediscover some properties of one of the most useful statistical tools to fit current conceptual and theoretical needs. This will require a change in set with respect to the nature of many research questions, then the adoption of appropriate statistical designs that not only reframe traditional restrictive dependency assumptions, but also make them a device for advancing knowledge.

2. Interaction Phenomena: The Challenge. Since Bell (1968) challenged traditional parent-effect models in developmental psychology, more and more researchers have acknowledged that in the "real world," parents and children actively *influence each other,* so neither can realistically be conceived as an independent or dependent variable. They are *interdependent,* as exemplified in conceptual analyses such as Patterson and Reid's (1970) coercion paradigm. In such analyses, it often appears that what people do is less related to their own behavior than to that of an interactant.

The recognition of these interdependencies has not been reflected in interaction research. Despite the compelling evidence of contingent probabilities and other strong correlations between behaviors of interactants, researchers still try to explain these data with one-way cause-effect models. This seems to represent a startling misfit between experimental procedure and data analyses in the face of evidence that the world operates to the contrary. The alarming issue is that when we consistently adhere to our one-way cause-effect models, we are artificially constraining the world through experimental procedures. Or at the very least, we are only selectively investigating artificial slices of our world.

Of course, designs can be generated that artificially create one-way effects, just as rats can be food-deprived and confined to Skinner Boxes in order to sufficiently constrain or control their behavior. However, the thrust of much of the research, theorizing, and clinical programs described in this chapter represents a shift of interest away from the traditional question, "What *can* we manipulate to produce an effect?" to an interest in "How do these interactants influence each other, and how are they as a unit influenced by independent environmental variables?"

Consistent with a shift of focus to ongoing interaction is an encounter with a new set of statistical problems, not to mention conceptual difficulties in unraveling cause and effect (if such a concept is still meaningful). In encountering this new set of statistical problems, however, one should bear in mind that the nature of these "problems" is related to possibly inappropriate theories of human behavior. Researchers are trying to play interaction ball in a "people-as-individuals" methodological ballpark. If researchers adhere to notions of a human being as a cause-effect individual, then they are required to view dependence as problematic. In contrast, if researchers adopt an interactionist perspective, dependence can take on new meaning.

3. *The Interactant Effect.* As described in Myers (1966), members of dyads and larger groups have systematic effects on one another that create non-additive impact. That is, in one sense, a new variable is created, the "interactant effect," which is often unexplored in the statistical design. If this effect is ignored, the traditional independence assumptions of ANOVA are violated and results become distorted in ways that we cannot interpret. On the other hand, if we do accept this interactant effect as a statistical phenomenon, we move away from an individual as the focus of our interest. The smallest unit of interest then becomes a person as a part of a larger unit. When we redefine this unit, we also reframe some fundamental statistical assumptions.

Researchers can, of course, resort to such solutions as ignoring all but one of the subjects in each interacting unit, though pragmatically one also loses degrees of freedom. More importantly, however, it is our contention that this "interactant effect" should not be avoided, since it is a phenomenon of major theoretical interest. As such, it must be included in our designs.

This point is central, because conventional analyses are the most graphic example of how our assumptions of the nature of man are described by contemporary ANOVA statistics. We attempt to set up our experiments and analyses as though people, in reference to our earlier sections, are a crop. Translated statistically, people have been treated as a random effect, and they or their impact on behavior, as a main effect. These analyses characterize people in a restrictive fashion, and the nature of these assumptions leads to traditional assertions that dependence is problematic. If we posit some forms of nonrandom dependence at outset, or *interactant* effects, people can be described in much different ways. Researchers become less tied to their additive assumptions of independent sources of variance, or main effects, and focus instead on interaction terms. At this point, interaction can become the basic building block in research designs, and all assertions are qualified by the interacting effects of man and the manipulated variables.

4. Designing a Solution. Figure 3 represents the type of design and source table which represents an avenue for conceptualizing and resolving the dependency issue. For purposes of discussion, it represents a simplified hypothetical study of rates of defensiveness in adaptive and maladaptive couples (the status variable) consisting of husbands and wives (the role variable). To appropriately apply the analysis of variance to interaction data that systematically is influenced by the couple interdependence, the *interactant* effect must be formally introduced into the design. This will permit the researcher to systematically separate interactant effects from the other effects of interest. Thus the design separates error, role (husband, wife), interactant effect (called the couple effect), and status. In sum, a hierarchical design is created with a within-effect (role) nested within a second within-effect (couples), which is in turn nested within the between-effect of status. The nesting of couples within condition has actually increased the independent variables from two to three. That is, couples have been added to the independent variables of role (husband, wife) and status, or condition (adaptive, maladaptive). This has allowed the separation of the *interactant effect* from error, using the appropriate term (couples within status) to test the between effect of condition, and the appropriate term to test the effect of role using the error term (couples by role within status) with the interdependency of the couple effect systematically accounted for.

Thus, at the very least, the design allows us to avoid isolating an important ANOVA assumption, thereby ending up with uninterpretable or biased results. However, the design also *forces* us to begin to look at the interactant effect *per se*. We have found that as scientists we have begun to be uncomfortable with simply adding the interactant effect as a statistical ploy; we have begun to look at it as a phenomenon itself. Of

Figure 3. Hierarchical Between-Within-Within Design (Nested Interactant) and Source Table

	Status: Adaptive				Maladaptive			
	Couple H1	CH2	. . .	CHn	Couple 1U	C2U	. . .	CnU
Role: Husbands								
Wives								

Source	*df*	*F*
Between	a*c-1	
Status (A)	a-1	$MS_{A}/MS_{C/A}$
Couples within A C/A (error)	a (c-1)	
Within		
Role (B)	b-1	$MS_{B}/MS_{CB/A}$
A x B	(a-1) (b-1)	$MS_{AB}/MS_{CB/A}$
CB/A (error)	a (b-1) (c-1)	

* *Note:* C represents couples. Note that couples or C appear only within error terms in this particular model.

course, adherents of Gestalt, systems, and other relational theories have been discussing the interactant effect—in other terms—for quite some time. Perhaps now that it can be conceptualized as a statistical concept, we can also begin to create designs that will allow us to evaluate it empirically.

At this point, it should be emphasized that *Ss* have actually been redefined as couples × role/status. *Subjects* are typically the least common denominator or error in traditional methodologies, since it has been assumed in the past that they are independently sampled, passive recipients. Under those conditions, it made sense that they could and should be considered as random sources of error in interaction studies. Note, however, in a layout such as the nested interactant design that inferences about subjects as sources of error are much different. In the couple × role/status error term, we recognize that dependent interacting environmental properties, which man presumably impacts, describe sources of error variance. When systematically considered, dependence concerns therefore suggest that looking at man as a different form of experimental error may render our designs more appropriate.

5. Scope and Limitations. As a statistical procedure, this model can be easily extended to numerous situations. If instead of having interactants blocked or assigned to only one per cell, there are two or more *Ss* per cell—a case of N children within a group, N members of a class, and so on—the design simply becomes a group (nested) within treatment design (Meyers, 1966). In such a design, of course, subject variability within cells again becomes a source of variance as it interacts with independent variables, and the researcher doesn't face the unique problem of only one subject per cell, which creates the interesting conceptual issue to which we have already alluded.

The nested-interactant model can also be easily expanded to include additional (between) independent variables, as well as another within effect representing repeated measurements (as in a pre-post design). Once the nature of the *interactant effect* has been properly identified, additional truly independent variables can be easily added to the design, though admittedly source tables appear somewhat intimidating, and four- and five-way interactions may lose meaning. In this respect, the researcher may find a situation comparable to deciphering a multivariate analysis of variance (MANOVA). We must remember, however, that while we have computers and programmers to handle the computational complexity of the data, we often don't have the theories that can predict and/or explain the data.

Of equal concern, but with added dimension, is the usual assumption of homogeneity of variance throughout the data set. In this particular nested interactant design, this assumption requires (among other things) that the degree of dependency between interactants is relatively constant across conditions. When this is not the case, biased computations can result. Experimenters are then forced to use the same types of "solutions" to differential dependence found in typical ANOVA designs: data transformations, manipulations of degrees of freedom and significance levels, and *post hoc* "partitioning" of parts of the data (as if two or more separate experiments had been performed). These "solutions" are, of course, compromises at best, and make it clear that the complexity of the *interactant effect* is only beginning to be unraveled. The model presented above has not dealt with statistical dependence in its myriad forms, or offered higher order and novel statistical solutions. We think, however, that to pursue more sophisticated statistical means with which to impose our traditional views of the nature of the world on the world itself may be a sad ordering of priorities. At another level, the problems created by heterogeneity of the interactant effect merely serve to reiterate the main point of this paper. If, for example, the interdependence of happy versus unhappy couples is *differentially* affected by an experimental situation, it will create problematic heterogeneity of the interactant effect. Yet this problematic effect may be one of the most important phenomena that can be studied. Why do some married partners reciprocate pleasing behaviors and others do not? Why do delinquent families reciprocate defensiveness, while adaptive families reciprocate supportiveness (Alexander, 1973)? Why do some groups respond in unison to stress, while others fragment? Though not usually phrased in such terms, these questions are issues of group (or couple, or family, etc.) interdependence, that is, questions about the interactant effect. Thus, while it may create statistical problems, the interactant effect also represents (at least for the systems-behavioral theorist) a fundamental focus of theory and research.

6. *Conclusions.* Two thrusts have been represented in this section. On the one hand, the goal was to present the rudiments of an analysis of variance model that provides the researcher with a device for removing troubling dependence when studying interaction among dyads and larger groups. This model, however, is no panacea, and statisticians and researchers have considerable work ahead to extend and refine the model, as well as find more satisfactory resolutions to continued problems of heterogeneity of interdependence and the like.

The second major thrust is less technical in nature, but potentially more far-reaching in scope and implication. In this thrust, it has been argued that some forms of dependence are not merely problems to be controlled or statistically rendered impotent. Instead, they reflect real-world phenomena that should become a focus of psychological theory and research. If we are going to appropriately examine both the world and our *Ss* in a realistic fashion, it therefore appears that we will need to recognize two implications for our research:

a. We cannot randomly sample most of our phenomena of interest. People can't be randomly assigned to families, or to roles within their families. Interaction researchers should therefore attend to the *within* forms of the analysis of variance, as well as the *hierarchical* strategies of analyzing data.
b. If phenomena are sampled in this *within* or hierarchical fashion, we recognize that an appropriate estimate of error is not an individual, but is rather a larger social unit within a situational context. This process is worth review as a statement of larger philosophical issues.

The statistical dependency found in interacting dyads and groups calls into question one of the most pervasive themes in psychological research:

people as passive recipients of externally applied independent variables. No one questions that human beings respond to such stimuli as light, stress, and food. Also, no one questions that variations in these stimuli can be responsible for variations in behavior. However, hardly a single philosophical, psychological, or theological system views man as a totally passive recipient. People influence their influencers. Young children learn to influence parents, students learn to influence teachers, and subjects often figure out how to influence even the most ingenious and devious researchers. In fact, the extent to which researchers must deceive subjects (Rosenthal and Rosnow, 1969), and parents repeatedly reread manuals (Patterson, 1975), attests to the powerful impact supposedly passive recipients can have.

The implications of the mutual influence of interactants suggest that the typical unidirectional cause-effect paradigm in the study of human behavior has serious limitations. Experiments designed to show how independently applied variables *can* operate on individuals provide essential information, but they cannot adequately describe *how* several types of social units *interact*. Stated differently, researchers can demonstrate powerful experimental causes and effects in well controlled experiments, when in fact these causes and effects are neither as powerful or independent in the real world. Unfortunately, behavioral scientists do not have a well-developed set of alternatives to the traditional cause-effect laboratory experiment. Except in some relatively distant fields such as astrophysics, cybernetics, and the like, theorists haven't been able to develop alternative concepts that can create and describe "control" (e.g., feedback) in a fashion as reliable as our traditional experimental paradigms. Only when we begin systematically including the *interactant effect* in our research designs, statistical models, and theories will we be able to move from the constraining effects of the "one-way set" to the interactionist perspective. In this respect, this section represents only a modest, though hopefully persuasive, beginning.

IV. SUMMARY AND CONCLUSIONS

Reviewing the systems-behavioral approach to treating families has generated simultaneous feelings of complacency, excitement, and challenge for the occasionally overwhelmed authors. In our less energetic moments, the sense of complacency emerges from the strong empirical support generated by the program. We have nonetheless been consistently surprised by the persuasive variance accounted for by examination of heretofore unexplored sources of program variance such as therapists and families, and certainly we are consistently surprised in the clinical arena. These same surprises have pointed out new directions for systems-behavioral researchers and clinicians to refine techniques, and enhance the model's bases of empirical support and clinical utility.

This process of program development has generated a proliferation of conceptual challenges. These challenges generate a sense of excitement and enthusiasm for continued development. Rather than forming any basis for conceptual complacency, the research and clinical activities have to date contributed to identification of whole new classes of important issues.

These issues are formidable and complex; many of them seem at this point to be much more complex than our current conceptual and methodological tools. These concerns lead to our sense of feeling overwhelmed. The unit of analysis problem is a case in point. Our traditional sequential interaction tools do not seem to translate well (either methodologically or conceptually) from descriptions of simultaneous molecular dependency to the more molar questions of their role in defining the outcomes of interpersonal relationship.

The arena of assessment has certainly assumed new saliency for the systems-behavioral program. Current data argue for a stronger consideration of other dimensions of family life than an analysis of their overt behavior, such as attributional sets about relationship structure in the family. The data also suggest that the arena of therapists as delivery systems for intervention certainly merits attention as well. Assessment will necessarily have to be more inclusive in focus, dimension, and complexity.

In order to increase our practical and conceptual understanding of these phenomena, it also appears that systems-behavioral researchers will need to reexamine and reevaluate some fundamental dimensions of traditional empirical paradigms. It seems clear, for example, that therapists and individual family members are neither sufficiently homogenous or independent from each other to be relegated the role of independent variables. Clearly, innovative methodological and quantitative solutions are necessary for continued development of an understanding of interactional phenomena.

We are optimistic that these concerns and issues do not necessarily pose unresolvable constraints. Rather, they will hopefully spawn more meaningful models to examine families and therapists and to better describe them. As a clinical mandate, they will surely enhance our ability to serve them.

REFERENCES

Agras, S. W. *Behavior modification: Principles and clinical applications*. Boston: Little, Brown and Company, 1972.

Alexander, J. F. Videotape recorded family interaction: A systems approach. Paper presented at the meeting of the Western Psychological Association, Los Angeles, April, 1970.

——— *Evaluation summary: Family groups treatment program*. Tech. Report 1, Ogden Juvenile Court, District 1, Contract No. S–72–G–2–a–1 5644. Washington, D.C.: National Institute of Mental Health, 1971.

——— *Journal of Consulting and Clinical Psychology,* 1973, *40,* 223–231.

——— In J. C. Cull & R. E. Hardy (Eds.), *Behavior modification in rehabilitation settings*. Springfield, Ill.: Charles C. Thomas, 1974.

Alexander, J. F., & Barton, C. In D. H. Olson (Ed.), *Treating relationships*. Lake Mills, Iowa: Graphic Publishing Company, 1976.

Alexander, J. F., Barton, C., Schiavo, R. S., & Parsons, B. V. *Journal of Consulting and Clinical Psychology,* 1976, *44,* 4, 656–664.

Alexander, J. F., & Parsons, B. V. *Journal of Abnormal Psychology,* 1973, *81,* 219–225.

Barton, C., & Alexander, J. F. In G. Harris (Ed.), *The group treatment of human problems: A social learning approach*. New York: Grune & Stratton, 1977.

Bell, R. Q. *Psychological Review,* 1968, *75,* 81–95.

Buckley, W. (Ed.). *Modern systems research for the behavioral scientist*. Chicago: Aldine, 1968.

Duncan, P. Family interaction in parents of neurotic and social delinquent girls. Unpublished doctoral dissertation, University of Wisconsin, 1968.

Fiedler, F. E. *Journal of Abnormal and Social Psychology,* 1955, *51,* 227–235.

——— *Journal of Experimental Social Psychology,* 1966, *2,* 237–264.

Gerard, H. B. *Human Relations,* 1954, *7,* 313–325.

Gibb, J. R. *Journal of Communications,* 1961, *3,* 141–148.

Haley, J. *Strategies of psychotherapy*. New York: Grune & Stratton, 1963.

——— *Changing families: A family therapy reader*. New York: Grune & Stratton, 1971.

Hand, I., Lamontague, Y., & Marks, I. M. *British Journal of Psychiatry,* 1974, *124,* 588–692.

Hawkins, R. P., Peterson, R. F., Schweid, E., & Bijou, S. W. *Journal of Experimental Child Psychology,* 1969, *4,* 99–107.

Kiesler, D. J. *Psychotherapy Bulletin,* 1966, *65,* 110–136.

Klein, N. C., Alexander, J. F., & Parsons, B. V. *Journal of Consulting and Clinical Psychology,* 1976, 469–474.

Liberman, R. *British Journal of Psychiatry,* 1971, *119,* 535–544.

Malouf, R. E., & Alexander, J. F. In R. E. Hardy & J. C. Cull (Eds.), *Therapeutic needs of the family*. Springfield, Ill.: Charles C. Thomas, 1974.

Mischler, E., & Waxler, N. *Interaction in families*. New York: Wiley, 1968.

Morton, T. L., Alexander, J. F., & Altman, I. In G. R. Miller (Ed.), *Annual reviews of communication research, Volume V: Interpersonal communication*. Beverly Hills: Sage Publications, 1976.

Myers, J. L. *Fundamentals of experimental design*. Boston: Allyn & Bacon, 1966.

Parsons, B. V., & Alexander, J. F. *Journal of Consulting and Clinical Psychology,* 1973, *41,* 195–201.

Patterson, G. R. *Applications of social learning to family life*. Champaign, Ill.: Research Press, 1975.

Patterson, G. R., & Reid, J. B. In C. Neuringer & J. L. Michael (Eds.), *Behavior modification in clinical psychology*. New York: Appleton-Century-Crofts, 1970.

The President's Commission on Law Enforcement and Administration of Justice. *Juvenile delinquency and youth crime*. Washington, D.C.: U.S. Government Printing Office, 1967.

Rosenthal, R., & Rosnow, R. L. (Eds.). *Artifacts in behavioral research*. New York: Academic Press, 1969.

Srole, L., Langer, T. S., Michael, S. T., Opler, M. K., & Rennie, T. A. C. *Mental health in the metropolis: The midtown manhattan study*. New York: McGraw-Hill, 1962.

Stuart, R. B. In R. Rubin & C. Franks (Eds.), *Advances in behavior therapy*. New York: Academic Press, 1968.

——— *Journal of Behavior Therapy and Experimental Psychiatry*, 1971, *2*, 1–11.

Stumphauzer, J. S. *Behavior therapy with delinquents*. Springfield, Ill.: Charles C. Thomas, 1973.

Tharpe, R. G., & Wetzel, R. J. *Behavior modification in the natural environment*. New York: Academic Press, 1969.

Turner, C. W., & Dodd, D. K. In R. L. Ault (Ed.), *Selected topics in child development*. Santa Monica: Goodyear Publishing Company. In press.

Traux, C. B., & Carkhuff, R. R. *Toward effective counseling and psychotherapy*. Chicago: Aldine, 1967.

Wahler, R. G. *Journal of Applied Behavior Analysis*, 1969, *2*, 159–170.

Wahler, R. G., Winchel, G. H., Peterson, R. F., & Morrison, D. C. *Behavior Research and Therapy*, 1965, *3*, 113–134.

Winter, W. D., & Ferreira, A. J. *Journal of Abnormal Behavior*, 1969, *74*, 574–575.

BEHAVIORAL ECOLOGY AS A PERSPECTIVE ON MARRIAGES AND FAMILIES

Edwin P. Willems, UNIVERSITY OF HOUSTON

Dennis G. Stuart, CALIFORNIA SCHOOL OF PROFESSIONAL PSYCHOLOGY

In this paper, we will try to highlight some of the flavor, values, and guiding principles of behavioral ecology, and illustrate the relevance of behavioral ecology to understanding marriages and families. Despite the fact that behavioral ecology is a loosely connected perspective rather than one unified theory or method, we believe that some of its values and strategies have important implications for theoretical and clinical work on the problems of families and marriages. We realize that we fall into the trap of emphasizing approaches that are most similar to ours. Thus, in

Advances in Family Intervention, Assessment and Theory, Volume 1, pages 89–128.

ISBN: 0-89232-137-7

what follows, we will mention the work of family *system* theorists more often than the work of other theorists.

In his review of systems theories of marriage, Steinglass (1978) outlines three conditions that are necessary for a model to be successful: (1) the model must direct attention to relevant data (selectivity), (2) the model must provide a conceptualization of family pathology, and (3) the model must suggest strategies for therapeutic intervention. We agree with these criteria, and they help to make clear that we will be discussing a perspective, context, or prolegomenon rather than a specific model of families. In a word, we will present a set of issues with which, we believe, the family theorist must deal in specifying relevant data and procedures, characteristics of family pathology, and techniques of therapeutic intervention.

SOME BACKGROUND

One of the major lines of development toward behavioral ecology came from within psychology. Roger Barker, one of the pioneers of the movement, summarizes the guiding questions as follows:

> . . . in varied and changing environments, the contribution of environmental input to the variance of behavior is enhanced. In a restless world, the nature of the environment is the intriguing scientific problem. And the applied fields and neighboring sciences ask: What are environments like? . . . it does not seem likely that our own curiosities and the demands of engineers, economists, educators, and political leaders will allow us to be content with a psychology of people to the neglect of a psychology of the environment of people (1965, p. 13) . . . the present methods, concepts, and theories of the psychological sciences *cannot* answer the new questions, . . . a new science is required to deal with them. (1969, p. 31)

The phrase "ecological psychology" has been circulating around American psychology for about twenty-five years, with a positively accelerating curve of visibility and acclaim. During the first ten or fifteen of those years, the major authors and agents of ecological psychology were Roger Barker and Herbert Wright, who, in turn, were co-workers and intellectual descendants of Kurt Lewin (Barker, 1960, 1963a, 1963b, 1965, 1968, 1969; Barker and Schoggen, 1973; Barker and Wright, 1955; Wright, 1967, 1969/1970). Lewin (e.g., 1951) had developed his field theory around the well-known dictum that behavior is a joint function of person and environment. However, "environment" in Lewin's formula was the environment as perceived by the person. Thus, Lewin's psychology was a postperceptual psychology as far as the environment was concerned. Lewin recognized this problem and he coined the phrase "foreign hull" to represent the outside, preperceptual world of the environment. He even suggested the phrase "ecological psychology" to denote the attempt to study influences from the foreign hull on the person, but he never pursued the development of ecological psychology to any sophisticated degree.

Ecological psychology in the hands of Barker and Wright was the formal, systematic attempt to include the preperceptual environment (foreign hull) in a field theoretical analysis of human behavior and apply the approach of the naturalist to psychology. These pioneers made remarkable advances in developing methods of research, in understanding the naturally occurring structure and pattern of behavior, in documenting and measuring units of the environment, and in developing models of the ways in which behavior and environment come to terms with each other.

The second major line of development into behavioral ecology comes from a convergence of forces outside of psychology. Ecology has its origin in the biological sciences and it refers traditionally to the study of relationships between living things and their habitats and the formalization of the natural rules by which those interactions are governed. Complex interdependencies that implicate organisms and their environments in exchanges of energy over time are the scientific coinage of the ecologist and dramatic advances have been made in understanding such interdependencies in areas outside of psychology (Benarde, 1970; Chase, 1971; Colinvaux, 1973; Dubos, 1965, 1968; Margalef, 1968; McHale, 1970; Shepard and McKinley, 1969; Smith, 1966; Wallace, 1972; Watt, 1966, 1968). These advances are important, but the formulation of the ecological perspective is still very spotty. This spottiness is most evident in the arena of human *behavior*. Much is known about the ways in which man's biological functioning and well-being are caught up in the complex webs of the environments he inhabits. However, very little is known about the laws of human use of environmental systems, the interrelations of those systems with behavior, and the paths by which behavioral problems emerge in those systems. The most pressing need in ecological science is to develop *behavioral* ecology in a systematic way.

As just one example of these needs, consider ecological problems of community mental health or community psychology. Professionals in community psychology operate on at least two basic assumptions: (1) that human development and performance are shaped profoundly by the settings and institutions people inhabit; and (2) that it is legitimate for mental health professionals to promote sound development and prevent maladaptive development by influencing such settings and institutions (Cowen, 1973). However, if we simply ask the question, "How *do* settings and institutions affect human development?", then we immediately see the dim outlines of a large domain of needed research in social and behavioral ecology. We need systematic frameworks for describing and classifying settings, institutions, and their involvements. We need to understand the mechanisms and processes by which they function, as well as the principles of organization and articulation they display. We need to understand the ways in which behavior is linked to them. And we need to develop new methods for extensive and long-term monitoring so that we can assess their effectiveness.

In recent years, an ecological approach to human behavior has been urged with increasing frequency and urgency. Among the central themes of behavioral ecology are:

(1) Human behavior must be viewed and studied at levels of complexity that are quite atypical in behavioral science.
(2) The complexity lies in systems of relationships linking person, behavior, social environment, and physical environment.
(3) Such systems cannot be understood piecemeal.
(4) Such behavior-environment systems have important properties that change, unfold, and become clear only over long periods of time.
(5) Tampering with any part of such a system will probably affect the other parts and alter the whole.
(6) We must develop an ecological awareness of the many ways in which (a) simple intrusions can produce unintended effects, (b) indirect harm may follow from narrowly-defined good, and (c) long-term harm may follow from short-term good.
(7) The focal challenge is to achieve enough understanding of such systems so that the effects of interventions and planned changes can be anticipated in comprehensive fashion.

In other contexts, the implications of behavioral ecology have been discussed for research and theory in psychology (Barker, 1965, 1968, 1969; Moos, 1973, 1974; Willems, 1973a, 1977a, 1977b, in press), technologies of behavior change (Willems, 1973b, 1974, 1977c), humanistic approaches to behavior (Alexander, Dreher, and Willems, 1976), environmental design (Willems, 1973c, 1973d; Wicker, 1972), and problems of health status and health care (Insel and Moos, 1974; Moss, 1973; Willems, 1976; Willems and Campbell, 1975).

At many levels of analysis, behavior is implicated in very complex organism-environment-behavior systems. "The significant feature is that the social, physical, and biological components function as an integrated system, and any tampering with any part of the system will affect each of the other parts and alter the whole" (Benarde, 1970, p. 24). Agents of change, including economic planners, housing authorities, architects, psychotherapists, social workers, industrial consultants, community psychologists, educational planners, psychopharmacologists, and operant behavior modifiers have at their disposal various means to affect behavior-environment systems. The questions of larger and unintended effects within interpersonal and environmental contexts and over long periods of time beg for evaluation and research, because lessons learned in other areas suggest that we should always be sensitive to "other" effects of interventions. It is hard to think in terms of systems and we eagerly warp our language to protect ourselves and our favorite approaches from the necessity of thinking in terms of interdependent systems. It is quite foreign to psychologists and psychiatrists to think of the physical and behavioral environment as inextricable parts of the behavioral processes of organisms and as relating to them in ways that are extremely complex. Two results that follow are (1) relatively splintered, bit-like attempts to understand large-scale, complex phenomena, and (2) blithe forms of bit-like tinkering in complex, interdependent systems.

Behavioral science must overcome its sense of futility about understanding and changing the seemingly pell-mell course of problems of human behavior and must develop the means to influence and shape that course in more reflective, purposeful, and humane directions. Otherwise, its venerable traditions may disappear and "become like those of a buggy whip factory, interesting and nostalgic but totally useless" (Thoreson et al., 1972, p. 134). A necessary condition for these developments is a willingness to change our old modes of thinking about human behavior in favor of an approach that accepts and understands the complexity and interdependency of the ecological systems in which behavior is embedded.

Both behavioral ecology and family systems theory have emerged in the last half of the twentieth century and have been influenced heavily by general systems theory, biological ecology, cybernetics, and the development of large, complex organizations and technologies. They share in a general philosophical trend toward understanding more and more complex systems that characterize our intellectual milieu. Aside from this common philosophical background, however, the two fields do not share any direct roots. Behavioral ecology has strong ties with social psychology and behaviorism and shares many concepts and concerns with the current areas of social ecology and environmental psychology.

Family systems theory and the techniques of family therapy have developed from two major sources, one developing from the treatment of children under the models of child guidance and psychoanalysis, and the other following from communications theory. Ackerman (1958) and Bowen (1978) are most clearly identified with the psychoanalytic tradition. Each became disenchanted about working with individuals and realized quickly that it was necessary to understand the whole family in order to understand the child. They added mothers and fathers to the treatment process and studied how family members interact with and influence each other.

At about the same time, Bateson (1972), Watzlawick, Beavin, and Jackson (1967), and Haley (1971) were approaching family processes through an analysis of communications and the theory of logical types. They studied the kinds of messages people send, the ways in which messages at different conceptual levels can interfere with or enhance one another, and the effects this interference has on behavior and human relationships. Meanwhile, Minuchin (1974) was developing a system of structural/ecological analysis for families. His approach falls somewhere between these other approaches. Minuchin's language and approach are perhaps the closest to behavioral ecology. All of these developments in approaches to families have been reviewed by Guerin (1976), Bowen (1978), Haley (1971), Beels and Ferber (1969), and Steinglass (1978). Prior to the emergence of family systems thinking, most attempts to describe family processes came from anthropology, sociology, or social psychology. In therapy, the techniques of small groups or marital counseling were all that were available. Family systems theory is sufficiently different from those precursors to justify the claim that family systems theory came into existence in the 1950s.

Until now, there has been little interplay between family therapists and behavioral ecologists. Perhaps this is more a function of their differing backgrounds than an indication that they have nothing to say to one another.

We turn now to several issues on which the behavioral ecologist and the family theorist or therapist have a great deal to offer each other.

DISTRIBUTIONS OF PHENOMENA

Behavioral ecology is not primarily a methodological orientation, but it has many implications for methodology (Barker, 1965, 1968; Willems, 1973a, 1977a, in press; Alexander, Dreher, and Willems, 1976). Thus, behavioral ecology is largely naturalistic in its methodological orientation; "largely" because it is not defined by any particular methodology and because this is an emphasis rather than a necessary condition (Willems, 1973a). Pluralism of methods is crucial to behavioral ecology, but the ecologist's methodological statement of faith has two parts. First, with Keller and Marian Breland (1966), the ecologist says, ". . . you cannot understand the behavior of the animal in the laboratory unless you understand his behavior in the wild" (p. 20). Second, contrary to widely held canons in psychology, the ecologist believes that the investigator should manipulate and control only as much as is absolutely necessary to answer his questions clearly, an argument that has been made by many writers (Barker, 1965, 1969; Brandt, 1972; Chapanis, 1967; Gump and Kounin, 1959/60; Menzel, 1969; Willems, 1965, 1969).

At a more substantive and theoretical level, behavioral ecology concerns itself with documenting the distribution of phenomena in nature; that is, the range, intensity, and frequency of behavior-environment relations in everyday systems. Somehow, this basic issue is poorly understood by psychologists, and such research is not yet widely accepted, valued, or promoted (Barker, 1965, 1969; Elms, 1975; McGuire, 1969; Willems, 1969). Perhaps this is so because the model of experimental and analytical science and the development of technology is so appealing. By and large, psychologists favor manipulations, demonstrations, standard tests, and experiments that tell us little about natural distributions, and we smile condescendingly at those few behavioral scientists who engage in what we call "only observational research; only descriptive research."

A friend of ours who is a psychologist and owns some farm land reported that he was having trouble with a well on his farm. The water was affected by nitrates, which can be a serious problem in a well. Our friend consulted a county agricultural extension agent who referred him to a data sheet on nitrates in water. The sheet contained detailed information on nitrates—their overall abundance, their geographical distribution, and the geological conditions under which they occur. This information provided our friend a basis to plan some remedial steps and also to decide where a new well should be located. However, this experience also puzzled and troubled our friend as a behavioral scientist. He wondered where he could go to find analogous data sheets on significant human behavior and experience. There are no such data sheets, of course, at least not on a large scale. It is a curious collective oversight, if not a distinct embarrassment, that the social and behavioral sciences have not developed detailed, systematic tables of information on the distribution, range, and frequency of behavior and behavior-environment relations.

If professionals in other areas proceeded in the way social and behavioral scientists do, we would question their competence and judgment. We assume that geologists and other scientists have plotted out the characteristics of the earth's crust in such a way that they know the distribution of layers and relationship between subsurface crustal formations and occurrence of crude oil, and we assume that a company in search of oil will use that information to reduce the likelihood of drilling a dry hole. We expect the planners of buildings and roads to benefit from information on the distributions and characteristics of soils, rocks, subsurface moisture, and fault lines to avoid expensive and tragic mistakes. We would scarcely feel sorry for the person who did not take advantage of what hydrologists know about rainfall before putting in a large and expensive pecan orchard.

We have nothing comparable in the sciences of human behavior. In what proportions and frequencies should laughing, cooperating, solving problems, playing, fighting, resting, becoming angry, and self-instigated performance be engaged in by developing children? What are their critical concentrations? We do not know. In what proportions and frequencies should various kinds of behavior occur around them, or be delivered to them? Again, we have no idea. At least in part, attempts to influence quality of life and health will involve accelerating, decelerating, producing, eliminating, and shaping various behaviors. If such attempts are going to intensify and spread, then, at some point, we must end our blind tinkering with them. We must grow far beyond the hit-or-miss grounds we now use to decide where and when to intervene and tinker. To grow in that way, we must know much more about the distribution of social and behavioral phenomena.

Ecosystems seem to function according to laws of conservation and succession, by which events in the systems become distributed and redistributed over time (Margalef, 1968). In the United States, only one of the top three causes of death in 1900 appeared among the top ten causes of death in 1967 (Chase, 1971), and cancer and heart disease now kill proportionately five times as many persons as they killed in 1900. Disturbing forms of interpersonal violence are changing in distribution, sometimes in ways that can be predicted according to type of neighborhood and dwelling complex (Newman, 1972). Not only are distributional aspects of behavior important to the basic ecological understanding of behavior, but if we are to continue our attempts to influence, change, and accommodate human behavior, then we must begin taking account (1) of the much larger organism-behavior-environment systems within which our activities take place, (2) of distributions of behavior within those systems, and (3) of optimal proportions and combinations of behaviors across populations and subpopulations.

Despite the relatively low status of such research, significant steps have been taken. Some important anthropological, sociological, and ethological studies have gathered distributional data. Closer to a direct focus on human behavior, Ebbesen and Haney (1973) made more than 13,600 observations of drivers at intersections and the environmental conditions under which the drivers took the risk of turning in front of oncoming traffic. The resulting tables of frequencies are full of implications for understanding the everyday behaviors of drivers and the factors that affect such risk taking. The pioneering descriptive work of Barker and Wright and their associates on behaviors of persons in their home communities is so rich and diverse that it defies a brief characterization (see Barker, 1963b, 1965, 1968; Barker and Schoggen, 1973; Barker and Wright, 1955; Wright, 1967, 1969/1970).

In addition to providing descriptive characterizations of ecological systems, distributional data can also suggest where scientific straw men are.

Many early theories of child development placed singular importance on the concept of frustration. Fawl (1963) analyzed records representing over 200 hours of observation of children. Occurrences of blocked goals (frustration) were relatively few. When they did occur, the child usually did not appear disturbed, and the few disturbances were of a mild intensity. In another area, it has often been assumed that disfigurement of the face produces widespread negative effects in a person's life because of the social stigma surrounding the face as a crucial social stimulus. After fifty-six days of monitoring the everyday social and behavioral lives of children and adolescents with grotesque facial disfigurements resulting from burns (as well as matched control children), Schmitt (1971) and Ronnebeck (1972) found that facial disfigurement produced almost no disruptions of the subjects' daily lives. Stuart (1973) conducted a similar study of wheelchair-bound college students for seven days and found that the overall frequencies of various types of behavior, participation in various settings, and time spent in various activities and places for wheelchair-bound students was almost indistinguishable from the behavioral topographies of matched, nondisabled students.

Family theorists share this interest in naturalistic methodology. The majority of family research has used observation rather than experimentation. When manipulation has been involved, it has typically been in a quasi-experimental design rather than a true experiment. Most of the theory has come from clinical observation of families.

> Fifty years of a voluminous literature devoted to schizophrenic thought processes, emotional states, logic, ànd ego characteristics contain only an occasional anecdote which shows how a schizophrenic actually behaves. Yet the point of the voluminous literature was to explain his behavior. (Haley, 1976, p. 102)

> When the aim is to get a fresh and fundamental view of any object of study, the natural history method of looking directly at raw observational data is often the most appropriate. (Bateson, Weakland, and Haley, 1976, p. 107)

The need to look at naturally occurring events follows in part from the fact that many of the phenomena of interest to family theorists do not occur in laboratory situations. Abeles (1976) notes that most experimental studies of the double bind hypothesis have been of limited usefulness because they do not reproduce the phenomena they purport to study. However, the importance of careful observation of families also follows from the fact that only extensive documentation of the distribution of phenomena in family and family-environment systems can guide us in avoiding the kind of shortsightedness and error mentioned earlier.

Despite the importance of such work for both theorists and clinicians, relatively few extensive studies have been done on families in the field, and there is almost no information on the distribution of the phenomena of family systems in the general population. Perhaps much of this follows from the development of family systems theory primarily as a clinical tool. There are some important exceptions. For example, Henry (1971) has conducted extended observations of families, and he comments:

> I do not believe in the "commonplace." If a woman peels an onion; if a man reads a newspaper or watches television; if there is dust or no dust on the furniture; if a parent kisses or does not kiss his child when he comes home; if the family has eggs or cereal for breakfast, orange juice or no orange juice, and so on through the "trivia" of everyday life—this is significant to me. . . . I proceed on the basis that science advances by relentless examination of the commonplace; that some of the greatest discoveries have been made through fascination with what other men have regarded as not worthy of note. (p. xix)

Research on ecosystems begins with *extensive* research—the description and measurement of distributions—and then elaborates the process of investigation to include *intensive* research, that is, the more discrete study of parts of the system and the testing of specific hypotheses (Southwood, 1966; Watt, 1966). There is no reason to assume that the specific case of family systems should be an exception. The phenomena are so complex, so hard to define and observe, that the area will remain a challenge to researchers for some time to come. However, it is unquestionable that naturalistic studies and distributional studies will be central in this area.

COMPLEXITY, INTERDEPENDENCY, AND THE ILLUSION OF SIDE EFFECTS

It is common for the ecologist to couch much of what he does and thinks about in the terminology and concepts of systems. This happens for several reasons. Sometimes it is because of the extensiveness of the phenomena under study, sometimes because of their complexity or because of the emphasis on interdependence of many variables at many levels, sometimes because systems theory brings to bear an appropriate and powerful set of formal principles, and sometimes simply because *system* is the best metaphor or image the ecologist can conjure up to communicate what he is trying to say when dealing with complexity. It is only reasonable that ecologists would turn to this discipline for tools of conceptual representation and analysis. There is a growing awareness that we need new and sophisticated forms of analysis and synthesis that are not amenable to the traditional, either-or methodology that permeates Western scientific thinking. Systems theory and its various derivatives offer promising tools for representing *interdependence* and simultaneous, time-related complexity (Berrien, 1968; Bruhn, 1974; Buckley, 1968; Laszlo, 1972).

General ecology has become quite sophisticated in its use of formal quantitative representation and systems theory, but behavioral ecology's use of such concepts is still in its infancy. Systems concepts in behavioral ecology are often commonsensical, crude, and analogical in form—for example, frequent use of the phrase "environment-behavior system" in contexts where the speaker or writer cannot specify precisely what that means.

Even in crude form, however, the concept of the system can serve the behavioral ecologist in important ways. To understand how this can work, we need to make a distinction. On the one hand, the behavioral ecologist might try to use the formal structure of systems theory, construct an explicit theory in those terms, and derive hypotheses and testable models in the terminology of systems theory. This has not been done much as yet. On the other hand, even if he does not use all the rules and formalisms of systems theory, the behavioral ecologist can conduct an extensive and detailed study or a conceptual analysis with general systems concepts as a kind of pervading background. He can operate with the notion of *system* as a guiding metaphor, with the guiding belief that what he is studying is involved in complex interdependencies which he has not discovered as yet. Proceeding in that fashion makes a difference in his work.

Humane efforts to apply proven technology and to alleviate human suffering can go awry in the most surprising and vexing ways. The building of large dams leads to increased rates of infectious disease, decreases in fish harvests, and disruptions of social and cultural patterns (Murdoch and Connell, 1970; Sterling, 1972). The green revolution, which involves breeding crops toward genetic uniformity, increases the vulnerability of the crops to epidemics (Wade, 1972). The large-scale use of pesticides and the introduction of new species of animals into an area lead to new, ecologically volatile problems. In the case of crops, insecticides, and other pesticides, and large dams—indeed, in many cases outside the behavioral sciences—we have learned that they are ecological phenomena whose complexity was not anticipated. We know now what happened and we have discovered the principles that govern such events. When it comes to human *behavior*, an analogous ecological perspective has not been formalized as yet, primarily because, with few exceptions, behavioral scientists have not conceived of human behavior as being implicated in complex, ecological systems.

Ecological principles and system principles often can be dramatized best by demonstrating that a given intervention or change leads to complicated and unintended ramifications. The same is true for systems that behavioral scientists are involved with. One of the significant features of many social, physical, and biological systems is that they function as integrated wholes; manipulation of any part of such a system will affect each of the other parts and change the whole. Even the most positively motivated intrusions into interdependent systems can lead to all sorts of unanticipated effects, many of which are unpleasant and pernicious. To label these unintended effects as "side effects" only compounds the problem. Anticipated and unanticipated effects are all functions of the system's processes. Side effects do not occur in the real world. They exist in our images of events for which we *expect* some things and not others.

In society's growing awareness of ecological phenomena, we are reluctant to introduce new biotic elements and new chemicals into our ecological systems, but we do not display the same judiciousness about intervening in behavioral and behavioral-environmental systems. Almost every day, we hear of projects or technologies being changed, slowed down, stopped, or disapproved on ecological grounds, because of the known complexity or delicacy of eco-systems. The location of a proposed factory is switched, a bridge is not built, a planned freeway is rerouted, a smokestack is modified, someone is restrained from introducing a new animal into an area, or a pesticide or other chemical is taken off the market. Those who think that no changes are required in the behavioral sciences, or that arguments for a new effort in behavioral ecology are just so much window dressing should ask one question: how often have I heard of a program or project whose target is human *behavior* being changed, slowed down, stopped, or disapproved on *behavioral*-ecological grounds, because of the *known* complexity and delicacy of eco-behavioral systems? The answer should sober us quickly. Every intervention, every human artifice, has its price, no matter how well-intentioned the agent of intervention may be. The places, programs, and times for which this is true need to be documented and understood much better by behavioral scientists. To clarify what we mean here, we can present briefly a hierarchical series of illustrations.

Partly because of their rigor and partly because of the explicitness with which their intended effects can be spelled out, various programs of applied behavior analysis or behavior modification illustrate these problems very clearly for human behavior (Willems, 1974, 1977c). Buell et al. (1968) used teacher attention to reinforce a withdrawn girl's use of play equipment in a preschool setting. The intervention was successful (the intended effect), but it also affected the girl's interactions with other children, such as touching, verbalizations, and cooperative play (positive unintended effects). Twardosz and Sajwaj (1972) found that increasing the rate of sitting in a retarded and hyperactive boy also decreased his rate of weird posturings and increased his rate of proximity to other children.

Unintended effects of a more unpleasant and pernicious sort also occur. Herbert et al. (1973) trained parents in the use of differential attention to increase appropriate behaviors and decrease deviant behaviors in six children. One child showed some improvement and one showed no change. In the cases of four children, dramatic, intense, and *durable* (but unintended) effects showed up, both in the treatment setting and in other settings. Examples were assaulting mother, scratching self until bleeding, enuresis, and throwing furniture. Robert Wahler (1975) found that the successful induction of planned treatment effects in one setting (either home or school) was accompanied by unplanned effects in the other setting. Sajwaj, Twardosz, and Burke (1972) found various so-called "side effects" of manipulating single behaviors in a preschool boy. They taught the teacher to extinguish the child's nagging in one setting of the preschool. This tactic was successful in reducing the nagging, but it produced systematic changes in other behaviors by the child in the same setting and in another setting as well. Some of the unintended effects were desirable, such as increasing speech initiated to children and increasing cooperative play; some were undesirable, such as decreasing task-appropriate behavior, and increasing disruptive behavior; and some were neutral, such as use of girls' toys. The investigators were able to show that the covarying effects were not due to differential attention by the teacher applied directly to those behaviors, but were somehow, as yet mysteriously, a function of modifying the nagging in one setting. It seems clear that the simplistic models and technologies of change used by the applied behavior analyst are not comprehensive enough to lead to the understanding of complex human behavior or to predictable interventions.

There are other examples that fall higher on a hierarchy of setting size and complexity. In a mental hospital ward, Proshansky, Ittelson, and Rivlin (1970) used some amenities of interior design to increase the rate of sociable occupancy and the use of a solarium and they found that the rate of detached, withdrawn, standing behavior went down. However, they had only succeeded in changing the *location* of the troubling behavior—a great deal of it now occurred at the other end of the corridor, by the nurses' station.

In 1974 and 1975, because of the energy crunch, administrators of a V.A. hospital decided to decrease the amount of electricity consumed (David M. Bailey, personal communication). They disconnected one-half to two-thirds of the fluorescent lights in several wards. When they did this, they found that the noise level in those wards decreased so much that they could cancel their plan to spend thousands of dollars to soundproof the wards. This was a simple intervention in a behavioral-environmental system that resulted in two positive unintended effects. We do not know whether there were other, less positive effects, such as a decrease in rates of activity and interactions.

Several years ago, a group of educators mobilized a new program of early intervention to train disadvantaged children in cognitive skills (Dale Johnson, personal communication). All available measures showed that the program achieved *none* of its *intended* effects on cognitive skills in the children. However, community participation and political involvement by the children's families increased markedly.

According to a TV news report, the police department in San Diego tried an experiment to reduce excessive automobile speed in an area in which the speed limit was 20 miles per hour. Without issuing tickets, the police gathered baseline data and found the average speed to be 23 miles per hour. In order to reduce the average speed, they then posted a new speed limit of 19 miles per hour, hoping, perhaps, to capitalize on the attention-getting value of unusual numbers on signs. After waiting for a period of time for stabilization of driving habits, the police found, to their surprise, that the new average speed had increased to *26 miles per hour*!

At the level of residential systems, the work of investigators such as Newman (1972) and Galle, Gove, and McPherson (1972), and the accumulation of experiences with arrangements such as the Pruitt-Igoe apartment complex in St. Louis all suggest that a torrent of troubling effects can follow from the concatenation of people in large groupings, high population density, and physical designs whose behavioral principles are very poorly understood. More and more frequently, engineers, architects, and other agents of environmental planning and policy are turning to the social and behavioral sciences with various forms of the question: how should we design this environment to make it best suited for human inhabitants? We must confess that mostly we know *after the fact* that some things have *not* worked and we can offer almost no prospective prescriptions.

We must recognize a common tendency here that is fed by pressures on us to demonstrate our ability to solve human problems. This is the tendency to devote less effort to *understanding* complexity and more effort to setting up interventions and programs of human change. Leon Eisenberg (1972) argues:

> With each decade, scientific findings translated into technology radically reshape the way we live. Technical capacity has been the ruling imperative, with no reckoning of cost, whether ecological or personal. If it could be done, it has been done. Foresight has lagged far behind craftsmanship. At long last we are beginning to ask, not *can* it be done, but *should* it be done? The challenge is to our ability to anticipate second- and third-order consequences of interventions in the ecosystem before the event, not merely to rue them afterward. (p. 123)

Behavioral scientists often believe that their favorite approaches to research ultimately will yield comprehensive understanding of human behavior. We think they are wrong in many cases because their conception of the research problems is too narrow and too short-sighted. On the other hand, in seeking to alleviate human problems, *applied* behavioral scientists often believe that, in order to be successful, they need mainly to do more of what they are already doing and do it more intensely. Again, we think they often are wrong and we think many of their best efforts are doomed because they do not understand the complexity of the systems in which they are dabbling. The perspective of behavioral ecology offers one hope for both problems.

On September 14, 1976, a commentator on an NBC news program spoke of some recent findings regarding aerosols and then said that, so often these days, we hear of severe and sometimes permanent damage being done by the very things we have been invited to use and consume. *Where are the scientists ahead of time?* That question and what we can do to answer it for techniques of behavior change represent major unfinished business for us. Often, science is sold in terms of the technological innovations it can produce and technological innovations are sold in terms of their basis in scientific research. People are beginning to see that many of these innovations have indirect and secondary effects that are far greater than anticipated. Being closely linked, science and technology have both come under a cloud of suspicion. We should ask ourselves, for substantive, theoretical, and professional reasons, "Where are we ahead of time, with some anticipatory understanding of the effects of our behavioral interventions and technologies?" Gaining such anticipatory understanding is a central issue in behavioral ecology.

Behavioral science can benefit from the use and the implications of the concept of *synergism*; that is, combined action of discrete agents such that the resultant effect is greater than or different from the sum of the effects of the agents taken singly or independently. In environmental pharmacology, this concept has become so much a part of the conceptualization that it is seldom mentioned anymore. Several hundred drugs, insecticides, herbicides, hormones, carcinogens, and other environmental chemicals are now known to enhance, inhibit, and become involved in complex interactive effects with ingested drugs in both man and animals (Conney and Burns, 1972; Lichtenstein, Liang, and Anderegg, 1973). Assuming synergism, environmental pharmacologists have pressed for explanations. At present, one common denominator appears to be the variable nature of liver enzymes that process and deal with chemicals having diverse structures and diverse biological effects. Many synergistic effects of chemicals are now predictable. In applied behavioral science, where we affect the rate, intensity, presence, absence, and combinations of behaviors and their linkages, we have made only a few bare attempts to ask questions about synergism, and there are even fewer answers. Adopting the belief in a synergistic world is an important step we can take.

In systems approaches to marriages and families, the use of the assumptions and concepts of systems is also somewhat analogical and crude. Some of the major figures in the area—Bowen, Watzlawick, Jackson, Hill, Minuchin, Steinglass, and Sluzki—would probably agree that marriages and families should be seen as *system-like*, rather than strictly as systems. Such a use of systems allows one to avoid some of the awkward and overly demanding formalisms of systems theory.

Family therapists also are sensitive to the ways in which an intervention can resonate through a family system. It is desirable to have a focused, simple intervention, not only for the sake of parsimony, but because too strong an intervention is likely to produce many unintended effects. Family therapy interventions sometimes appear trivial or paradoxical because they are based on this idea that a simple input can result in a very complex reaction. It is important to monitor the changes produced by these interventions because they provide needed information on how the system processes input. For instance, Minuchin (1974) cites a case of a family with a schizophrenic boy. Based on the judgment that the mother-child relationship was too strong while the spouse subsystem was too weak, the parents were instructed to go out once a week and leave the son at home. The first time this happened the boy slashed all his clothes with a razor. The therapist interpreted this as a sign that the treatment was working and told the parents to continue going out. The next time, the boy slashed his wrists and was hospitalized. Here, the therapist's original assessment of the problem may have been correct, but his intervention was poorly directed and he failed to monitor the process.

It may not be too long before therapists may be required to write *therapy-impact statements*, or *eco-behavioral impact statements* before proceeding with an intervention. Such statements include analyses of net costs and benefits, and must take account of wider ramifications of interventions. The conceptualization of behavioral ecologists and systems theorists of human behavior will lead the way in solving this problem. However, to reach the solution successfully, a great deal of related empirical research will have to be done.

SETTING DEPENDENCIES

One of the central conceptual issues of behavioral ecology is the transactional character of organism-environment systems. Studying behavior by itself is always short-sighted because behavior points two ways, or relates in two directions—organism and environment—and to mediating processes between them. Behavior represents the coming-to-terms that occurs in organism-environment systems. Organism and environment are part of the same system, with behavior being the major interface between them. Thus, the behavioral ecologist would argue, we must study *behavior-environment* units rather than just behavior units.

From this perspective, bits of behavior or bits of environment taken independently (as in an S-R model), the "independent" and "dependent" variables of most experiments, and the bits and pieces of behavior with which we tinker so blithely in psychotherapy, counseling, operant behavior modification, and behavioral pharmacology are all abstractions that have lost much of their scientific and practical meaning because they are separated from the larger, contextual interdependencies in which they occur. What is worse, when changing such abstracted bits of behavior, we may create unintended effects in the ecological systems with which the behaviors are linked (Willems, 1973b, 1974). As Rhodes (1972) argues, the credo of behavioral ecology is that, in both its positive and negative manifestations, behavior is a property of ecological systems rather than an attribute of the individual.

> The ecosystem, within the ecological perspective, is an active, energetic composite. . . . It is not only the individual members of the system who act and react, but the total ecosystem "behaves" as a whole. In this sense, behavior is not only a function of an individual, it is also a function of the ecosystem or its subsystems. Therefore, territory is not merely an inert geographical mass. It is also a set of forces which encompasses the behavioral forces of the individual. Together, they form living patterns which have their own, inbuilt self-sustaining behavior-selecting regularity. (pp. 558–559)

Closely related to the issue of behavior-environment units is the issue of predictability from place, or setting, to behavior. In order to clarify what we mean, we need to distinguish between intrabehavioral complexities and eco-behavioral complexities. *Intrabehavioral complexities* are the complicated effects and behavioral outcroppings that arise as a function of behavior-behavior relationships; for example, response chains and response classes. Such complexities should be (and have been) of great concern because they operate in producing unintended effects of interventions. However, they are largely intrinsic to repertoires of behavior. *Eco-behavioral complexities* are the complicated effects, patterns, and discontinuities in behavior that arise as a function of behavior-environment relationships and the properties of settings. Thus, eco-behavioral complexities are at least partially extrinsic to repertoires of behavior. Since these complexities are at least a partial function of the properties of settings, they are poorly understood because so little effort has been devoted to the analysis of contexts.

Where organisms are located is never unimportant because behavior and place combine into lawful, functioning systems (Barker, 1963a; Moos, 1973; Wicker, 1972; Willems, 1976). In the conduct of everyday affairs, not only do we depend upon location specificity in behavior for predictability and social order, but we often use departures from such correlations to label persons as sick, crazy, deviant, etc., and in need of help or control. Roger Barker points out that place-behavior systems have such strong principles of organization and constraint that their standing patterns of behavior remain essentially the same, though individuals come and go. Allan Wicker (1972) calls this "behavior-environment congruence." Barker (1968) calls it "behavior-milieu synomorphy" and argues that the appropriate units of analysis for studying such relationships are behavior settings, whose defining attributes and properties he has spelled out in detail (1963a, 1968).

A clear example of the importance of place dependencies is found in the work of Harold Raush and his colleagues in their studies of normal children and children diagnosed as hyperaggressive or disturbed (Raush, 1969; Raush, Dittman, and Taylor, 1959a, 1959b; Raush, Farbman, and Llewellyn, 1960). By observing the children for extended periods of time in various settings and then examining the frequencies of various kinds of behavior by the children toward peers and adults, the investigators were able to demonstrate several aspects of place dependency. First, the interpersonal behavior of all the children varied from one setting to another. Second, and perhaps most revealing, the place dependence of behavior was much stronger for normal children than for disturbed children; that is, the influence of the setting was greater for normal children. Finally, as the disturbed children progressed in treatment, the place dependence of their behavior came to approximate the normal children more and more.

Robert Wahler (1975) observed two troubled boys periodically for three years in home and school settings. He found (1) that behaviors clustered differently in home and school settings, (2) that the clusters within each setting were very stable over time, and (3) that different patterns of deviant behaviors occurred in stable fashion in the two settings. Lichstein and Wahler (1976) observed behaviors of an autistic child and adults and peers for approximately six months. Observations were made in three different settings, and covariation of behaviors across time and settings was analyzed by means of cluster analysis. Again, the investigators found that the child's behavior was relatively stable across time within a given setting and that none of the child's behavior clusters appeared in more than one setting.

These principles are also illustrated and elaborated by our program of research on persons with spinal cord injuries (Willems, 1976). First, when we look at distributions of patient behavior within different settings, we find that these profiles of behavior vary dramatically from one setting to another (LeCompte and Willems, 1970; Willems, 1972a, 1972b). Some behaviors that occur in one setting do not occur at all in others, and the relative frequencies and percentage weights of behavior show strong variation between settings. *What* patients do varies systematically from one setting to another.

Second, in addition to these topographical dependencies on settings, we find setting dependencies in the more dynamic aspects of patient behavior. From the observations, we extract behavioral measures of *independence* (i.e., the proportion of performances that patients initiate and execute alone). Because an increase from very low rates in this measure reflects a relative normalization of the patient's behavior repertoires, it relates closely to important goals of the hospital's treatment system. Many traditional, person-based theories of human behavior assume that independence is largely a matter of individual motivation and thus should reflect a high degree of personal constancy across situations. We find instead that behavioral independence varies dramatically when patients move from one hospital setting to another.

Third, we find in many cases that differences between settings account for more variance in patient performance than do differences between patients. Fourth, and most interestingly, there are powerful variations among settings in the rate of behavioral growth and development displayed by individual patients over time. That is, patients show much more *change* of behavior over time in some hospital settings than in others. Thus, not only do we find that persons perform differently in different settings when we make simple comparisons between settings, but persons change in different ways and at different rates in different settings (Willems and Halstead, 1978).

These are important phenomena with regard to which we all should take some procedural and empirical steps because there is too much mystery. The behavioral ecologist is intrigued by place dependency as a fundamental issue in eco-behavioral relationships. More specifically, we are concerned about their relevance to the delivery of health care. For example, we have discovered that the place dependency in patient behavior affects staff judgments and assessments of patients and, therefore, probably influences their treatments of patients. When these central principles of behavioral ecology really soak in, they will affect psychology and related disciplines in profound ways. One area that will be affected strongly is the area of human assessment and diagnosis. It no longer will be so tenable or defensible to assess *a person's* performance. Rather, we will have to assess performance-by-settings, simply because variations in settings produce variations in performance.

For many types of behavioral problems and disabilities, the person is most dependent upon ministration and intervention by the social and physical environment for survival and adaptation when his problem is most acute. Thus, common sense and conventional social wisdom suggest

(1) that the person's performance should show the most intersetting variability when he is sickest, and (2) that the intersetting variability (setting dependency) should diminish as the person gets better, perhaps because his performance comes more and more under the control of his own internal processes. The findings of Raush and his group mentioned earlier suggest that just the opposite is the case for some behavioral disturbances. The more normal the disturbed boys became, the more differentiated their behavior became according to the disparate programs of the various settings they entered. We find something similar in our work with spinal cord injured persons. Early in their hospitalizations, the clients display little intersetting variability in performance. As they get better, their behavior rapidly shows more variability among settings.

In offering these arguments, we are not advocating the relatively superficial environmentalism of learning theory, which argues that a wide variety of specific behaviors can be conditioned to a wide variety of environmental cues. Rather, we are advocating the deep, evolutionary environmentalism of ethology, behavioral ecology, and sociobiology. On this view, specific patterns of behavior that can be learned are less important than the more generic idea that the evolutionary process has produced behavioral responsiveness to settings, because the location appropriateness of behavior has functional survival value (Sells, 1969; Skinner, 1971). If that is so, then several implications follow. First, we must engage in the investigative effort to describe and classify the general types and patterns of congruence between behavior and environment. Second, we must enrich our theoretical models of human functioning to include this generic environmentalism. Finally, we must enrich our classifications of human problems to take account of eco-behavioral complexities rather than only intrabehavioral or intrapersonal events.

Perhaps the most basic theme of behavioral ecology is this need to understand the complex relationships that link person, behavior, and the social and physical environments. It is axiomatic that an organism cannot be understood apart from an understanding of its environment and the laws by which the two are linked. Family systems theory takes a very similar position, although it focuses primarily on the social environment, with less interest in the physical environment. For the family theorist, the individual always exists as part of a social network that influences and shapes his behavior and thinking in many ways. Even the hermit or recluse has been shaped by a social history. Behaviors that appear paradoxical or self-destructive, such as fire-setting, anorexia nervosa, and suicide, may take on meaning when seen in the context of relationships surrounding the person.

Behavioral ecology puts much emphasis on where behavior occurs, on the site specificity of behavior. At the most sophisticated conceptual level, behavior and environment are combined in the concept of behavior setting, which includes both regular patterns of behavior and a given physical setting. Setting effects are believed to be very powerful, and indeed, one definition of pathology for the behavioral ecologist is behavior that does not respond to setting influences.

Family therapists generally have not been sensitive to these types of ecological variables, although they probably would consider them important. A behavioral ecologist, for instance, might look at a high rise apartment complex and make predictions about the effects of such an environment on the people living there, while a family therapist working with a family in such a setting would probably focus on the ways in which the family has organized itself to deal with the environment. In the latter case, a therapeutic intervention might focus on shifting roles or responsibilities in the family, or might attempt to mobilize the family to seek a different living arrangement.

One family therapist, however, does conceptualize problems very much as a behavioral ecologist would (Minuchin, 1974).

> An Italian widow, in her late sixties, who had lived in the same apartment for twenty-five years, came home one day to find the apartment robbed. She decided to move and called the moving company. It was the beginning of a nightmare. As she described it, the people who came to move her things tried to control where she went. When they moved her belongings, they purposefully misplaced and lost precious possessions. They left sinister markings—cryptograms—on her furniture. When she went outside, people followed her, secretly signaling to each other. She went to a psychiatrist, who gave her tranquilizers, but her experiences did not change. . . .
>
> She went to see another therapist, whose interventions were based on an ecological understanding of the old and lonely. He explained to the woman that she had lost her shell—the previous home where she had known each object, the neighborhood, and the people in the neighborhood. At this point, like any crustacean that has lost its shell, she was vulnerable. Reality had a different experiential effect. These problems would disappear, he assured her, when she grew a new shell. They discussed how to shorten the time this would take. She was to unpack all her belongings, hang up the pictures that had decorated her previous apartment, put the books on the shelves, and organize the apartment so it became familiar. All her movements were to become routinized. She was to get up at a certain time, shop at a certain time, go to the same stores, the same checkout counters, and so on. She was not to try to make new friends in the new neighborhood for two weeks. She was to go back to visit her old friends, but in order to spare her friends and family, she was not to describe any of her experiences. If anyone inquired about her problems, she was to explain that they were merely the problems of illogical, fearful old people. (pp. 11–12)

Although this case is far too rich to analyze completely here, it illustrates the way in which person and environment can interact to produce what some would call clinical phenomena. A change in the woman's environment changed her attitude toward it and led to behavior that unfortunately reinforced further changes in the environment, which in turn led to more negative perceptions. Her behavior began to pull negative reactions from others (the psychiatrist). Yet with help, she was able to act on the environment in such a way as to make it more supportive (by fixing her apartment and visiting old friends while avoiding any odd actions that might pull negative reactions from them). Her behavior became understandable when interpreted as part of the total context, and the intervention was both effective and rapid. An attempt to understand the woman's reactions without reference to her environment probably would have led to attributing psychopathology to her, possibly a form of senility. A younger person might have been able to handle the situation with less turmoil, but the woman's behavior was quite comprehensible given the total situation. This type of willingness to look at complex person-environment transactions characterizes both the behavioral ecologist and many family therapists.

Even though the behavioral ecologist and family theorist or therapist overlap somewhat in attaching importance to the context or situation in which behavior occurs, there are some important differences. The family theorist emphasizes the communication networks and social networks of families and friends. The behavioral ecologist insists that we also consider ways in which physical contexts shape behaviors and produce outcomes of interest to the family theorist or therapist. Several examples will illustrate this point.

Powerful site specificity, or place dependence, of behavior is found in the case of the yellow-faced grassquit (Pulliam et al., 1972). Observations of the grassquits indicate that they are far more communal on the Central American mainland than on nearby islands, such as Jamaica, where they are highly territorial and selfish. Klopfer and Klopfer (1973) generalize about subhuman animals by saying that leadership in groups of animals (which animal will have preference or take initiative) depends upon the specific context and cannot be seen as a trait that resides within particular animals.

The power of situational dependencies as compared to person dependencies is illustrated further in a study by Quilitch and Risley (1973). It is common to assume that a person's sociability, the rate at which he interacts with others, is primarily a matter of his inclinations, motives, attitudes, or dispositions. Quilitch and Risley found that the type of toys provided to children dramatically influenced their rate of social (interactive) play, probably even more than the types of children or differences between children. When the same children were presented first one set of toys and then another, their rate of playing together varied by as much as eighty-nine percent. More importantly, when the membership of the group was allowed to shift and evolve over time, the same pattern of situation dependence emerged. That is, groups with changing membership engaged in social play at a rate of about fifteen percent when provided with the "isolate" toys while similarly evolving groups engaged in social play at a rate of about eighty-two percent when provided with "social" toys. The situations and their props, rather than the stable traits of the children, produced the social-behavioral topography of the situations. Professionals concerned with families would be quite interested in the sociability of children. And yet, the physical context and its physical props shape sociability in powerful ways.

Finally, consider a family with a quadriplegic son, and imagine the home environment being such that the door sills to the bathroom door and outside door are a fraction of an inch too high to be negotiated by the quadriplegic in his wheelchair. The whole family and its community involvement and freedom probably would be affected profoundly by a simple smoothing of the door sills to that the paralyzed son could negotiate the environment independently.

Often in recent years, we have heard complaints that sexism is so pervasive and ingrained in our society that sexist responses are almost automatic. We would argue that *personism* is just as pervasive, if not more; that is, explanations and interpretations of behavior that point inside the person are almost automatic, even among psychologists and psychiatrists. Contexts also produce behavior. It is just as accurate to speak of incompetent, confused, maladjusted, crazy *contexts* as it is to speak of incompetent, confused, maladjusted, crazy persons. Furthermore, the work of Norris-Baker (1978) suggests that precise environmental assessment and diagnosis is possible.

ECOLOGICAL DIAGNOSIS

The next issue we want to mention, diagnosis, is closely related to the issue of place dependency of behavior. An ornithologist with a European zoo wished to add a small, rare bird called the bearded tit (sometimes called the reedling) to the zoo's collection (Robert B. Lockard, personal communication). Noting that other attempts to maintain the bird in captivity had been unsuccessful, he devoted a great deal of time and effort to summarizing what was known about the tit's habitat and life style. Armed with all this information, including many photographs, the ornithologist built an extensive setting for the tits in his zoo, being careful to include exactly the right proportion and distribution of shrubs, trees, grasses, rocks, arrangements for feeding, nesting materials, and lighting. After the designed environment satisfied him, he introduced a male and female to it. The birds sang, ate, drank, flitted about, groomed, mated, built an appropriate nest, laid eggs, hatched babies, and fed them. If birds can be said to enjoy their environments, then, by all these behavioral criteria, the ornithologist had designed an environment whose habitability the family of bearded tits enjoyed thoroughly.

Within a day or two, however, he came to check the tits, only to find the babies dead on the ground. Since the parents were still so clearly enjoying themselves, he assumed that some accident or illness had befallen the infants, and he waited for the reproductive cycle to recur. When a new brood was hatched, the ornithologist observed carefully and found, to his dismay, after a period of time, that the parents pushed the babies out of the nest, onto the ground, where they died. This cycle, beginning with mating and ending with the babies dead on the ground, repeated itself over and over again.

The ornithologist tried several modifications, but none forestalled the systematic infanticide. In desperation, he went back out to observe tits in the wild. After many hours of observation, he noted three clear patterns of behavior. First, throughout most of the daylight hours, the parent tits were almost frantically active at finding and bringing food for the infants. Second, the infants, with whose food demands the parents could hardly keep pace, spent the same hours with their mouths open, apparently crying for food. The third pattern was that any inanimate object, whether eggshell, leaf, or beetle shell, was quickly shoved out of the nest by the parents.

With these observations in hand, the ornithologist went back to observe his captive tits and what he found astounded him because of its subtlety and, yet, its clarity. During the short time a new brood of infants lived, the parents spent only brief periods feeding them by racing between the nest and the food supply, which the ornithologist had supplied in abundance. After a short period of such feeding, the infants, apparently satiated, fell asleep. The first time the infants slept for any length of time during daylight hours, the parents shoved them out of the nest (they were two inanimate objects, after all). When he made the food supply *less* abundant and *less* accessible and thereby made the parents work much longer and harder to find food, the ornithologist found that the infants spent more daylight time awake, demanding food, and that the tits then produced many families and cared for them to maturity. Here is a clear illustration of the micro-ecology of behavior.

We would all agree that infanticide is an important behavior problem in a family and that the ornithologist cured it. But the case of the bearded tits also points out some important issues about diagnosis. Diagnosis is a process that begins with careful scrutiny of a set of indicators and ends with a judgment, a statement, regarding the events to which those indicators point. In psychology and psychiatry, judgments of what is wrong (that is, diagnoses) are often highly constrained by prior theoretical commitments that lead one to look for the underlying problem *inside* the target person. It is important to recognize this tradition because diagnostic judgments usually carry with them either implicit or explicit strategies of intervention. If the underlying problem is seen to lie inside the person, then remedial steps will usually be focused on the person (Caplan and Nelson, 1973; Ryan, 1971). The bearded tit story raises some fundamental conceptual questions about the use of behavior as a source of indicators, the process of diagnostic judgment, and the targets of intervention.

After he had confirmed his suspicion that the parent tits were engaging in infanticide, the ornithologist could have followed the example provided by diagnosticians of human affairs. That is, he could have assumed that the mainsprings of the behavior resided inside the skins of the parents and he could have diagnosed *them* as crazy or sick and in need of some form of help, perhaps psychotherapy. Instead, he used a series of careful observations to scrutinize the organism-environment system and to converge on a contextual, *ecological* diagnosis of the problem. Then, he engaged in an ecological course of remedial action that makes great sense in retrospect; that is, he intervened with the accessibility of the food supply. We have little difficulty accepting this kind of ecological, contextual approach to infra-human animals, but we manage to blind ourselves to its implications for human behavior. The problem lies in our models, theories, and research, which are preoccupied with the unity and integrity of persons taken one at a time and are preoccupied with what goes on inside them, rather than with behavior-environment systems. After all, it is the *person* who behaves, whose behavior we must understand, who misbehaves, and it is the *person* who comes or is referred for help because of some serious internal disturbance, isn't it? This is the way it has been in psychology, but psychology needs much more if it is to deal effectively with human problems.

The traditional mode of diagnosis, in which the person is seen as the repository of the problems, can lead to results that are too facile and too quick-and-dirty in their execution. The ease with which this can happen is illustrated by the work of Rosenhan (1973), who asked eight sane persons to gain admission to twelve different mental hospitals over a period of time. With only fleeting reference to hearing voices in otherwise straightforward presentations, all were admitted with diagnoses of schizophrenia except one. The investigators who arranged the study told the pseudopatients that they would have to get out of the hospitals by their own devices. The average length of stay was nineteen days, with a range from seven to fifty-two days. Even though several of the hospitals had excellent reputations, other patients—never staff members—were the ones who spotted the pseudopatients as pretenders. Furthermore, each of the pseudopatients was discharged with a diagnosis of schizophrenia in remission. Note that they were not judged never to have been sick; they were judged to have been sick and somehow remitted. In other words, the original label remained in effect.

Rosenhan reports other data and his study certainly has far-reaching implications. The important point for present purposes is to note how simplistic and facile the classical mode of diagnosis can be. Assuming that the person carries around the roots of his problems inside him, the classical mode often involves a few logical steps to respond to a simple set of verbal signals about what is presumably going on inside the person and to conclude, diagnostically, that his life is fouled up. What such a process disregards about the person's behavioral life and his functioning beyond the simple, verbal, inward-pointing signals should give us all pause.

Our traditional models lead us to focus on persons. The points in the ecological system in which we sample determine where we locate the behavioral problem. When our pet models lead us to attach our disturbance detectors to the individual, we will detect disturbance in the individual and we will make the individual our target of intervention and change. In the process, we disregard the fact that the problem or the disturbance may lie at the level of a system of which the individual is only one component. Our scientific understanding of behavior, our principles of diagnosis, and our interventions must be adjusted to a new level of complexity. One of the most important steps toward credibility and long-range impact that behavioral science can take is to develop sound procedures for new forms of contextual, ecological diagnosis.

The behavioral ecologist and family therapist overlap each other in the area of diagnosis. More than any other group, family therapists have developed the tools of contextual diagnosis. That is, some of them have developed models and interventions to deal with behavior problems that arise in a person because of difficulties in the forces operating in networks of family members or acquaintances (Minuchin, 1970, 1974; Rueveni and Speck, 1969; Sluzki, 1978; Speck and Attneave, 1973; Speck and Rueveni, 1969; Steinglass, 1978). If adopted widely, this approach will help to revolutionize the processes of diagnosis and treatment. Though it is an important step in the right direction in pointing to problems in systems of forces, the network therapy movement has a severe limitation. That is, the movement tends to restrict its focus to communications, social influences, pressures, and counterpressures that permeate the relations among persons in a defined network. The behavioral ecologist would argue that the revolution should be extended much more widely because behavioral difficulties in persons or groups of persons also may arise from problems or disruptions in person-environment-behavior systems wherein "environment" includes much more than social forces.

BEHAVIORAL EMPHASIS

Traditionally, psychologists have studied many aspects of human functioning: thoughts, feelings, moods, structures of personality, habits, motives, judgments, cognitions, self-concepts, beliefs, attitudes, perceptions, sensory processes, ego strength, and a host of other traits and dispositions. The anchoring point for the behavioral ecologist is individual and collective behavior, the molar performances of persons vis-à-vis the environment and their molar responses to it—where persons go, what they do with their time, how they use resources, how they interact with each other. This emphasis has emerged for several reasons. First, the great strides made in animal ecology and ethology have had an influence. In those areas, investigators have been forced to focus on overt behavior because the subjects cannot report feelings and subjective states.

Second, not only do attempts to measure subjective and dispositional variables often evolve into endless psychometric jungles of checking, cross-checking, and validation, but more distressingly, they often yield very weak correlations to behavior (Mischel, 1968; Wicker, 1969, 1971; Willems, 1967). On the basis of his review of the attitude-behavior field, Wicker (1969) concluded that there is

> little evidence to support the postulated existence of stable, underlying attitudes within the individual which influence both his verbal expressions and his actions. . . . Most socially significant questions involve overt behavior, rather than people's feelings, and the assumption that feelings are directly translated into action has not been demonstrated. (p. 75)

Third, with a shift in emphasis to problems of everyday life and to naturalistic research, psychologists have begun to question some old, dearly held assumptions, one of which asserts that affective, attitudinal, and cognitive variables affect behavioral variables in a simple and unidirectional way. Bakeman and Helmreich (1975) argue:

> Much of the laboratory research of the last two decades in fact has viewed cognitive variables as affecting behavioral ones. Perhaps it is worthwhile to speculate why this is so. The experimentalist . . . manipulates what he can most effectively manipulate, and cognitions are far easier to manipulate than actual behavior. Perhaps feasibility comes to bias views of causality, and then theorists working from laboratory data are likely to become convinced that cognitive variables determine behavioral ones. (p. 488)

Fourth, behavioral performance and response are the major means by which person-environment adaptations are actually mediated. The ecologist does not argue against the reality of subjective phenomena.

Rather, his position is a matter of emphasis in his seeking to understand human functioning in relation to the environment. Nor does the relative emphasis on behavior imply a simplistic advocacy of behaviorism. To the ecologist, overt behavior simply is more important than many other psychological phenomena. For him, it is more important to know how parents *treat* their children than how they feel about being parents; more important to observe whether or not passersby *help* someone in need than what their beliefs are about altruism and kindness; more important to note that a person *harms* someone else when given an opportunity than to know whether his self-concept is that of a considerate person; more important to know what persons *do* with trash than to measure their attitudes about waste disposal; more important to know what one *does* in the way of consuming alcohol or hiring women than to infer community beliefs regarding alcohol or women. To the behavioral ecologist, person-environment-*behavior* systems represent problems to be understood and solved that are simply more important than person-environment-*cognition* systems or person-environment-*attitude* systems. Ecologically speaking, the crucial issues are the ways in which individuals and groups actually relate to, adapt to, connect with, and make their way in the environment. Subjective states—subjective responses such as happiness, sadness, *joie de vivre*, satisfaction—are inevitably transient. They are fleeting *accompaniments* of the match between person and environment, and that match is the important problem.

Between behavioral ecologists and family theorists and therapists, there is likely to be considerable diversity of opinion regarding relative emphasis on behavior. The behavioral ecologist sees it as fundamental. Most family therapists consider behavior very important, but tend to see behavior as a special instance of the more general set of communications. These family therapists operate on the assumption that all human behavior can have a communicative function. In social systems, it is impossible not to communicate, because an attempt to avoid communicating is itself a message defining the desired relationship between people (Haley, 1971). This message quality of behavior is so important for the family therapist that the specific behaviors are seen as something like carrier waves or message channels for the information being conveyed. Many different behaviors can be used to transmit the same message and many different messages can be transmitted by the same behavior, with interpretation depending on the context.

The interpretation will depend on the history of the relationship and on the current situation. This historical component, part of any behavioral transaction, is one of the things that makes predicting behavior difficult or impossible. It is also the reason that achieving change can be so difficult—new behaviors tend to be interpreted as part of the old context, as when a man buys his wife a present because he wants to improve their relationship, but she gets angry because she thinks he has done something to make him feel guilty. Similarly, a change in context, as when a couple decides to enter therapy, can produce dramatic improvement in a relationship because old behaviors are reinterpreted in the context of a desire to improve the relationship.

On the other hand, some marital therapists take a stricter behavioral view that is closer to the view of the behavioral ecologist. For example,

> When observing couples' interactions, a system-oriented therapist will take into consideration effects, rather than intentions. The effects of behavior upon behavior, the way interpersonal sequences are organized, will be carefully noted, while, on the contrary, no inference will be made about the motivations of the participants. Even further, issues about motivation or intention will be considered irrelevant to the understanding of interpersonal processes. This choice must not be taken as the blunt denial of the existence of motivation, intention, or human volition in general. It only happens that those inferences do not add any relevant information for purposes of conceptualizing and/or treating marital disorder from a systems perspective. (Sluzki, 1978, p. 367)

Dialogue between behavioral ecologists and family therapists about the concepts of behavior and information might benefit both disciplines.

THE LONGER TIME FRAME

In keeping with the characteristics of behavior-environment systems and the kinds of behavioral dimensions with which he often works (e.g., adaptation, accommodation, functional achievement, long-range behavior, and sometimes even survival), the ecologist not only allows, but sometimes demands, unusually long time periods and time perspectives in his research. Over and above the more traditional search for early antecedents (as in developmental psychology), such long-range research often takes the form of monitoring interdependencies continuously, or nearly continuously, for extended periods of time. At least three concerns lead to this emphasis. First, sequential, temporal, emergent phenomena are among the most important properties of behavior (Barker, 1963b; Nesselroade and Reese, 1973; Raush, 1969). Second, ecosystems in general (and, therefore, probably behavioral-ecological systems) follow rules of succession and internal distribution in which the longitudinal perspective becomes critical. Third, we know by now from other areas (e.g., crop diseases, pollution, public health problems, insecticides) that empirical monitoring of very long sequences can be both scientifically illuminating and pragmatically critical. Psychologists must become willing to participate in such long-range concerns.

> Whatever is done to the environment is likely to have repercussions in other places and at other times. Because of the characteristic problems of ecology some of the effects are bound to be unpredictable in practice, if not in principle. Furthermore, because of the characteristic time-dependence problem, the effects may not be measurable for years—possibly not for decades. (Murdoch and Connell, 1970, p. 61)

Three examples illustrate these issues. First, Watt (1968, pp. 30–31) demonstrates how continuous monitoring of ecological phenomena over long periods of time can enable researchers and resource managers to avoid mistaken explanations. From 1941 to 1947, the catch of whitefish in Georgian Bay, Lake Huron, dropped alarmingly, by 88 percent. Many persons, noting an accompanying rise in the population of smelt and lamphreys, believed that the drop in whitefish was caused partly by smelt eating whitefish eggs. However, the data-gathering process went on. Beginning in 1948, the catch of whitefish began to rise to a spectacular new record in 1953 (724 percent higher than 1941), even though the population of smelt did not decline appreciably. The continuous gathering of data over a long period of time (twelve years) made it possible to eliminate the smelt-egg hypothesis; smelt just happened to build up while the whitefish declined.

Second, noting that a person's adaptation to the noxious stimulation of high-intensity noise can produce negative aftereffects in behavior (Glass and Singer, 1972), Cohen, Glass, and Singer (1973) studied the long-term effects of noise on children living in a high-rise apartment building. The apartment building was situated directly over a busy interstate highway that produced high noise levels and an echo-chamber effect in the building. Measurements of decibel levels showed that noise levels were much more intense in the lower floors than in the upper floors. Testing of the children showed that the lower the floor of residence (noisier), the more impairment of auditory discrimination and reading ability the children displayed. Most importantly, these relationships increased in strength as length of residence increased. If a long time perspective had not been adopted in the research, this cumulative effect of noise on the behavioral performances of hearing and reading would have been missed.

Third, Lee (1972) shows how misleading a data-gathering period of even a whole year can be in understanding the behavior and social life of a tribe of hunter-gatherers. The typical field worker observes at most one or two annual cycles in the life of a tribe. He may well observe the hunting and gathering population in a state of mobility that puzzles him and he is likely to conclude that they are moving more than necessary because of social deterioration, or breakdown of the groups. However, from a very long time frame, Lee has shown in the case of the !Kung Bushmen that such an hypothesis, based on a one-year observation, misrepresents what is happening because it underestimates the amount of movement of such tribes. With data from the !Kung, Lee shows that a group of hunter-gatherers often is able to satisfy subsistence requirements within an area of 100 square kilometers (already a large area) for four out of five years. However, the group must have access to a much larger area every fifth year, on the average, in order to survive. To survive cycles of environmental fluctuations, over the course of fifty years, or up to two hundred years, the group must maintain access to areas of up to 1000 square kilometers. This pattern of extreme environmental mobility and its relation to environmental resources can only be understood within a very long time perspective. Adaptation by the !Kung is a long-term, cyclical process—a very small part of which can be captured by one year of observation.

An additional problem is that what seems sound, correct, humane, satisfying, and pleasurable in the short run may be painful, harmful, or tragic in the longer term. Short-term criteria of good can be very misleading. A classic argument regarding such cumulative entrapment is found in Hardin's paper, "The Tragedy of the Commons" (1968). One example of a commons is a public grassland available to all the local herdsmen for grazing their cattle. It is to the immediate advantage of each individual cattleman to increase the number of cows in his herd and feed them by taking advantage of the free good, the commons. However, if all herdsmen follow the same logic, the effect is that the common grasslands eventually are overgrazed and are destroyed in the long run. The long-run result of a short-term, individual good is negative for both the group and each individual. Platt (1973) has generalized this model to specific cases of human behavior.

The ecological point is that many of our positive but short-sighted views of good lead to serious negative consequences in the long run. The selection of criteria for evaluating the humaneness of our interventions into complex systems must recognize the interrelated nature and functioning of these systems over time.

It is both striking and ironic how seldom behavioral scientists gather truly longitudinal data, even for relatively short periods of time. In fact, the two safest generalizations about human behavior—(1) every behavior takes place some*where*, and (2) every behavior takes place at some particular *time*—very seldom become translated into data in programs of research. That is, investigators seldom keep data on where or when behavior occurs. Lacking that information, the investigators very seldom can make inferences about environmental or spatial dependencies (see above), or about temporal or longitudinal dependencies. As Steinglass (1978) points out, it is impossible to understand process or to make clear distinctions between structure and process without information on temporal sequence.

Of course, not all of the important phenomena of human functioning and behavior require very long periods of study. The *ecological* problem is that behavioral scientists often are distressingly unwilling to differentiate those behavioral issues that require the emergent time frame from those that do not and even less willing to knuckle down and tackle those that do. Many psychologists would much rather do several discrete studies with many subjects each year than work on a phenomenon whose important properties unravel and cycle over a period of months or years. Research with very long time frames is absolutely necessary for the development of an ecological perspective on behavior.

Most family therapists probably would agree that, within the current network of a family and its functioning, some attention to process and sequence over the short term is important in understanding the family. However, there is some disagreement on how long a time frame must be taken. Some of those in the communications school (Haley, 1971) are not much interested in the history of a family; they believe it is desirable to work with the current family situation without seeking to understand how it got to be the way it is. They are more interested in the process of therapy than in understanding the theoretical processes of development. This position is very similar to that of the behaviorists who, in clinical situations, are interested primarily in the factors reinforcing a behavior now and not in how the behavior first started. Haley believes that a suitable change in the family's communications patterns will be maintained by the homeostatic properties of the system so that a very rapid intervention can have long-lasting results. In addition, he feels that it is not necessary for the family members to gain any particular insight into their problem or their functioning; it is only necessary that a change occur in the patterns of communication.

At the other end of this spectrum is Murray Bowen, who speaks of a multigeneration transmission of pathology and therapy that may span a number of years. Bowen discusses a family projection process by which parental problems are solved by projection of pathology onto the children. The process operates in a differential fashion so that perhaps only one child in the family is selected to carry the pathology and so comes to function at a lower level than his parents. The other children escape the projection process and are free to function at a higher level than their parents. This selection process acts as a focusing mechanism that concentrates dysfunctions in succeeding generations until finally a schizophrenic child is produced. Bowen has his clients study their family history so they can learn how this process works and so they can identify family problems that have been handed down for generations (Bowen, 1978).

TAXONOMY

Behavioral ecology concerns itself with one of the great voids in American psychology—the problem of taxonomy. Together with naturalistic description of the distribution of behavioral phenomena, basic taxonomic research has been grossly neglected by psychologists (Frederiksen, 1972). What are the units of environment, of behavior, and of environment-behavior linkages? Into what types of classifications do situations, behaviors, and environments fall? It is sometimes argued that behavior is too ephemeral, too spontaneous, and too malleable to be fitted into taxonomies. That is an evasion, because the fleeting and malleable qualities of many chemical and biological phenomena have not prevented the creation of useful taxonomies. Furthermore, the fact that the behavioral sciences "are in a historical position analogous to 100 to 200 years prior to Mendeleev and Linneaus" (Altman, 1968, p. 57) is no excuse to avoid the necessary work. It is tempting to view the great advances now occurring in biology and physiology and assert that those scientists are not going through the drudgery of basic taxonomic research. Why should a sophisticated molecular biologist, who is pressing his search for the cause of cancer, worry about taxonomy? He does worry about taxonomy and uses it in his work, but he does not have to develop the taxonomies because other persons have done it. His work and all other current work *presupposes* and rests upon the work of taxonomists going all the way back to Linneaus, Fritsch, Hitzig, and others who developed a rich tradition of developing classifications of tissues and cellular and organic structures.

Taxonomies are important for several reasons. First, there is the aesthetic pleasure that accompanies scientific orderliness. Second, systems of classification represent the only comprehensive way to avoid being smothered by a great host of splintered, separate facts (Altman, 1968; Studer, 1972). The development of comprehensive theory depends, in part, upon a coherent classification of the empirical domain. Third, a good taxonomy "can provide a standard metalanguage to describe all concepts and variables in a field" (Altman and Lett, 1970, p. 182). Such translation into a common system permits comparison of various findings and concepts with each other. Fourth, as Altman and Lett point out (1970), an effective taxonomy can help scientists pinpoint well-established results, confused or contradictory results, and areas of research that have been neglected; that is, missing data. Fifth, Altman and Lett also argue that a taxonomy can lead to predictions of new relationships that have not become obvious from separate studies. Sixth, a generally used taxonomy allows any particular investigator to classify what he is working on and to classify it with sufficient precision in a general system so that he is fully aware of how his phenomenon relates to what other investigators are working on, and it allows him to communicate it with enough precision so that other investigators know what he is working on. Consider how far we are from that state of affairs in psychology and related behavioral sciences. The behavioral ecologist would argue that the infinite splintering and disparate quality of the behavioral sciences is due, in large part, to the lack of coherent, consensual systems classifications.

Seventh, it is not difficult to see from all this that good taxonomies become particularly important to persons engaged in the applied, mission-oriented efforts of environmental design. Moos (1974) argues that

> Psychologists and behavioral scientists are being asked to help design physical and social systems that will maximize the possibilities for human growth, and that will facilitate effective functioning and excellence. We need information about the common task requirements for effective functioning in different milieus. . . . We need to identify the behaviors related to survival, learning, and adaptation in different social systems. . . . We cannot obtain definitive information on any of these areas without learning more about the dimensions of social and physical environments and about the different types of initiatives, adaptive behaviors, and preparatory and coping mechanisms likely to be successful in each. . . . The optimal arrangement of environments is probably the most powerful behavior modification technique currently available. Psychologists and other behavioral scientists will be important in predicting the probable behavioral . . . effects of environmental changes that human beings can control. . . . it may be cogently argued that the most important task for the behavioral and social sciences is the systematic description and classification of environments and their differential costs and benefits for adaptation. (pp. 24–25)

Finally, we would argue that scientific disciplines mature in direct proportion to the seriousness with which they conduct taxonomic work and to the sophistication of their taxonomies. However, we can take that argument a step further, at least theoretically, as follows. Whether it is learned or instinctive, the ability of organisms and groups of organisms to discriminate and respond to effective distinctions among environmental events, and to do it reliably and consistently, is critical to survival. Perhaps something similar happens with scientific and clinical disciplines; that is, those function best and survive best that have reliable, consistently applied, consensual classifications on the basis of which they make discriminations and respond. Perhaps it is no accident that the most sophisticated and prestigious disciplines have the most sophisticated taxonomies.

Family systems theory has been weak in the area of taxonomy. Few adequate systems exist for classifying the phenomena of family systems. Toman (1969) developed a system for describing sibling position in a family and for drawing inferences from this and other characteristics of the person. Bowen has developed a differentiation of self scale which he uses to classify clients, but he has not operationalized it in a way that is very useful to other workers. Minuchin's system of diagramming family structure is a useful device. However, much work needs to be done in defining and classifying variables and processes of interest to the family theoretician. Here again, a dialogue with behavioral ecology may prove fruitful.

CONCLUDING COMMENTS

We have discussed some of the major earmarks and guiding assumptions of behavioral ecology and some of its more obvious relationships to the work of family theorists and therapists. We believe that these issues relate in important ways to the three criteria that Steinglass (1978) spelled out for effective models of families: (1) pointing to appropriate data, (2) understanding and defining pathology, and (3) offering guidelines for intervention. We will have to take another opportunity to sharpen the issues we have raised in this paper.

In his review of marriage from a systems perspective, Steinglass (1978) says:

> Systems theory, as it has been applied to marriage and marital disorders, is at the moment more a series of loosely connected concepts than an integrated theory of marriage. . . . However, if the *essence* of a systems approach is defined as attention to organization, to the relationship between parts, to concentration on patterned rather than on linear relationships, to a consideration of events in the context in which they are occurring rather than on isolation of events from their environmental context, then the systems approach may be found both masterable and useful. (pp. 300, 304)

If we were to substitute "behavioral ecology" in place of "the systems approach," then Steinglass's comments would apply just as well to our feeling about behavioral ecology.

REFERENCES

Abeles, G. Researching the unresearchable: Experimenting on the double bind. In C. E. Sluzki and D. C. Ransom (Eds.), *Double bind: The foundations of the communications approach to the family*. New York: Grune and Stratton, 1976.

Ackerman, N. W. *The psychodynamics of family life*. New York: Basic Books, 1958.

Alexander, J. L., Dreher, G. F., & Willems, E. P. Behavioral ecology and humanistic and behavioristic approaches to change. In A. Wandersman, P. Poppen, & D. Ricks (Eds.), *Humanism and behaviorism*. Elmsford, N.Y.: Pergamon, 1976.

Altman, I. Choicepoints in the classification of scientific knowledge. In B. P. Indik & F. K. Berrien (Eds.), *People, groups, and organizations*. New York: Teachers College Press, 1968.

Altman, I., & Lett, E. E. The ecology of interpersonal relationships: A classification system and conceptual model. In J. E. McGrath (Ed.), *Social and psychological factors in stress*. New York: Holt, Rinehart and Winston, 1970.

Bakeman, R., & Helmreich, R. Cohesiveness and performance: Covariation and causality in an undersea environment. *Journal of Experimental Social Psychology*, 1975, *11*, 478–489.

Barker, R. G. Ecology and motivation. In M. R. Jones (Ed.), *Nebraska symposium on motivation*. Lincoln, Neb.: University of Nebraska Press, 1960.

——— On the nature of the environment. *Journal of Social Issues*, 1963, *19*, No. 4, 17–38. (a)

——— (Ed.). *The stream of behavior*. New York: Appleton-Century-Crofts, 1963. (b)

——— Explorations in ecological psychology. *American Psychologist,* 1965, *20,* 1–14.
——— *Ecological psychology.* Stanford, Calif.: Stanford University Press, 1968.
——— Wanted: An eco-behavioral science. In E. P. Willems & H. L. Raush (Eds.), *Naturalistic viewpoints in psychological research.* New York: Holt, Rinehart and Winston, 1969.
Barker, R. G., & Schoggen, P. *Qualities of community life.* San Francisco: Jossey-Bass, 1973.
Barker, R. G., & Wright, H. F. *Midwest and its children.* New York: Harper & Row, 1955.
Bateson, G. *Steps to an ecology of mind.* New York: Ballantine, 1972.
Bateson, G., Weakland, J. H., & Haley, J. Comments on Haley's "history." In C. E. Sluzki & D. C. Lawson (Eds.), *Double bind: The foundation of the communications approach to the family.* New York: Grune and Stratton, 1976.
Beels, C. C., & Ferber, A. Family therapy: A view. *Family Process,* 1969, *8,* 280–318.
Benarde, M. A. *Our precarious habitat.* New York: W. W. Norton, 1970.
Berrien, F. K. *General and social systems.* New Brunswick, N.J.: Rutgers University Press, 1968.
Bowen, M. *Family therapy in clinical practice.* New York: Aronson, 1978.
Brandt, R. M. *Studying behavior in natural settings.* New York: Holt, Rinehart and Winston, 1972.
Breland, K., & Breland, M. *Animal behavior.* New York: Macmillan, 1966.
Bruhn, J. G. Human ecology: A unifying science? *Human Ecology,* 1974, *2,* 105–125.
Buckley, W. (Ed.). *Modern systems research for the behavioral scientist.* Chicago: Aldine, 1968.
Buell, J., Stoddard, P., Harris, F. R., & Baer, D. M. Collateral social development accompanying reinforcement of outdoor play in a preschool child. *Journal of Applied Behavior Analysis,* 1968, *1,* 167–173.
Caplan, N., & Nelson, S. D. On being useful: The nature and consequences of psychological research on social problems. *American Psychologist,* 1973, *28,* 199–211.
Chapanis, A. The relevance of laboratory studies to practical situations. *Ergonomics,* 1967, *10,* 557–577.
Chase, A. *The biological imperatives.* New York: Holt, Rinehart and Winston, 1971.
Cohen, S., Glass, D. C., & Singer, J. E. Apartment noise, auditory discrimination, and reading ability in children. *Journal of Experimental Social Psychology,* 1973, *9,* 407–422.
Colinvaux, P. A. *Introduction to ecology.* New York: Wiley, 1973.
Conney, A. H., & Burns, J. J. Metabolic interactions among environmental chemicals and drugs. *Science,* 1972, *178,* 576–586.
Cowen, E. L. Social and community interventions. *Annual Review of Psychology,* 1973, *24,* 423–472.
Dubos, R. *Man adapting.* New Haven, Conn.: Yale University Press, 1965.
——— *So human an animal.* New York: Charles Scribner's Sons, 1968.
Ebbesen, E. B., & Haney, M. Flirting with death: Variables affecting risk taking at intersections. *Journal of Applied Social Psychology,* 1973, *3,* 303–324.
Eisenberg, L. The *human* nature of human nature. *Science,* 1972, *176,* 123–128.
Elms, A. C. The crisis of confidence in social psychology. *American Psychologist,* 1975, *30,* 967–976.
Fawl, C. L. Disturbances experienced by children in their natural habitats. In R. G. Barker (Ed.), *The stream of behavior.* New York: Appleton-Century-Crofts, 1973.
Frederiksen, N. Toward a taxonomy of situations. *American Psychologist,* 1972, *27,* 114–123.
Galle, O. R., Gove, W. R., & McPherson, J. M. Population density and pathology: What are the relations for man? *Science,* 1972, *176,* 23–30.

Glass, D. C., & Singer, J. E. *Urban stress.* New York: Academic Press, 1972.

Guerin, P. J. (Ed.). *Family therapy.* New York: Gardner Press, 1976.

Gump, P. V., & Kounin, J. S. Issues raised by ecological and "classical" research efforts. *Merrill-Palmer Quarterly,* 1959/1960, *6,* 145, 152.

Haley, J. (Ed.). *Changing families: A family therapy reader.* New York: Grune and Stratton, 1971.

——— Development of a theory: A history of a research project. In C. E. Sluzki & D. C. Ransom (Eds.), *Double bind: The foundations of the communications approach to the family.* New York: Grune and Stratton, 1976.

Hardin, G. The tragedy of the commons. *Science,* 1968, *162,* 1243–1248.

Henry, J. *Pathways to madness.* New York: Random House, 1971.

Herbert, E. W., Pinkston, E. M., Hayden, M. L., Sajwaj, T. E., Pinkston, S., Cordua, G., & Jackson, C. Adverse effects of differential parental attention. *Journal of Applied Behavior Analysis,* 1973, *6,* 15–30.

Insel, P. M., & Moos, R. H. (Eds.). *Health and the social environment.* Lexington, Mass.: Lexington Books, 1974.

Ittelson, W. H., Rivlin, L. G., & Proshansky, H. M. The use of behavioral maps in environmental psychology. In H. M. Proshansky, W. H. Ittelson & L. G. Rivlin (Eds.), *Environmental psychology.* New York: Holt, Rinehart and Winston, 1970.

Klopfer, P. H., & Klopfer, M. S. How come leaders to their posts? The determination of social ranks and roles. *American Scientist,* 1973, *61,* 560–564.

Laszlo, E. *The systems view of the world.* New York: Braziller, 1972.

LeCompte, W. F., & Willems, E. P. Ecological analysis of a hospital: Location dependencies in the behavior of staff and patients. In J. Archea and C. Eastman (Eds.), *EDRA-2: Proceedings of the 2nd annual environmental design research association conference.* Pittsburgh: Carnegie-Mellon University, 1970.

Lee, R. B. !Kung spatial organization: An ecological and historical perspective. *Human Ecology,* 1972, *1,* 125–147.

Lewin, K. *Field theory in social science.* New York: Harper, 1951.

Lichstein, K. K., & Wahler, R. G. The ecological assessment of an autistic child. *Journal of Abnormal Child Psychology,* 1976, *4,* 31–54.

Lichtenstein, E. P., Liang, T. T., & Anderegg, B. N. Synergism of insecticides by herbicides. *Science,* 1973, *181,* 847–849.

Margalef, R. *Perspectives in ecological theory.* Chicago: University of Chicago Press, 1968.

McGuire, W. J. Theory-oriented research in natural settings: The best of both worlds for social psychology. In M. Sherif & C. W. Sherif (Eds.), *Interdisciplinary relationships in the social sciences.* Chicago: Aldine, 1969.

McHale, J. *The ecological context.* New York: Braziller, 1970.

Menzel, E. W., Jr. Naturalistic and experimental approaches to primate behavior. In E. P. Willems & H. L. Raush (Eds.), *Naturalistic viewpoints in psychological research.* New York: Holt, Rinehart and Winston, 1969.

Minuchin, S. The use of an ecological framework in the treatment of a child. In E. J. Anthony & C. Koupernil (Eds.), *The child in his family.* New York: Wiley, 1970.

——— *Families and family therapy.* Cambridge: Harvard University Press, 1974.

Mischel, W. *Personality and assessment.* New York: Wiley, 1968.

Moos, R. H. Conceptualizations of human environments. *American Psychologist,* 1973, *28,* 652–665.

——— Systems for the classification of human environments: An overview. In R. H. Moos & P. M. Insel (Eds.), *Issues in human ecology.* Palo Alto, Calif.: National Press Books, 1974.

Moss, G. E. *Illness, immunity, and social interaction.* New York: Wiley, 1973.

Murdoch, W., & Connell, J. All about ecology. *The Center Magazine,* 1970, *3,* No. 1, 56–63.

Nesselroade, J. R., & Reese, H. W. (Eds.). *Life-span developmental psychology: Methodological issues*. New York: Academic Press, 1973.

Newman, O. *Defensible space*. New York: Macmillan, 1972.

Norris-Baker, C. Surveys of environmental negotiability in homes of disabled persons. Unpublished master's thesis, University of Houston, 1978.

Platt, J. Social traps. *American Psychologist*, 1973, *28*, 641–651.

Proshansky, H. M., Ittelson, W. H., & Rivlin, L. G. (Eds.). *Environmental psychology*. New York: Holt, Rinehart and Winston, 1970.

Pulliam, R., Gilbert, B., Klopfer, P., McDonald, D., McDonald, L., & Millikan, G. On the evolution of sociality with special reference to the grassquit *Tiaris olivacea*. *Wilson Bulletin*, 1972, *84*, 77–89.

Quilitch, H. R., & Risley, T. R. The effects of play materials on social play. *Journal of Applied Behavior Analysis*, 1973, *6*, 573–578.

Raush, H. L. Naturalistic method and the clinical approach. In E. P. Willems & H. L. Raush (Eds.), *Naturalistic viewpoints in psychological research*. New York: Holt, Rinehart and Winston, 1969.

Raush, H. L., Dittman, A. T., & Taylor, T. J. The interpersonal behavior of children in residential treatment. *Journal of Abnormal and Social Psychology*, 1959, *58*, 9–26. (a)

——— Person, setting and change in social interaction. *Human Relations*, 1959, *12*, 361–379. (b)

Raush, H. L., Farberman, I., & Llewellyn, L. G. Person, setting and change in social interaction: II. A normal-control study. *Human Relations*, 1960, *13*, 305–333.

Rhodes, W. C. An overview: Toward synthesis of models of disturbance. In W. C. Rhodes & M. L. Tracy (Eds.), *A study of child variance*. Ann Arbor, Mich.: University of Michigan Press, 1972.

Ronnebeck, R. W. A naturalistic investigation of community adjustment of facially disfigured burned teenagers. Unpublished doctoral dissertation, University of Houston, 1972.

Rosenhan, D. L. On being sane in insane places. *Science*, 1973, *179*, 250–258.

Rueveni, U., & Speck, R. V. Using encounter group techniques in the treatment of the social network of the schizophrenic. *International Journal of Group Psychotherapy*, 1969, *19*, 495–500.

Ryan, W. *Blaming the victim*. New York: Pantheon, 1971.

Sajwaj, T., Twardosz, S., & Burke, M. Side effects of extinction procedures in a remedial preschool. *Journal of Applied Behavior Analysis*, 1972, *5*, 163–175.

Schmitt, R. C. Some ecological variables of community adjustment in a group of facially disfigured burned children. Unpublished doctoral dissertation, University of Houston, 1971.

Sells, S. B. Ecology and the science of psychology. In E. P. Willems & H. L. Raush (Eds.), *Naturalistic viewpoints in psychological research*. New York: Holt, Rinehart and Winston, 1969.

Shepard, P., & McKinley, D. (Eds.). *The subversive science: Essays toward an ecology of man*. Boston: Houghton Mifflin, 1969.

Skinner, B. F. *Beyond freedom and dignity*. New York: Knopf, 1971.

Sluzki, C. E. Marital therapy from a systems theory perspective. In T. J. Paolino & B. S. McCrady (Eds.), *Marriage and marital therapy*. New York: Brunner/Mazel, 1978.

Smith, R. L. *Ecology and field biology*. New York: Harper and Row, 1966.

Southwood, T. R. E. *Ecological methods*. London: Methuen, 1966.

Speck, R. V., & Attneave, C. L. *Family networks*. New York: Pantheon, 1973.

Speck, R. V., & Reuveni, U. Network therapy—a developing concept. *Family Process*, 1969, *8*, 182–191.

Steinglass, P. The conceptualization of marriages from a systems theory perspective. In

T. J. Paolino & B. S. McCrady (Eds.), *Marriage and marital therapy.* New York: Brunner/Mazel, 1978.

Sterling, C. Superdams: The perils of progress. *The Atlantic,* 1972, *229,* No. 6, 35–41.

Stuart, D. G. A naturalistic study of the daily activities of disabled and non-disabled college students. Unpublished master's thesis, University of Houston, 1973.

Studer, R. G. The organization of spatial stimuli. In J. F. Wohlwill & D. H. Carson (Eds.), *Environment and the social sciences: Perspectives and applications.* Washington, D.C.: American Psychological Association, 1972.

Thoreson, R. W., Krauskopf, C. J., McAleer, C. A., & Wenger, H. D. The future for applied psychology: Are we building a buggy whip factory? *American Psychologist,* 1972, *27,* 134–139.

Toman, W. *Family constellations.* New York: Springer, 1969.

Twardosz, S., & Sajwaj, T. Multiple effects of a procedure to increase sitting in a hyperactive, retarded boy. *Journal of Applied Behavior Analysis,* 1972, *5,* 73–78.

Wade, N. A message from corn blight: The dangers of uniformity. *Science,* 1972, *177,* 678–679.

Wahler, R. G. Some structural aspects of deviant child behavior. *Journal of Applied Behavior Analysis,* 1975, *8,* 27–42.

Wallace, B. *Essays in social biology* (Three volumes). Englewood Cliffs, N.J.: Prentice-Hall, 1972.

Watt, K. E. F. (Ed.). *Systems analysis in ecology.* New York: Academic Press, 1966.

Watt, K. E. F. *Ecology and resource management.* New York: McGraw-Hill, 1968.

Watzlawick, P., Beavin, J. H., & Jackson, D. D. *Pragmatics of human communication.* New York: Norton, 1967.

Wicker, A. W. Attitudes versus actions: The relationship of verbal and overt behavioral responses to attitude objects. *Journal of Social Issues,* 1969, *25,* No. 4, 41–78.

——— An examination of the "other variables" explanation of attitude-behavior inconsistency. *Journal of Personality and Social Psychology,* 1971, *19,* 18–30.

——— Processes which mediate behavior-environment congruence. *Behavioral Science,* 1972, *17,* 265–277.

Willems, E. P. An ecological orientation in psychology. *Merrill-Palmer Quarterly,* 1965, *11,* 317–343.

——— Behavioral validity of a text for measuring social anxiety. *Psychological Reports,* 1967, *21,* 433–442.

——— Planning a rationale for naturalistic research. In E. P. Willems & H. L. Raush (Eds.), *Naturalistic viewpoints in psychological research.* New York: Holt, Rinehart and Winston, 1969.

——— The interfact of the hospital environment and patient behavior. *Archives of Physical Medicine and Rehabilitation,* 1972, *53,* 115–122. (a)

——— Place and motivation: Complexity and independence in patient behavior. In W. J. Mitchell (Ed.), *Environmental design: Research and practice.* Los Angeles: University of California at Los Angeles, 1972. (b)

——— Behavioral ecology and experimental analysis: Courtship is not enough. In J. R. Nesselroade & H. W. Reese (Eds.), *Life-span developmental psychology: Methodological issues.* New York: Academic Press, 1973. (a)

——— Go ye into all the world and modify behavior: An ecologist's view. *Representative Research in Social Psychology,* 1973, *4,* 93–105. (b)

——— Behavior-environment systems: An ecological approach. *Man-Environment Systems,* 1973, *3,* No. 2, 79–110. (c)

——— Behavioral ecology as a perspective for man-environment research. In W. F. E. Preiser (Ed.), *Environmental design research,* vol. 2. Stroudsburg, Pa.: Dowden, Hutchinson and Ross, 1973. (d)

——— Behavioral technology and behavioral ecology. *Journal of Applied Behavior Analysis,* 1974, *7,* 151–165.

——— Behavioral ecology, health status, and health care: Applications to the rehabilitation setting. In I. Altman & J. F. Wohlwill (Eds.), *Human behavior and environment: Advances in theory and research.* New York: Plenum, 1976.

——— Relations of models to methods in behavioral ecology. In H. McGurk (Ed.), *Ecological factors in human development.* Amsterdam: North-Holland Pub. Co., 1977. (a)

——— Behavioral ecology. In D. Stokols (Ed.), *Perspectives on environment and behavior.* New York: Plenum, 1977. (b)

——— Steps toward an ecobehavioral technology. In A. Rogers-Warren & S. Warren (Eds.), *Ecological perspectives in behavior analysis.* Baltimore: University Park Press, 1977. (c)

——— Behavioral ecology as a perspective for research in psychology. In C. W. Deckner (Ed.), *Methodological perspectives for behavioral research.* Springfield, Ill.: Charles C. Thomas, in press.

Willems, E. P., & Halstead, L. S. An eco-behavioral approach to health status and health care. In R. G. Barker (Ed.), *Habitats, environments, and human behavior.* San Francisco: Jossey-Bass, 1978.

Willems, E. P., & Campbell, D. E. Behavioral ecology: A new approach to health status and health care. In B. Honikman (Ed.), *Responding to social change.* Stroudsburg, Pa.: Dowden, Hutchinson and Ross, 1975.

Wright, H. F. *Recording and analyzing child behavior.* New York: Harper and Row, 1967.

——— *Children's behavior in communities differing in size* (Five volumes). Lawrence, Ks.: University of Kansas, 1969/1970.

CIRCUMPLEX MODEL OF MARITAL AND FAMILY SYSTEMS II:

EMPIRICAL STUDIES AND CLINICAL INTERVENTION*

David H. Olson, UNIVERSITY OF MINNESOTA

Candyce S. Russell, KANSAS STATE UNIVERSITY

Douglas H. Sprenkle, PURDUE UNIVERSITY

This is the *second* in a series of articles which describes the value of the Circumplex Model in bridging the domains of theory, research, and counseling with couples and families. One goal of the current paper is to review the empirical studies demonstrating the salience of the two dimensions in

Advances in Family Intervention, Assessment and Theory, Volume 1, pages 129–179.

ISBN: 0-89232-137-7

the model—family cohesion and family adaptability—and to test the hypotheses derived from the model. The second goal is to demonstrate the clinical utility of the model for diagnosing marital and family systems, for establishing treatment goals, and for evaluating the effectiveness of the treatment program.

The first paper on the Circumplex Model (Olson et al., 1979) provided an overview of the theoretical importance of cohesion and adaptability dimensions in the family literature and across several different social science fields. Combining family cohesion and family adaptability into a circumplex model enables one to identify sixteen types of marital and family systems. Descriptions of the concepts related to each of these two dimensions enables one to empirically describe and clinically diagnose a marital or family system.

Three empirical studies have been completed to test the construct validity of the Circumplex Model with couples (Sprenkle and Olson, 1978), with family triads with an adolescent female (Russell, 1979), and with families with a female status offender (Druckman, 1979). Two other empirical studies are nearly completed comparing family triads with an adolescent who has run away (Bell, 1980) and family triads with an adolescent in treatment (Portner, 1980) with control family triads. The clinical utility of the model with marital and family systems with an alcoholic member is described in another paper (Killorin and Olson, 1980). These and other relevant research projects will be reviewed in greater detail later in this chapter.

Conceptual Definitions of Family Cohesion and Adaptability Dimensions

Family cohesion and adaptability are two dimensions of family behavior that initially emerged from a conceptual clustering of over fifty concepts developed to describe marital and family dynamics. While some of these concepts have been used for decades (power and roles, for instance), many of the concepts have been developed recently by individuals observing problem families who had a general systems perspective (pseudo-mutality, double binds). After reviewing the conceptual definitions of many of these concepts, it became apparent that despite the creative terminology, the terms were conceptually similar and dealt with highly related family processes. One family process had to do with the degree to which an individual was separated from or connected to his or her family system. This was called family cohesion. Family adaptability focused on the extent to which the family system was flexible and able to change.

Family cohesion is defined as the *emotional bonding that family members have toward one another and the degree of individual autonomy they experience*. Within the Circumplex Model, some of the specific concepts or variables that can be used to diagnose and measure the family cohesion dimensions are: *emotional bonding, independence, boundaries, coalitions, time, space, friends, decision-making,* and *interests* and *recreation*. There are four levels of cohesion, ranging from extremely low (disengaged) to moderately low (separated), moderately high (connected), and extremely high (enmeshed). The operational definitions of each of the cohesion concepts at these four levels are indicated in Table IV.

It is hypothesized that *balanced* levels of moderately low to moderately high cohesion are most viable for family functioning. The extremes of being disengaged or enmeshed are seen as problematic and most couples and families who come for treatment often fall into one of these extremes. When cohesion levels are extremely high (enmeshed systems), there is overidentification so that loyalty to and consensus within the family prevent individuation of family members. At the other extreme (disengaged systems), high levels of autonomy are encouraged and family members "do their own thing" with limited attachment or commitment to their family. It is the central area (separated and connected) of the model where individuals are able to *experience* and *balance* being independent from and connected to their family.

The salience of the cohesion dimension is underscored by the wide range of social science disciplines that have used the dimension or concepts related to it. Psychiatrists, family therapists, family sociologists, small-group theorists, group therapists, social psychologists, and anthropologists all have utilized the concept in their work. They have been highly creative in developing concepts to describe high or low levels of cohesion. Extremely high cohesion has been called pseudo-mutuality (Wynne et al., 1958), undifferentiated family ego mass and emotional fusion (Bowen, 1960), binding (Stierlin, 1974), enmeshment (Minuchin, 1974), extraordinary mutual involvement (Scott and Askworth, 1968), and consensus-sensitive families (Reiss, 1971). Extremely low cohesion has been described as emotional divorce (Bowen, 1960), schism and skew (Lidz et al., 1957), disengagement (Minuchin, 1974), pseudo-hostility (Wynne et al., 1958), expelling (Stierlin, 1974) and scapegoating (Bell and Vogel, 1962). There are fewer terms to describe the more balanced and moderate areas of cohesion, but some of the terms reflecting this are differentiated self (Bowen, 1960), interdependence (Olson, 1972), and mutuality (Wynne et al., 1958).

Family adaptability is the second dimension and is defined as *the ability of a marital or family system to change its power structure, role relationships, and relationship rules in response to situational and developmental stress*. In order to describe, measure, and diagnose couples on this dimension, a variety of concepts have been taken from several social science disciplines, with heavy reliance on family sociology. These concerns include: *family power* (assertiveness, control, discipline), *negotiation styles, role relationships, relationship rules,* and *feedback* (negative and positive). The four levels of adaptability range from *rigid* (extremely low) to *structured* (low to moderate) to *flexible* (moderate to high) to *chaotic* (extremely high). The operational definitions of each of the concepts for these four levels are presented in Table V.

As with cohesion, it is hypothesized that central levels of adaptability (structured and flexible) are more conducive to marital and family functioning with the extremes (rigid and chaotic) being the most problematic. Basically, this dimension focuses on the ability of the marital and family system to *change*. Much of the early application of systems theory to families emphasized the rigidity of the family and its tendency to maintain the status quo (Haley, 1962, 1963, 1964). Morphostasis was the systems term used to describe the pattern of rigidity to change, and morphogenesis was the potential to develop and grow as a system. Until the work of recent theorists (Speer, 1970; Wertheim, 1973, 1975), the importance of potential for change was minimized. They helped to clarify that systems need both stability and change and that it is the ability to change when appropriate that distinguishes functional couples and families from others. In line with this thinking, the Circumplex Model postulates that the *balance* is critical and that problematic families often function at either the extreme of continual change leading to chaos or that of no change, which results in rigidity.

Because the definition of *balance* is so critical to the Circumplex Model, it will be briefly discussed here and further elaborated later. For the moment, the operational definition of balance is that the family scores on dimensions of cohesion and adaptability fall into the two central levels. It should not be assumed, however, that family systems in the two central levels will *always* function in that area or that they function in a moderate manner. In fact, family members in a balanced system can *experience* both extremes of the dimension when it is appropriate but they usually do not stay at these extremes for extended periods of time. For example, a family system balanced in the cohesion dimension would mean that family members are able to be alone at times (disengaged) and also are able to be highly connected with their family (enmeshed), but they do not continuously stay at either extreme. Extreme family types are generally able to function only at that extreme and, therefore, have a *smaller* behavior repertoire.

The difference between balanced and extreme family systems can be further illustrated by examining how each group handles problems or stress. A balanced family system might shift to a more extreme type in an attempt to deal with the problem and will continue shifting until they resolve the problem. After the problem is resolved, they will probably return to functioning at the central levels. Also, their new level of functioning might be somewhat different from where they were before the problem occurred. When an extreme family type encounters problems, they will have difficulty functioning at any other level even though the situation demands some change in the system. In other words, the extreme family types are more resistant to change and have a more limited behavior repertoire compared to the more balanced family systems.

CIRCUMPLEX MODEL OF MARITAL AND FAMILY SYSTEMS

Once the two dimensions of family cohesion and adaptability were independently identified as being important both conceptually and empirically, the first author discovered that there were numerous advantages in combining the two dimensions to form a circumplex model. After the Circumplex Model was developed, it was then possible to identify *types* of couples and families based on their location in these two dimensions. There has been increasing awareness of conceptual and empirical power of typologies as compared to simple descriptions of couples based on single variables or factors. Since it appeared that problem couples and families tended to fall at either extreme of both dimensions, couple or family types at the extremes would be predicted to have more relationship problems than those types in the central area of both dimensions. Based on this initial idea, specific hypotheses were derived from the Model that could be further investigated both clinically and empirically.

Figure 1 illustrates the two dimensions and the four levels of each dimension. The four levels of cohesion were named (from low to high): *disengaged, separated, connected, enmeshed.* The four levels of adaptability were called (from low to high): *rigid, structured, flexible, chaotic.* In selecting the adjectives for each level, an attempt was made to avoid the traditional diagnostic labels.

Combining the dimensions enables one to identify and describe sixteen distinct types of marital and family systems. Although it is assumed that it is possible to conceptually identify, empirically measure, and clinically observe all sixteen types, it is also assumed that some of the types would occur more frequently than others. As with any circumplex model, the more central types are the most common, but it is hypothesized that couples and families coming for treatment would fall more into the extreme types. Once the types are identified and located within the model, it then becomes clear that there are three basic groups of types. One group had scores at the two central levels on both dimensions (four types); another group was extreme on both dimensions (four types); and the third

Figure 1: Sixteen Possible Types of Marital and Family Systems Derived from the Circumplex Model

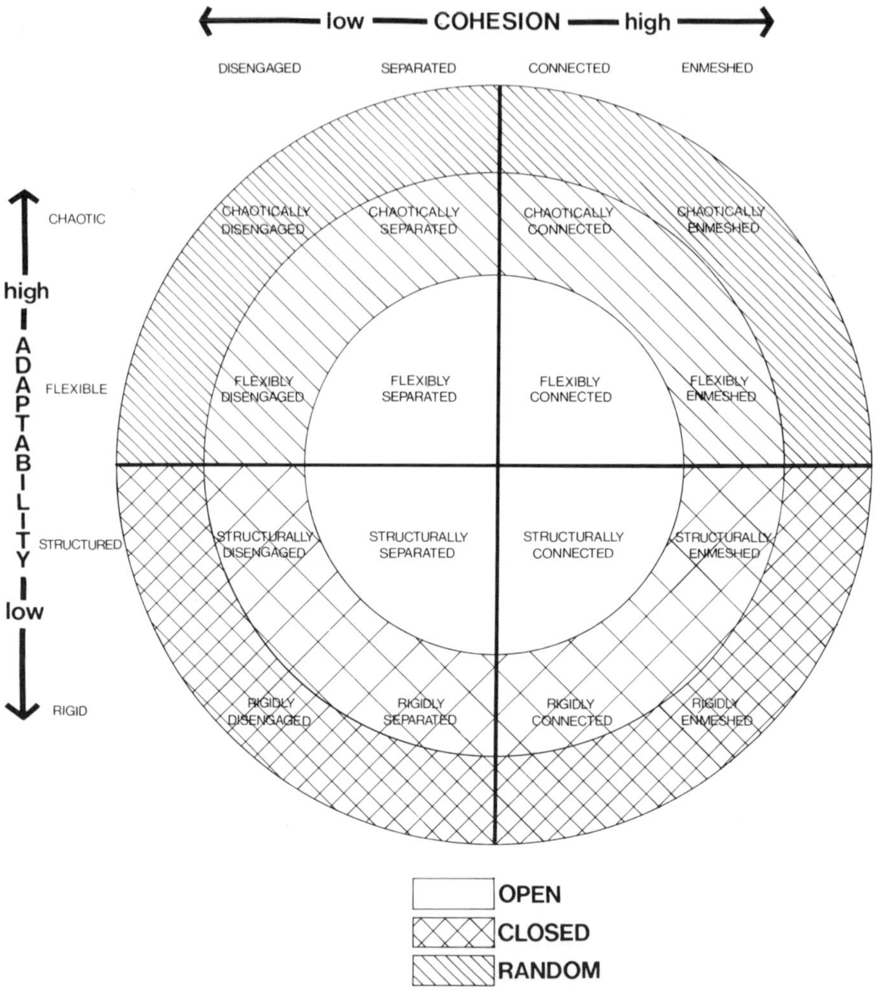

group was extreme on only one dimension (eight types). It then became evident that regions within the model corresponded to some of the recent theoretical work by Kantor and Lehr (1975) and Wertheim (1973, 1975), who described marital and family systems as being *open, closed,* and *random*. These three types of systems are also indicated in the Circumplex Model (see Figure 1). A more complete discussion of open, closed, and random systems and the clinical application of the Circumplex Model with chemically dependent families is described in a paper by Killorin and Olson (1980).

As the model began to take shape, it became apparent that several objectives could be accomplished by using the Circumplex Model. The following are the general goals and objectives that are being used to further develop this model:

1. Identify and describe the salience of family cohesion and adaptability and the types of marital and family systems in our culture.
2. Demonstrate the theoretical, clinical, and empirical utility of these two dimensions and the model.
3. Demonstrate how systems need to balance both dimensions in order to function most effectively.
4. Describe group properties of marital and family systems rather than individual characteristics or dyadic properties.
5. Describe how couples and families change as a result of situational stress or changes in the family life cycle.
6. Bridge the domains of research, theory, and practice and provide a framework for designing educational and treatment programs.

In general, the Circumplex Model attempts to provide a parsimonious framework for reducing the enormous complexity of marital and family systems. It attempts to describe two dimensions of marital and family systems that have emerged from a conceptual clustering of a wide range of theoretical concepts and empirical studies of marital and family systems. Although the Model may, at first glance, seem simplistic, it becomes more complex as one begins to implement it. Furthermore, it allows one to focus on and understand a rich variety of individual and group behavior. Viewed from this perspective, the Model facilitates a more systematic understanding of these systems. Also, the Model enables one to make predictions about couples and families that can be further tested to increase the validity and utility of the Model.

It should be remembered, however, that the Circumplex Model is still in its early stage of development and is continually being modified and expanded to more adequately describe and clinically treat couples and families.

Although the Model has been applied primarily to marital and family systems, some work is being done to attempt to understand other social groups and systems such as small work groups and large-scale organizations (such as churches and businesses). For example, the deaths of over 800 followers of Rev. James Jones in Jonestown, Guyana in 1979 can be understood using the Circumplex Model. As a group, they would be described as *Rigidly Enmeshed* because they were extreme on both the cohesion and adaptability dimensions (see Figure 1). The viability of such systems is easily threatened. When tension increases, they are unwilling to change (rigid) and they increasingly turn to each other for all their support (enmeshed). They become rigidly under the control of their leader and when that leader can no longer cope, the system is prone to destruction. The unfortunate result was mass suicide and murder of most of the members of the People's Temple Commune in Guyana.

Hypotheses Derived from the Circumplex Model

One of the assets of a theoretical model is that hypotheses can be deduced and tested in order to evaluate and further develop the model. The following are hypotheses derived from the model, some of which have been or are currently being tested and others of which can be tested.

The first general hypothesis postulates a *curvilinear* relationship between the dimensions of cohesion and adaptability and successful or effective family functioning. The exception to this general hypothesis is indicated in Hypothesis 1c, where the normative expectations in the family support extreme behavior on these dimensions.

1. *Couples/families with balanced (two central levels) cohesion and adaptability will generally function more adequately than those at the extremes of these dimensions.*
    a. Couples/families without serious problems will tend to have more balanced scores on both of these dimensions.
    b. Couples/families with serious problems will tend to have more extreme scores on one or both of these dimensions.
    c. Couples/families with normative expectations which support behaviors extreme on these dimensions will *not* develop problems as long as *all* the members accept these expectations.

An important issue in the Circumplex Model relates to the definition of *balance*. The Model postulates that a balance on the dimensions is related to more adequate family functioning. Even though a balanced family system is placed at the two central levels of the Model, it should not be assumed that these families always operate in a moderate manner. Being balanced means a family system can experience the extremes on the dimensions when appropriate, but that they do not typically function at these extremes for long periods of time. For example, families in the central area of the cohesion dimension allow family members to experience being both independent from and connected to their family. Both extremes are tolerated and expected, provided an individual does not continually function at the extreme. Conversely, extreme family types tend to function only at the extremes and are not expected or able to change their behaviors. As a result, the more balanced family types have a larger behavioral repertoire and are more able to change compared to extreme family types.

The operational definition of balance is that a couple or family falls into the two central levels of each dimension. Each dimension is divided into four levels, with the extremes representing the lowest and highest levels. The concepts and definitions related to each level for the adaptability and cohesion dimension are indicated in Tables IV and V. As will be described later in the paper, a self-report scale called FACES can be used to obtain scores on each of the concepts and dimensions. FACES, the acronym for Family Adaptability and Cohesion Evaluation Scales, was recently developed by Olson, Bell, and Portner (1978).

Although a curvilinear relationship is generally predicted, some important qualifications must be made in terms of the *normative expectations* and *cultural bias* in this hypothesis. The normative expectations in our culture provide two conflicting themes that can create double and often confusing messages. One theme is that family members are expected to do things together as a family; yet, the second theme encourages individuals to "do their own thing." This second theme becomes more prominent as children approach adolescence and has taken on greater importance for increasing numbers of women in our culture. As a result, many American families find that a balance of these two themes has become a personal issue.

Families in our culture still vary greatly in the extent to which they encourage and give support to individuals to develop in ways that may differ from the family's values. While parents would prefer their children to develop values and ideas similar to theirs, most parents can enable their children to become somewhat autonomous and differentiated from the family system. A sizable minority, however, have normative expectations that strongly emphasize family togetherness, often at the expense of individual development. Their family norms emphasize emotional and physical togetherness and they strive for high levels of consensus and loyalty. Some ethnic groups in this country such as the Slovak-Americans (Stein, 1978), Puerto Rican (Minuchin et al., 1967), and Italian families (Goetzl, 1973), and religious groups such as the Amish (Wittmer, 1973) and Mormons (Schvaneveldt, 1973) have high expectations regarding family togetherness. These expectations are also common, but less predominant, in many other American families regardless of their ethnic or religious orientation. Many of these families could be described as extreme on the cohesion dimension, that is, enmeshed, and they will *not* necessarily have problems in their families as long as the family members are willing to go along with those expectations (see Hypothesis 1c).

In general, the hypothesized curvilinear relationship between effective family functioning and the cohesion-adaptability dimensions primarily applies to families that accept the current cultural norms that support both family togetherness and individual development. The general hypothesis would *not* apply, however, for families that have very high expectations for family togetherness.

Another important qualification of the hypothesis relates to our definition of "problem families." We tend to define problem families as those that voluntarily or involuntarily are involved in some treatment program. There is good clinical evidence that those couples or families in treatment programs are often extreme in one or both of these dimensions. However, there are many families that are extreme in these dimensions that do function well and never seek treatment. There are also families extreme in these dimensions that do have problems but never choose to seek treatment. Unfortunately, most studies have relied on problem families that seek or are placed in treatment and, hence, we know very little about those that do not. Hopefully, future studies will attempt to gather data from families not seeking or receiving treatment and ones with extreme normative expectations, so that these hypotheses can be more adequately tested.

2. *Couples/families will change their cohesion and adaptability to deal with situational stress and changes in the family life cycle.*
    a. Couples/families without serious problems will change their cohesion and adaptability to an adjacent level (type) to deal with situational or developmental stress.
    b. Couples/families with serious problems will either not change their cohesion and adaptability or will flip to an opposite extreme (on one or both dimensions) to deal with situational or developmental stress.

This second general hypothesis deals with change in the family system to deal with stress or to accommodate changes in family members, particularly as family members change their expectations. The Circumplex Model is *dynamic* in that it assumes that individuals and family systems will change and it hypothesizes that change can be beneficial to the maintenance and improvement of family functioning. When one family member desires change, the family system must deal with this request. For example, increasing numbers of married women want to develop more autonomy from their husbands (cohesion dimension) and also want more power and equality in their relationships (adaptability dimension). If their husbands are unwilling to understand and change in accordance with these expectations, the marriages will probably experience increased amounts of stress. Another common example of changing expectations is when a child reaches adolescence. Like the wife in the previous example, adolescents often want more freedom, independence, and power in the family system.

3. *Positive communication skills will facilitate couples and families to balance cohesion and adaptability.*
   a. Couples/families with balanced scores (two central levels) on cohesion and adaptability will tend to have more positive communication skills than those at the extremes of the dimensions.
   b. Couples/families at the extremes of the cohesion and/or adaptability dimensions will tend to have more negative communication skills than those not at the extremes.

Positive communication skills include the following: sending clear and congruent messages, empathy, supportive statements, and effective problem-solving skills. Conversely, negative communication skills include the following: sending incongruent and disqualifying messages, lack of empathy, non-supportive (negative) statements, poor problem-solving skills, and paradoxical and double-binding messages (Olson, 1972). Although many studies have investigated communication and problem-solving skills in couples (Vincent et al., 1975; Sprenkle and Olson, 1978) and families (Alexander and Barton, 1976; Guerney, 1976; Patterson, 1976), these studies have not specifically tested the relationship of these skills to the hypotheses derived from the Circumplex Model.

In general, positive communication skills are seen as helping marital and family systems facilitate and maintain a balance on the two dimensions. Conversely, negative communication skills prevent and minimize marital and family systems from moving into the central areas and thereby increase the probability that extreme systems will remain extreme. Carlfred Broderick (personal communication) proposed that communication was the critical dimension missing in the Circumplex Model and has recently developed specific hypotheses that relate family communication and system processes to child behavior (Broderick and Pulliam-Krager, 1979). There is need for research that will more adequately assess the relationship between communication skills, types of marital and family systems, and the extent to which positive skills facilitate movement within the Model.

The Circumplex Model also allows one to begin an integration of general systems theory with family development, a proposal made several years ago by Reuben Hill (1971) in a paper comparing these theoretical orientations. Building on the family development approach as described by Hill and Rodgers (1969), it is asserted that families must change and adapt to normal transitions in the family (Rappoport, 1962). It is expected, therefore, that the stage of the family life cycle and composition of the family will have considerable impact on the type of family system. Although marital and family systems at the same stage will differ, it is hypothesized that many of them will cluster together at certain critical stages or transition points because they are dealing with similar development tasks (see Table I). For example, it would be predicted that premarital couples would tend toward the high range on cohesion (enmeshed and connected) and toward the lower range on adaptability (structured to rigid). In other words, they would fall into the lower right quadrant of the Circumplex Model (see Figure 1).

Table I indicates the levels of family cohesion and adaptability that are expected at critical stages of the family life cycle and indicates how distressed and non-distressed couples and families will differ. Unfortunately, there is not sufficient space to elaborate on all the predicted changes that may occur at critical transitions in marriage and family relationships. Future papers will elaborate on these ideas and hypotheses and, hopefully, future studies will evaluate and refine them.

Bridging Research, Theory, and Practice

The hallmark of some of the more recent and comprehensive intervention models with couples and families is their ability to bridge theory, research, and therapeutic intervention. Traditionally, most of the research with couples and families has tested hypotheses and theories which have not been therapeutically relevant. On the other hand, the majority of outcome studies on the effectiveness of marital or family intervention have not been theoretically based (Gurman and Kniskern, 1978). The few exceptions that have integrated these three domains have been therapy outcome studies in behavioral areas (Alexander and Barton, 1976; Stuart, 1976; Patterson, 1976; Weiss, 1974, 1978) or with communication skills (Epstein et al., 1978; Guerney, 1976; Miller et al., 1976).

The numerous advantages of integrating research, theory, and practice have been reviewed elsewhere (Olson, 1970, 1976; Sprenkle and Olson, 1978; Sprenkle, 1976), but bear repeating. Integrating these three domains into a single project not only bridges the traditional gaps between these domains, but improves the quality of each area. Theory and research are no longer seen as irrelevant to clinical practice. The use of clinical populations increases both the validity and generalizability of the findings. While therapists, researchers, and theorists have much to gain from each other, these groups have rarely worked together and only a few professionals (often psychologists) have designed and conducted these integrative projects.

The advantages of combining research, theory, and practice into an integrated package become most apparent when one is concerned with assessing the relative effectiveness of treatment programs. In designing outcome studies, it is advantageous to be clear about the specific theoretical outcomes and to be able to identify and operationalize both the outcome variables and the treatment variables. Then one needs to select

Table I: Typical Types of Systems at Critical Stages of Family Life Cycle

	Cohesion	*Adaptability*	*Quadrant of Model*
Premarital	Connected and Enmeshed	Structured and Rigid	Lower Right
Newlyweds	Connected	Flexible and Chaotic	Upper Right
Early Marriage	Separated and Connected	Flexible and Structured	Central Area
Later Marriage			
(a) Non-distressed	Separated and Connected	Flexible and Structured	Central Area
(b) Distressed	One or both spouses Disengaged or Enmeshed	One or both spouses Disengaged or Enmeshed	Extreme Areas
Birth of First Child	Connected and Enmeshed	Initially Chaotic; later Structured and Rigid	Initially Upper Right; later Lower Right
Child Rearing			
(a) Non-problem Families	Separated and Connected	Flexible and Structured	Central Area
(b) Problem Families	Disengaged and Enmeshed	Chaotic and Rigid	Extreme Areas
Adolescent in Family			
(a) Non-problem families	Primarily Separated; some Connected	Flexible and Structured	Central Area
(b) Problem families	Enmeshed or Disengaged	Rigid or Chaotic	Extreme areas
Older Couples w/o children			
(a) Non-distressed	Separated and Connected	Flexible and Structured	Central Area
(b) Distressed	Disengaged or Enmeshed	Rigid	Lower Left or Right

1) This table summarizes modal patterns for each stage. It is assumed that there will be high variability within these stages, and this summary obscures many of the complexities that need to be more fully described and empirically evaluated.
2) The concepts used to describe the four levels of cohesion and adaptability are presented in the Circumplex Model (Figure I).

from the available research methods those that are most relevant for assessing the specific outcome variables. The excellent review of diagnostic tools by Cromwell et al. (1976) provides a range of self-report and behavioral methods that can be used. Then it becomes possible to make an initial diagnosis of the marital and family system, use that information in the treatment program, and finally assess the changes on the same variables after the treatment has been completed.

Several integrative projects have been done by investigators interested in testing the value of behaviorally oriented and communication programs for couples and families.

One of the most systematically developed intervention programs for couples and families that is based on systems theory and effectively integrates research, theory, and intervention is the McMaster Model developed by Epstein, Bishop, and Levin (1978). The theoretical concepts that they use for diagnosis and intervention are very similar to the variables that are related to the cohesion and adaptability dimensions in the Circumplex Model (see Table II).

Brief Review of Theoretical Models of Family Systems

This review will describe theoretical models that have focused independently on variables related to the cohesion and adaptability dimensions. Most of these models have been developed in the last five years by individuals having a systems perspective of the family. One bit of evidence regarding the value and importance of the cohesion and adaptability dimensions is the fact that these theorists and therapists quite independently concluded that the variables they selected were critical for understanding and treating marital and family systems.

Table II summarized the work of seven theorists who have worked on describing marital and family systems. Before reviewing the definitions of the variables they have identified, it should be mentioned that another paper (Olson et al., 1978) reviews other theoretical concepts that relate to each of these two dimensions. That review indicated that cohesion was considered a significant variable in several social science fields including social psychology, sociology, small-group research, group therapy, family therapy, and anthropology. Many of the traditionally important variables in the family field have related directly to the adaptability dimension; these include assertiveness, power, discipline, role relationships, negotiation skills, and relationship rules.

Most of the recent theorizing about family dynamics and intervention has been strongly influenced by general systems theory as described by Von Bertalanffy (1968) and applied to the family by Jackson (1957, 1965), Haley (1962, 1963, 1964), Speer (1970), Hill (1971) and Wertheim (1973, 1975). The current work has focused on describing both clinical and

Table II: Theoretical Models of Family Systems Utilizing Concepts Related to Cohesion—Adaptability and Communication Dimensions

	Cohesion	*Adaptability*	*Communication*	*Others*
Benjamin (1974, 1977)	Affiliation	Interdependence		
Epstein, Bishop, and Levin (1978)	Affective Involvement	Behavior Control Problem-Solving Roles	Communication Affective Responsiveness	
French and Guidera (1974)		Capacity to Change Power		Anxiety; Role as Symptom Carrier
Kantor and Lehr (1974)	Affect Dimension	Power Dimension		Meaning Dimension
Leary (1957) and Constantine (1977)	Affection-Hostility	Dominance-Submission		
Lewis et al. (1976) and Beavers (1977)	Closeness Autonomy Coalitions	Power Negotiation	Affect	Mythology
Parsons and Bales (1955)	Expressive Role	Instrumental Role		

nonclinical families (Kantor and Lehr, 1975; Lewis et al., 1976) or has been concerned with clinical intervention (Benjamin, 1974, 1977; Constantine, 1977; Epstein et al., 1978). Only the early work by the psychologist Timothy Leary (1957) and Talcott Parsons (1955) was less influenced by the recent systems perspective, although Parsons's work had a strong systems orientation relating the family to other social systems.

In summary, the cohesion and adaptability dimensions have become critical for understanding and treating marital and family systems. The diversity of concepts can, therefore, be conceptually clustered to primarily the two dimensions, with communication being an important third dimension. The operational definitions of these concepts by various writers are also similar to those used in the Circumplex Model. A review of the empirical studies attesting to the value of these dimensions will now be presented.

EMPIRICAL STUDIES RELATED TO THE CIRCUMPLEX MODEL

Empirical Studies of Marital and Family Cohesion

In the last few years, there has been an increasing amount of research of concepts related to the cohesion dimensions in couples and families. In spite of the large variety of concepts used to describe aspects of cohesion and the diversity of operational measures used in these studies, most of the findings have been supportive of the principles and hypotheses in the Circumplex Model. The congruence of findings across studies using different conceptual and operational definitions attests to the potency of this dimension.

One of the earliest intensive outcome studies of family therapy, conducted by Minuchin et al. (1967), compared multi-problem families with more than one delinquent child to ten matched families without a delinquent child. A major discovery was the existence of enmeshed and disengaged families, which are the two extremes of family cohesion in the Circumplex Model. In describing the twelve multi-problem families, they stated: "Our families can be seen at either extreme of the enmeshed-disengaged axis or as alternating in time between the two poles" (1967, p. 211). The importance of this dimension is indicated by the fact that the disengaged-enmeshed dimension provided "distinguishing patterns or profiles of family structure which differentiated among these families in a surprisingly consistent fashion despite an array of differences in personality organization of individuals in families falling into the same family category" (1967, p. 352). At both extremes, the mothers tended to assume absolute responsibility for their children's behavior and discouraged autonomous exploration and mastery of the environment by the children.

In the enmeshed families, there was "tight interlocking" and extraordinary resonance between individual members. "Their quality of connectedness is such that attempts on the part of one member to change elicit fast complementary resistance on the part of the others" (1967, p. 358). In dramatic contrast, the individuals in disengaged families seem oblivious to the effects of their action on each other. "Actions of its members do not lead to vivid repercussions. . . . The over-all impression is one of an atomistic field; family members have long moments in which they move as in isolated orbits, unrelated to each other" (1967, p. 354).

Although Minuchin et al. (1967) emphasized the potency of the enmeshed-disengaged axis for describing multi-problem families, they also observed variables that are major concepts on the adaptability dimension of the Circumplex Model (see Table IV). They indicated that one should look at: "(1) the lines of power and leadership; (2) the labeling of members and their assignment to particular roles; (3) subgrouping alliances and shifts around different significant themes; and (4) the fluidity of assigned labels" (1967, p. 218). These variables correspond to the adaptability concepts of power, roles, and flexibility. They also discussed the importance of observing and changing the ways families negotiate and deal with conflict. In treating the families, they emphasized the importance of changing the rigid family system and increasing its adaptability. They stated: "We stress the obtaining of impressions of the family's elasticity within its own internal framework. . . . While he(she) is studying the family system by these means, he(she) is also changing it. By unbalancing and loosening the family's customary patterns, he(she) is forcing them to organize around conflicts in new ways" (1967, p. 292).

One of the most careful and systematic studies on the cohesion dimension with normal, delinquent, and schizophrenic families was done by David Reiss (1971a, 1971b). In an attempt to develop a middle range theory of family consensual experience, he identified three variables to investigate: family problem-solving effectiveness, coordination, and penchant for closure. Studying family interaction on a card-sorting procedure, he identified three patterns of behavior which he described as *environment-sensitive* (normal families), *interpersonal distance-sensitive* (delinquent families), and *consensus-sensitive* (schizophrenic families).

More specifically, he found that normal families experienced the environment as patterned, logical, and masterable. They perceived the problem as "out there" and did not react to the problem personally. They operated on objective accuracy and final solutions were based on input from all the family members. These families would fall at the mid-point on the cohesion dimension (see Table III). The interpersonal distance-sensitive families would fall at the lower end of the cohesion dimension. Here individuals experienced the rejection of their ideas as rejection of

Table III: Empirical Studies of Family Cohesion*

Extremely Low Family Cohesion	Moderate Family Cohesion	Extremely High Family Cohesion
Multiple Delinquent Families (Minuchin, 1967)	Normal families (Reiss, 1971)	Working class families (Straus, 1968)
Distressed marriages (Levinger, 1965)	White collar families (Kohn, 1969)	Jewish families (Strodtbeck, 1958)
Delinquent families (Van der Veen, 1975, 1976; Reiss, 1971; Glueck and Glueck, 1950; Druckman, 1978)	Adjustment to War separation (Hill, 1949)	Slovak-American Families (Stein, 1978)
Blue collar families (Kohn, 1969)	Non-delinquent families (Van der Veen, 1975, 1976)	Schizophrenic families (Reiss, 1971)
Southern Italian family (Strodtbeck, 1958)	Non-problem marriages (Levinger, 1965)	Multiple Delinquent Families (Minuchin, 1967)

* The classification of couples and families in this table are only suggestive of how different groups can be arrayed on the cohesion dimension. Labeling families by social class, race, ethnic background, or type of presenting symptom is heavily value-laden and falsely assumes homogeneity within these groups.

themselves as persons. Individuals attempted to demonstrate their independence and made decisions based on little information. Furthermore, they refused to come to closure without considerable distress. Conversely, the consensus-sensitive families would fall at the high end of the cohesion dimension. They often maintained an implicit level of agreement and dissent was not tolerated. These families achieved closure very early, regardless of how good the solution was, because they wanted to maintain harmony and consensus.

At least three sociological studies relating family membership to success in the American culture (as defined by attained social class) offer distinctions analogous to the one Reiss made between environment and consensus-sensitive families. Although heavily value-laden, degree of success in the socioeconomic structure may be taken as a measure of system viability or functionality. Strodtbeck (1958), in his study of family values and achievement, compared the typical world view of Eastern European Jewish families with that of Southern Italian families. Though the external world of the Jews was hostile, there was a "belief in a rational mastery of the world'' (p. 151). These families were described by Strodtbeck as intensely aware of and open to the technical and nonpersonal aspects of the wider community. These are qualities similar to Reiss's environment-sensitive families, which was seen among a ''normal'' population, and would be expected of families near the mid-range of our model. In contrast, Strodtbeck described the Southern Italian family as seeing the external world as unpredictable and unmasterable. ''Destino,'' or fate, could intervene for good or bad and was always present. The basic code was family solidarity. Strodtbeck's description of the Southern Italian family is rather similar to Reiss's consensus-sensitive category, which were comprised of families of schizophrenics. The Southern Italian family may be located five-eighths of the way out on the cohesion axis, but not quite as far out as schizophrenic families.

Melvin Kohn (1969), in a large survey study of white-collar and blue-collar families in Washington, D.C., found that working-class parents typically view the outside world as unchangeable and tend to teach their children obedience. Middle-class parents, on the other hand, view the world as masterable and encourage curiosity and self-direction in their children. While sociologists tend to emphasize the anticipatory socialization function of such world views for the type of work the offspring will eventually perform, it is equally plausible that the world view of white-collar families facilitates morphogenic or adaptive processes. White-collar families may occupy the central region of the model, with blue-collar families, on the average, somewhat more distant from the mid-point of cohesion.

Straus's (1968) description of working-class families in Bombay, Minneapolis, and San Juan bears some similarity to Reiss's description of ''interpersonal distance-sensitive'' families. These families appeared not to share enough information during a family game to achieve a rapid solution to the experimental task. As a result, their problem-solving involved a lot of individual autonomous behavior and little family cohesion. Reiss's ''interpersonal distance-sensitive'' families are typified in his sample by families with delinquents. Reiss believes that these families experience acceptance of suggestions, observations, and ideas from others as a sign of weakness. Straus suggested that a normal group of working-class parents may exhibit the same behavior, but for different reasons. Experiences in crowded environments may have made necessary the development of a norm of ''civil inattention.'' Strodtbeck (in Framo, 1972) has made explicit the similarity he observed between ''sick'' families and lower-class families:

> I think the gap between the interaction of sick families and the interaction of lower class families is narrower than the interaction differences between lower class and upper class families. I am basing this comparison on their verbal skills and methods of dealing with one another, the speed with which they can survey a large number of

> cognitive differences and bring about reconciliation, and the amount of humor and so forth, they display. (p. 81)

This suggests, then, that blue-collar families are located somewhere between the midpoint of cohesion and low group identification.

The Gluecks' (1950) studies of juvenile delinquents indicated that they would be located at the low end of the cohesion dimension, characterized by extreme individual autonomy and limited identification with the family group. The Gluecks sent out field workers with instructions to describe the quality of relationships among family members. What resulted was a three-class category of cohesion: (1) good—strong "we-feeling" as evidenced by cooperativeness, group interests, pride in the home, affection for each other; (2) fair—elements of cohesiveness, but some members pulling away from the family group; (3) poor—unintegrated; home is just a place to "hang your hat"; self-interest of the members exceeds group interest.

An evaluation of each family (N = 499 delinquents, 500 nondelinquents) on the basis of data from social investigations and psychiatric interviews showed a far lower proportion of families of delinquents than of non-delinquents to be cohesive (16 percent as compared with 61.8 percent). In 24 percent of the families of delinquents, self-interest clearly exceeded group interest. This was true of less than one percent of the families of non-delinquents. Putting the cohesiveness dimension into a "Social Predictive Table" with four other variables, they found that if families were extremely low on cohesion (unintegrated), they predicted 97 percent of the time the child would be delinquent.

Hill (1949) in his Iowa study of war separation and reunion, investigated integration, a variable which is conceptually related to what we have been calling cohesion. In Hill's study, family integration involved the unifying bonds of economic and emotional independence: strong emotional ties among family members, pride in family traditions, and high participation as a family in joint activities. Taken as a composite index, Hill found that while highly integrated families had the best adjustment to war reunion, *moderately* integrated families had the best adjustment to the somewhat more difficult crisis of war separation. Perhaps "highly" integrated families are so emotionally interdependent that they are disrupted more than "moderately" integrated families by a crisis such as war separation.

Another sociological study of family cohesiveness was conducted by Sandberg et al. (1969) in which adolescents in India were compared to those in the United States. Family cohesiveness was defined as the reporting of joint family activities and a positive attitude toward family interaction and was assessed by a twenty-five-item scale. Generally, these investigators found greater perceived family cohesion in both males and females in India and, conversely, greater perceived autonomy in the U.S. sample.

Family cohesion was found to be the best predictive dimension of a one-year follow-up of treatment outcome for ninety-two couples in which the husband was diagnosed and treated for alcoholism (Oxford et al., 1976). Cohesive marriages were twice as likely to have a favorable treatment outcome and non-cohesive marriages were three times as likely to have an unfavorable treatment outcome. Cohesion was a composite measure which emerged from several scales that were factor analyzed, resulting in a single cohesion factor that contained these variables: mutual affection, husband's involvement in family tasks, favorable spouse perceptions and meta-perceptions, and optimism about the future of the marriage. Three other variables were also related to positive outcome (husband's job status, husband's self-esteem, and wife's reported hardship), but when these variables were partially controlled, it was found that cohesion remained predictive for husbands with low status jobs and low levels of self-esteem. A composite index of dominance balance was also identified which relates to the adaptability dimension in the Circumplex Model. This dimension was *not* predictive of outcome.

While the previous studies focused on family cohesion, the remaining studies will examine marital cohesion as it relates to other aspects of marriage. Levinger (1965) reviewed the literature on marital cohesion and dissolution and identified the following three factors that differentiated high and low cohesive marriages: sources of attraction, sources of barrier strength, and sources of alternative attraction. He hypothesized that marital cohesion was a direct function of *psychological attraction* (affectional rewards, socioeconomic rewards, and similarity in social status) and *barrier forces* (feelings of obligation, moral proscriptions, and external pressures), and inversely related to the *attractiveness of alternative relationships* (affectional rewards and economic rewards). Marital cohesion was seen as a special case of group cohesion which has been used extensively in small group research. Levinger indicated that high-cohesive families are much easier to identify than low-cohesive relationships that terminate because many couples stay together because of high barrier forces, in spite of the fact that they have an "empty shell" marriage that is low on psychological attraction variables.

Hawkins (1968) developed a scale of marital cohesion that discriminated between a group of twenty clinic and twenty-eight non-clinic couples. The final thirty-six-item scale had a high split-half reliability (r = .92), a low correlation (r = .28) with the Marlowe-Crown Social Desirability, a high correlation (r = .72) with marital satisfaction, and was not significantly correlated with socioeconomic variables. The mean score for the non-clinic group was 135 while the clinic group had a mean of 111, with very little overlap between the two groups. The cohesion scale consists of items dealing with the degree of hostile interaction, open affection, mutual activities, supportiveness, and dialogue. The specific items that had the highest correlation with the total score were caressing and kissing, laughing and having fun, and being romantic and communicative. A useful methodological innovation was to have the couple discuss each item and agree, so that a couple score was obtained rather than individual husband and wife responses. Unfortunately, this scale has been used only in this study but it deserves further use.

Paul Rosenblatt and colleagues at Minnesota have done a series of systematic studies on the dimension of cohesion, which they describe on the continuum of togetherness-apartness. In a review of mechanisms that families use to maintain apartness, Rosenblatt and Titus (1976) emphasized that there might be considerable difference between the feelings of togetherness-apartness and objective assessment that rely on time and space measures. As postulated in the Circumplex Model, they also indicated that family members need to arrive at a balance on togetherness-apartness. This balance will vary within dyadic combinations in the family and different expectations can often be problematic for families. As they indicated: "Teenagers may see parental demands for greater togetherness as controlling, while parents may see teenagers' moves toward greater apartness as threatening in many ways. Thus it can be expected that in any family relationship there may be power battles and strong emotions experienced over togetherness and apartness" (1976, p. 369).

In order to more adequately understand how American families with norms for togetherness manage to obtain separateness in socially acceptable ways, such as watching television, working away from home, sleeping, and participating in voluntary activities, Rosenblatt has conducted studies with different types of families. Rosenblatt and Budd (1975) investigated territoriality and privacy in married and cohabiting couples. As hypothesized, they found married couples had higher levels of territoriality than cohabiting couples and cohabiting couples had more places in their residence for being alone. In studying farm families where the potential for too much togetherness and too much apartness exists, Rosenblatt, Nevaldine, and Titus (1978) found that these families developed ways of finding time and places to be apart and together.

One mechanism that families sometimes use to handle too much togetherness at home is watching television. Rosenblatt and Cunningham (1976) found high tension levels for families that watched more television. It appeared that families who were more crowded together often used television to prevent tension. Studying togetherness-apartness in couples experiencing tension, Rosenblatt et al. (1979a, 1979b) found that couples high in disrespect tended to stay apart more after a fight or disagreement, whereas couples low in disrespect tended to stay together more than they usually did. In other words, couples not only differ in how much time they spend together and apart, but some couples deal with tension in their relationship by spending greater time together while others prefer spending greater time apart.

Another study assessed cohesion by investigating the time a couple spends together and alone in recreational activities (Birchler, Weiss, and Vincent, 1975). In a study of distressed and nondistressed couples, they studied how marital and stranger dyads interacted in problem-solving situations. The Marital Activities Inventory, which consists of eighty-five typical recreational activities, was also used to determine what individuals did alone, with others, or together as a couple. While individuals in both distressed and nondistressed marriages spent about the same time in individual activities, the individuals from distressed marriages engaged in significantly fewer activities together and significantly more activities with others. It appeared that individuals in distressed marriages avoided the aversiveness of the spouse by participating more in recreational activities alone or with others. Whether this type of participation is a cause or an effect of marital distress was not assessed.

In a related study, Williams (1977) focused on togetherness-apartness in terms of marital interaction. She studied ten happily married and ten distressed couples according to the quality and quantity of their marital interaction. She found that husbands and wives disagreed on the *quality* of time but agreed on the *quantity* of time spent together. Using the quantity of time variable, the distressed couples felt that they either spent too much or too little time together. This finding again attests to the need for achieving a balance on the dimension of being connected or cohesive.

Although many studies have examined cohesion in ad hoc groups, only the study by Wheaton (1974) will be included here because it demonstrates the important relationship between conflict and cohesion. Wheaton used 102 female dyads who were roommates in college, a total of 204 subjects. Seashore's Group Cohesiveness Index (Miller, 1964) was modified for two-person groups and a factor analysis revealed an attitudinal and behavioral factor. Basically, it was found that the degree of cohesion was unrelated to the total undifferentiated level of conflict. However, principled conflict (related to what one *ought* to do) had a negative effect on cohesion, whereas communal conflict (how or when something should be done) produced higher levels of cohesion than when there was no conflict. In summary, this study demonstrated the positive contribution that some types of conflict can have on increasing cohesion in a relationship.

Empirical Studies of Marital and Family Adaptability

Many of the variables that historically have been of interest to family sociologists and other family professionals are concepts related to the adaptability dimension. These variables are indicated in Table IV and include *power* (assertiveness and control), *discipline*, *negotiation*, *roles*, and *rules*. The variable of power (assertiveness and control) has been given considerable conceptual and methodological attention elsewhere by Cromwell and Olson (1975). Discipline has been studied extensively and many of the salient findings have been summarized by Rollins and Thomas (1975).

Negotiation in couples has been studied both empirically and clinically by Weiss, Birchler, and Vincent in a series of studies (Weiss et al., 1974; Birchler et al., 1975; Vincent et al., 1975). Role relationships have been a fruitful arena of family sociology for the past decade and a recent empirical update of this work was done by Nye (1976). The importance of family rules, both implicit and explicit, has been an interest of many family therapists since the early work by Jackson (1965), but little empirical work has been done to operationalize and measure family rules.

Because of the extensive literature related to these concepts, only the studies most relevant to the Circumplex Model will be reviewed. Many hypotheses in the Model were based upon the research findings in these studies. Hence, it is no accident that the studies support the Model. What is important is that despite the diversity of conceptual and operational definitions, the basic curvilinear hypothesis between adaptability and family functioning is generally supported.

The first study to explicitly test hypotheses related to the *power* concept in the adaptability dimension was done by Sprenkle and Olson (1978). They studied the marital interaction of twenty-five couples receiving marriage counseling with a matched control group of twenty-five couples while they took part in an interaction game called SIMFAM. It was predicted that couples in counseling would either have no leadership or authoritarian leadership (two extremes on adaptability), whereas nonclinic couples would have more equalized leadership so that power could shift between the husband and wife. Under the nonstressful condition, no difference was found between the two groups. However, when the stress level increased, the hypothesis was strongly supported. Nonclinic couples were also more responsive to each other's attempts to control. Significantly more of the counseling couples had a wife-dominant leadership pattern. When the variable of supportiveness (communication dimension—see Hypothesis 3 earlier in this paper) was included, the combination of support and equalized leadership was the pattern most characteristic of nonclinic couples. In summary, this paper provided considerable support for the curvilinear hypothesis of adaptability and marital functioning.

In another study of family power using the SIMFAM game, Tallman and Miller (1974) demonstrated the importance of examining role expectations as they related to leadership patterns (see Hypothesis 1c). While they found white-collar egalitarian families performed best, this same leadership style was problematic for blue-collar families. Post hoc analysis indicated that the role expectations in the blue-collar families was that the husband-father should be the leader and that any other pattern was seen as inadequate. For the white-collar families, the egalitarian leadership pattern was congruent with their role expectations and, hence, this pattern facilitated more effective problem-solving.

Bahr and Rollins (1971) found that couples with more democratic leadership patterns pre-crisis were more likely to change leadership in the SIMFAM crisis. Since, as Tallman (1970) suggests, more competent families may have greater leadership adaptability, measuring leadership changes may be a promising technique. Miller and Westman (1966) used changes in leadership patterns as a measure of adaptability. They found that the variable discriminated between a control group and families of severely retarded readers. They used a technique conceptually similar to the SIMFAM crisis in that the rules of the experiment were changed mid-stream.

In a rather good study of conflict behavior among clinically distressed couples, Epstein and Santa-Barbara (1975) found that couples could be classified as Doves, Dominant-Submissive, Hawks, or Mugwumps on the basis of their behavior in a mixed-motive interaction game. They found that the Doves indicated adaptability by the shift from an initially exploitative to a cooperative strategy. Both the Doves and the Dominant-Submissive couples were also responsive to the structural aspects of the game. On the other hand, Hawks and Mugwumps rigidly adhered to the same strategy throughout the game and were also insensitive to the structural aspects of the game. This was a good attempt to relate types of couples to their behavioral changes in an experimental interaction situation. Kieren and Tallman (1972) attempted to specifically measure family adaptability in a systematic manner. They defined adaptability as: "A spouse's ability to deal effectively with a problematic situation by changing roles and strategies in terms of new or modified assessments of the situation with which s/he is confronted" (p. 248). The components of spousal adaptability were: flexibility, empathy, and motivation. Husbands and wives were interviewed separately about the last time they had had disagreements in fifty-three different topic areas. These scores were then factor analyzed and a General Adaptability factor emerged that was independent from other variables. No significant relationship was found between the spouse's adaptability scores and the marital happiness scores of the spouses.

Goldstein and Kling (1975) developed a scale which they called family solidarity, but which most clearly measures what we are calling family adaptability. High scores represent interdependence and flexible role relationships, democratic decision-making, and free communication patterns. They had fifty items covering the six areas of family tasks and behaviors. They found some relationships between this scale and other related ffamily behavior and also found that the scale did discriminate between a group of forty clients after treatment and a waiting list control group.

In terms of *parental discipline*, there is considerable evidence for the curvilinear hypothesis that states that either highly permissive or highly restrictive (authoritarian) patterns of discipline are counterproductive compared to the more democratic pattern (Rollins and Thomas, 1975). In studying perceived parental behavior and adolescent rebellion, Balswick and Macrides (1975) found in a sample of 417 college students that either extreme restrictiveness or permissiveness was related to significantly greater amounts of rebellion. At a time when marijuana use was considered to be a measure of adolescent rebellion, Hunt (1974) also found that perceived parental permissiveness (laissez faire) related to high marijuana use, parental restrictiveness (autocratic) related to moderate marijuana use, while democratic parenting had the lowest level of marijuana use. In general, these studies support the predicted hypothesis that the extremes of parental behavior are related to more problematic behavior in children.

The following studies have focused on what is called *family flexibility*, a concept closely related to family adaptability. The problem is that these studies have been so poorly operationalized that it is difficult to decipher what they are actually studying. Most of these studies have compared clinic and nonclinic families in a laboratory setting. In general, the empirical research on this topic suggests that normal families tend to be more flexible than distressed families. Conversely, patterns of interaction tend to be maintained more rigidly in the latter (Bell, 1962; Jackson and Weakland, 1961).

Flexibility has been operationalized primarily in two ways: (1) the amount of intrusion, interruption, sarcasm, or laughter in families; and (2) randomness or relationship patterns such as who speaks after whom (assuming that a random order suggests flexibility). Because of difficulties encountered with these two measures, it is suggested that future studies *not* rely on these measures to assess family adaptability. Several studies using these measures will, however, be reviewed to demonstrate the problems in measurement.

Conceptually, the validity of the first approach appears to be the weakest. Mishler and Waxler (1968) found that in asymptomatic families, as opposed to families with a schizophrenic male offspring, there was more disruption of communication and fragmentation of speech patterns (such as intrusive laughter, repetitions, joking, and incomplete sentences). They interpreted their findings to indicate that there was greater flexibility and spontaneity in normal family systems and that consequently members were freer to offer relevant and creative input. A rather important finding was that normal family members were responsive to each other and sensitive to each other's inputs in spite of the interruptions.

Becker and Iwakami's (1969) results were similar. They found that normal family members engaged in reliably higher incidences of simultaneous speech, aggressive verbalizations, disagreements, and interruptions in problem-solving interaction than did families attending a child psychology clinic. The work of Riskin and Faunce (1970) found similar results concerning interruptions and intrusions. Minuchin et al. (1967), in their study of slum families, found that control mothers, as opposed to those with delinquent children, displayed more disruptive verbal behavior in a family task situation. Lennard et al. (1965) found that members of asymptomatic families were more likely to intrude when intrusion was defined as "an entry by a third person into a two person interaction which is not requested or elicited by the persons in the interaction."

The problem with these studies is that interruptions and intrusions and, especially, laughter and sarcasm are difficult to code reliably. It is interesting to note that Mishler and Waxler's interpretation of these characteristics as indicating flexibility was post hoc. They had actually predicted the reverse—that there would be more intrusions in the interaction of families with schizophrenics. Indeed, several studies have found more interruptions and intrusions in troubled families (O'Connor and Stachowiak, 1971; Farina and Dunham, 1963). In other words, there is conflicting data regarding whether there are more interruptions and so forth in normal or disturbed families.

Haley (1964) was among the first to use the second methodology, studying forty normal and abnormal families with a noninferential measure that indicated "who speaks after whom." Hypothesizing that organization means limitation, Haley reasoned that normal families would use more of the possible speech sequences more often, while disturbed families would use less and, hence, their interaction patterns would be more rigid. This is consistent with the theory of neurosis that disturbed people limit the range of responses they exhibit in comparison with normals. The hypothesis was strongly supported with the family triads.

The limits of this methodology became more evident when Haley (1967) attempted to replicate his research with family quads. There were no overall differences between normal and abnormal families. The normal families increased their deviation from random participation in this second study. This may have been due in part, however, to the fact that the chances of unequal participation in a four-person group are greater than in a three-person group, since the latter is composed of only three possible pairs while the former has six possible pairs. However, the abnormal families shifted only slightly toward more unequal participation with the addition of another child.

Lennard et al. (1965) found that in normal triads, as opposed to family triads with a schizophrenic, all three possible dyads operated with relatively equal saliency with regard to rate and direction of intrafamily communication. In the schizophrenic triads, one dyadic unit tended to dominate.

Research by Winter and Ferreira (1967) suggests yet another limitation with this methodology. They used a "who speaks after whom" measure and found that disturbed families had a less equal or less random pattern of participation in family discussions. However, they also discovered that a large portion of the variance could be accounted for by the fact that the schizophrenic children in the abnormal families did not talk very much. In short, when schizophrenic children are used, or any children who are unusually silent, it is easy to achieve significance on this measure. The difference between normal families and those with emotionally disturbed, but not psychotic, children was very slight.

In summary, this brief view of the relevant studies related to family adaptability indicates the importance of several family concepts: power, discipline, negotiation, roles, and rules. In spite of the diversity of operational and conceptual definitions, the curvilinear hypothesis between adaptability and family functioning was generally supported.

Empirical Studies Combining Cohesion and Adaptability

While the previous section focused on studies that examined *either* cohesion or adaptability, this section will focus on studies that incorporated *both* dimensions. There is evidence from these studies that significant gains are made by cross-partitioning the two dimensions so that a couple or family's location can be considered relative to each dimension. This also enables one to classify couples or families into *types*, as has been done within the Circumplex Model.

Historically, the first major family study to include both family cohesion and adaptability and to combine them into family types was done in 1936 by Angell in his classic book on how families coped with the depression. His two concepts were "family integration," which is very similar to cohesion, and "family adaptability." He defined integration as "the bonds of coherence and unity running through family life, of which common interests, affection, and a sense of economic interdependence are perhaps the most prominent" (1936, p. 15). Family adaptability related to how the family functioned as a unit, their flexibility in meeting difficulties, the family's readiness to adjust to changes, and its manner of making decisions. Dividing families into high, medium, and low categories on each dimension, he formed nine types of families, eight of which he empirically located and described. The conceptual and empirical value of forming family types was discovered after trying many other analyses using single variables and combinations of other variables. The importance of this discovery seemed obvious after it was made, which is common for most discoveries. In this regard, Angell said:

> I am ashamed of the fact that I did not see clearly from the start that integration alone would be no basis for predicting the effect of a decrease in income from accustomed sources. It seems now perfectly obvious that if one wished to define types in relation to a change of any kind, flexibility or adaptability with reference to that change was a very important consideration. (1936, p. 290).

In two subsequent studies, Reuben Hill also used both integration and adaptability and combined them into a measure he called dynamic stability. In 1949, Hill studied *Families Under Stress* to learn how 135 families dealt with war separation and reunion. He also formed family types by cross-classifying family integration and adaptability. He concluded that "taken as a whole, family integration is highly significant in predicting success both in separation and reunion, but . . . its relationship is higher with reunion adjustments than separation adjustments. The most highly integrated families did best in reunion and second best in separation" (1949, p. 132). Family adaptability related more directly to family adjustment to separation than reunion. The most adaptable families were not the most successful in adjusting to these two situations. In the typological analysis which combined integration and adaptability, it was found that the medium integration and high adaptability type had the best overall adjustment to both separation and reunion. Hill et al. (1953) also used these two dimensions in a study of personal and family adjustments to rapid urbanization in a monograph entitled *Eddyville's Families*. Although cross-classification was done with adaptability and other variables, it was not done with integration.

Only recently, in a series of studies of military separation by Ham McCubbin and colleagues, has there been an attempt to build upon and extend the classic studies of Angell and Hill. McCubbin (1975, 1976, 1977, 1979, in press) and Boss (in press), in their research on occupationally (military and business) induced family separations, underscore the central importance of family adaptability and cohesiveness. These recent investigators arrived at this conclusion by focusing on the coping behaviors and coping patterns that families employ in the management of stress. In three different studies, the two dimensions emerged as significant factors. A recent study by McCubbin et al. (1979) found in a second-order factor analysis that wives' coping behaviors focused on two dimensions: (1) maintaining family integrity and integration, and (2) promoting individual members' independence and self-sufficiency. In summary, they found that the management of family stress involves maintaining a delicate balance between both individual development and growth *and* family unity and integration.

A study that empirically demonstrates that cohesion and adaptability are underlying dimensions in assessing family behavior was conducted by van der Veen (1976). He developed a Family Concepts Test (FCT) which contained a nontheoretical set of eighty items that were thought to provide a comprehensive picture of family dynamics. This scale focused on an individual's perception of attitudes, feelings, and expectations toward one's family to obtain a "family concept" that was analogous to the self concept. This FCT was administered, using the Q-sort technique, to a large sample of families (parents, adolescents, and siblings) where some adolescents were disturbed and others were nondisturbed. Using factor analysis to condense the eighty items, fifteen first-order factors with eigen values greater than one were found. After a second-order factor analysis, the two higher order dimensions that emerged were *family integration* and *adaptive coping*. Family integration was very similar to cohesion and it was composed of the following first-order factors: family loyalty, togetherness vs. separateness, consideration vs. conflict, open communication, and closeness vs. estrangement. Adaptive coping, which is similar to the adaptability dimension, was composed of the following first-order factors: family actualization, community sociability, and locus of control. The similarity of these second-order factors to the circumplex dimensions is noteworthy since the item pool was not constructed with any theoretical orientation in mind.

Van der Veen's findings in the previous study (1976) and earlier studies (Novak and van der Veen, 1970; van der Veen, 1965) are also very congruent with the hypothesized relationships derived from the Circumplex Model (see Hypotheses section). Members of disturbed families had lower family concepts than members of nondisturbed families on all of the adaptive coping factors and the first three factors of family integration.

In order to assess what variables would distinguish healthy family functioning from problem functioning, Westley and Epstein (1969) studied 170 college students and 88 families in Canada. The major variables that they focused on were *problem solving, power, authority,* and *roles,* which are related to the adaptability dimension of the Circumplex Model, and the development of *autonomy,* which is related to family cohesion. They found that the quality and harmony of the husband-wife relationship was critical for the emotional health of the adolescent. Children from mother-dominated and father-dominated homes had more emotional problems and fewer strengths, whereas those from father-led and democratic families had few problems and major strengths. Autonomy dealt with the extent to which individual family members could make their own decisions and were differentiated from the family system. Families that encouraged autonomy had significantly more emotionally healthy adolescents than those that minimized it. This study demonstrates again the importance of the variables related to the two circumplex dimensions. All of their findings are congruent with the hypothesized relationships among the variables in the cohesion and adaptability dimensions as illustrated in Tables IV and V.

In a rather systematic study of family interaction with healthy and patient families, Lewis et al. (1976) developed the Family System Rating Scales, which contain several of the variables central to the cohesion and adaptability dimensions in the Circumplex Model. Their sample consisted of thirty-three nonpatient families and seventy patient families with one member having one of the following three symptoms: behavior disorders (forty-five), psychoses (eighteen), and neuroses (seven). Family members were video-taped while they were completing five interaction tasks: (1) discussing what they disagreed about; (2) planning something together; (3) discussing the greatest pain in the relationship; (4) discussing placement of family members on a Family Closeness Board; and (5) discussing family strengths.

The Family System Rating Scale (FSRS) used to rate the video tapes had thirteen subscales that relate to the Circumplex Model in the following ways: Cohesion Dimension (Closeness, Coalitions, and Autonomy—four scales); Adaptability Dimension (Power and Negotiation); Communication Dimension (Affect—four scales; Mythology)—see also Table I. Their findings are complicated by the lower inter-rater reliabilities that were in part caused by the confusing operational definitions of the variables. However, by using sum scores across these scales, the researchers did obtain interesting findings. The sum total of the FSRS correlated very closely to the one-item Global Family Health-Pathology Scale ($r = .90$), even though that scale also had low inter-rater reliability. The FSRS also correlated with the sum of the Gossett-Timerlawn Adolescent Psychopathology Scale ($r = .42$), but the FSRS intercorrelations with the sub-scales of this measure were very low, but significant. In general, this research was an ambitious study of family interaction and demonstrated the value of the cohesion, adaptability, and communication dimensions in discriminating types of family systems.

Moos and Moos (1976) utilized a Family Environment Scale (FES) with one hundred families and identified six typologies of families using cluster analysis of mean scores of family members. Of the ten concepts assessed by the FES, several related directly to the cohesion and adaptability dimensions. The cohesion dimension was measured by two scales (cohesion and independence), adaptability was assessed by two scales (control and organization), and the communication dimension was measured by two scales (expressiveness and conflict). Although it was hoped that the FES could be used to study the Circumplex Model, a validity study by Russell (1978) found that the FES lacked construct validity for the cohesion and adaptability dimensions. As a result, a new self-report instrument, Family Adaptability and Cohesion Evaluation Scales (FACES), was developed (Olson, Bell, and Portner, 1978) and will be described later.

In order to determine how important family cohesion, family adaptability, and family communication concepts are to healthy family functioning and as goals for family therapy, Fisher and Sprenkle (1977) conducted a survey of 310 marriage and family therapists. These family therapists made ratings and rankings on the ten family cohesion concepts, seven family adaptability concepts, and seventeen family communication concepts in terms of how important these concepts were to (1) healthy family functioning and (2) goals for guiding their therapeutic intervention with couples and families.

Considering *healthy family functioning,* the mean rating for cohesion and adaptability was 3.9 and 4.0 for communication, which indicates that all three dimensions were seen as *very* important (5 = crucial; 4 = very important; 3 = important; 2 = somewhat important; 1 = not important). In the upper third of the ranking were thirty percent of the cohesion concepts, twenty-nine percent of the adaptability concepts, and thirty-five percent of the communication concepts. Considering the *goals of therapy,* the mean rating for cohesion was 3.6, while adaptability was 4.1, and communication variables were 4.0, which indicates these three dimensions are *usually* used to guide therapy (5 = always; 4 = usually; 3 = often; 2 = seldom; 1 = never). In addition, there was considerable congruence between the descriptions of healthy family functioning and goals for family treatment on cohesion ($r = .54$), adaptability ($r = .56$), and communication ($r = .65$). In general, this study demonstrates the value of cohesion, adaptability, and communication dimensions for describing healthy family functioning and for setting goals for family intervention.

Another study of family therapists found that the cohesion, adaptability, and communication dimensions were important goals for treatment. The Group for the Advancement of Psychiatry (1970) conducted a survey of family therapists. Of the 290 respondents, forty percent were social workers, another forty percent were psychiatrists and psychologists, and the remaining twenty percent were marriage counselors and other helping professionals. These therapists were asked to indicate the primary goals they had for family therapy from a list of eight. *Improved communication* was rated as primary for eighty-five percent of the therapists, *improved empathy* (communication) was fifty-six percent, *im-*

proved autonomy and individuation (cohesion) was fifty-six percent, *more flexible leadership* (adaptability) was thirty-four percent, *improved role agreement* (adaptability) was thirty-two percent, *reduced conflict* (communication) was twenty-three percent, *individual symptomatic improvement* was twenty-three percent, and *improved individual task performance* (adaptability) was twelve percent. It is interesting that all of the goals selected for this study except improved symptomatic improvement related to the cohesion, adaptability, and communication dimensions. Also, ninety percent of the respondents said that *all eight goals* were either of primary or secondary importance for some families. This study, like the one by Fisher and Sprenkle (1977), indicates the importance of these three dimensions as goals for family therapy.

In a recent book, Minuchin (1974) emphasized the importance of the disengaged-enmeshed continuum (cohesion dimension), but also devoted attention to family adaptation (adaptability dimension). Not only did Minuchin focus directly on these two dimensions in family therapy, but his comments about the dimensions are very congruent with those presented in the paper and will, therefore, be highlighted. He indicated that while many families tend toward enmeshed and disengaged subsystems at times in the family life cycle, such as an enmeshed mother-child relationship, the subsystems should move toward disengagement as the children grow older. However, systems that continue to function at the extremes of this dimension often have problems. He states:

> Operations at the extremes, however, indicate areas of possible pathology. A highly enmeshed subsystem of mother and children, for example, can exclude father, who becomes disengaged in the extreme. The resulting undermining of the children's independence might be an important factor in the development of symptoms. . . . Members of disengaged subsystems or families may function autonomously but have a skewed sense of independence and lack feelings of loyalty and belonging and the capacity for interdependence and for requesting support when needed. . . . Both types of relating cause family problems when adaptive mechanisms are evoked. (1974, p. 55)

In describing family adaptation, Minuchin (1974) indicated that stress often produces the need for family change. He believes that many families in treatment are simply going through transitions and need help in adapting to the new situations. "The label of pathology would be reserved for families who in the face of stress increase the rigidity of their transactional patterns and boundaries, and avoid or resist any exploration of alternative" (1974, p. 60). Stress could be produced because of external or internal pressures in the family. It usually occurs when new members are added to or dropped from the family system, or because of developmental changes in family members, such as when a child becomes an adolescent.

In conclusion, there are a growing number of studies that have found the two circumplex dimensions to be important for understanding marital and family systems. The earliest work by Angell (1936) and Hill (1949, 1953) also demonstrated the value of cross-classifying the dimensions to form family types. Their studies and more recent work by McCubbin, Boss, and colleagues demonstrated how these dimensions help to describe how families deal with stress. The empirical potency of these dimensions was demonstrated by the fact that they emerged as second-order factors in the Family Concept Test developed by van der Veen (1976). Variables related to the circumplex dimensions were found to be statistically discriminating in several large studies of family interaction conducted by Westley and Epstein (1969), Lewis et al. (1976), and Moos and Moos (1976). The value of these two dimensions to family therapists was specifically investigated by Fisher and Sprenkle (1977) and both emerged as useful for describing healthy family functioning and for goals in family therapy. A survey of family therapists (GAP, 1970) also found that variables related to these dimensions were important, and a well-known family therapist, Minuchin (1976), has integrated these two dimensions into his diagnostic and treatment program.

Empirical Studies Validating the Circumplex Model

The studies reviewed in the three previous sections have demonstrated the salience of the cohesion and adaptability dimensions in describing marital and family systems, discriminating between different groups of couples and families, and in planning and conducting marital and family therapy. While the analysis of the previous studies was post hoc, the studies reviewed in this section used the Circumplex Model as the theoretical base and specifically tested hypotheses derived from the Model.

The first study was done by Sprenkle and Olson (1978), in which they compared clinic and nonclinic couples on variables related to the adaptability dimension. Using the SIMFAM interaction game, they found that under stressful conditions, the nonclinic couples tended to share leadership whereas the clinic couples had a wife-leadership pattern. This and related findings demonstrated support for the curvilinear hypothesis that more balanced leadership (adaptability) was related to better marital functioning (see Hypothesis 1).

A second study by Russell (1979) focused on both dimensions and compared thirty-one families with female adolescents that were divided according to level of functioning (high and low). Using the SIMFAM game, she found that high-functioning families had moderate scores on both family adaptability and cohesion, while low-functioning families had extreme scores on these two dimensions. Placing the families into types based on the two dimensions, she found that all of the low-functioning families fell into the extreme areas. Most (ten of fifteen) of the high-functioning families fell into the central area, but no low-functioning families were in this central area. These findings generally supported the curvilinear hypothesis between family functioning and the circumplex dimensions.

One of the basic assumptions of the Circumplex Model is that the two dimensions in the model are independent. In two separate studies conducted by Russell (1978, 1979) which utilized self-report and behavioral measures of both cohesion and adaptability, factor analysis revealed that measures of these dimensions loaded on separate factors. Hence, the independence of the two dimensions was empirically demonstrated and validated.

The first study by Russell (1978) involved thirty family triads and used four behavioral measures of adaptability and one self-report measure. There was also one self-report and one behavioral measure of cohesion, family support, and family creativity. A factor analysis revealed that the first rotated factor contained all four behavioral measures of adaptability (average r = .77) and negative loadings (average r = .54) on the two family creativity measures, which is conceptually related to adaptability. The self-report measure of adaptability did not load on any factor. The second factor contained high loadings on both the self-report (r = .76) and behavioral (r = .75) measures of cohesion and a high loading (r = .75) on the behavioral measure of family support, which is conceptually related to cohesion.

The second study by Russell (1979) involved twenty family triads and similar measures of cohesions and adaptability in addition to some relevant measures from the Moss Family Environment Scale (1977). In this study, both the four behavioral measures of adaptability and the one self-report measure loaded on the first factor (average r = .73). The second factor contained the four self-report and the one behavioral measure of cohesion (average r = .53). As would be expected, the Moss Conflict scale correlated negatively (r = .68) with the cohesion dimension. In conclusion, this second analysis confirmed and replicated the findings of the first study and indicated the independence of the cohesion and adaptability dimensions.

Another recent study by Druckman (1979) considered the effectiveness of family-oriented treatment for adolescents. Twenty-nine families with female juvenile offenders were assessed using the Moss Family Environment Scale (1976) on the cohesion and adaptability dimensions before and after family-oriented treatment. As predicted by the model, families at pre-testing had low scores on family cohesion and high scores on adaptability. At post-testing, both program completers and dropouts became more moderate on both of these dimensions. Those with very high family cohesion had the highest rate of recidivism. In general, these findings offer support for the Model.

The most comprehensive test of the Circumplex Model is nearing completion in dissertations by Richard Bell and Joyce Portner, supervised by the first author. They are comparing families with runaways and families in family therapy to a control group of about one hundred families without problems. A self-report scale, *Family Adaptability and Cohesion Evaluation Scales* (FACES), was specifically developed to measure these dimensions. In addition, an interaction instrument called the *Inventory of Parent-Adolescent Conflict* (IPAC) was used to describe their style of communication. Both of these instruments were developed by the first author in collaboration with Bell and Portner (Olson et al., 1977, 1978). It is predicted that families with runaways and those in family therapy will be more extreme on both the adaptability and cohesion dimensions than the control group.

Clinical evidence of the value of the Circumplex Model in diagnosing and setting treatment goals for marital and family therapy will be described later in the paper.

CLINICAL APPLICATION OF CIRCUMPLEX MODEL

One of the major goals in developing the Circumplex Model was to provide a conceptual framework that could be used by marital and family therapists. More specifically, the Model was designed so that it could be used in diagnosis, in establishing treatment goals, and in assessing the effectiveness of the treatment program. The Model does *not* specify treatment techniques, since it is assumed that most techniques are atheoretical and should be chosen from those that the therapist has in his/her repertoire. Also, the Model assumes that the circumplex types are dynamic, can be changed, and are not as static or stable as personality types.

Diagnosis of Marital and Family Systems

There are basically two ways of making a diagnosis using the Circumplex Model: the clinical and/or the empirical approach. Both approaches rely on the variables related to the cohesion and adaptability dimensions. Table IV indicates the variables related to cohesion and how they are described at the four levels of cohesion. Table V lists the variables related to the adaptability dimension. In a *clinical assessment*, the therapist would rate the marital or family system on each of these variables based on interviews and direct observation. The *empirical assessment* would be based on some objective scale or interaction method

Table IV: Family Cohesion Dimension: Clinical and Research Indicators

	DISENGAGED *(Very Low)*	*SEPARATED* *(Low to Moderate)*	*CONNECTED* *(Moderate to High)*	*ENMESHED* *(Very High)*
Emotional Bonding	Very Low	Low to Moderate	Moderate to High	Very High
Independence	High independence of family members.	Moderate independence of family members.	Moderate dependence of family members.	High dependence of family members.
Family Boundaries	Open external boundaries. Closed internal boundaries. Rigid generational boundaries.	Semi-open external and internal boundaries. Clear generational boundaries.	Semi-open external boundaries. Open internal boundaries. Clear generational boundaries.	Closed external boundaries. Blurred internal boundaries. Blurred generational boundaries.
Coalitions	Weak coalitions, usually a family scapegoat.	Marital coalition clear.	Marital coalition strong.	Parent-child coalitions.
Time	Time apart from family maximized (physically and/or emotionally).	Time alone and together is important.	Time together is important. Time alone permitted for approved reasons.	Time together maximized. Little time alone permitted.
Space	Separate space both physically and emotionally is maximized.	Private space maintained; some family space.	Family space maximized. Private space minimized.	Little or no private space at home.
Friends	Mainly individual friends seen alone. Few family friends.	Some individual friends. Some family friends.	Some individual friends. Scheduled activities with couple and family friends.	Limited individual friends. Mainly couple or family friends seen together.
Decision-Making	Primarily individual decisions.	Most decisions are individually based, able to make joint decisions on family issues.	Individual decisions are shared. Most decisions made with family in mind.	All decisions, both personal and relationship, must be made by family.
Interests and Recreation	Primarily individual activities done without family. Family not involved.	Some spontaneous family activities. Individual activities supported.	Some scheduled family activities. Family involved in individual interests.	Most or all activities and interests must be shared with family.

Table V: Family Adaptability Dimensions: Clinical and Research Indicators

	Assertiveness	***Control***	***Discipline***	***Negotiation***	***Roles***	***Rules***	***System Feedback***
CHAOTIC (Very High)	Passive and Aggressive Styles	Limited leadership	Laissez faire Very lenient	Endless negotiation. Poor problem-solving	Dramatic role shifts	Dramatic rule shifts. Many implicit rules. Few explicit rules. Arbitrarily enforced rules.	Primarily positive loops; few negative loops
FLEXIBLE (High to Moderate)	Generally Assertive	Egalitarian with fluid changes	Democratic; Unpredictable Consequences	Good negotiation; good problem-solving	Role making and sharing. Fluid change of roles	Some rule changes. More implicit rules. Rules often enforced.	More positive than negative loops.
STRUCTURED (Moderate to Low)	Generally Assertive	Democratic with stable leader	Democratic; Predictable Consequences	Structured negotiations, good problem-solving	Some role sharing	Few rule changes. More explicit than implicit rules. Rules usually enforced.	More negative than positive loops.
RIGID (Very Low)	Passive or Aggressive Styles	Authoritarian leadership	Autocratic; Overly strict	Limited negotiations; Poor problem-solving	Role rigidity; Stereotyped roles.	Rigid rules; Many explicit rules. Few implicit rules. Strictly enforced rules.	Primarily negative loops; few positive loops.

that assessed the variables related to these dimensions. A variety of self-report and behavioral methods have been reviewed in the empirical studies related to the dimensions; however, none of them were specifically developed to assess all of these variables. Recently, the Family Adaptability and Cohesion Evaluation Scales (FACES) was specifically developed for this purpose and will be described later in greater detail.

In a *clinical* assessment on the cohesion and adaptability dimensions, the therapist would first need to interview and observe the couple or family. The session(s) would be conducted to provide information on the variables or indicators of cohesion and adaptability. In terms of cohesion, the therapist would determine how the system dealt with the following variables indicated in Table IV: *emotional bonding, independence, boundaries, coalitions, time, space, friends, decision-making, interest,* and *recreation.* In terms of adaptability, the therapist would identify the variables indicated in Table V: *assertiveness, control, discipline, negotiation style, role relationships, relationship rules,* and *system feedback.*

In the assessment, the therapist would need to look at how each member, each dyadic unit, other member combinations, and the entire system functions. As family size increases, the number of combinations (dyads, triads, tetrads, pentads, etc.) of family members makes the system even more complex (Lindsay, 1976). For example, while a three-person family has only three dyads and one triad, a six-member family would have fifteen dyads, twenty triads, fifteen tetrads, and one pentad–fifty-six total combinations.

It should be emphasized that *not* all combinations of family members within a family will be classified in the same manner. In fact, the unique groupings of members are rich sources of clinical information that can be used later in treatment. For example, Minuchin commented about a common family grouping where "A highly enmeshed sub-system of mother and children . . . can exclude father, who becomes disengaged in the extreme" (1974, p. 55).

Another factor that influences the complexity of marital and family systems is that they may function differently depending on the situation and kind of problem. In a post hoc analysis of conflict resolution styles in couples, Craddock (1977, 1978) found that one couple's predominant style changed when they dealt with religious issues. The couple was highly religious and in these areas both partners felt that the husband should be the authority. Their general style of dealing with problems reflected a democratic form power structure and role sharing. They also had balance on the cohesion dimension between autonomy and togetherness. As a result, they typically functioned as a *flexibly connected* couple (central area of model). However, when dealing with religious issues, such as their child's attendance at Sunday school, the husband became the authority and they demonstrated an extreme level of cohesiveness. They then functioned as a *rigidly enmeshed* couple. Because of the potential changes in systems in some situations, it is therefore important to learn of family interaction in a wide variety of situations.

Once the clinical observation is completed, the therapist needs to determine the *general system functioning* of the various combinations of family members on *each* of the *seven* variables of cohesion and the *nine* variables of adaptability. This more global assessment is used to classify the system at one of the four levels of cohesion (disengaged, separated, connected, enmeshed) and four levels of adaptability (rigid, structured, flexible, chaotic). Basically, if four or more of the seven ratings on adaptability fall on the *same* level, this would be considered the *modal* pattern for that system. It should be remembered, however, that this more global assessment might conceal some of the clinical richness revealed by the ratings. This additional information should be retained and used in the clinical intervention.

The therapist's assessment is certainly important, but it should be warned that this assessment might differ from each family member's own perception of their system. Also, these assessments might differ from a more empirical assessment using a self-report scale or behavioral task. There is considerable evidence that insiders' and outsiders' views of the same relationship may differ in both systematic and unsystematic ways, but these differences can be clinically and empirically useful (Olson, 1977).

Although a variety of self-report and/or behavioral instruments can be used to do an *empirical assessment,* we now will discuss a self-report scale that was specifically developed to measure each of the sixteen variables related to the cohesion (nine variables) and adaptability (seven variables) dimensions. The *Family Adaptability and Cohesion Evaluation Scales* (FACES) is a 111-item self-report instrument recently developed by Olson, Bell, and Portner (1978). There are six items for assessing each of the sixteen variables related to the model and a fifteen-item social desirability scale, making a total of 111 items in FACES. Each family member completes FACES in terms of his or her perception of the marital and family system. Each member, therefore, has a score on each of the sixteen variables, a total score in the two dimensions, and a social desirability score. These individual scores can then be plotted so that it is possible to compare family members. Couple or family scores can be obtained by summing individuals, and discrepancy scores can also be obtained between individuals. A scoring template enables one to hand-score FACES so that it can be more readily used for clinical diagnosis. A sample packet of FACES, which includes the materials and a manual describing its development and validity, can be obtained by writing to the first author.

Common Problems in Marital and Family Systems

The Circumplex Model enables one to focus on two central themes in marital and family dynamics that go beyond presenting symptoms. One theme (cohesion) is concerned with how much individual members want to be connected to each other versus how much they want to maintain their own autonomy. The second theme (adaptability) relates to how much they would like the system to change. Trying to handle or balance these two themes to satisfy all family members is one reason couples and families have problems. No matter what *type* of system within the Circumplex Model best describes the couple or family, if one person has highly discrepant expectations or behaviors from others in the system, there is strong likelihood that problems will develop.

To explore and further develop one of the hypotheses related to problems, let us consider Hypothesis 1b. Couples/families coming for counseling will tend to be extreme on either or both the cohesion and adaptability dimensions. One frequent problem with couples coming for counseling is that each spouse is at an *opposite extreme* on the *same* dimension. On the cohesion dimension, one partner might want more cohesion in the relationship, while the other person might want more autonomy and freedom. On the adaptability dimension, one partner might want more change in the system while the other wants it to stay the same. In this example, both are at opposite poles on each dimension and are unable to balance the extreme differences in their expectations and/or behaviors. Napier (1978) described in greater detail the struggle that divorcing couples often have in dealing with their conflicting needs for closeness and autonomy.

A second type of problem encountered by couples is when *both* partners are at the *same extreme* on one or both dimensions. On the cohesion dimension, they may both be disengaged or enmeshed. Disengaged couples spend so much energy doing "their own thing" that they have little to give each other. On the other hand, enmeshed couples are so invested in each other that they have little autonomy. Neither of these couples will necessarily have problems unless it is discrepant from what they want in the relationship.

As mentioned earlier, the complexity of diagnosis and placement of *all* family members within a type becomes more difficult as the number of family members increases. Also, as different sources and methods are used for the diagnosis (i.e., therapist's ratings, family members' perceptions, scores on objective measures), the richness of the diagnosis increases but the degree of agreement on the *type* of system decreases.

Unfortunately, there is no easy solution to this dilemma. However, it is maintained that this multi-method approach to diagnosis is generally advantageous since it enables the therapist to more adequately assess the richness and complexity of marital and family systems that have so often been elusive.

In conclusion, once the diagnostic assessment is completed, the therapist has information on the nine variables related to cohesion and the seven variables related to adaptability. Also, the therapist has placed the couple or family into one of the *sixteen types* indicated in Figure 1. It is possible that some of the dyadic subsystems in a family might occupy different regions in the Model. This information will enhance the complexity and, one hopes, the validity of the diagnosis.

Setting Treatment Goals and Treatment Strategies

Once the diagnosis is completed, the therapist is then ready to begin setting the treatment goals. Therapists vary in the extent to which they involve the couple or family in deciding on the goals of treatment. From the perspective of the Circumplex Model, several general guidelines are suggested. *First*, the couple or family should be consulted about how they would like to change in each dimension. *Second*, if a couple is extreme in one or both dimensions, it is suggested that the goal of treatment be to move them only *one* level toward the central area. It has been found that if a shift is attempted through more than one level in the dimension, the couple will either resist change or flip to the opposite extreme.

The therapist then needs to decide with the couple or family what dimension and what specific variables related to the dimension to work to change. The setting of the treatment *goals* is critical and often neglected. As Feldman stated:

> In many ways, the most important initial task for the family therapist is goal-setting. Unfortunately, this process is often not carried out. In too many instances, family therapists (especially beginning family therapists) start to "intervene" before having formulated (in conjunction with the family) a clear set of goals for the therapy. As a consequence, the therapy often gets bogged down, meanders aimlessly, or is precipitously terminated. (1976, p. 111)

While the Circumplex Model is designed to assist the therapist in making a diagnostic assessment and choosing treatment goals, it does *not* indicate what intervention techniques to use. Techniques, are for the most part, atheoretical and can be used regardless of the therapist's theoretical orientations. The therapist must, therefore, choose the techniques from his/her repertoire that seem most appropriate for achieving the specific goals. As Minuchin emphasized:

> Although different therapists might agree on a therapeutic goal for a particular family, their techniques for achieving that goal will vary. Therapists, having individual personalities and skills, develop idiosyncratic ways of relating. They can use themselves better if they learn to know and accept their own styles. (1974, p. 256)

TREATMENT OF A CHEMICALLY DEPENDENT FAMILY SYSTEM

In order to illustrate the use of the Circumplex Model in the diagnosis and treatment of a chemically dependent family, a case study of the Davis family will be presented. This family system was diagnosed as *rigidly enmeshed* (extreme on both dimensions) and the treatment plan focused on changing the system to being *structurally connected,* which is in the central area of the model. This was accomplished by working on two variables on each of the cohesion and adaptability dimensions. The diagnostic assessment of the family systematically goes through the variables for both dimensions indicated in Tables IV and V. Although multiple-family therapy was initially used with this family, more progress was made when intervention shifted to marital therapy.

This case study is one of four that are more fully described in a more comprehensive paper on family therapy with chemically dependent families written by Killorin and Olson (1978). One interesting finding in that paper was that even though all four families had the same presenting problem—that is, one alcoholic member—the diagnosis indicated that they all had different family systems within the Circumplex Model. While they were all extreme on both dimensions, they fell at different extremes and represented all the extreme types: rigidly enmeshed, rigidly disengaged, chaotically enmeshed, and chaotically disengaged. This demonstrates the importance of diagnosis based on some theoretical model rather than on the basis of the presenting symptom. This finding raises some questions about treatment programs that use the same approach for all cases with the same presenting symptoms. It is proposed that a more pragmatic approach would be to design treatment programs related to types of families and their unique potentials.

The Davis Family: A Rigidly Enmeshed System

The Davis family is composed of parents Mary and Don, 18-year-old Ann, 16-year-old Julie, and 9-year-old Peter. Mary is chemically dependent. Her chemical use functioned to relieve her feelings of inadequacy in a family where the husband and oldest daughter are high achievers. Mary was consoled by daughter Julie, who also felt inadequate and maintained enough responsibility to over-mother the youngest child, Peter. Don went along with her drinking because it allowed him to feel more responsible as she became less so. He did not miss an intimate relationship as he never had one with her and feared any closeness to his wife. The family came for therapy shortly after Mary began treatment for chemical dependency. Ann had left the home, being very angry at her mother. Julie was painfully trying to find a place in the family as her mother no longer needed her for support.

On the cohesion dimension, the Davis family showed *high emotional bonding* as well as high mutual dependency. Mary, Ann, and Julie were in intense conflict for approval from each other and from Don. Youngest child Peter was quietly, but painfully, seen as keeping the connection between Julie and the rest of the family intact. *Internal boundaries* were blurred. Members sought to have one another meet their needs but did not know how to do so. Intense conflict arose as they fought to get approval from one another. The *external boundary* was closed in the sense that others were not allowed to freely interact outside the family. Julie's attempt to connect with the therapist was angrily rejected by the rest of the family.

The *parental coalitions* were strong but the *marital coalition* was weak. Parents were unable to achieve intimacy with each other. Their only point of connection was to argue and/or band together in the face of misbehavior from one of the children. Father-daughter coalitions between Don and Julie and Don and Ann were strong. Also, the mother-son coalition was strong as Mary continued to protect Peter. Oldest child Ann was given a lot of parental power, especially in setting rules and providing consequences to sister Julie. The father-daughter coalition of Don and Ann in a real sense operated as the parental unit.

The variables of *time, space, friends, interests,* and *recreation* all emphasized extreme togetherness. Individual activities were permitted but only within family-approved guidelines. Tennis was an approved outlet; Ann and Don spent a lot of time away from the family with this activity. Julie's desire to spend the same amount of time "partying" with her friends was seen as without purpose and thus was not approved. Intimate friendships were not allowed. The family worked at having fun at their cabin on weekends and all members were expected to go. The result was that none of them enjoyed the experience. Each had separate space at home but borrowed one another's possessions, which caused much family conflict. Mary insisted the home was mutual space and demanded that everyone feel responsible about sticking to her extremely high standards of housekeeping.

Likewise, while the system did permit some individual *decisions,* especially by Don and Ann, others were prohibited. Julie's individual decisions were not supported by the family. Mary made no individual decisions as she felt incapable of it. Peter was seen by the family as too young to make responsible age-appropriate choices. Thus, while family behavior showed a moderately high range of connectedness, the emotional climate seemed to demand extreme connectedness or enmeshment.

Much of the conflict in this family seems due to their low level of *adaptability*. The system, as well as individual members, suffers from too much *rigidity* as the response to a chemically dependent parent, while two teenagers seek developmentally appropriate independence. At the time of therapy, no one knew how to be *assertive*. Requests were not made but demanded in an aggressive fashion. Parents traded positions of passivity and aggression with each other and with the children. Ann was aggressive when anyone got close to her. Julie attempted to be passive in order to gain approval and then would erupt aggressively. Peter remained passive and dependent. *Control* was authoritarian and traditional. Don was looked to as the rule enforcer. He kept his place in the family by remaining passive. When things got out of hand, *discipline* was enforced in an overly strict fashion. Mary tended to impose consequences that were excessively harsh but were not followed. *Negotiation* was limited by angry outbursts after just a few minutes and then Don or Ann would cut it off by walking away. *Roles* were rigid and stereotyped. Mary saw herself as in charge of the house and wanted Don to be boss with the children. *Rules* were arbitrary and, although somewhat reasonable, consequences were strict. Defiance against the rigidity was met with increasingly severe consequences. Many rules were implicit and consequences given for not following through when one should have known what was expected. Thus, while the rules, roles, and leadership format may have been reasonable, the rigidity of the format and the lack of an ability to communicate and negotiate the individual desires for change, especially by Ann and Julie, caused the system to be dysfunctionally rigid. The Davises were thus seen as *rigidly enmeshed*.

Goals and Treatment Plan

Attempts to intervene with this system could be made on several variables. It seemed most therapeutic to focus on those issues where the family was already indicating some movement. On the cohesion dimension, the goal was to increase the level of individual autonomy and strengthen the marital dyad. In terms of adaptability, the family was taught negotiation skills and was helped to make roles and rules less rigid. Because the family occupies an extreme position in both dimensions, helping the system to move to a central level in either the adaptability or the cohesion dimension would presumably increase their ability to function.

When the family as a whole was discharged from multiple-family group at their request, Mary and Don continued in marriage counseling, and then dramatic shifts began to occur. On the *cohesion* variable, we see many attempts at individual expression of unique personal interests. Although the system was not supportive of its members, the members were capable of some individual expression and were strongly encouraged. As the *marital coalition* strengthened, the children's need to fight diminished. It became less necessary for Julie and Ann to struggle for a position in coalition with Dad as Mary took back her place in that position. As Mary became more secure in her relationship with Don, she could be more supportive of Julie's individuality as well as her own. The family was free to separate and connect more freely.

Because of the ages of the two oldest children, it seemed appropriate to help the family become more adaptable. Teaching them how to communicate increased their *negotiation* skills. They were then able to handle a family discussion and to relax the roles, rules, and consequences so that each person felt heard and responded to. The structure, which had previously been rigid, became more flexible and it was then met with less defiance. The parents were able to clarify rules and establish consequences which were more situationally appropriate. A *rigidly enmeshed* family became *structurally connected.*

* Funding for work on the theoretical and empirical aspects of this project was provided to the first author by the Agricultural Experiment Station at the University of Minnesota. The first author wishes to thank the following colleagues who have made constructive suggestion which have helped in clarifying and expanding this model: Carlfred Broderick, Larry Constantine, Alan Craddock, James Hawkins, Reuben Hill, and Paul Rosenblatt. Special thanks to Elinor Killorin for her assistance in modifying Tables IV and V and to Garth Rockcastle for designing Figure 1.

REFERENCES

Alexander, J. F., & Barton, C. Behavioral systems therapy for families. In D. H. Olson (Ed.), *Treating relationships.* Lake Mills, Iowa: Graphic Publishing, 1976.

Angell, R. *The family encounters the depression.* New York: Charles Scribner & Sons, 1936.

Bahr, S. J., & Rollins, B. C. Crises and conjugal power. *Journal of Marriage and the Family,* 1971, *33,* 360–367.

Balswick, J. O., & Macrides, C. Parental stimulus for adolescent rebellion. *Adolescence,* 1975, *10,* 253–266.

Becker, J., & Iwakami, E. Conflict and cominance within families of disturbed children. *Journal of Abnormal Psychology,* 1969, *74,* 330–335.

Bell, J. C. Recent advances in family group therapy. *Journal of Child Psychology and Psychiatry,* 1962, *2,* 1–15.

Bell, N. W., & Vogel, E. F. *The family.* Glencoe, Ill.: Free Press, 1960.

Bell, R. Parent-adolescent interaction in runaway families. Unpublished doctoral dissertation, University of Minnesota, St. Paul, 1980.

Benjamin, Lorna S. Structural analysis of a family in therapy. *Journal of Counseling and Clinical Psychology,* 1977, *45,* 391–406.

——— Structural analysis of social behavior. *Psychological Review,* 1974, *81,* 392–425.

Birchler, G., Weiss, R., & Vincent, J. Multimethod analysis of social reinforcement exchange between maritally distressed and non-distressed spouse and stranger dyads. *Journal of Personality and Social Psychology,* 1975, *31,* 349–360.

Boss, P., McCubbin, H., & Lester, G. The corporate executive wife's copying patterns in response to routine husband-father absence: Implications for family stress theory. *Family Process.* In press.

Bowen, M. The family as the unit of study and treatment. *American Journal of Orthopsychiatry,* 1961, *30,* 346.

Broderick, C. B., Williams, P., & Krager, H. Family process and child outcomes. In W. Burr, R. Hill, I. Nye, & I. L. Reiss (Eds.), *Contemporary theories about the family.* New York: Free Press, 1979.

Constantine, L. A verified system theory of human process. Paper presented at University of Minnesota, Family Social Science, October, 1977.

Craddock, A. E. Marital problem solving as a function of couple's marital power expectations and marital value system. Unpublished manuscript, 1978.

——— Social influence and conflict within the marital dyad. Unpublished doctoral dissertation, University of Sydney, Australia, 1977.

Cromwell, R. E., & Olson, D. H. (Eds.). *Power in families.* New York: John Wiley and Halsted Press, 1975.

Cromwell, R. E., Olson, D. H., & Fournier, D. G. Diagnosis and evaluation in marital and family counseling. In D. H. Olson (Ed.), *Treating relationships.* Lake Mills, Iowa: Graphic Publishing, 1976.

Druckman, J. A. Family oriented policy and treatment program for juvenile status offenders. *Journal of Marriage and the Family.* In press.

Epstein, N. B., Bishop, D. S., & Levin, S. The McMaster model of family functioning. *Journal of Marriage and Family Counseling,* 1978, *40,* 19–31.

Epstein, N. B., & Santa-Barbara, J. Interpersonal perceptions and stable outcomes of conflict behavior in clinical couples. *Family Process,* 1975, *14,* 51–66.

Farina, A., & Dunham, R. M. Measurement of family relationships and their effects. *Archives of General Psychiatry,* 1963, *9,* 64–73.

Feldman, L. B. Goals of family therapy. *Journal of Marriage and Family Counseling,* 1976, *2,* 103–113.

Fisher, B. L., & Sprenkle, D. H. Assessment of healthy family functioning and its relation to goals of family therapy. Unpublished manuscript, Purdue University, 1977.

Framo, J. L. (Ed.). Family interaction: A dialogue between family researchers and family therapists. New York: Springer Publishing, 1972.

French, A. P., & Guidera, B. J. The family as a system in four dimensions: A theoretical model. Paper presented at American Academy of Child Psychiatry, San Francisco, 1974.

Glueck, S., & Glueck, E. *Unraveling juvenile delinquency.* Cambridge, Mass.: Harvard University Press, 1950.

Goetzel, V. Mental illness and cultural beliefs in a southern italian immigrant family. *Canadian Psychiatric Association Journal,* 1973, *18,* 219–222.

Goldstein, H. K., & Kling, F. The measurement of family solidarity. Unpublished manuscript, Florida State University, 1975.

Group for the Advancement of Psychiatry. *Treatment of families in conflict.* New York: Science House, 1970.

Guerney, L. F. Filial therapy program. In D. H. Olson (Ed.), *Treating relationships.* Lake Mills, Iowa: Graphic Publishing, 1976.

Gurman, Alan S., & Kniskern, D. P. Research in marital and family therapy: Empirical, clinical and conceptual issues. In S. L. Garfield & A. E. Bergin (Eds.), *Handbook of psychotherapy and behavior change* (Revised Edition). New York: Wiley, 1978.

Haley, J. Family experiments: A new type of experimentation. *Family Process*, 1962, *1*, 265–293.

——— *Strategies of psychotherapy*. New York: Grune and Stratton, 1963.

——— Research on family patterns: An instrument measurement. *Family Process*, 1964, *3*, 41–65.

———Experiment with abnormal families. Testing done in a restricted communication setting. *Archives of General Psychiatry*, 1967, *17*, 53–63.

Hawkins, J. L. A measure of marital cohesion. Unpublished manuscript, University of Minnesota, 1968.

Hill, R. *Families under stress*. New York: Harper, 1949.

——— Modern systems theory and the family: A confrontation. *Social Science Information*, 1971, *10*, 7–26.

Hill, R., & Rodgers, R. The developmental approach. In H. T. Christensen (Ed.), *Handbook of marriage and the family*. Chicago: Rand McNally, 1969.

Hill, R. J., Moss, J., & Wirths, C. G. *Eddyville's families*. Chapel Hill, North Carolina: University of North Carolina, 1953.

Hunt, D. G. Parental permissiveness as perceived by the offspring and the degree of marijuana usage among offspring. *Human Relations*, 1974, *27*, 267–285.

Jackson, D. The question of family homeostasis. *Psychiatry Quarterly*, 1957, *31*, 79–90.

——— Family rules. *Archives of General Psychiatry*, 1965, *12*, 589–594.

Jackson, D. D., & Weakland, J. H. Conjoint family therapy: Some considerations on theory, technique and results. *Psychiatry*, 1961, *24*, 30–45.

Jacob, T. Family interaction in disturbed and normal families: A methodological and substantive review. *Psychological Bulletin*, 1975, *82*, 33–65.

Kantor, D., & Lehr, W. *Inside the family*. San Francisco: Jossey-Bass, 1975.

Kieren, D., & Tallman, I. Spousal adaptability: An assessment of marriage competence. *Journal of Marriage and the Family*, 1972, *34*, 247–256.

Killorin, E., & Olson, D. H. Clinical application of the circumplex model to chemically dependent families. Unpublished manuscript, 1980.

Kohn, M. *Class and conformity*. Homewood, Ill.: The Dorsey Press, 1969.

Leary, T. *Interpersonal diagnosis of personality*. New York: Ronald Press, 1957.

——— *Interpersonal diagnosis of personality*. New York: Ronald Press, 1957.

Lennard, H., Beaulieu, M., & Embrey, N. Interaction in families with a schizophrenic child. *Archives of General Psychiatry*, 1965, *12*, 166–183.

Lennard, H., & Bernstein, A. *Patterns in human interaction*. San Francisco, Calif.: Jossey-Bass, 1969.

Levinger, G. Marital cohesiveness and dissolution: An integrative review. *Journal of Marriage and the Family*, 1965, *27*, 19–38.

Lewis, J. M., Beavers, W. R., Gossert, J. T., & Phillips, V. A. *No single thread: Psychological health in family systems*. New York: Brunner/Mazel, 1976.

Lidz, T., Cornelison, A. R., Fleck, S., & Terry, D. The interfamilial environment of schizophrenic patients. *American Journal of Psychiatry*, 1957, *114*, 241–248.

Lindsay, J. S. B. Balance theory: Possible consequences of number of family members. *Family Process*, 1976, *15*, 245–249.

McCubbin, H. Integrating copying behavior in family stress theory. *Journal of Marriage and the Family*. In press.

McCubbin, H., Boss, P., Wilson, L., & Lester, G. Developing family invulnerability to stress: Coping strategies wives employ in managing separation. In Jan Trost (Ed.), *Proceedings: World congress of sociology*. Beverly Hills: Sage, 1979.

McCubbin, H., Dahl, B., Lester, G., & Ross. The returned prisoner of war: Factors in family reintegration. *Journal of Marriage and the Family,* 1975, *37,* 471–478.

McCubbin, H., & Lester, G. Coping behaviors in the management of the dual stressors of family separation and reunion. Paper presented at the Military Family Research Conference, San Diego, Calif., September, 1977.

McCubbin, H., Barbara, B., Dahl, B., Lester, G., Benson, D., & Robertson, M. Coping repertoires of wives adapting to prolonged war-induced separations. *Journal of Marriage and the Family,* 1976, *38,* 461–471.

Miller, D., & Westman, J. Family teamwork and psychotherapy. *Family Process,* 1966, *5,* 49–59.

Miller, S., Nunnally, E. W., & Wackman, D. Minnesota couples communication program: Premarital and marital groups. In D. H. Olson (Ed.), *Treating relationships.* Lake Mills, Iowa: Graphic Publishing, 1976.

Minuchin, S. *Families and family therapy.* Cambridge, Mass.: Harvard University Press, 1974.

Minuchin, S., Rosman, B. L., & Baker, L. *Psychosomatic families.* Cambridge, Mass.: Harvard University Press, 1978.

Minuchin, S., Montalvo, B., Guerney, B. G., Rossman, B. L., & Schumer, F. *Families of the slums.* New York: Basic Books, 1967.

Mishler, E., & Waxler, N. *Interaction in families.* New York: John Wiley, 1968.

Moos, R., & Moos, B. A typology of family social environments. *Family Process,* 1976, *15,* 357–371.

Napier, A. Y. The rejection-intrusion pattern: Central family dynamic. *Journal of Marriage and Family Counseling,* 1978, *4,* 5–12.

Novak, A. L., & Van der Veen, F. Family concepts and emotional disturbance in the families of disturbed adolescents with normal siblings. *Family Process,* 1970, *9,* 157–171.

Nye, F. I. *Role structure and analysis of the family.* Beverly Hills: Sage Publications, 1976.

O'Connor, W., & Stachowiak, J. Patterns of interaction in families with high adjusted, low adjusted and mentally retarded members. *Family Process,* 1971, *10,* 229–241.

Olson, D. H. Bridging research, theory and application: The triple threat in science. In D. H. Olson (Ed.), *Treating relationships.* Lake Mills, Iowa: Graphic Publishing, 1976.

——— Marital and family therapy: Integrative review and critique. *Journal of Marriage and the Family,* 1970, *32,* 501–538.

——— Empirically unbinding the double bind: Review of research and conceptual reformulations. *Family Process,* 1972, *11,* 69–94.

——— Insiders' and outsiders' view of relationships: Research strategies. In G. Levinger & H. Raush (Eds.), *Close relationships.* Amherst, Mass.: University of Massachusetts Press, 1977.

Olson, D. H., Portner, J., & Bell, R. Inventory of parent-adolescent conflict (IPAC). Unpublished manuscript, 1978.

Olson, D. H., Bell, R., & Portner, J. Family adaptability and cohesion evaluation scales (FACES). Unpublished manuscript, 1978.

Olson, D. H., Sprenkle, D., & Russell, C. Circumplex model of marital and family systems I: Cohesion and adaptability dimensions, family types and clinical applications. *Family Process,* 1979, *14,* 1–35.

Oxford, J., Oppenheimer, E., Egert, S., Hensman, C., & Guthrie, S. The cohesiveness of alcoholism-complicated marriages and its influence on treatment outcome. *British Journal of Psychiatry,* 1976, *128,* 318–339.

Parsons, T., & Bales, R. F. *Family socialization and interaction process.* Glencoe, Ill.: Free Press, 1955.

Patterson, G. R. Parents and teachers as change agents: A social learning approach. In D. H. Olson (Ed.), *Treating relationships*. Lake Mills, Iowa: Graphic Publishing, 1976.

Patterson, G. et al. Interpersonal skills training for couples in early stages of conflict. *Journal of Marriage and the Family*, 1975, *37*, 295–302.

Portner, J. Parent-adolescent interaction of families in treatment. Unpublished doctoral dissertation, University of Minnesota, St. Paul, 1980.

Rappoport, R. Normal crises, family structure and mental health. *Family Process*, 1962, *2*, 68–79.

Reiss, D. Varieties of consensual experience. I. A theory for relating family interaction to individual thinking. *Family Process*, 1971, *10*, 1–27. (a)

——— Varieties of consensual experience. II. Dimensions of a family's experience of its environment. *Family Process*, 1971, *10*, 28–35. (b)

Riskin, J. M., & Faunce, E. E. Family interaction scales III: Discussion of methodology and substantive findings. *Archives of General Psychiatry*, 1970, *22*, 527–537.

Rollins, B. C., & Thomas, D. L. A theory of parental power and child compliance. In R. C. Cromwell & D. H. Olson (Eds.), *Power in families*. New York: Halsted and John Wiley, 1975.

Rosenblatt, P., & Budd, L. Territoriality and privacy in married and unmarried cohabiting couples. *The Journal of Social Psychology*, 1975, *97*, 67–76.

Rosenblatt, P. C., & Cunningham, M. R. Television watching and family tensions. *Journal of Marriage and the Family*, 1976, *38*, 105–111.

Rosenblatt, P. C., Nevaldine, A., & Titus, S. L. Farm families: Relation of significant attributes of farming to family interaction. *International Journal of Sociology of the Family*, 1972, *8*, 89–99.

Rosenblatt, P., & Russell, M. The social psychology of potential problems in family vacation travel. *Family Coordinator*, 1975, *24*, 209–215.

Rosenblatt, P. C., & Titus, S. L. Together and apart in the family. *Humanities*, 1976, *12*, 367–379.

Rosenblatt, P. C., Titus, S. L., Nevaldine, A., & Cunningham, M. R. Togetherness-apartness and tensions in marriages of elementary and high school teachers with summer-long vacation. *International Journal of Family Counseling*, 1979. (a)

Rosenblatt, P. C., Titus, S. L., & Cunningham, M. R. Disrespect, tension, and togetherness-apartness in marriage. *Journal of Marriage and Family Counseling*, 1979. (b)

Russell, C. A methodological study of family cohesion and adaptability. *Journal of Marriage and Family Counseling*, 1979.

——— A factor analysis of family cohesion and adaptability scales. Unpublished manuscript, 1978.

——— Circumplex model of marital and family systems III: Empirical evaluation of families. *Family Process*, 1978, *18*, 29–45.

Sandberg, N. et al. Family cohesiveness and autonomy of adolescents in India and the United States. *Journal of Marriage and the Family*, 1969, *31*, 403–407.

Schvaneveldt, J. D. Mormon adolescents: Likes and dislikes toward parents and home. *Adolescents*, 1973, *8*, 171–178.

Scott, R. D., & Askworth, P. L. Closure at the first schizophrenic breakdown: A family study. *British Journal of Medical Psychology*, 1967, *40*, 109–145.

Speer, D. Family systems: Morphostasis and morphogenesis, or is homeostasis enough? *Family Process*, 1970, *9*, 259–278.

Sprenkle, D. The need for integration among theory, research and practice in the family field. *Family Coordinator*, 1976, *25*, 261–263.

Sprenkle, D., & Olson, D. H. Circumplex model of marital systems IV: Empirical study of clinic and non-clinic couples. *Journal of Marriage and Family Counseling,* 1978, *4,* 59–74.

Stein, H. F. The Slovak-American "swaddling ethos": Homeostat for family dynamics and cultural continuity. *Family Process,* 1978, *17,* 31–45.

Stierlin, H. *Separating parents and adolescents.* New York: Quadrangle, 1974.

Straus, M. Power and support structure of the family in relation to socialization. *Journal of Marriage and the Family,* 1964, *26,* 318–326.

——— Communication, creativity, and problem solving ability of middle-and-working-class families in three societies. Reprinted in M. Sussman (Ed.), *Sourcebook in marriage and the family,* (3rd ed.). Boston: Houghton Mifflin, 1968.

Strodtbeck, F. Family interaction, values, and achievement. In D. McClelland et al (Eds.), *Talent and society.* Princeton: D. Van Nostrand, 1958.

Stuart, R. B. An operant interpersonal program for couples. In D. H. Olson (Ed.), *Treating relationships.* Lake Mills, Iowa: Graphic Publishing, 1976.

Tallman, I. The family as a small problem solving group. *Journal of Marriage and the Family,* 1970, *32,* 94–104.

Tallman, I., & Miller, G. Class differences in family problem solving: The effects of verbal ability, hierarchical structure, and role expectations. *Sociometry,* 1974, *37,* 13–37.

Van der Veen, F. Content dimensions of the family concept test and their relation to childhood disturbance. Unpublished manuscript, Institute for Juvenile Research, Chicago, 1976.

——— The parent's concept of the family unit and child adjustment. *Journal of Counseling Psychology,* 1965, *12,* 196–200.

Vincent, J. P., Weiss, R. L., & Birchler, G. R. A behavioral analysis of problem solving in distressed and nondistressed married and stranger dyads. *Behavior Therapy,* 1975, *6,* 475–487.

Von Bertalanffy, L. *General systems theory.* New York: Braziller, 1968.

Weiss, Robert L. The conceptualization of marriage from a behavioral perspective. In T. J. Paolino & B. S. McCardy (Eds.), *Marriage and marital therapy.* New York: Brunner/Mazel, Inc., 1978.

Weiss, R., Birchler, G., & Vincent, J. Contractual models for negotiation training in marital dyads. *Journal of Marriage and the Family,* 1974, *36,* 321–330.

Wertheim, E. Family unit therapy and the science and typology of family systems. *Family Process,* 1973, *12,* 361–376.

——— The science and typology of family systems II. Further theoretical and practical considerations. *Family Process,* 1975, *14,* 285–308.

Westley, W. A., & Epstein, N. B. *Silent minority: Families of emotionally healthy college students.* San Francisco: Jossey-Bass, 1969.

Wheaton, B. Interpersonal conflict and cohesiveness in dyadic relationships. *Sociometry,* 1974, *37,* 328–348.

Williams, A. Behavioral interaction in married couples. Unpublished doctoral dissertation, Gainesville, Fla.: University of Florida, 1977.

Winter, W. D., & Ferreira, A. J. Interaction process analysis of family decision making. *Family Process,* 1967, *6,* 155–165.

Wittmer, J. Amish homogeneity of parental behavior characteristics. *Human Relations,* 1973, *26,* 143–154.

Wynne, L. et al. Pseudo-mutuality in the family relations of schizophrenics. *Psychiatry,* 1958, *21,* 205–222.

RECIPROCITY AND DOMINANCE IN MARITAL INTERACTION

Gwendolyn Mettetal, UNIVERSITY OF ILLINOIS

John M. Gottman, UNIVERSITY OF ILLINOIS

In a recent paper on social communication, von Cranach and Vine (1973) described what they called the "Structural Approach" to the study of communication. In their review, they listed the "theoretical commitments" of the structural approach, which included the following: (1) communication is governed by rules and these rules are the topic of investigation (2) all behavior is communicative and (3) "the relations between parts of the system are not probabilistic but deterministic" (p. 3). Von Cranach and Vine never defined the term "structure" very carefully; it remains an attractive, technological-age metaphor.

Advances in Family Intervention, Assessment and Theory, Volume 1, pages 181–228.

ISBN: 0-89232-137-7

By the term "structure" we mean *constraint,* particularly temporal constraint, imposed on both behavior between individuals and behavior within an individual over time. The goal of detecting structure, pattern, and social rules in the stream of social behavior is a venerable objective. In this chapter, we will consider two elements in the structure of social interaction that often have been proposed as central to the discovery of social rules, namely, reciprocity and dominance.

The approach we take is, in some ways, directly opposite to that which von Cranach and Vine (1973) referred to as the "Structural Approach." Our approach is that *not all behavior is communicative,* and, furthermore, that *social relationships are characterized by probabilistic rules;* in fact, we hold that *the stream of behavior is best viewed as a stochastic process, the parameters of which we will attempt to estimate.*

Our approach is not new. In fact, it has been applied fruitfully in ethological research. In this research tradition, behavior X by organism A is considered to have social communicative value if it reduces uncertainty in predicting a subsequent behavior Y by organism B. The stream of behavior is thus seen as a code that we are attempting to break; we search for repetitive patterns. Once we find these patterns, we attempt to summarize them succinctly.

The theoretical model for any type of relationship ought to be able to discriminate between extreme examples of that type of relationship, such as the well and the poorly functioning. Reciprocity and dominance are two important aspects of all relationships, especially intense, long-term relationships such as marriage. This paper presents a new formulation of these concepts and describes a series of studies by Gottman and his associates that tests the reciprocity and dominance hypotheses in his *Structural Model* of marital interaction.

The first section reviews the literature on previous concepts of reciprocity and dominance in social and clinical psychology. There have been numerous definitions of these terms and, consequently, a range of methods for studying them. We have reconceptualized both reciprocity and dominance in terms of sequential connections. Subsequent sections describe the methodology used in the Gottman research (in particular, those studies using observational methods), its content and affect coding systems, their reliability, and the data analysis techniques which were used. The Structural Model of marital interaction is presented, each of the studies on marital interaction is described briefly, the results on reciprocity and dominance are reported, and all are summarized across studies. Finally, the advantages of the research methods are noted, their limitations are discussed, and some hypotheses concerning the causes of reciprocity and dominance are presented.

I. HISTORY AND DEFINITION OF RECIPROCITY AND DOMINANCE

A. Reciprocity

Reciprocity could be loosely defined as "Doing unto others as they have done unto you." This slight, perhaps cynical, rewording of the Golden Rule seems to cover the basic concept of reciprocity as seen by the lay public and by the social sciences. In other words, if people have done something positive to you, do something positive to them. But, if they have done something negative to you, do something negative to them.

1. Research in Reciprocity. *a. The social psychology tradition.* In the fields of sociology and social psychology, reciprocity is described as a norm that guides people's interactions with family, friends, and strangers. This norm was first described by the sociologist Gouldner (1960), who said that it was a universal norm. Two forms of the norm were described: the strong form, which says we must *help* those who have helped us; and the weaker form, which says we must not *hurt* those who have helped us. This imposes an obligation, which is contingent upon the other person's actions. Gouldner described the reciprocity norm as an "all-purpose moral cement" that keeps the powerless from being exploited.

The experimental investigation of the reciprocity norm conducted by social psychologists focused on how the norm operates among strangers. Instead of being studied as an independent topic, reciprocity usually has been studied as one of the causes of altruism and cooperation. For this reason, most studies have looked only at the reciprocity of positive behaviors in strangers, rather than reciprocity of behaviors in long-term relationships such as marriage.

An example of a study that examined the effects of the reciprocity norm on altruism is an investigation with children by Staub and Sherk (1970). Two children listened to a tape-recorded story; one of the children had been given some candy that could either be shared or kept. Later in the session, the children were asked to draw a picture, and the child who had *not* been given candy was given the only crayon. As the reciprocity norm predicted, the more the first child shared the candy, the more likely the second child was to share the crayon. When the candy was not shared, neither was the crayon. While this study allowed face to face contact, there is another group of studies that placed strangers in situations allowing little or no communication.

The effects of reciprocity in a minimal contact situation have been assessed using the Prisoner's Dilemma paradigm. In the Prisoner's Dilemma game, an operationalization of Thibaut and Kelley's behavior exchange theory (1959), each member of a dyad must decide whether or not to cooperate with the other person for mutually high payoffs, or to defect, with the possibility of winning a very high payoff at the partner's expense. Subjects are usually instructed not to communicate in any way and are often playing against a confederate who has been instructed to use a certain strategy. Oskamp (1971) reviewed the effects of various programmed strategies on cooperation. The most effective strategy seems to be "tit for tat," or *quid pro quo*. In this strategy, the confederate always reciprocates the subject's previous choice—if the subject cooperated, then the confederate cooperates, but if the subject defected, the confederate defects. With this strategy, the subject soon begins to pick cooperative choices, knowing that the confederate will match them. This contingent strategy produces significantly more cooperation than either free play (no set strategy) or a noncontingent strategy having the same level of cooperation.

These studies indicate that, even among strangers, there is reciprocity of altruism and cooperation. Another group of studies examined reciprocity of a different nature—the reciprocity of self-disclosures among strangers. For example, Jourard and Jaffe (1970) paired subjects with confederates who varied the length of their self-disclosures. Subjects tended to speak for a long time if their confederate spoke for a long time and to speak for a short time when the confederate spoke for a short time. These results were interpreted as a form of reciprocity in self-disclosure. Worthy et al. (1969) had subjects exchange notes in a free exchange situation—that is, the experimenter did not introduce any manipulations or restrictions. The notes were then coded for the degree of intimacy of the topics mentioned. In this study, too, there was evidence of reciprocity in the disclosures. Subjects disclosed more intimate information to those who had previously disclosed such information to them.

In Altman's (1973) review, he concluded that the reciprocity of self-disclosure was reasonably well confirmed, but that most research was descriptive and not explanatory. He proposed a model of the reciprocity of interpersonal exchange in which initial trust leads to trial disclosure, which is followed by positive outcomes and the strengthening of trust, which leads to more disclosure, and so on. He hypothesized a maximum of reciprocity in early stages of relationships and when superficial, nonintimate topics are being discussed, as in the typical reciprocity of disclosure experiment. However, he did not expect to find reciprocity of disclosure in long-term, committed relationships (such as marriages).

In summary, the social psychology literature has shown evidence for the operation of a norm of reciprocity among strangers. This norm seems to operate on such diverse behaviors as sharing toys, cooperating in a game, and disclosing information about oneself. However, these findings are limited to the behaviors of strangers during brief encounters and may not be applicable to the marital dyad.

b. The clinical psychology tradition. Clinical psychologists, operating primarily from a social learning perspective, have used a different strategy for investigating the operation of reciprocity. Because social learning theory holds that positive reciprocity is indicative of good relationships and that negative reciprocity is indicative of poor relationships (Azrin, Naster, and Jones, 1973; Lederer and Jackson, 1968; Rappaport and Harrell, 1972; Stuart, 1969; Weiss, Hops, and Patterson, 1973), clinical research has concentrated on ongoing relationships, such as those in families. The clinical research tradition differs from the social psychology in another fundamental way—while the social tradition examines a single instance of reciprocal behavior, the clinical tradition is more likely to examine long-term interaction, in which several instances of reciprocal behavior might occur. To accomplish this, much of the clinical literature employs an observational methodology, in which the interactions of people are observed over some time span.

For example, Patterson and Reid (1973) observed seven families, each with a problem child. During a two-week observation period, the families' interactions were coded according to the behavior emitted and the consequences of that behavior. In three of the seven families, there were significant differences in the number of social reinforcers given to the various family members. Mothers tended to give the largest number of social reinforcers and fathers the smallest. The deviant children in the families seemed to receive the greatest share of these reinforcers. Patterson and Reid, who defined reciprocity as interaction in which two persons reinforce one another at an equitable rate, concluded that these families were not showing reciprocity in their interactions. A case study was described in which a behavior modification program was used to increase the reciprocity of social reinforcers in a problem family. In line with their definition of reciprocity, they attempted to increase the frequency of social reinforcers emitted by each family member until all members were reinforcing each other at an equitable rate.

Alexander (1973) compared the interaction of normal families with that in families with a delinquent child and examined the reciprocity of negative (defensive) as well as positive (supportive) behaviors. The families were videotaped during both a general discussion and interaction around a revealed-differences task. The verbal and nonverbal behaviors were then coded using a system that examined defensive and supportive communication. To examine reciprocity, Alexander studied the rate of these types of communications within each possible dyad (father-child, child-father, mother-child, etc.). Both supportive and defensive behaviors from one member of a dyad tended to elicit similar rates of that behavior from the other dyad member in both normal and problem families. When the groups were examined separately, in normal families there was supportive parent-child reciprocity, but not defensive reciprocity. Problem families exhibited reciprocity in defensiveness, but not in supportiveness. In this study, both positive and negative reciprocity discriminated between normal and problem families; however, these findings were contradicted by a study in which spouses rated their mates' behavior.

Nondistressed spouses were studied by Wills et al. (1974). For two weeks, the spouses made daily observations of their mates' positive and negative behaviors and the overall pleasantness of the relationship. Both affective and instrumental acts were included. As a measure of reciprocity, each person's positive behaviors were correlated with the spouse's positive behaviors, and the negative behaviors were correlated with the spouse's negative behaviors over the course of the fourteen day study. They found reciprocity of displeasurable behaviors, but no reciprocity of pleasurable behaviors or displeasurable instrumental behaviors. These findings, that nondistressed spouses showed only negative reciprocity, differ from the results of Alexander (1973), who found that normal families showed only positive reciprocity.

A different approach to the reciprocity question was taken by Murstein et al. (1977). They suggested that "individuals can be placed on a continuum according to the degree to which they believe equity of exchange should characterize relationships" (p. 543). They asked spouses to complete scales of exchange orientation and marital satisfaction, while same-sex friends completed the exchange orientation scale and a friendship intensity scale. Thus, they examined the philosophy of people rather than their actual behavior. Their results indicated that a high exchange orientation correlated positively with friendship satisfaction, but negatively with marital satisfaction. This finding would suggest that high levels of reciprocity are not necessary to marital satisfaction and that excessive concern about reaching high levels may actually have an adverse effect on satisfaction. Levinger (1979) also noted that:

> Either member's preoccupation with the reward-cost balance could be considered a signal of danger. (p. 178)

It is thus possible that when dimensions of a relationship such as equity become a concern, this is an *index* of distress. In the marital dyad most variables that have been used to describe the quality of the marriage correlate with marital satisfaction. It could simply be the case that, on any reasonable dimension on which a relationship can be assessed, distressed spouses judge the marriage to be awry.

To summarize, the clinical tradition has not found clear evidence to indicate a relationship between positive and negative reciprocity and marital satisfaction. Disturbed relationships have been connected with a lack of positive reciprocity (Patterson and Reid, 1970), defensive, but not supportive, reciprocity (Alexander, 1973), and a high equity of exchange orientation (Murstein, Cerreto, and MacDonald, 1977). Normal relationships have been connected with supportive, but not defensive, reciprocity (Alexander, 1973), reciprocity of displeasurable affectional behaviors, but not with pleasurable affectional behaviors (Wills, Weiss, and Patterson, 1974), and with a low equity of exchange orientation (Murstein, Cerreto, and MacDonald, 1977). While such inconsistent results are discouraging, they are perhaps understandable in view of the wide variety of subjects (from families with problem children to nondistressed spouses), methods (from direct observation to questionnaire data), and operationalizations of reciprocity. It is particularly important to distinguish between contingency-based and noncontingency-based definitions of reciprocity.

2. *Definitions of Reciprocity.* Not all studies of reciprocity have used the same conceptualization of the term. This is especially apparent in each study's description of how reciprocity was measured. In this chapter, we will distinguish between those definitions based on the idea of contingency and those that are not.

a. Noncontingency-based definitions. The most common type of definition is *not* based on the contingency of responses. Instead, it is based on a mutually high or low rate of response between two people. For example, the Jourard and Jaffe study (1970) defined reciprocity as both persons' disclosing for equal amounts of time. Patterson and Reid (1970) described their target family as showing high positive reciprocity when all family members were reinforcing one another at an equitable rate. Alexander (1973) also looked at the rates of behavior in each member of the dyad, defining reciprocity as high correlations of rates of supportive or defensive behavior in each dyad member. In the study by Wills et al. (1974), each person's positive (negative) behaviors were correlated with the spouse's positive (negative) behaviors over the fourteen days. These definitions do not determine whether or not one dyad member's behavior had any temporal effect on the other's behavior; they merely demonstrated that both were performing the behavior with the same frequency.

b. Contingency-based definitions. In the contrast to those noncontingency-based definitions, several conceptualizations are based on the idea of contingency. For example, in the study on self-disclosure by Worthy et al. (1969), reciprocity is operationally defined as self-disclosure following disclosure by another person. Another example of contingency-based reciprocity is Brazelton et al.'s (1974) description of the cycle of inattention, initiation, orientation, attention, acceleration, excitement, deceleration, withdrawal, and turning away in mother-infant interaction. One of their descriptions of a mother-infant dyad provides an illustration of contingency-based reciprocity:

> One of our mothers was particularly striking in her capacity to subside as [her infant] decreased his attention to her. She relaxed back in her chair smiling softly, reducing other activity such as vocalizing and moving, waiting for him to return. When he did look back, she began slowly to add behavior on behavior, as if she were feeling out how much he could master. She also sensed his need to reciprocate. She vocalized then waited for his response. When she smiled, she waited until he smiled before she began to build up her own smiling again. (p. 67)

Thus, when the mother initiated an action, she waited for the infant to respond with action before she continued.

The notion of contingency would seem to be an essential element in any definition of reciprocity that has meaning in terms of the detection of a social rule that operated within a dyad. Thus, reciprocity is said to occur when A's behavior is contingent upon B's behavior. This is a conditionally probabilistic definition, which means, for example, that the probability of a husband being positive after the wife is positive is *greater* than the probability of the husband being positive regardless of the wife's prior behavior. It is important to point out that the frequent temporal co-occurrence of two codes, A and B, does not establish the sequential connection, A→B. This is true because B may occur extremely frequently. We need to demonstrate that the occurrence of A enhances the likelihood of B's subsequent occurrence. Thus, we must compare the conditional probability, $p(B|A)$ to the unconditional probability of B's occurrence, $p(B)$. If we are interested in whether or not husband and wife reciprocate positive behavior, the comparison of the conditional probability $p(H+|W+)$ with the unconditonal probability $p(H+)$ establishes the sequential connection $W+ \rightarrow H+$; the comparison of $p(W+|H+)$ with $p(W+)$ establishes the sequential connection $H+ \rightarrow W+$.

c. Positive reciprocity and the time unit. We should note, in passing, that we have discussed positive reciprocity as a concept in a microanalytic time frame, within one interaction. Previous uses of the term have indirectly suggested the utility of a positive reciprocity model on a micro-time frame within an interaction (for example, Alexander, 1973), or on a longer time frame, over days or years, or both (Patterson and Reid, 1970). Our research found no support for positive reciprocity's ability to discriminate clinic from nonclinic marriages on the micro time frame within an interaction. However, there is currently no evidence to suggest that a positive reciprocity concept will fare any better on a longer time frame. Evidence from Murstein, Cerreto, and MacDonald (1977) suggests that a couple's belief that positive reciprocity is how the marriage should operate predicts marital *dissatisfaction*.

The Murstein *et al.* study did not observe *behavior,* and this expensive procedure would of course be necessary over long time units to test the positive reciprocity concept. We should point out that the couple's self-monitoring of behavior is of course, not the same thing as observing behavior. The mechanism for testing the concept is, nonetheless, the same: Within couples, we would have to demonstrate that conditional probabilities exceed unconditional base rates. A correlation of base rates of positive behaviors between husband and wife across couples is not an adequate test. A correlation of the husband's positive behavior across days with the wife's behavior across days is also not adequate, unless both time-series were not autocorrelated (see Jenkins and Watts, 1968).

B. Dominance

1. Research on Dominance. Although dominance has been proposed as an important factor in marital satisfaction, there is wide disagreement about the effects of different dominance patterns. Some researchers (Haley, 1964; Murrell, 1971) found evidence that normal families are egalitarian, but the results of other studies (Schuham, 1972) supported the hypothesis that normal families have a clear power hierarchy.

Jacob's (1975) review of research in family interaction found no major differences in measures of power and dominance in schizophrenic and nonschizophrenic (but distressed) families. Ten of the seventeen studies reviewed showed significant differences between the two types of families, but there was no clear pattern in the findings. Results of studies comparing disturbed, nonschizophrenic families to normal families generally indicated that normal families were more likely to have differentiated power structures (hierarchical vs. egalitarian) than disturbed families. However, even the significant results were complex, and might lead to the conclusion that the concept of dominance has not been of great value in distinguishing well-functioning from distressed families.

In sociological writings on marriage, the view has been proposed that well-functioning marriages are egalitarian. This hypothesis has not been directly tested in observational research on marital interaction; nevertheless, it is widely accepted. For example, social learning theories (Patterson and Reid, 1970) view dominance as an example of coercive control. Communication theorists (Watzlawick, Beavin, and Jackson, 1967) suggest that "symmetrical" relationships are less dysfunctional than "complementary" relationships. Social-exchange theorists (Kelley and Thibaut, 1978) describe mutual control as more desirable than unilateral control in achieving an interdependent relationship.

On the other hand, ethological investigations have studied the functional aspects of dominance patterning. Wilson's (1975) essay noted that dominance patterning reduces aggression within a group and has adaptive functions for the group's survival. A dominance hierarchy provides leaders who both keep order within the group and repel enemies. Maslow (1936) observed the dominance rankings of monkeys and apes in the zoo and noted that these rankings were relatively stable within the group (see also Stephenson, 1973). The overall picture of dominance patterning is equivocal; further, it is unclear whether the concept is defined in the same way across research traditions.

2. *Definitions of Dominance.* In research on family interaction, operational definitions of dominance always refer to some asymmetry in the frequency of a variable presumed to reflect power. For example, the person who speaks first, who speaks most frequently, or who stages the most successful interruptions has been considered to be the dominant member of the group in research on family interaction (Hetherington and Martin, 1972). The ethological definitions also refer to asymmetry of some variable, such as territory controlled, resources utilized, freedom of mobility, and/or the outcome of aggressive bouts. However, the dominant individual in a group might be a person who does not speak often, but who is highly influential—a type of dominance these definitions ignore. Conversely, a person might speak first and most frequently, but be largely ignored by the others.

To assess dominance by identifying the most influential person, it is necessary to study the *effects* of influence attempts, and to detect asymmetry in *patterns* of attempts at influence, rather than asymmetry in *attempts* to influence. Thus, dominance, like reciprocity, should be defined in terms of contingent actions. Person A is dominant in an interaction when B's actions are contingent upon A's actions, but the reverse is *not* true. When influence operates in only one direction ($A \rightarrow B$) the pattern is called dominance. When influence operates in two directions ($A \rightleftharpoons B$), an egalitarian relationship is said to exist. When there is no influence at all, it is probable that A and B are not interacting; that is, their behavior is not communicative. Thus, to determine who is influencing whom, we must look for asymmetry in the *effects* of influence (contingent behavior), not for asymmetry in attempts to influence (such as the frequency of interruptions).

C. Probability Change

1. Concept of Probability Change. The concept of probability change is a basic part of the definition of reciprocity. The probability that an event will occur can be estimated by comparing the number of times an event occurs to the number of times it could have occurred. For example, the probability that the husband will speak with positive affect, p(H+), is estimated by dividing the number of times the husband actually spoke with positive affect by the total number of times the husband spoke (with either positive or negative affect). If the husband spoke one thousand times, and one hundred of those times he spoke with positive affect, the p(H+) would equal 100/1000, or 0.10. This would mean that the husband was positive about ten percent of the time, regardless of the wife's affect.

Likewise, given certain antecedent conditions, it is possible to calculate the conditional probability that an event will occur. The probability that the husband would be positive, given that the wife had been positive in the preceding utterance, denoted p(H+|W+), can be found by dividing the number of times the husband was positive after his wife was positive by the total number of times the wife was positive. If the husband was positive fifty times after his wife spoke with positive affect, and if the wife was positive on a total of one hundred and fifty utterances, then p(H+|W+) would be 50/150 or 0.33. This would mean that thirty-three percent of the time, the husband would respond positively to his wife's positive affect.

We now have two values, the unconditional probability p(H+), and the conditional probability p(H+|W+). The question is, can we more accurately predict the husband's affect using the conditional probability than the unconditional probability? That is, if we wish to predict his affect at time X, will it help to know his wife's previous affect? In our hypothetical case, knowledge of the wife's affect *does change* the probability that the husband will be positive (the probability changes from 0.10 to 0.33). If the value of p(H+|W+) had been 0.12, we would probably conclude that there had *not* been a probability change when information about the wife's behavior was added. Knowledge of the wife's previous behavior thus reduces uncertainty in predicting the husband's behavior.

2. Reciprocity and Probability Change. If p(H+|W+) is greater than p(H+), then there is positive reciprocity in one direction, W+ → H+; that is, a positive sequential connection has been obtained. If a connection is demonstrated in the other direction as well, H+ → W+, then the positive reciprocity is symmetrical. We can define negative reciprocity similarly. This symmetry could be called bidirectionality in social influence. This general notion was described by the Brazelton et al. (1974) research on infant-mother interaction in which the mother responded to the infant *and* the infant responded to the mother. For example, in the passage we quoted when the mother smiled, the infant tended to respond by smiling back. In the symbolic language of probability, p(baby smiling|mother smiling) was greater than p(baby smiling) *and* p(mother smiling|baby smiling) was greater than p(mother smiling). Each person was reciprocally affected by the other's behavior.

3. Dominance as Asymmetry of Predictability. Dominance can be defined as a one-way influence process. There is asymmetry in predicting one person's behavior based on another's. This is similar to the definition Maslow (1936) proposed in his study of primate interaction. He defined the dominant animal as "one whose behavior patterns (sexual, feeding, aggressive, social) are carried out without deference to the behavior patterns of his associates." He wrote, "The subordinate animal is one whose behavior patterns (sexual, feeding, aggressive, social) are suggested, modified, limited, or inhibited by the behavior patterns of its more dominant associates" (p. 263). This differs from the reciprocal relationship in two ways. First, in reciprocity the second person responds with the *same* behavior as the first. For example, H+ → W+ or H− → W−. In dominance, the second person does not necessarily respond with the same behavior as the first. A chain such as H+ → W− would be possible, indicating that when the husband is positive the wife is likely to respond in a negative manner. Second, in reciprocity it is possible for each person to reciprocate the other's behaviors, a situation which would lead to long chains of behavior such as H+ → W+ → H+ → W+. However it is *not* possible for both members of a dyad to be dominant at the same time, since dominance indicates asymmetry in predictability. (Note, however, that the spouses might each be dominant in *different components* [see p. 208].)

Asymmetry in predictability is operationalized through the time-series techniques, discussed in section V.B.

II. HYPOTHESES ABOUT RECIPROCITY AND DOMINANCE

A model of marital interaction that suggested hypotheses about dominance and reciprocity was proposed by Gottman. According to this model, the structure of marital interaction has three dimensions: a positive/negative dimension, a reciprocity dimension, and a dominance dimension.

Gottman (1979), based on a review of the literature, hypothesized that the reciprocation of negative behavior would discriminate distressed from nondistressed couples, with more reciprocity of negative behavior evident in distressed than in nondistressed couples. Gottman's review of the literature led him to expect no similar discrimination between distressed and nondistressed couples in the reciprocation of positive behaviors. However, this positive reciprocation might have been predicted by a temporally based *quid pro quo* theory—that is, *quid pro quo* theory would predict that nondistressed couples would reciprocate positive behaviors, and distressed couples would not. Concerning dominance, Gottman hypothesized that the interaction of distressed couples would show more asymmetry in predictability than the behavior of nondistressed couples. Regarding the positiveness dimension, Gottman hypothesized that nondistressed couples would be more positive and less negative than distressed, especially in the area of nonverbal behavior. Furthermore, Gottman proposed that the interaction of distressed couples would be more structured than those of nondistressed couples. The results of the tests of these latter hypotheses will not be included in this paper.

The dimensions of this model of marital interaction are ubiquitous. For example, the positiveness, dominance, and structure components of this model are similar to the evaluation, potency, and activity factors of Osgood's (1966) three-dimensional model of human judgments. Dimensions similar to dominance and positiveness have been found in developmental data (e.g., Schaefer, 1971; Becker, 1964) and in the circumplex model of the Interpersonal System of Personality Diagnosis (see Wiggins, 1973). A model of interpersonal behavior proposed by Schutz (1960) had affection, inclusion, and control dimensions. The affection dimension, which is the interpersonal need people have to receive and extend affection, is similar to positiveness; inclusion is, in some senses, similar to reciprocity; and control is similar to dominance.

Models of behavior have also used similar dimensions. Mehrabian's (1972) model of nonverbal behavior consisted of three dimensions: positiveness, status, and an active-passive dimension. His active-passive dimension represents the nonverbal social counterpart of the orienting reflex, which is similar to the responsiveness inherent in a reciprocity dimension. The status dimension relates to social control, social influence, and territoriality, which could be considered a dominance dimension.

While the three dimensions of Gottman's Structural Model are similar to those of other models, using the probabilistic concepts of information theory discussed previously, and using specific assessments of nonverbal behavior, each of the three dimensions has been reconceptualized and sharpened. Essentially, the differences between the Structural Model of marital interaction and the other interpersonal models are: (1) all dimensions in the Structural Model are derived from observational data; (2) positiveness is reconceptualized specifically in terms of the role of agreement, and positive and negative nonverbal behaviors; (3) reciprocity is reconceptualized specifically in terms of the contingent nature of (primarily) negative nonverbal behavior; and (4) dominance is reconceptualized specifically in terms of asymmetry in predictability of one person's behavior from the other's.

III. BASIC METHODOLOGY

A. Observational Methods

1. The Advantages of Observational Methods. Well-planned observational research can be a rich source of data about human behavior. If the experimenter observes reasonably natural behavior, the data collected is presumed to be representative of everyday behavior outside the laboratory. There have been two main objections to observational methodology: (1) it is difficult to code the data reliably, and (2) the situation cannot be controlled as well as a laboratory experiment can. Weick's (1968) excellent essay suggested how to minimize these problems.

There are several difficulties in coding the data reliably. For example, it is difficult to code the interaction as it occurs—a process that usually requires making many complex judgments in a small amount of time with no chance to go back and reconsider the coding. Reliability coders must be present at the same time, alerting the coder to the fact that he or she is being checked (and possibly changing the coding process). Problems with reliability in coding live behavior have been solved with very complex coding systems and the aid of electronic keyboard systems (see, for example, Sackett, 1978). This problem can also be solved effectively by videotaping the interaction to be coded. There is no reason to believe that videotaping equipment is more disturbing to subjects than the presence of one or more coders—and its advantages are numerous. Once the interaction is on tape, it is possible to code it carefully, rechecking troublesome sections as needed. Videotaping also makes it possible for the reliability checker to select random samples of the taped interaction to code, without the coder's knowledge. The importance of this will be discussed in section IV.C. In coding nonverbal behavior, it is often desirable to use slow-motion photography, and this is possible with videotape.

Another difficulty in collecting reliable data is that coding systems themselves have been difficult to use. Many systems (e.g. Bales IPA) are vague and nondescriptive, requiring subjective inferences on the part of the coder. A good system should describe each category clearly and specifically. Coders should be able to code data without having to make difficult inferences from what the subjects "really" meant.

Another complaint about observational methods is that they do not allow the experimenter to control the situation. While it is true that the observational study will never reach the same *degree* of control as the laboratory experiment, it is possible to structure a situation in many ways that will improve control without losing the naturalness of the situation. One method for controlling a situation is to elicit the specific classes of behaviors under investigation. For example, conflict may be elicited in a group by requiring subjects to come to a consensus about a set of pre-administered items on which they expressed the most disagreement. Another strategy in controlling interactions is to take a sample from those situations in which the desired responses usually occur. For example, a study of parent-child conflict might observe behavior from dinner until bedtime, or another such period of high stress likely to produce conflict.

2. *Observational Methods in the Study of Group Interaction.* *Process,* defined as the nature of the interaction within a group, is considered a primary factor in group productivity (Steiner, 1972). Although many studies examine process through the use of periodic questionnaires or other techniques (e.g., Davis et al., 1976), the most efficient way to study process seems to be via observational methods. One of the better known studies using this method to examine group process is a study of group problem-solving by Bales and Strodtbeck (1951). Observers watched the group interaction and coded the process as it occurred. By examining the process during the first, second, and last third of the discussions, Bales and Strodtbeck were able to propose that there were three phases of group process: (1) orientation, when all group members shared their knowledge about the problem; (2) evaluation, when they judged the information and proposed solutions; and (3) control, which concerned the regulation of members and their common environment. Bales (1953) also found that the content of group discussions was fairly stable, which he summarized as consisting of about twenty-five percent positive reactions, eleven percent negative reactions, fifty-seven percent attempted answers to the problem, and about seven percent questions. He hypothesized that these stable rates reflect the equilibrium processes within the group. Bales also studied the temporal factor in group process and found that clustering of codes does occur. Two types of sequencing were examined: one speaker following another, and one person speaking twice in a row. It was found that there were similar amounts of each type of patterning. For

example, questions were usually followed by answers from a different person, while disagreements were likely to be followed by an opinion from the same person.

A second study of group process examined the frequency of oral contributions to the group (Stephan and Mishler, 1952). Observers counted the number of times each student spoke during an informal class meeting. The groups included from four to twelve members; there were four groups of each size. Within each group, the students were rank-ordered by the number of times they spoke. The researchers found a constant ratio of speaking frequency across adjacently ranked pairs; for example, if person A talked most frequently, then B, C, and so on, then if B spoke one-third as often as A, it was found that C spoke one-third as often as B and so on down the line. The model did not specify what the ratio would be, but it predicted this ratio would be constant within the group.

In a different type of study, Kendon (1970) examined the relationship between verbal and nonverbal behavior. He filmed the interaction of a group of men in the lounge of a hotel (a pub-like atmosphere). The films were later analyzed using slow motion to look for synchrony in the verbal and nonverbal behavior of people who were speaking, and the nonverbal behavior of the people listening to them. The speech and body movements (of head, trunk, arms, and hands) of each person were plotted on a chart on which the intervals represented successive frames of the film. (Speech was broken into its phonetic components.) This chart was then inspected for evidence of synchronous movement. This synchrony was found, even when the listener was not looking at the speaker, and was described as if the speaker and listener were dancing to the same beat. In many sequences, the listener was actually mirroring the speaker's behaviors. This analysis emphasizes the interrelation between speakers and listeners.

In summary, these observational studies of group process have indicated that interaction in groups is not random; rather, it is highly patterned. The phases of group discussion are stable across groups (Bales and Strodtbeck, 1951), the ratio in frequency of speech is constant within a group (Stephan and Mishler, 1952), and the behavior of speaker and listeners is synchronous (Kendon, 1970). If such high degrees of structure are found in the interactions of groups of strangers, it seems probable that the interactions of married couples would also show high degrees of patterning.

B. General Methodology of the Marital Studies

Most of the studies reported in this chapter used similar procedures. This section describes the general methodology. Any deviations from this method in a particular study will be included in the discussion of that study.

1. Subjects. An attempt was made to recruit couples who were either very happily married or who were experiencing definite problems with their marriage. Happily married couples were usually recruited through a newspaper advertisement asking for people who felt that their marriages were mutually satisfying. These couples were identified as the *nonclinic* couples. Couples with unhappy marriages were recruited through a similar advertisement asking for people who felt that their marriages were unsatisfactory. Couples were also referred by marital counseling agencies. These couples were called the *clinic* couples. In some studies, more extreme groups were identified by giving all recruited couples the Locke-Wallace Marital Relationship Inventory (MRI) and selecting those with the highest and the lowest scores. When this practice was used, those couples in which at least one spouse's MRI score was below 85 were called *distressed* couples and those in which *both* husband and wife had MRI scores above 102 were called *nondistressed* couples.

2. Setting. The spouses were videotaped as they interacted in a laboratory room. They sat facing each other across a table and a videotape camera filmed their discussion. Experience with these couples has shown that a videotape camera is no more obtrusive than a coder. Most people seem to adapt easily to its presence within the first five minutes of filming, sometimes becoming surprisingly uninhibited during their conversation.

3. Procedure and Tasks. Spouses individually completed a demographic information sheet, the MRI, and a problem inventory. The problem inventory asked each spouse to rate separately the perceived severity of a list of problem areas and to provide a specific description (like a play-by-play account) of an incident, providing situational context, and a typical conversation illustrating the problem.

Tasks in the various experiments included reaching a solution for one of the marital problems described in the problem inventory, role-playing situations selected for their ability to produce conflict between spouses, completing consensus decision-making tasks, and creating joint stories for Thematic Apperception Test cards.

IV. THE CODING SYSTEM

In an observation study, one of the major problems is data reduction. The data must be categorized in a meaningful way using one or more coding systems. These coding systems must be detailed enough to capture the information needed, but general enough to be a data reduction tool. These requirements are usually met by developing a coding system that is suitable to the researcher's area of interest, as well as to the subjects and the context. The studies presented here were coded according to two systems, a content coding system geared to describing conversation in a problem-solving situation, and a nonverbal coding system that classified nonverbal behavior on a positive-negative basis.

A. Content Codes

1. Other Content Coding Systems. Many coding systems, varying in complexity, have been used to code marital and family interaction. One scheme, borrowed from social psychology, is Bales's (1970) Interaction Process Analysis (IPA). This system, which was designed to code group interaction, contains categories such as "gives opinion" and "shows tension." Several investigators tried to use the system to code family interaction, but they had difficulty in obtaining agreement between independent coders (Winter and Ferreira, 1967; Waxler and Mishler, 1965; Raush et al., 1974). They concluded that family interaction was more private, and thus harder to judge, than group interaction.

The Marital Interaction Coding System (MICS), as the name implies, has been widely used to code marital interaction. This system, developed by Hops et al. (1972), was designed to assess the effects of marital therapy. While much more applicable to marital interaction than the IPA, it still posed problems of coder agreement, probably attributable to the high degree of judgment needed by coders to categorize the data. The Olson and Ryder Inventory of Marital Conflict (IMC) coding system (Olson and Ryder, 1970), which is somewhat similar, was developed to assess decision-making on specific problems of varying degrees of programmed conflict.

2. The Codes Used in This System. The Couples Interaction Scoring System (CISS) was developed for coding couples' interaction over a variety of decision-making situations. It was developed partly from the MICS system and the IMC system, and partly from experience with the videotaped decision-making of over three hundred couples resolving a marital issue or interacting on structured laboratory tasks that induced varying degrees of conflict.

The basic coding unit is the thought unit, which consists of the utterances used to express a single idea. A thought unit may be a phrase, a sentence, or a paragraph, but it always contains one and only one idea. When a coder begins to work on a new transcript, the first task is to break it down into thought units. This can be done reliably between coders. Then each thought unit is coded. In analysis, the behavior unit is used so that the final unit of analysis is demarcated by transitions between codes.

a. Description of codes. The CISS is comprised of eight codes, some of which have several subcodes. The coder must give one of these codes to each thought unit. Although the coders make their decision based on the subcode categories, only the major category is used in the analysis of the data. The coding system is exhaustive; that is, each unit on the transcript fits into one of the categories. The system is designed so that the categories are defined precisely, and require minimal inference on the part of the coder.

Detailed coding manuals and training materials are used to train coders; thus, any summary of the coding system runs the risk of appearing overly simplistic. With this caveat in mind, a brief outline of the coding system is given in Table I.

b. Selection of codes. The original content coding system consisted of twenty-four distinct subcodes. While transcripts were coded reliably using this system, data analysis proved unwieldy, and the decision was made to group the subcodes into larger categories. Because one of the major aims of the research was to examine the sequences of interaction, the summary categories were obtained by clustering subcodes according to their sequential connections. Thus, codes were grouped together when they usually led to the same criterion code. For example, the subcodes

Table I. Eight Summary Content Codes of the C.I.S.S.

Code	*Definition*	*Example*
AG	Agreement	(a) Yeah. (b) You're right.
DG	Disagreement	(a) No. (b) Yes, but. . . .
CT	Communication Talk	We're getting off the issue.
MR	Mindreading: attributing thoughts, feelings, motives, etc. to spouse	You always get mad in those situations.
PS	Proposing a solution to a problem or information exchange	Let's take out a loan.
SO	Summarizing Other	(a) What you're saying is I drink too much. (b) We're both suggesting that we take a vacation.
SS	Summarize Self	I told you that I'm not going because it's just too late.
PF	Problem information or feelings about a problem	(a) The problem is that we don't have enough money. (b) That makes me sad.

Plan and Relationship Information were usually followed by the same code. In this way, the original twenty-four codes were lumped into the present eight categories.

3. Description of the Coding Process. Each videotape is coded by a single coder. After the tape is transcribed, the coder watches the tape and divides the transcript into thought units. Each unit is given one of the eight major codes. Then the coder reviews the videotape, paying special attention to any sections in which there were difficulties in coding. When the transcript has been completed, a randomly-chosen segment is coded by the coder coordinator. Reliability will be discussed in section IV.C.

B. Nonverbal Codes

1. Description of the Codes. The content coding system provides a usable summary of the verbal content of an interaction, but a large part of the communication process is nonverbal. Nonverbal cues can add to, modify, or completely reverse the meaning of the spoken word. Examples are the raised eyebrow, which adds skepticism to the content, and the sarcastic tone of voice, which gives negative meaning to positive content. There is some evidence that nonverbal cues may be less subject to faking than content (Ekman and Friesen, 1969). Mehrabian (1972) studied the transmission of emotional messages during brief interaction between strangers and he estimated that total affect consists of seven percent verbal, thirty-eight percent vocal, and fifty-five percent facial. Our experience suggests that, with couples, voice tone would be weighted more heavily than in Mehrabian's equation.

a. Facial codes. According to Ekman and Friesen (1975), emotion is displayed on three regions of the face: the brow, the eye, and the lower face. Each region can show the same emotion (such as sadness), or there can be a blend (for example, sad eyes and brow with a slight smile). They listed six emotions that could be identified by people of various ages and cultures: happiness, sadness, fear, anger, surprise, and disgust. However, these identifications were of still photographs of actors simulating pure emotions. Our coding problem was slightly different—the expressions were videotaped, rather than still pictures, most of the facial expressions of the couples were neutral or attentive, and often their other expressions were blends. Fortunately, coding from videotape proved to be easier than coding from still pictures because most expressions last several seconds (which is a large number of frames), and videotape lets the coder see the build-up and fade-out of the expression. To avoid the coding problems presented by affect blends, only three codes were used—positive, neutral, and negative. A unit was coded "positive" when the person smiled, laughed, looked interested, etc. "Neutral" was coded when the person's face was in its normal resting state. A "negative" code was used when the person frowned, cried, looked bored, etc. Coders reached high levels of reliability using this system.

b. Voice codes. Voice tone is also an important nonverbal cue. Observers can agree on the emotional content of voice tone even when content has been removed (Davitz and Davitz, 1959). According to a study by Zahn (1975), in judgments of emotional content, vocal cues account for 1.39 times greater variance than verbal content. The two major methods used to code the voice are the electronic filtering method and the ignore-content method. Electronic filtering removes all cycles higher than a certain frequency, but this procedure may also remove some of the emotional content. Also, despite the fact that this method is often called "content filtering," coders can recognize the content after continued use of the method. In the ignore-content method, coders are simply instructed to ignore the content. There are obvious limitations to this procedure, but this method has also been shown to provide judgments of affect that are moderately independent of content.

In these studies, voice tone was coded either positive, neutral, or negative using the ignore-content method. The cue words for these codes were comparable to those used in the facial coding. One other code was used—the non-ah disturbance. These are speech errors—*not* the "ah," "um," or "er"—commonly used to hold the floor while thinking. The non-ah disturbances have been found to be generally related to speaker tension. Examples are sentence change in the middle of a sentence, repetition, stuttering, omissions, slips of the tongue, and intruding incoherent sounds.

c. Body codes. The body is a less reliable channel of expression because it is influenced by many situational, ethnic, and cultural variables. However, it is reasonable to code some body cues as positive, neutral, or negative. Positive cues are such things as relaxed posture or touching. (Some couples could be seen touching feet or knees under the table.) Negative cues are neck and arm tension, arms akimbo, and increase of distance between spouses.

2. *The Coding Process.* Affect coders work from videotapes and verbatim transcripts that have already been marked into thought units and content coded. Using the completed content coding sheets, the affect coder's task is to give a code (positive, neutral, or negative) to *each* spouse during *each* thought unit. The code for the person speaking is called the *affect* code, while the code for the person listening is called the *context* code.

The coder first views the entire tape to get a general idea of the affective tone of the couple's interaction. Then the tape is viewed slowly, with the coder stopping the tape after each thought unit to code the affect and context. A hierarchical model is used to arrive at a single code from the face, voice, and body cues. If the face is positive or negative, that code is used. If the face is neutral, the coder listens to voice tone. Again, if the voice code is positive or negative, that code is used. If it is neutral, the body cues are used. Thus, the affect will not be coded as neutral unless the face, voice, *and* body are neutral. Otherwise, the face is given precedence over the voice which has precedence over the body.

As in content coding, the coder checks with the coder coordinator about any problem areas. A randomly chosen segment of each transcript is coded by a reliability checker and a reliability score is computed.

C. *Reliability in Coding*

1. Observer Agreement. Many methods of calculating observer agreement have been proposed, from a simple percent agreement over an entire observation period for all codes to more complex calculations of agreement for a single code, taking chance probabilities of agreement into account. Perhaps the most general statement that can be made about these various reliability coefficients is that no one of them is appropriate for all situations. The investigator must choose the reliability test that is appropriate for a particular investigation.

Johnson and Bolstad (1973) reviewed the various methods of calculating reliability coefficients and the problems associated with each method. They suggested that an overall percent-agreement score over all codes tends to give more weight to behaviors that occur most frequently, and is therefore meaningless. An exception is Cohen's (1960) statistic Kappa, which calculates the proportion of agreement after chance agreement has been removed.

$$\text{Kappa} = \frac{P_o - P_c}{1 - P_c}, \qquad \text{Eq. (1)}$$

where P_o is the observed proportion of agreement and P_c is the chance proportion of agreement. Kappa, which can be calculated across all transcripts in a study, yields a single reliability coefficient. It can also be computed separately for each transcript to point out transcripts on which agreement was difficult for observers.

An important issue is the length of the time span within which common coding is counted as an agreement. When a large time unit is used, coders might agree on the number of times a particular code was observed but never agree as to when it was observed. Johnson and Bolstad wrote, "If one observer sees 10 occurrences of a behavior over a 30-minute period and the other sees 12, there is no assurance that they were ever in agreement'' (p. 13). When the researcher's interest is the sequence or patterning of codes, it is important to know that two observers saw the same behavior at the same time. In other words, for sequential analysis, agreement must be tied to specific codes on specific units of the transcript. On every unit of the transcript, coders will either agree or disagree.

According to generalizability theory (Cronbach et al., 1972), all assessments of reliability (and validity) are statements of the extent to which one may generalize along some dimension. Using an analysis of variance model, the total variance around the grand mean is partitioned into whatever independent sources of variance the investigator chooses, plus error variance. For example, variance might be partitioned into a person effect, a condition effect, and a residual (error) effect. In the design we have used frequently (Wiggins, 1973), the partitioning of variance produces a mean square term between dyads (MS_p), a mean square term between coders (MS_i, where N_i is the number of coders), and a residual (error) term (MS_r). The reliability coefficient obtained from the analysis of variance,

$$\alpha = \frac{MS_p - MS_r}{MS_p + (N_i - 1)MS_r} \qquad \text{Eq. (2)}$$

Facets of the analysis of variance design might include coders, videotapes, segment length coded, location of the segments, and so on.

2. *Reliability Drift and Decay*. Several investigations have suggested that interobserver agreement declines when observers are unaware that their coding is being checked (Reid, 1970; Taplin and Reid, 1973; O'Leary and Kent, 1973; Romanczyk et al., 1973). Taplin and Reid (1973) had three groups of coders; one group was told they would be checked at random times, one group was told they would be checked at specific times, and one group was told they would not be checked. Actually, reliability was continuously monitored. They found that the random-check group showed consistently high levels of reliability, while the no-check group had consistently low levels of reliability. The period spot-check group had higher reliabilities than the random-check group on the days when it was checked, but between those days it fell much lower.

Our procedures show that it is possible to avoid these problems of decay and actually *increase* reliability over time. This is accomplished by training observers to high levels of agreement on two consecutive tapes before coding begins, and by checking a random segment of *every* tape coded. This method is easily employed using videotapes—another advantage of taping interaction.

Another problem in coding reliability is observer ''drift,'' in which pairs of observers modify the coding system and stay reliably together, but drift apart from the other coders. This problem can be attenuated by having a written code manual, training sessions on coded material, and tapes that are coded unknowingly with subsequent discussion of disagreements; by using one major reliability checker to code samples of every tape; and by rotating the role of checker throughout the study. These procedures were used in the research reported here.

3. *Reliability of the CISS.* Several generalizability studies of the CISS have been conducted assessing the reliability of the content codes, the affect codes, and the content codes over time. The first study looked at the reliability of the content codes over different coders and different segment lengths checked. The transcripts and tapes of twenty-eight couples were content coded by five coders and one reliability checker. The analysis of variance design described by Wiggins (1973) was employed to determine the reliability of each code, using the unit criterion of agreement; that is, the reliability checker and the coder agreed only if they had coded independently the *same* thought unit in the same way. In half of the transcripts, four-page samples were checked by the reliability checker; from the other half, two pages were sampled, with clinic and nonclinic couples included in both groups.

The results showed that all codes had high reliabilities, ranging from 0.84 to 1.00 as measured by the Cronbach Alpha. The more extreme scores, in either direction, were in the codes that occurred with low frequency, such as summarize self and summarize other. The median reliability was 0.96. These findings indicate that the CISS content coding system has high generalizability over coders and over sample length.

The second study assessed the reliability of the CISS affect coding system. The same set of fourteen transcripts and tapes with four-page segments was used, and two coders coded affect and context for the same four pages sampled previously. The Cronbach alpha was calculated for each code (positive, neutral, and negative) when used as affect and again when used as context. Again, reliabilities were high. For affect, the reliability score of the positive code was 0.90, neutral was 0.96, and negative was 0.99. Context reliability scores were not quite as high; positive was 0.78, neutral 0.84, and negative 0.95. This is probably due to the fact that all videotapes used in this study involved a one-camera profile shot of the couple rather than full-face views. Positive and neutral listening may be difficult to detect in profile, while negative affect listening (such as the wrinkled nose of disgust) may be easier to detect in profile. Therefore, the CISS affect coding system is reliably coded across coders.

A third study was tested for reliability decay in the CISS content coding system. The same group of coders consecutively coded three separate sets of transcripts over the course of approximately one year. When the alphas were computed for each code at each of the three time periods, there was no evidence of reliability decay; in fact, reliability for most codes increased slightly from the first period to the third period. Only three codes showed significant changes in reliability, and two of those (mind-reading and communication talk) were *increases* in reliability from the second to the third period. The summarize self code (an infrequent code) was coded most reliably during the second time period. In summary, there was *no* evidence of a steady decline in reliability over time for *any* code. All codes remained at the initial acceptable levels, with a median reliability over all periods of 0.98.

V. DATA ANALYSIS

A. Sequential Analysis

Since our definition of reciprocity hinges on the identification of *contingent* behaviors, it is necessary to look at behavior across time. The question we must ask is "Did A's behavior at time 1 affect B's behavior at time 2?" In other words, we are interested in the probability of certain *sequences* of behaviors.

In a previous section, we discussed the concept of probability change as a means of determining whether one person's behavior was influenced by the behavior of another person. A change in probability was said to occur when there was a significant difference between the conditional and the unconditional probabilities of a behavior's occurrence. The *z-score* is the method used to determine the significance of the probability change.

As an example, consider the case of positive affect in the husband. Is the unconditional probability of the husband being positive (H+) significantly different from the conditional probability of the husband being positive, given that the wife has been positive (H+|W+)? To test this difference, calculate the z-score:

$$Z(H+|W+) = \frac{X - NP}{NPQ} \qquad \text{Eq. (3)}$$

where X = observed joint frequency of H+ and W+
N = frequency of W+
P = unconditional probability of H+
Q = 1 − P

If the resulting Z is greater than or equal to ±1.96, then the difference between the conditional and unconditional probabilities is significant at the 0.05 level, meaning that the wife *is* influencing the husband's behavior (Sackett, 1977). If the Z is positive, then the husband matched the wife's behavior *more* than would be expected by chance (that is, he was more likely to be positive if she had previously been positive). If the Z is negative, then the husband matched *less* than would be expected by chance (so he was less likely to be positive if she had previously been positive).

The discussion to this point has concerned reciprocity at lag one. However, there can be sequences of reciprocal interaction lasting several lags. For example, there might be a sequence H+, W+, H+, W+, indicating that each spouse is reciprocating the other's positive behavior. The probability of such a sequence can also be assessed using z-scores by using the following steps:

1. Select a criterion behavior code, and compute the conditional probabilities of the other codes at each lag. For example, if behavior code H+ has the highest conditional probability with respect to W+ at lag one, and W+ has the highest conditional probability with respect to W+ at lag two, a possible sequence, W+, H+, W+ is suggested.
2. To test the sequence W+, H+, W+, make H+ the criterion behavior and see if the transition probability of W+ with respect to H+ at lag one from H+ shows a peak (i.e., is above the transition probabilities of other codes).
3. Z-scores that test conditional against unconditional probabilities should be greater than 1.96, or the transition probabilities are at base rate level, which would argue against a sequence.

A sequence W+, H+, W+, H+, W+ is identified if and only if the lag one z-scores connecting intermediate codes are greater than 1.96. When z-scores are less than 1.96, consider the sequence ended.

B. *Time-series Analysis*

Dominance was previously defined as asymmetry in predictability. To operationalize dominance using this definition, it is necessary to create a variable that gives some index for the behavior of each dyad member over time. To accomplish this, Gottman et al. (1977) scaled positive, neutral, and negative verbal and nonverbal codes to create a continuous variable that (1) discriminated distressed from nondistressed couples; and (2) provided *an index of the affect of a discussion within a conversation.* Cumulative point graphs for each spouse's behavior were constructed by giving each spouse a score for his or her behavior during each floor switch. The behaviors were scaled according to the following system: (a) each positive speaker or listener nonverbal behavior = +1; (b) each negative speaker or listener nonverbal behavior = −1; (c) mind-reading with negative affect = −2; (d) problem-solving = +1 if followed by an agreement within the floor switch; (e) agreement = +1, and disagreement = −1. Each spouse's score for the floor switch was plotted on that spouse's graph. The scores were cumulative over floor switches. The general effect of this scoring system was that the graph tended to go up when the spouse was positive and down when the spouse was negative. Gottman (1979) reported, "The shape of the curves fit the intuitions we had as we watched the videotapes" (p. 273).

These graphs were the data base for frequency-domain time-series analyses. In frequency-domain analysis, the basic question is, What are the component oscillations in the series? Figure 1 depicts the general

Figure 1. Schematic Illustration of the Superposition of Two Sine Waves of Different Frequencies, the Reverse of Decomposition of a Complex Wave.

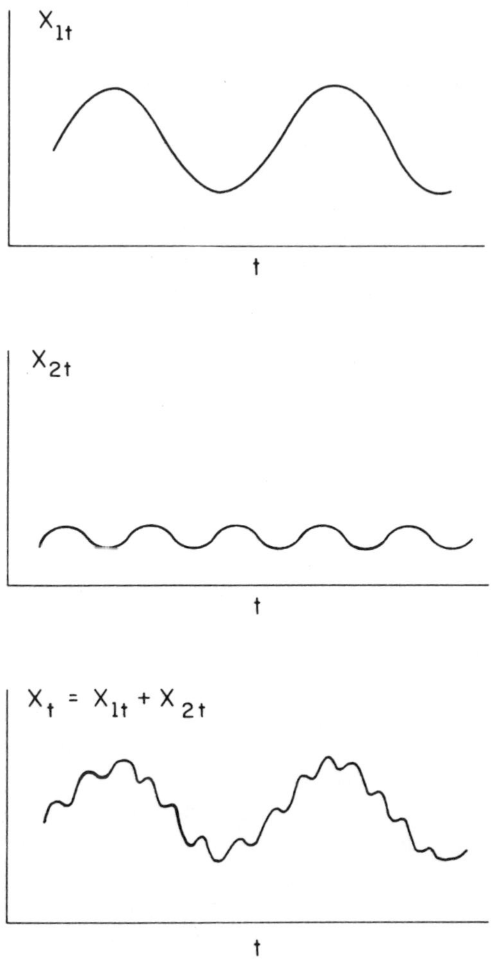

idea. X_t is composed of two superimposed components, a slow sine wave of large amplitude and a fast wave of small amplitude.

Two time-series (e.g., those of a husband and wife) can be compared in order to determine the lead-lag relationship between them. The phase spectrum is the statistic that shows whether frequency components in one series lead or lag the same frequency component in the other series. If the slope of the phase spectrum is non-zero, the dyad has a lead-lag relationship across all frequencies and the sign of the slope indicates which spouse is leading the interaction.

A two component model, as suggested by Granger and Hatanka (1964), would divide the frequency range into two parts, slow and rapid frequency components. The first component, which included the slower overall changes in affect, was termed the *mood* component, and the faster moment-to-moment changes were designated the *expressive* component. Each component was analyzed separately for dominance patterning. Theoretically, it is possible for one spouse to be dominant in the mood component while the other is dominant in the expressive component. Several books on time-series analysis offer a complete description of these methods (e.g., Jenkins and Watts, 1968; Koopmans, 1974).

VI. RESULTS OF STUDIES OF MARITAL INTERACTION

These studies are described more fully in Gottman's (1979) book on marital interaction.

A. The Topography of Marital Conflict

The role of description in scientific research has been minimized, but without careful description, theories are often based on little more than intuition. This study (reported in full in Gottman, Markman, and Notarius, 1977) was designed to describe the interactions of distressed and nondistressed couples as they resolved existing marital problems. Examined was the hypothesis that reciprocity of positive exchange is a crucial aspect of good marriages.

The subjects were two groups of fourteen married couples. Fourteen clinic couples were referred by marital counseling agencies or responded to an advertisement asking for research subjects who felt that their marriages were unsatisfactory. The nonclinic couples responded to an advertisement asking for couples who felt that their marriage was mutually satisfying. All couples took the MRI, and the five couples with the highest scores and the five with the lowest scores were identified as nondistressed and distressed subgroups. Each of the twenty-eight couples was asked to discuss one problem and come to a mutually satisfying resolution. Their discussion was taped and these tapes were analyzed using the procedures described in the preceding sections.

Reciprocity results for the twenty-eight clinic and nonclinic couples were calculated to lag six. Negative affect cycles were likely for both groups, although the z-scores were larger for clinic couples, supporting the popular hypothesis that clinic couples were characterized by negative affect cycles. The groups also differed in positive reciprocity. In the earlier lags, the clinic couples showed the highest degree of positive reciprocity, but the nonclinic couples showed more reciprocity in later lags. Both groups showed less reciprocity of positive affect than of negative affect. Thus, positive affect reciprocity was not as consistent a discriminator as was negative reciprocity.

Reciprocity was also analyzed by using the point system graphs for the five distressed and five nondistressed couples. These graphs combined positive and negative content and affect behaviors for each floor switch. These analyses used the base rate unconditional probabilities as the covariate for conditional probabilities. The results indicated that there is greater positive reciprocity in the interaction of nondistressed couples than in interaction of distressed couples. But this finding was useful only in predicting the wife's reciprocation of the husband's positive behavior.

B. *A Recoding Study*

To provide a comparison with the results from another laboratory, a subset of the data from a study by Raush et al. (1974) was recoded and analyzed. The Raush et al. study was the only sequential study from another laboratory on the interaction of couples in conflict situations. By contacting newlyweds who had recently received marriage licenses in Washington, D.C., they had recruited forty-six couples. Audiotapes of these couples' interactions were obtained during pregnancy, soon after the birth of the first child, and then later after the birth.

In the taping sessions, the couples interacted in improvised conflict situations. Although the basic situations were constant across couples, an effort was made to make the improvisations relevant to each couple by asking the husband and wife for input on the details of the situation. There were four improvisations; two "issue oriented," presenting conflict about a specific issue (e.g., which television program to watch), and two "relationship oriented," in which one spouse was instructed to try to get close and the other to try to maintain psychological distance.

The tapes were recoded using the CISS because the summary codes used by Raush et al.—Cognitive, Resolving, Reconciling, Appealing, Rejective, and Coercive—were too general to compare to the findings of the topography study. Affect coding from audiotapes was more difficult than coding from videotapes, so a slightly different coding procedure was used. Each tape was coded independently by two affect coders and the reliability checker coded all the tapes. A thought unit was coded positive or negative only if the coders agreed; otherwise it was coded neutral. Listener affect could not be coded unless the spouse laughed or cried audibly, so listener affect was not coded.

The couples' scores on marital satisfaction scales were unavailable, so the couples were compared to those in the Gottman et al. (1977) study by using agreement to disagreement ratios and the affect codes. This comparison showed that both of the Raush et al. groups were in the distressed range of the Gottman study. However, the discordant and harmonious couples differed to the same degree as the distressed and nondistressed couples, suggesting that the variables in the Structural Model may be able to distinguish among levels of distress as well as between the extremes of distressed and nondistressed couples.

The negative reciprocity results for the harmonious and discordant couples were calculated to lag six. The discordant couples were more likely to show negative reciprocity than the harmonious couples, as evidenced by higher z-scores and conditional probabilities, although in both groups there was a tendency for the more negative spouse to continue in a negative manner, while the partner remained unresponsive. In this analysis as well, the results replicate the Gottman et al. (1977) findings. In both groups, there was strong evidence of positive reciprocity up to lag six. Discordant couples showed higher positive reciprocity than harmonious couples, but only in earlier lags.

Therefore, even though both of the Raush et al. groups were within the distressed range of the Gottman study, the analysis of reciprocity discriminated between the groups.

C. The Issue Focus

In a dissertation conducted in Gottman's laboratory, Rubin (1977) designed a study to examine the effect of the issue being discussed on the marital interaction. As in the Raush et al. (1974) study, couples interacted in the context of improvisations; however, in the Rubin study the six improvisations were empirically derived from transcripts of interviews with sixty couples, each of whom had described three problem areas. The tapes were transcribed and summarized into short vignettes that were then reduced to eighty-five nonredundant situations. It was found that six issues were the most common for both clinic and nonclinic couples: sharing the events of the day, money, in-laws, sex, whether to have children or to have more children, and how to discipline children. Improvisations were devised for each of these problem areas. One other nonconflict task was devised. Called the "fun deck," it consisted of a deck of cards. Each card contained the description of an activity that the couples had said they enjoyed. Subjects were instructed to look through the deck and talk about the various activities.

Nineteen clinic and nineteen nonclinic couples were recruited through newspaper advertisements and agency referrals. Each couple was videotaped as they discussed the fun deck and interacted in the improvisations. (The six improvisations were presented in a random order, but the fun deck was always the first task given.)

Positive and negative reciprocity was calculated for all tasks combined, and for each task separately. Over all tasks combined, positive reciprocity was not dramatically different for the two groups. In fact, clinic couples showed slightly more positive reciprocity than nonclinic couples in later lags. On the other hand, large differences were found between groups in negative reciprocity. Clinic couples showed far more negative reciprocity than nonclinic couples.

The different improvisations induced different levels of conflict, as measured by agreement to disagreement ratios. The highest degree of conflict was induced by the sex improvisation, followed by having children, money, in-laws, sharing events of the day, disciplining children, and the fun deck. On the high-conflict sex improvisation, both clinic and nonclinic spouses were very likely to have cycles of positive reciprocity through lag six. The nonclinic group showed negative reciprocity, but not at the high levels evidenced by the clinic group. Greater discrimination between groups was seen on the fun deck, a task designed to create little or no conflict. Again, both groups were likely to have positive reciprocity cycles. The nonclinic groups had no negative reciprocity, as might be expected on a low-conflict task. But the clinic spouses were as likely to show high rates of negative reciprocity in the fun deck as in the sex improvisation, even in later lags. It seems that the nonclinic couples vary their interaction style to suit the task, with no negative reciprocity on the low-conflict task and fairly high negative reciprocity on the high-conflict task. However, the clinic couples showed high rates of negative reciprocity on both tasks.

D. Dominance in Marital Interaction

Dominance was defined as asymmetry in predictability within a dyad and it was hypothesized that a clearly defined dominance pattern would be characteristic of clinic couples, while an egalitarian pattern would be characteristic of nonclinic couples. To test this hypothesis, the data from the Rubin (1977) study was reanalyzed using time-series analysis. The Rubin study used improvisations that produced varying degrees of conflict. For this analysis, the three highest-conflict improvisations were combined for one analysis and the four lowest-conflict improvisations were combined for the other. Cumulative point graphs were constructed for each couple on each task and the mood and the expressive components were analyzed separately.

On the high-conflict tasks, both the clinic and the nonclinic groups were likely to have *no* dominance patterning on the mood component. That is, in the slow cyclic changes of affect, neither spouse was more likely to lead the interaction. However, when dominance was present, the dominant person was equally likely to be either the wife or husband in nonclinic couples, but only the husband in clinic couples. The two groups were discriminated on the more rapid expressive component. The nonclinic couples still showed no dominance patterning, but the husband was dominant in clinic couples.

In summary, the clinic couples were most likely to show the pattern of husband dominance in the expressive components. However, the most common nonclinic pattern was egalitarian, with neither person leading the interaction. This supports the hypothesis that clinic couples will be characterized by dominance patterning while nonclinic couples will be characterized by egalitarian patterns. Further, dominance in clinic couples was of a particular type, in which the husband's behavior predicted the wife's behavior, but only for rapid changes in affect expression.

On the low-conflict tasks, the most prevalent pattern for all couples, in both mood and expressive components, was the egalitarian pattern. Thus, dominance patterning may be a function of situational aspects of interaction, which are more likely to appear on high-conflict tasks than on low-conflict tasks. To check this hypothesis, the time-series of the highest-conflict task, the sex improvisation, were analyzed separately. In all four clinic couples, the husband was dominant in the expressive component. In the three nonclinic couples, the wife was dominant in two and the husband in one, not suggesting a clear pattern.

E. The Talk Table Studies

Earlier in this chapter, we described the Prisoner's Dilemma game, an operationalization of Thibaut and Kelley's exchange theory (1959). While behavior-exchange theory is conceptually appealing, there have been several methodological problems in using it to study complex interactions. First, it is difficult to operationalize the concept of "behavioral repertoire," the set of behaviors a person might choose to use in a given situation. Second, there is the problem of obtaining a measure of the rewards and costs that result from a behavior exchange.

The most usual way of dealing with these problems is for the experimenter to limit each person to a certain set of behaviors and set a value for each behavior. This strategy is typified by the Prisoner's Dilemma paradigm, in which each person is limited to two behavioral choices, and the joint payoffs are predetermined by the experimenter. Far from being involved in a complex social interaction, often the people do not communicate during the entire experiment except to choose their behaviors. Speer (1972) used this paradigm with sixty clinic and sixty nonclinic couples, but found that, of four forms of the game, none of the response variables discriminated the two groups. However, this lack of discrimination may have been due to the restricted nature of the interaction.

In this series of studies (reported in Gottman et al., 1976), spouses interacted in a paradigm that: (1) made it possible for each spouse to rate the satisfaction of a particular exchange; (2) minimally constrained the couple's behavior repertoire; and (3) allowed the couple to interact on a wide range of possible tasks. These aims were met by having the couple interact on several tasks using the "talk table."

The talk table is a double sloping table. A toggle switch on the side of the table lit a button on the side of the spouse who had the floor to speak. There were two rows of five buttons on each spouse's side of the table. The five buttons on the left were used by the speaker to code the "intended impact" of his or her message: the five buttons on the right were used by the receiver to code the "impact" of the message received. The buttons were labeled "super negative," "negative," "neutral," "positive," and "super positive." Although partners could see one another, a metal shield blocked the buttons from the view of the other person so that, throughout the experiment, neither spouse could see the codes assigned by his or her partner.

1. *Study 1.* Twenty-six nonclinic couples and fifteen clinic couples were recruited through newspaper advertisements and clinic referrals. From this group, ten distressed couples and six nondistressed couples were selected on the basis of their MRI scores. The two groups of couples did not significantly differ in age, educational level, or the number of years married. Couples were, on the average, twenty-five years old and had been married about three years.

The couples interacted on three low-conflict tasks and two high-conflict tasks while using the talk table. The low-conflict tasks were: (1) the choice questionnaire (Haley, 1964), a consensus decision-making task that required an agreed-upon ranking of personal preferences; (2) three Thematic Apperception Test cards (Locke, 1951), which required the couples to create jointly one story for each set of cards; and (3) one of two tasks administered first individually and then again for consensual ranking. One of the tasks involved rank ordering items for their survival value on the moon and the other involved rank ordering items according to their nutritional value. The high-conflict tasks were: (1) the Inventory of Marital Conflict (IMC) (Olson and Ryder, 1970), in which the couple is presented with three short vignettes of marital conflict and required to agree on which spouse in the vignette is primarily responsible for the problem, and (2) the couple was asked to discuss a current problem and try to come to a mutually satisfactory resolution of this problem. Within each session, the five tasks were randomly ordered.

The reciprocity dimension was originally tested using an analysis of covariance on conditional probabilities, with unconditional probabilities as the covariate (Gottman et al., 1976), but that method is extremely conservative in making Type II errors. Therefore, the reciprocity analyses presented in that paper may have been too hasty in concluding that there was no evidence for reciprocity effects in the talk table data. This data was reanalyzed in Gottman (1979) using the z-score analysis, which was developed subsequent to the publication of the Gottman et al. paper (see Bakeman and Dabbs, 1976; Sackett, 1977; Gottman and Bakeman, 1978).

In the analysis of reciprocity, there was insufficient data to go beyond lag three. The negative reciprocity results showed that while clinic couples were likely to reciprocate negative affect, the nonclinic couples were not. The positive reciprocity results did not differentiate between the clinic and nonclinic groups, since both were very likely to show positive reciprocity cycles. As in previous studies, it was negative reciprocity, not positive reciprocity that discriminated the clinic from the nonclinic couples.

2. *Study 2.* A second study was undertaken to test the generality of these results. The same methods were used to recruit thirty couples, fourteen clinic and sixteen nonclinic. The groups did not differ on demographic variables; however, they averaged 32.5 years of age and had been married an average of nine years.

The procedure was the same as in Study 1 with two exceptions. Only one high-conflict task (the IMC) and one low-conflict task (rating the nutritional value of food items) were used. Also, more explanation was given for the use of the talk table, and a specific example was provided for the intent codes.

The amount of data allowed negative reciprocity analyses to lag three for nonclinic couples and to lag four for clinic couples. Results replicated Study 1. Negative reciprocity analyses showed clinic couples at much higher rates of reciprocity than nonclinic couples. The nonclinic wives reciprocated their spouses' negative affect at lag one, but otherwise the couples showed no negative reciprocity. However, the clinic couples showed strong reciprocity cycles through lag four. With analyses to lag six, both groups had strong positive reciprocity cycles through all lags.

In a related study, Markman (1977) investigated the predictive capability of the talk table. Couples planning to marry used the talk table as they completed several questionnaires and intereacted on a range of decision-making tasks, including a marriage contract task and resolving a relationship issue. Followups one year and two and one-half years later involved the same tasks. The impact of messages, that is, the partner's perception of the affect, was the crucial variable. The impact ratings at the initial assessment were highly correlated (correlations in the .60s) with satisfaction ratings at the second followup two and one-half years later. Negative impact predicted low satisfaction at a later time, while positive impact predicted high satisfaction. Thus, the important variable in the prediction of marital satisfaction was the perception of the partner's affect.

In summary, both groups showed high positive reciprocity, but the clinic groups had much higher rates of negative reciprocity. These results are in line with the previously described findings, indicating that the data derived from the couples' own perceptions of their interaction are consistent with data obtained from the observational coding system.

F. Interaction at Home

The preceding studies have shown consistently that distressed and nondistressed couples are discriminated by reciprocity of negative affect, but not by reciprocity of positive affect. However, these studies were done in a laboratory setting. Is it possible to generalize from laboratory-based results to marital interaction at home?

In the only investigation of this question, O'Rourke (1963) used a shortened form of the Bales IPA to study the interaction of families on two tasks—making up a story about several Thematic Apperception Test cards, and solving a set of standardized family problems. The results suggest that family interaction tends to be more positive at home than in the laboratory, but there were several methodological problems in the study including lack of attention to observer bias and observer reactivity, no assessment of interobserver reliability, and no control of possible order effects.

However, many of the couples participating in the marital studies in the Gottman laboratory found the laboratory assessment procedures therapeutic, even though the procedures were not designed as therapy. This observation would lead to a hypothesis precisely opposite to O'Rourke's, namely that the interactions in the laboratory are likely to be more positive than similar interactions at home without the presence of strangers. It is logical that being videotaped in the presence of strangers in a relatively public and unfamiliar setting should have the effect of increasing politeness and decreasing negative interaction.

Nineteen couples responded to a newspaper advertisement announcing two weekend "couples communication workshops" to be held in a local church. The workshops are described in detail in Gottman et al.'s (1976) book designed for couples. During a laboratory interview, couples completed the demographic information form, the MRI, and the problem inventory, and the major marital issue was identified. Then couples were randomly assigned to a condition in which they returned to the laboratory to be videotaped as they tried to reach a mutually satisfactory resolution to their problem. Eight of the nine other couples were given a portable audio cassette recorder and a cassette and asked to complete a tape at home when they were alone during the next week. One of the nine couples cancelled their appointment. All ten couples completed the videotape and seven of eight completed the cassette tape. The two groups of couples did not significantly differ in age, years married, or number of children. Also, they did not differ on MRI scores; however, their mean scores were intermediate to the scores of the distressed and nondistressed couples in the study of the topography of marital conflict. This would suggest that the interaction patterns of these couples should be intermediate to the patterns of distressed and nondistressed couples, with interactions resembling those of nondistressed couples in the laboratory and those of distressed couples in the home.

In this study, affect was coded solely from the speaker's voice tone. A screen was attached to the videotape monitor to conceal the picture so that face and body cues would not inadvertently influence the coders. Reliabilities of affect coding from voice cue alone were very high, with a median score of 0.97.

Results indicated that reciprocity of positive affect was equally likely at home and in the laboratory. Only lag one conditional probabilities were computed because of low rates of positive affect. At home, both husband and wife were likely to reciprocate the spouse's affect. In the laboratory, wives were more likely to reciprocate husband's positive affect, but the husband's reciprocity remained at the same level as at home.

In contrast to these results, there were large differences in the likelihood of negative reciprocity at home and in the laboratory. In the laboratory, neither wife nor husband showed reciprocity of negative affect. However, at home negative affect cycles continued with highly significant z-scores into the sixth lag.

Therefore, couples were equally likely to reciprocate positive affect in the home and in the laboratory. However, while couples showed *no* negative reciprocity in the laboratory, they were very likely to have long cycles of negative reciprocity in the home. These results provide strong support for the hypothesis that interactions in the laboratory would be more positive than interactions at home. Results also supported the hypothesis that interaction patterns of these couples would be intermediate to the patterns of distressed and nondistressed couples in the

Gottman et al. (1977) study. In the laboratory, these couples resembled the nondistressed couples of the earlier study, with reciprocity of positive affect. However, at home, their long cycles of negative reciprocity resembled the interactions of the earlier distressed group.

Additional analyses were performed to see if couples within the distressed and nondistressed range of the MRI would also show these differences in interaction in the home and laboratory. In the laboratory group, three couples were within the low satisfaction range of previous studies and two couples were within the high satisfaction range. Two couples in the home group were in the low range, but only one couple was within the high range. There were no significant differences in demographic data among the four groups. There was insufficient data to go beyond lag two. In the laboratory, spouses did not reciprocate negative affect, although the spouse who was negative was likely to be negative again on the second lag. However, the home groups showed wide differences between high and low satisfaction groups. In the high satisfaction group, spouses showed the same reactions as in the laboratory, but the low satisfaction home group showed a high degree of patterning with negative reciprocity to lag two. In summary, there was little difference in negative affect patterning between the high and low satisfaction laboratory groups, but there were large differences between the high and low satisfaction home groups. At home, the high satisfaction couples showed no negative reciprocity, but the low satisfaction couples were very likely to engage in negative reciprocity cycles.

While the low satisfaction groups identified above had MRI scores similar to clinic groups in other studies, these couples were not in therapy and had not necessarily identified their marriage as in need of professional help. A group of seven couples in marital therapy was recruited to compare to the overall home workshop group. These couples completed a cassette tape at home, and these tapes were intermixed with the tapes of the home workshop group so that coders were unaware of the source of the tapes. The home clinic couples and the home workshop couples were not significantly different on age, years married, number of children, or marital satisfaction scores. Results indicated that the two groups were very similar in both positive and negative affect reciprocity. There were low but significant probabilities of positive affect reciprocity, and high probabilities of negative affect reciprocity.

These results indicate that home interaction contains more negative affect reciprocity than interaction in the laboratory and that the differences between low and high marital satisfaction couples are more extreme in the home than in the laboratory. As a generalizability study, these results suggest that laboratory studies are valid indicators of the differences between low and high marital satisfaction couples, although they tend to underestimate the extent of these differences. Therefore one can place confidence in the differences previously reported to hold for the interaction of couples home alone.

G. Summary of Results Across Studies

These investigations have presented a consistent view of the differences between distressed and nondistressed spouses. Throughout these studies, groups were discriminated by negative, but not positive, reciprocity. More specifically, although both groups showed high rates of positive reciprocity, the distressed groups were much more likely to engage in negative reciprocity than the nondistressed groups. This lack of negative reciprocity in nondistressed couples seems to be due to the nondistressed wife, who does not reciprocate her husband's negative affect past lag one. This discrimination among groups becomes greater during interaction at home alone.

Distressed and nondistressed couples were also discriminated in the dominance dimension. Nondistressed couples showed an egalitarian dominance pattern in both mood and expressive components. While distressed couples showed an egalitarian pattern in the mood component, the husband dominated the interaction in the expressive component.

VII. DISCUSSION

A. A Precise Interpretation of Dominance

The equation of dominance with asymmetry in predictability has some advantages as well as some serious limitations. Recent theorizing on dominance supports the proposed definition of dominance. In the literature on animal behavior, a recent attempt was made to extend the dominance concept beyond the arena of aggressive interactions. Chance suggested that the asymmetrical patterning of attention, usually assessed by visual gaze, could be used as an index of dominance even in nonaggressive encounters (Chance, 1967; Chance and Jolly, 1970; Chance and Larsen, 1976). This suggestion is entirely consistent with the asymmetry in predictability definition, although the predictability definition is more general; for example, the measure could be excitement or activity levels during play as well as gaze.

However, there is an important limitation of this equation of asymmetry in predictability with dominance. For example, in caretaking interactions the fact that a mother's behavior is more predictable from her baby's behavior than conversely may be purely a function of the caretaking context; in play interactions the same asymmetry may be indicative of the social/cognitive developmental level of the infant. If a mother waits for her baby to be interested in play and her behavior is thus highly predictable from her baby's, but not vice versa, it does not make much sense to refer to the baby's behavior as "dominant" in the same sense as an alpha male monkey's aggressive behavior toward a beta male may be called dominant. In short, asymmetry in predictability need not always imply dominance. Dominance is a function of both the participants and the situational context of the interaction. The conceptual label given to asymmetry in predictability should vary as a function of the dependent measures, the situational context (e.g., the goals and tasks of the interaction), and the nature of the interaction.

In the case of marital interaction, the dependent measure that was used to tap the nature of interaction *within* a discussion was based entirely on agreement and the affect codes. The phase spectrum, which is the measure of assymmetry, assesses lead-lag relationship. Husband dominance thus means the husband leads and the wife responds affectively. Therefore, asymmetry on this variable between husband and wife is more precisely interpreted as an asymmetry in emotional responsiveness, with the male less responsive emotionally than the female in a distressed marriage.

Rubin's (1977) exceptionally insightful interview study of working class and professional couples observed a similar pattern of asymmetry in emotional responsiveness. She wrote:

> . . . Thus, they talk *at* each other, *past* each other, or *through* each other—rarely *with* and *to* each other. He blames her: "She's too emotional." She blames him: "He's always so rational." In truth, neither is blameworthy. (p. 116)

Rubin notes the differences in masculine and feminine role in our culture with respect to affect, and, she concludes:

> This equation of emotional with nonrational, this inability to apprehend the logic of emotions lies at the root of much of the discontent between the sexes, and helps to make marriage the most difficult of all relationships. (p. 117)

In our own laboratory we are currently investigating a hypothesis that relates this asymmetry to the high levels of negative affect and negative affect reciprocity that characterizes distressed marriages. The hypothesis is that the husband in a distressed marriage is not responsive to *low intensity* affective expressions by his wife (e.g., mild sadness, worry) whereas the husband in a nondistressed marriage is responsive to these low intensity affective expressions. The distressed wife must escalate the intensity of her affective expressions to get her husband to respond. High intensity negative affect is coercive in the sense of Patterson and Reid (1970) and its response is, predictably, more negative affect.

In this manner, an asymmetry in emotional responsiveness may produce negative affect reciprocity.

B. Advances

The program of research presented here revealed a pattern of variables that consistently distinguished distressed from nondistressed couples. These variables, reciprocity and dominance, were conceptualized in terms of the *patterning* of interaction, rather than as frequency rates of behavior. The use of sequential analysis and time-series analysis allowed a quantitative approach to the study of this patterning. When faced with the masses of data often generated by observational studies, the investigator cannot rely on the simple inspection of data to reveal patterns in the interaction. Often participants themselves may be unaware of the sequential aspects of their behavior. It is only through the use of the data analysis techniques of time-series and sequential analysis that these patterns of reciprocity and dominance emerge.

These investigations made extensive use of nonverbal cues of affect in the face, voice, and body. We are currently developing new, more detailed coding systems for the face and voice. The voice tone coding system will involve giving specific codes such as sarcasm, bitterness, or tenderness to the voice tone.

The new facial coding system is now in use. It is a micro-level analysis of facial expressions designed for frame-by-frame analysis of each person's face. Split-screen filming gives a three-quarter face view of two people who sit face to face during the filming. This videotape is viewed frame by frame, using slow motion so that the exact beginning and end of the expression can be determined. A code-generator/frame-counter numbers each frame as it is filmed so that there is a standard reference point.

Because so many expressions in normal conversations are blends of the pure expressions, this micro system separately codes the brow, the eyes, and the mouth. For example, the brow could be coded as "asymmetrically raised," the eyes as "slightly closed with laugh lines," and the mouth as "asymmetrical nasolabial grooves." The total effect would be a bemused, quizzical look. Gaze, tilt of head, and hand manipulations are among the other variables coded. This detailed coding system is actually more reliably coded than the former positive-neutral-negative system, probably because it requires almost no inference on the part of the coder. When the expression is broken down into facial sub-areas, it is possible to have a separate code for each possible facial expression within that sub-area.

This micro-coding technique makes it possible to look for dominance and reciprocity of affect on a very different level. Instead of looking for probability changes in global affect scores, it is possible to look for probability changes in certain facial expressions over a very short period of time. An example would be "lag-mirroring," which occurs when person B shows the same facial expression as person A, with a slight time delay. Figure 2 shows the lag-mirroring of a raised nasolabial groove (one side of the mouth raised as if in doubt or disgust) in a pair of identical twins. The person on the right shows the expression first and then the person on the left mirrors it. This entire interaction lasted approximately two seconds.

C. *Limitations*

As in all research, there are limitations that must be mentioned. One problem was the sample of spouses. With few exceptions, the couples were in their twenties or early thirties and had been married less than ten years. Interaction patterns of older couples or those who had been married longer may differ from the patterns shown by this sample. However, similar patterns of interaction were shown by spouses in their mid-twenties who had been married approximately three years (Sections VI.A and VI.E) and by spouses who had been married an average of ten years (Sections VI.C and VI.F). This suggests that the results reported here should generalize to older spouses.

Another limitation of these studies was the task the couples completed. In most cases, couples engaged in problem-solving tasks, either their own marital problems or improvisations selected by the experimenters. The discussion of marital problems may not be a common activity of spouses, and may be one that many couples avoid. Therefore, the interaction patterns reported here may not generalize to the majority of spouse interactions. Research currently in progress asks couples to discuss the events of their respective days, a nonproblem-solving task that may generalize to more couple interaction, and also studies the interaction of these couples at home.

D. *Implications of Reciprocity and Dominance*

The general results of these investigations indicated that distressed and nondistressed couples showed similar rates of positive reciprocity. However, the distressed couples were much more likely to engage in negative reciprocity cycles. An additional difference between distressed and nondistressed couples was that while nondistressed couples showed egalitarian dominance patterns (that is, neither person is dominant), in distressed couples the husband is usually dominant, but only in the moment-to-moment expressive component.

Although we have now defined both dominance and reciprocity in terms of probability change, we have not explained *why* this probability change would occur. The question remains, why is one person so responsive to

Figure 2. The lag-mirroring of facial expressions in a pair of identical twins.

the other's behavior? We theorize that the crucial factor in predicting reciprocity and dominance may be symmetry or asymmetry in the perceived cost of leaving the relationship for each person. The higher this perceived cost, the more dependent a person is on the relationship and the more responsive he or she will be to the other person.

The cost of leaving the relationship can be conceptualized in the terms of Thibaut and Kelley's exchange theory (1959, 1978). If two people, A and B, are interacting in some sort of relationship, each person will obtain certain rewards from interacting with the other, but certain costs will also be involved. The overall worth of the relationship (reward minus cost) will be called the Value (V) of the relationship. The V may (and probably will) be different for A and B.

Both A and B have alternatives to this particular relationship. They could form similar relationships with other people or they could leave this relationship and stay alone. The value of the best of these possible alternative situations is known as the Comparison Level for Alternatives (CL_{alt}). Note that the CL_{alt} refers to alternative situations, not just alternative people. In this way, long-lasting effects to the person are taken into account. For example, many older women believe that divorce is a disgrace. For one of these women, the alternative situation to their marriage would consist of the stigma of divorce as well as other aspects of the alternative situation. The alternative of remaining alone is also included here.

From these components, a third variable, the Unique Value (UV), can be formed. The UV signifies the reward value gained from the present relationship that could not be gained from the CL_{alt}. This relationship can be expressed mathematically as:

$$UV = V - CL_{alt} \qquad \text{Eq. (4)}$$

Again, the UV for A and for B may be very different.

According to Thibaut and Kelley, the larger the UV, the more dependent the person is on the relationship. The greater this dependency, the more responsive he or she will be to the other person's actions and emotions, and the more predictable his or her behavior will be from the other person's behavior. If both people hold a high UV for the relationship, reciprocity will result because they will be equally responsive. If both hold a low UV, they will behave relatively independently because neither person will be responsive to the other. However, if one holds a higher UV than the other, that person will be more responsive, more predictable, and therefore subordinate. The person with the lower UV will be acting more independently, will be less predictable, and will be dominant.

This explanation has implications for the reciprocity and dominance results reported in this chapter. In the nondistressed couples, spouses reciprocated positive affect. However, the nonclinic husband's negative affect was often followed by neutral or positive affect by the nonclinic wife. This "editing" served to prevent a possible negative affect cycle, and may be a function of the wife's role in the dyad. The distressed couples also reciprocated positive affect, but were likely to reciprocate negative affect as well. In these couples, the wife was reciprocating the husband's negative affect rather than ignoring it, leading to the negative affect cycles. Her greater responsiveness could be explained by the husband-dominant pattern common to distressed couples. According to the exchange theory formulation, the wife is very dependent in a husband-dominant relationship. This dependency on the relationship causes her to behave more responsively, thus reciprocating the husband's negative affect and leading to negative affect cycles. This explanation is more plausible when one remembers that negative affect is not only anger, but also includes sadness, defensiveness, whining, etc. Thus, the distressed wife may respond defensively to her husband's accusation or cry when he is angry, whereas the nondistressed wife (who is not so dependent on the relationship) may respond less emotionally.

This formulation may also have implications for marital therapy. It seems plausible that the person with the highest UV (the most dependent person) will be the most responsive to therapy. Because this person is more dependent on the relationship, he or she should be more anxious to keep the relationship viable. This person will be able to compromise more, possibly raising costs or lowering rewards, before the UV reaches the zero point. On the other hand, if the person with the lower UV has to compromise much, his or her UV may soon reach zero, tempting the person to go to the alternative situation (CL_{alt}). (It is interesting to note that in a therapy study reported by Gottman, Markman, and Notarius (1977), the couples with the best prognosis were those in which the wife showed negative affect, but not negative reciprocity. In those wives, the negative affect might be seen as evidence of some specific problem that could be solved, rather than the effect of negative reciprocity caused by dependency.)

This explanation was formulated after the reported research was completed, so it has not been given a formal test. Pilot research is being conducted at the present time to construct valid and reliable measures of the V and CL_{alt} components.

E. Summary

Overall, the high degree of negative reciprocity and dominance in distressed couples can be seen as evidence of a higher degree of structure than is seen in nondistressed couples; that is, their behavior is more predictable. In such a structured situation, a disturbance in one part of the system is more likely to disturb other parts of the system. As Sander (1977) wrote:

> . . . *perturbation* of the "disjointed" or partially independent subsystem as a consequence of its adaptive encounter with the surround does not spread to the rest of the system. The subsystem is, in effect, insulated from the rest of the system. . . . On the other hand, when the system is tightly coupled and relatively poor in such states of equilibrium, perturbation of one subsystem preempts the function of the rest of the component subsystems to restore variables to their region of stability. (pp. 141–42)

Applied to the distressed marital dyad, this implies that events that cause negative affect in the husband should produce delayed negative affect in the wife. However, the more loosely structured nondistressed couples should be more adaptive to disturbance.

These investigations have described empirically some of the behavioral differences between distressed and nondistressed couples, specifically the patterns of reciprocity and dominance. The next task is to investigate possible determinants of this patterning, such as the concept of Unique Value described here; to look at the more typical discussions of couples; and to explore the reciprocity and dominance concepts with more detailed nonverbal coding systems.

REFERENCES

Alexander, J. Defensive and supportive communications in family systems. *Journal of Marriage and the Family,* 1973, *35,* 613.

Altman, I. Reciprocity of interpersonal exchange. *Journal of Theory of Social Behavior,* 1973, *3,* 249.

Azin, N. H., Naster, B. J., & Jones, R. Reciprocity counseling: A rapid learning based procedure for marital counseling. *Behavior Research and Therapy,* 1973, *11,* 365.

Bakeman, R., & Dabbs, J. M., Jr. Social interaction observed: Some approaches to the analysis of behavior streams. *Personality and Social Psychology Bulletin,* 1976, *2,* 335.

Bales, R. F. *Interaction process analysis.* Cambridge, Mass.: Addison-Wesley, 1970.

——— In T. Parsons, R. F. Bales & E. A. Shils (Eds.), *Working papers in the theory of action.* New York: Macmillan, 1953.

Bales, R. F., & Strodtbeck, F. L. Phases in group problem-solving. *Journal of Abnormal and Social Psychology,* 1951, *46,* 485.

Becker, W. C. In M. L. Hoffman & L. M. Hoffman (Eds.), *Review of child development research,* Vol. 1. New York: Russell Sage, 1964.

Brazelton, T. B., Koslowski, B., & Main, M. In M. Lewis & L. A. Rosenblum (Eds.), *The effect of the infant on its caregiver.* New York: Wiley, 1974.

Cohen, J. A coefficient of agreement for nominal scales. *Educational and Psychological Measurement,* 1960, *20,* 37.

Cronbach, L. J., Gleser, G. C., Nanda, H., & Ragaratnum, N. *The dependability of behavioral measurements: Theory of generalizability for scores and profits.* New York: Wiley, 1972.

Davis, J., Stasser, G., Spitzer, C. E., & Holt, R. Changes in group members' decision preferences during discussion: An illustration with mock juries. *Journal of Personality and Social Psychology,* 1976, *34,* 1117.

Davitz, J. R., & Davitz, L. J. The communication of feelings by content-free speech. *Journal of Communication,* 1959, *9,* 6.

Ekman, P., & Friesen, W. V. Nonverbal leakage and clues to deception. *Psychiatry,* 1969, *32,* 188.

——— *Unmasking the face.* Englewood Cliffs, N.J.: Prentice Hall, 1965.

Gottman, J. M. *Marital interaction: Experimental investigations.* New York: Academic Press, forthcoming.

Gottman, J. M., & Bakeman, R. In M. Lamb, S. Soumi & G. Stephenson (Eds.), *Methodological problems in the study of social interaction.* Madison: University of Wisconsin Press, forthcoming.

Gottman, J. M., Gonso, J., Notarius, C., & Markman, H. *A couple's guide to communication.* Champaign, Ill.: Research Press, 1976.

Gottman, J. M., Markman, H., & Notarius, C. The topography of marital conflict: A study of verbal and nonverbal behavior. *Journal of Marriage and the Family,* 1977, *39,* 461.

Gottman, J. M., Notarius, C., Markman, H., Bank, S., Yoppi, B., & Rubin, M. E. Behavior exchange theory and marital decision making. *Journal of Personality and Social Psychology,* 1976, *34,* 14.

Gouldner, A. W. The norm of reciprocity: A preliminary statement. *American Sociological Review,* 1960, *25,* 161.

Granger, C. W. J., & Hatanaka, M. *Spectral analysis of economic time series.* Princeton, N.J.: Princeton University Press, 1964.

Haley, J. Research on family patterns: An instrument measurement. *Family Process,* 1964, *3,* 41.

Hetherington, E. M., & Martin, B. In H. C. Quay & J. S. Werry (Eds.), *Psychopathological disorders of childhood.* New York: John Wiley & Sons, 1972.

Hops, H., Wills, T. A., Patterson, G. R., & Weiss, R. L. The marital interaction coding system (MICS). Unpublished manuscript, University of Oregon, 1972.

Jacob, T. Family interaction in disturbed and normal families: A methodological and substantive review. *Psychological Bulletin,* 1975, *82,* 33.

Jenkins, G. M., & Watts, D. G. *Spectral analysis and its applications.* San Francisco: Holden-Day, 1968.

Johnson, S. M., & Bolstad, O. D. In L. A. Hamerlynck, L. C. Handy & E. J. Mash (Eds.), *Behavior change: Methodology, concepts, and practice.* Champaign, Ill.: Research Press, 1973.

Jourard, S. M., & Jaffee, P. E. *Journal of Counseling Psychology,* 1970, *17,* 252.

Kelley, H. H., & Thibault, J. W. *Interpersonal relations: A theory of interdependence.* New York: John Wiley & Sons, 1978.

Kendon, A. *Acta Psychologica,* 1970, *32,* 100.

Koopmans, L. H. *The spectral analysis of time series.* New York: Academic Press, 1974.

Lederer, W. J., & Jackson, D. D. *The mirages of marriage.* New York: W. W. Norton and Co., 1968.

Locke, H. J. *Predicting adjustment in marriage: A comparison of a divorced and a happily married group.* New York: Henry Holt & Co., 1951.

Markman, H. J. A behavior exchange model applied to the longitudinal study of couples planning to marry. Unpublished doctoral dissertation, Indiana University at Bloomington, 1977.

Maslow, A. H. The role of dominance in the social and sexual behavior of infra-human primates: I. Observation at Vilas Park Zoo. *Journal of Genetic Psychology,* 1936, *48,* 261.

Mehrabian, A. *Nonverbal communication.* New York: Aldine-Atherton, 1972.

Murrell, S. Family interaction variables and adjustment of nonclinic boys. *Child Development,* 1971, *42,* 1485.

Murstein, B. I., Cerreto, M., & MacDonald, M. G. A theory and investigation of the effect of exchange-orientation on marriage and friendship. *Journal of Marriage and the Family,* 1977, *39,* 543.

O'Leary, K. D., & Kent, R. In L. A. Hamerlynck, L. C. Handy, & E. J. Mash (Eds.), *Behavior change: Methodology, concepts, and practice.* Champaign, Ill.: Research Press, 1973.

Olson, D. H., & Ryder, R. G. Inventory of marital conflicts (IMC): An experimental interaction procedure. *Journal of Marriage and the Family,* 1970, *32,* 443.

O'Rourke, J. M. Field and laboratory: The decision-making behavior of family groups in two experimental conditions. *Sociometry,* 1963, *26,* 422.

Osgood, C. E. Dimensionality of the semantic space for communication via facial expressions. *Scandanavian Journal of Psychology,* 1966, *7,* 1.

Oskamp, S. Effects of programmed strategies on cooperation in the Prisoner's Dilemma and other mixed-motive games. *Journal of Conflict Resolution,* 1971, *15.*

Patterson, G. R., & Reid, J. B. In J. Michaels & C. Neuringer (Eds.), *Behavior modification for psychologists.* New York: Appleton-Century-Crofts, 1970.

Rappaport, A. E., & Harrell, J. A behavior exchange model for marital counseling. *Family Coordinator,* 1972, *21,* 203.

Raush, H. L., Barry, W. A., Hertel, R. K., & Swain, M. A. *Communication, conflict, and marriage.* San Francisco: Jossey-Bass, 1974.

Reid, J. B. Reliability assessment of observational data: A possible methodological problem. *Child Development,* 1970, *41,* 1143.

Romanczyk, R. G., Kent, R. N., Diament, C., & O'Leary, K. D. Measuring the reliability of observational data: A reactive process. *Journal of Applied Behavior Analysis,* 1973, *6,* 175.

Rubin, M. E. Differences between distressed and nondistressed couples in verbal and nonverbal communication codes. Unpublished doctoral dissertation, Indiana University at Bloomington, 1977.

Sackett, G. P. In J. Osksky (Ed.), *Handbook of infant development.* New York: Wiley, 1977.

Sackett, G. P. (Ed.). *Observing behavior,* Vol. 2; *Data collection and analysis methods.* Baltimore: University Park Press, 1978.

Sander, L. W. In M. Lewis & L. A. Rosenblum (Eds.), *Interaction, conversation, and the development of language.* New York: Wiley, 1977.

Schaefer, E. S. In J. P. Hill (Ed.), *Minnesota symposia on child psychology,* Minneapolis, Minn.: University of Minnesota Press, 1971.

Schulman, A. Activity, talking time and spontaneous agreement in disturbed and normal family interaction. *Journal of Abnormal Psychology,* 1972, *79,* 68.

Schultz, W. C. *The interpersonal underworld: FIRO-B.* Palo Alto, Calif.: Science and Behavior Books, 1960.

Speer, D. C. Marital dysfunctionality and two-person non-zero-sum game behavior. *Journal of Personality and Social Psychology,* 1972, *21,* 18.

Staub, E., & Sherk, L. Need approval, children's sharing behavior, and reciprocity in sharing. *Child Development,* 1970, *41,* 243.

Steiner, I. D. *Group process and productivity.* New York: Academic Press, 1972.

Stephen, F. F., & Mishler, E. G. The distribution of participation in small groups: An exponential approximation. *American Sociological Review,* 1952, *17,* 598.

Stephenson, G. R. In E. W. Menzel, Jr. (Ed.), *Symposia of the fourth international congress of primatology,* Vol. 1. Basel, Switzerland: S. Karger, 1973.

Stuart, R. Operant-interpersonal treatment for marital discord. *Journal of Consulting and Clinical Psychology,* 1969, *33,* 675.

Taplin, P. S., & Reid, J. B. Effects of instructional set and experimenter influence or observer reliability. *Child Development,* 1973, *44,* 547.

Thibault, J. W., & Kelley, H. H. *The social psychology of groups.* New York: Wiley & Sons, Inc., 1959.

Von Cranach, M., & Vine, I. (Eds.). *Social communication and movement.* New York: Academic Press, 1973.

Watzlawick, P., Beavin, J. H., & Jackson, D. D. *Pragmatics of human communications: A study of interactional patterns, pathologies, and paradoxes.* New York: W. W. Norton, 1967.

Waxler, N. E., & Mishler, E. G. Scoring and reliability problems in interaction process analysis: A methodological note. *Sociometry,* 1965, *29,* 32.

Weick, K. E. In G. Lindzey & E. Aronson (Eds.), *The handbook of social psychology,* Vol. II. Reading, Mass.: Addison-Wesley, 1968.

Weiss, R. L., Hops, H., & Patterson, G. R. In L. A. Hamerlynck, L. C. Handy & E. J. Mash (Eds.), *Behavior change: The fourth Banff convention on behavior modification.* Champaign, Ill.: Research Press, 1973.

Wiggins, J. *Personality and prediction.* Reading, Mass.: Addison-Wesley, 1973.

Wills, T. A., Weiss, R. L., & Patterson, G. R. A behavioral analysis of the determinants of marital satisfaction. *Journal of Consulting and Clinical Psychology,* 1974, *42,* 802.

Wilson, E. D. *Sociobiology: The new synthesis.* Cambridge, Mass.: Kelknap Press of Harvard University Press, 1975.

Winter, W. D., & Ferreira, A. J. Interaction process analysis of family decision-making. *Family Process,* 1967, *6,* 155.

Worthy, M., Gary, A. L., & Kahn, G. M. Self-disclosure as an exchange process. *Journal of Personality and Social Psychology,* 1969, *13,* 59.

Zahn, L. G. Verbal-vocal integration as a function of sex and methodology. *Journal of Research in Personality,* 1975, *9,* 226.

STRATEGIC BEHAVIORAL MARITAL THERAPY: TOWARD A MODEL FOR ASSESSMENT AND INTERVENTION

Robert L. Weiss, UNIVERSITY OF OREGON

I. INTRODUCTION

Both conceptions of and the practice of marital therapy have grown phenomenally within the last decade. Among the most salient sources for this proliferation of interest are the proponents of "behavioral marital therapy" (Jacobson and Martin, 1976; Jacobson and Weiss, 1978; Weiss, Hops, and Patterson, 1973; Weiss, 1978). The presentation of behavioral forms of marital therapy in the literature stress the empirical basis for the technology (Jacobson, 1978; Weiss and Margolin, 1977), thereby making it possible for those of other persuasions to forcefully examine and

Advances in Family Intervention, Assessment and Theory, Volume 1, pages 229–271.

ISBN: 0-89232-137-7

critique the "reinforcement view" of adult intimacy (Gurman, 1978; Gurman and Kniskern, 1978). Further development can be seen in an ambitious symposium that presents marriage and marital therapy from the psychoanalytic, systems, and behavioral points of view (Paolino and McCrady, 1978), along with presentations of their respective therapeutic practices. We now enjoy far greater sophistication in the evaluation of marital therapies, particularly in the challenges to Behavioral Marital therapy (BMT), and the question of whether it can deal with phenomena heretofore excluded by what Gurman and Kniskern (1978a) have called "a simplistic Skinnerian framework." These authors hold that most behavioral therapists have abandoned learning theory reinforcement orthodoxy in favor of a more enlightened cognitive emphasis on private events (client phenomenology), and argue that BMT practitioners are no longer justified in failing to join them.

As is often the case, when a technology-based program is first presented many significant details of "practice" are omitted. The argument is often advanced that written accounts of BMT fail to mention the "other factors" deemed important to the practice of BMT. The central issue for all forms of therapy is how therapist behaviors are brought under rule control. That is, therapists' interventions must be under the stimulus control of a conceptual model for assessment and intervention. [In a related sense Wills (1978) has reviewed the literature on those factors which determine *therapist* perceptions of clients.] BMT has been challenged on two fronts: (1) Failure to incorporate "cognitive" events and (2) insufficient detailing of the role of nonspecifics in gaining client compliance. One assertion made in this chapter is that we are now ready to spell out ways in which cognitive elements and nonspecifics can be conceptualized within BMT.

The issue is not adherence to a "mindless behaviorism" instead of the promise of a richer phenomenology, but rather how conceptualizing cognitive factors facilitates the applications of BMT, and whether it leads us to clinical innovations. Similarly, it can be said that any attempt to gain compliance from another person is based upon some degree of artifice. Indeed, Frank (1973) has stressed that all therapy seems to involve the arousal of hope in persons who are demoralized; that this occurs within a formalized context of "help giving" that includes formal techniques for ministering to the patient. (See Murray and Jacobson, 1978, and Bergin and Lambert, 1978 for detailed consideration of "nonspecifics" in therapeutic outcome.)

A. The Nature of the Problem

Why should BMT include cognitive formulations? Some of the more recent persuasive arguments will be considered first.

1. Rejection of Behavioral Philosphy. Behavioral approaches to human problems do not enjoy a favorable press among consumers (and often among colleagues). That behavior is controlled by the manipulations of personal (rather than anonymous) "others," (e.g., a therapist rather than Madison Avenue), is considered generally unacceptable. That we should be paid off contingently for our efforts, or worse, that we ought to reward a spouse for doing what he/she should otherwise execute out of love, or devotion, contradicts the voluntary nature of egalitarian relationships. Addressing specific behaviors rather than employing familiar trait descriptors is not only a taxing bother, but it also fails to capture the essence of such important abstractions as love, devotion, etc. In a word, the humanistic thrust of the "Me" generation effectively tarnishes the silver lining of our behavioral cloud. This ideological rejection of BMT is often interpreted as client "defensiveness," although more simply, there are cultural grounds for such rejection.

2. Issues of Noncompliance. It is often difficult, once therapy has been started, to continually ensure client compliance with therapist prescriptions (assignments). In some instances clients may lack rudimentary cognitive skills (orderly record keeping, etc.) but more often it becomes a matter of one partner's using noncompliance as a within-relationship problem. ("See, what did I tell you? He simply won't do his assignments!") Or, a couple may accept the tenants of BMT but show specific noncompliances that are not readily amenable to usual forms of contingency control, such as extracting penalty deposits from clients. Noncompliance often occurs within the context of the relationship itself—one person fails to meet a commitment thereby punishing the other for having completed an assignment.

At some point compliance and relationship distress blend; compliance itself would be evidence that there was no problem with the relationship (Gurman, 1978). Thus it can be argued that to insist on compliance is tantamount to asking the clients not to exhibit the very symptoms that brought them to therapy in the first place. Compliance, therefore, cannot be a precondition of therapy!

3. Dyadic Focus Is Counterintuitive. Relationship distress is experienced as the failures of one's partner—either in behavior or in intentions. Although a person may enter individual therapy to present a catalogue of personal failings (even here one finds it easier to externalize blame to "others"), a couple is not likely to present their *relationship* for treatment. More typically they present the shortcomings of the other person. Such externalizing of problems may actually facilitate dealing with them. Not uncommonly a host of physical symptoms are presented by one partner (Weiss and Birchler, 1978) which further intensifies the externalization. Thus, when the marital therapist attempts to focus on the dyad, suggesting that the difficulties are relational in nature, the message correctly comes through as "You are contributing to your own distress." This dyadically focused message is counterintuitive and may lead to the conclusion that the therapist simply does not understand the intensity of the individual's upset. Yet, to accept the clients' version of their "problem" and to plan an intervention on that basis alone will prove ineffective. Therefore, a technique-oriented approach, such as BMT, can only be successful in a small number of cases.

4. Not All Problems Represent Skill Deficiencies. This point, mentioned when considering issues of noncompliance, suggests that some difficulties are relationship problems per se and not a case of responses occurring at either too high or too low a daily rate. Put bluntly: If a couple had every social skill teachable, would the partners necessarily choose to be married to one another? For those positions that emphasize intraindividual organization in developmental processes, it is not the topography of responses, but a melding of derivative needs that predicts marital satisfaction or stability. Although evidence of need and trait complementarity is lacking (Meyer and Peper, 1978; Bentler and Newcomb, 1978) relationship intricacies cannot, it is argued, be built up from segmental skills. On the other hand, one could argue that by engaging in an activity often enough it is possible to develop a positive sentiment about that activity. However, to suggest that a couple work on some behavioral task in order *to learn* to love one another would only encourage further popular rejection of BMT psychology.

5. Reward Devaluation. For many distressed couples there seems to be little that A does for B, and vice versa, that judged by objective standards is rewarding. From a behavioral framework the couple may be seen as exchanging negative behaviors or even actively punishing one another, yet they stay together. A simple Law of Effect, it is argued, would predict noncontinuation of the relationship.

Two alternatives are available at this juncture: (a) Specify the nature of rewarding exchanges within the observational system itself, or (b) Leave the behavioral model entirely and invoke a system which emphasizes inferential constructs, e.g., one involving symbolic encoding of behaviors. Let us consider each in turn.

(a) It is often inadvisable to focus on isolated behavioral exchanges when in fact it is the temporal extent of a transaction that contains the key to contingency control. A couple may develop a cycle of fighting-making-up-fighting, etc., which is really part of a complex chain of behavior. Because of their temporal extent, such chains are not readily observable as such. Although such chains might be possible in principle it is often the case that they are not spelled out within the behavioral point of view.

(b) The reliance on inferential constructs is of course more familiar to those working with behavior change. Stuart (1969) invoked the concept of Comparison Level for Alternatives (CLA) in his exposition of an operant interpersonal theory of marital interaction. That which could be defined as rewarding within a relationship was dependent upon the available alternatives for each person of the dyad. Without independent measurement of the CLA we are given the tautology that persons stay in a relationship because they have not left. We invoke relationship cohesion because alternative relationships are too costly, yet without independent measurement of the CLA.

Critics of the behavioral approach of course stress "motivational" constructs, either from a psychodynamic model (Sager, 1976) or from a systems theory viewpoint stressing the intent of a couple to protect one another in the relationship as defined. Thus a marriage may represent an *unelaborated* negotiation about self-worth, for example, I trade you X for your providing me with Y. Marriages of convenience have been recognized for some time, and those with far less explicit detailing of the rule of exchange are common in marital therapy practice.

In either case, the conclusion reached by critics is that BMT must extend itself considerably if it is going to accommodate problems of reward devaluation. Indeed, couples stay together for reasons not readily apparent to a behavioral exchange model, and without invoking motivational constructs such relationship stability is not well explained within such models.

6. Distinctions between Impact and Intent. Gottman's research has focused on the distinction between the impact of a communication and the intent of the sender (Gottman et al. 1976). It has been shown that both distressed and nondistressed couples rated the intent of their communications similarly, yet the distressed, relative to the nondistressed, couples rated the impact of messages as less positive: "Distressed couples were having less positive impact on their spouses than they intended" (p. xv). This finding, similar to our concern with reward devaluation, suggests that for distressed relationships, the receiver filters out the intentional positiveness and replaces it with a self-generated negativity. This perceptual processing is more similar to cognitive information processing considerations than it is to Skinnerian contingency management issues.

7. Success Rates of BMT. Gurman and Kniskern (1978b), in their review of outcome effectiveness, conclude that BMT is not appreciably more effective than other forms of marriage therapy (however, see also Jacobson, 1978). If indeed BMT was something special it should exceed the now familiar 66 percent success rate.

These represent some, certainly not all, of the reasons one can find for being critical of BMT and, perhaps more importantly, reasons for arguing that BMT must go cognitive, or at least take into consideration the widespread "resistance" one encounters in marital work. The immediate conclusion is that something more dynamic than tinkering with responses is needed.

B. Tinkering, Tactics, and Strategy

As even a cursory look at the behavioral journals would suggest (Marks, 1978), changing responses have been beneficial to persons exhibiting a vast array of troublesome behaviors. (For evaluations of the outcome of various forms of BMT see Jacobson, 1978; Gurman and Kniskern, 1978b.) Nor are behavioral therapists unaware of response changes that may be under specific situational control, for example, demand characteristics of the therapy setting. Rosen and Kopel (1977) report an instance of such limited "success" in their treatment of chronic deviant sexual arousal that turned out to be under the control of "demand characteristics," such as pleasing the therapists and/or the client's wanting a way out of therapy! Therapists also seem to be aware that generalization to broader response systems is better trained-in than its occurrence assumed.

Nevertheless, the growth of all forms of couples' therapy has advanced relatively unencumbered by theory development (Olson, 1970; Weiss and Margolin, 1977). Not surprisingly we often find a number of techniques having minimal conceptual dependence on one another applied to persons seeking some form of relationship therapy (Gurman and Kniskern's 1978b review). While not truly representing instances of response tinkering, earlier approaches to unhappily married couples were at a relatively low level of intervention complexity (Patterson, Weiss, and Hops, 1976); they were characterized more by technique than by theory, such as token exchanges or contracting. As BMT became more explicitly modular (Weiss, Hops, and Patterson, 1973; Azrin, Naster, and Jones, 1973; Stuart, 1976), it entered a tactile stage; technology *per se* gave way to the *ordering* of technological possibilities for accomplishing explicit, short-term outcomes. Such reports focused on the sequential application of technique-defined modules (e.g., Jacobson, 1977; Margolin, Christensen, and Weiss, 1975).

As application of behavioral tactics gained acceptance by therapists, it became apparent that couples and therapists were not always working toward the same relationship outcome. Client acceptance of BMT and compliance with assignments were causes of therapist frustration. Problems of noncompliance traditionally have been dealt with in psychoanalytic therapies as matters of resistance. The communications oriented systems theorists (e.g., Watzlawick, Weakland and Fisch, 1974) explain the inertia of a system using different concepts, notably those that have become identified with strategic therapy; impediments to change are the focus nonetheless. Because of its obvious emphasis on transactional behaviors, the strategic theories may be useful for BMT. BMT intervention is strategic to the extent that the therapist orchestrates the application of tactics in ways designed to overcome the usual problems of noncompliance.

Strategic therapy has taken on the specific meanings given it by the advocates of systems formulations of interpersonal distress that derive from communications models (Jackson, 1965; Haley, 1973, 1976; Watzlawick, Weakland, and Fisch, 1974; Sluzki, 1978). In at least two instances (Johnson and Alevizos, 1975; Weiss, 1976) attempts have been made to incorporate strategic approaches into behavioral therapy with adults. Largely because the strategic point of view claims success with "symptomatic" behaviors that are resistant to the direct behavior change attempts, it is of interest in those cases in which BMT seems to be ineffective with couples. The remainder of this section will consider strategic therapy as it may apply to BMT.

Haley (1973) defines therapy as strategic when the therapist initiates that which happens during sessions and is otherwise responsible for designing an approach to each problem.

> In strategic therapy the initiative is largely taken by the therapist. He must identify solvable problems, set goals, design interventions to achieve those goals, examine the response he receives to correct his approach, and ultimately examine the outcome of his therapy to see if it has been effective. (p. 17)

These attributes of strategic therapy are similar to those subscribed to by BMT. The BMT practitioner is active; he/she focuses on identified problems, makes use of empirical methods in evaluating the process of therapy, and utilizes outcome measures.

The differences between strategic and BMT approaches are defined best by comparing their parent models. It is axiomatic within strategic therapy that a relationship cannot present itself to an outsider for purposes of change. The communications of the partners represent analogic forms of relationship organization which is understandable as a metaphoric representation of the relationship's difficulties. As Watzlawick et al. have stated the matter, "The solution adopted by the couple to their problem is the *problem*." It is the partners' attempt to maintain relationship homeostasis which is getting in their way.

Within the BMT model, relationship difficulties are conceptualized largely in terms of faulty behavior change tactics; couples rely upon aversive behavior control techniques, exchanging negative reinforcers for positive reinforcers, for example, belittling the other's favors as a tactic for increasing the rate of such favors (Stuart, 1969). Not only is there a decreased rate of positive exchanges, but the couple reciprocally controls their use of negative reinforcement and punishment in what has been called the coercion model (Patterson, Weiss, and Hops, 1976). By focusing on behavior change tactics which are based upon positive control and increasing the exchange of positive reinforcers, one increases relationship satisfaction (Azrin, Naster, and Jones, 1973).

The two approaches differ in whether the nature of transactions are changed incrementally through step by step application of skills training (BMT), or by manipulating how the spouses interact with one another in light of a reassignment of meanings of specific acts (systems model). These meaning changes are not so much a matter of producing insight or awareness as they are a matter of therapist-induced change in the context of behaviors, for example, by changing the locus of the struggle for control from between the spouses to between a spouse and the therapist, or between spouses as a unit and the therapist.

Strategic forms of therapy are best known for their use of paradox and reframing the linear causality offered by clients as the explanation of their difficulties (Sluzki, 1978). Whereas the BMT practitioner often serves as a consultant to a relationship, providing new skills to be mastered by the couple, the strategic therapist utilizes the language and structure of the relationship of a particular couple as a means of applying leverage for change. The therapist may encourage the couple to engage in some exercise which, if viewed from a skills training point of view, would be patently absurd. For example, a couple might be encouraged to fight at specific times designated by the therapist "in order to understand your fighting better." It is not a case of fighting as catharsis, nor learning the rules for "fair fighting," but a strategic maneuver to bring fighting under therapist control and no longer under spouse control. The rules for ritualistic fighting (and thereby its meaning) have now been changed. By shifting the context of a particular struggle, the transaction can be changed.

It is well to caution at this point that blind application of paradox (as some form of "reverse psychology") is certain to lead to disastrous outcomes for couples. Strategic prescriptions (Haley, 1976; Sluzki, 1978) are based upon a careful analysis of a problem within the domain of a particular theoretical framework, and because of the heavy use of counterintuitive and nonlinear causality one should be very cautious in tinkering with such forms of intervention.

We can now use strategic forms of therapy as a model for reconsidering the criticisms of BMT noted earlier as these argue for changes in BMT itself. First, BMT has been strategic in the more general sense that it has made modular applications of techniques (sequenced tactics) that take order into account when addressing relationship skill deficits (Weiss and Birchler, 1978). Contracting skills may not be necessary for every couple, although problem solving skills may be; the temporal sequencing of such training will of course depend upon evidence of compliance with prior assignments.

BMT has not been strategic in the sense of making a direct attack on the typical "resistances" to such a therapy with couples. When one more closely analyzes the specific techniques described as strategic therapeutic intervention, two classes of activity standout: (1) Changing relationship attributions about causality, by various techniques of *cognitive restructuring;* an annoying spouse behavior can be redefined as "spouse being protective, solicitous, caring, etc;" (2) Effecting behavior changes by counting on spouses to predictably counter therapist prescriptions thereby making a given outcome the one actually desired by the therapist. When instructed to fight on schedule, a couple may find their fighting has stopped miraculously. Sudden shifts in transactional behaviors (patterns) can be brought about without attempting to change the theory of the relationship. One could put two squabbling siblings under a regime that reinforces increasing amounts of time together not spent in fighting; after some days this shaping procedure may be effective. However, one also could create a dyadic situation (context) that naturally leads to nonfighting, such as assigning them the task of simultaneously washing both sides of the same window! Given that particular context it is reasonable to assume that before long each will be making faces at the other, outdoing the other's washing behavior, etc. Such a contrived confrontation does not attempt to change the "theory" of their relationship ("why we can't get along"), but it does foster reciprocal interest and nonfighting. Similarly, it does not attempt to teach new skills for handling conflict between them.

Cognitive restructuring is not the exclusive domain of the strategic therapies, since it will be recognized that such techniques figure largely in cognitive behavioral therapies as well (Mahoney and Arnkoff, 1978). From the research in this area it appears that those cognitive-restructuring interventions that require active utilization of skills, so-called coping training, are more likely to be effective than attempts that simply alter cognitions (e.g., self statements) (Mahoney and Arnkoff, 1978). The explicit emphasis on situational engineering within the context of creating paradoxical outcomes, typical of systems oriented approaches, seems to have no parallel within behavioral approaches. This is largely explained by the fact that behavioral models are quite straightforward in postulating active ingredients of change that typically do not require decoding symbolic behaviors. BMT especially has not yet evolved a theory of practice beyond that offered by the specific content of the technology to be applied to a given relationship. As noted elsewhere (Weiss and Margolin, 1977; Patterson et al., 1976) marriage relationships are complex in the sense that it is very difficult to assess the reinforcing exchanges of intimates. The BMT practitioner may see only the tip of the iceberg at any one time, and may not be well-equipped to deal with the power struggles for control that system's theorists (Haley, 1976) find typical of marital therapy. However, it must be pointed out that, with very few exceptions, the strategic approaches considered here represent a nonempirical literature based more on art than clearly stated theoretical principles or controlled research. (Recent exceptions may be found in DeShazer, 1978; Rohrbaugh et al., 1977.)

The remainder of this chapter will consider an outline for the integration of BMT with these aspects of "strategic" therapies focusing on noncompliance problems. In a broadest sense our focus is on the use of cognitive restructuring in BMT. Since many of the ideas are drawn from systems theoretical points of view, it is labeled a Behavioral Systems Approach to marital interaction and change.

B. *The Competency-Based Model of BMT*

As noted above, BMT gained its position of eminence without an accompanying theory of practice. Once the goals for marital success were defined, usually involving repertories of communication and behavior change skills, the procedures for attaining these goals followed directly (Weiss et al., 1973.) Also as noted above, BMT seemed to ignore the "dynamics" of marital relationships, that indeed persons establish intimate relationships for a host of nonrational reasons. By implication, if not by direct inference, the application of skills training to behaviors based upon nonrational principles of organization would be doomed to failure, meaning one could not bring about responsible changes in distressed relationships.

It is becoming more and more the case that all models of marriage therapy view the transactions between the partners as critical for understanding the relationship. Thus, one finds exponents of intrapsychic theory espousing the relationship between intrapsychic organization and how a couple evolves patterns for dealing with their exchanges (Meissner,

1978; Gurman, 1978). At the transactional extreme it is far more important to know what the people are doing in an effort to accomplish their goals than who they are in a personality-descriptive sense. The choice of models, it would seem, is between one which argues that what the people are doing is limited by their premarital psychological development, or one that holds that contemporaneous patterns of interaction are sufficient for a theory of behavior change. [For an early, now classic, statement of the transactional point of view the reader may select Jackson's (1965) paper on marital *quid pro quo*.] Both points of view agree on the fundamental assumption that marriages are interactively patterned, that redundancies, and stereotypical transaction cycles are recognizable.

BMT is basically a competency-based model of human intimate interaction (Weiss, 1978). The motives for a particular relationship are somewhat less important to an understanding of that relationship than are the means available to the partners for accomplishing goals within that relationship. Partners may harangue or bludgeon one another with accusations, both for intrapsychically plausible reasons, according to a particular model for decoding ongoing behaviors. But alternatively, one could view the transactions as self-perpetuating, based not on intrapsychic dynamics but on either mutually reinforced aversive control tactics, or what often amounts to the same thing—marked skill deficits in communication and problem solving. Marriage can be viewed as a relationship that demands competencies on the part of the participants. A couple may persist in ritualized transactions because they are skill deficient in ways for changing the course of a transaction once it has started. Just as individuals may fail to master their responses to demanding social situations (Sundberg, Snowden, Reynolds, 1978, for a review of the literature on assessing competencies) a relationship may fail to reach its major goal—providing life-sustaining benefits to the partners. It is precisely this failure that we equate with marital dysfunctioning. From this point of view a relationship that generates considerable psychopathology or somatically-based disturbances may be said to be homeostatic, adjustive, and intrapsychically inevitable, but *not* beneficial to the partners. Thus while it may be possible to decode such relationships as serving the (postulated) needs of one or the other partner, such explanations do not speak to the life-sustaining aspect we defined as basic. To be sure, an alcoholic and his/her spouse may be symbiotically joined, displaying a teeter-totter alternating balance, but only unless they are incapable of any other adjustment should we argue for the truly adjustive basis of their symbiosis.

As stated earlier, it is precisely those relationships which appear to an outsider as least beneficial that are difficult to conceptualize in an exchange-of-benefits model without also invoking some collusive pact describing how each partner provides exactly what the other needs.

Strategic writers are quite correct in stressing the aim-discrepancy between therapist and marriage client; a couple's ability to *prevent* relationship change might seem brilliantly organized. Indeed, some might suggest that the partners are quite competent in providing benefits.

It is interesting in this regard to observe at least one functional explanation of our very high divorce rates, namely, that individuals believe they are capable of deriving greater benefit from a different relationship. Although disengaging is a major stressor for most, requiring still different competencies (Bloom, Asher, and White, 1978), the greater ease with which people now can leave a relationship may make some of our theories of why they stay together unnecessary. The motives we have postulated for why marriages continue, when reason would have suggested otherwise, may evaporate when we focus on the conditions which more easily allow people to disengage.[1] In some European countries divorce is simply financially unthinkable, thereby requiring accommodations based upon economic necessity rather than romantic love; such relationships would be congruent with a competency-based model. Thus, the conditions which hold people together may be in some measure a function of their cognitions (self-efficacy expectations as described below), the sociological realities of their time, and their competencies in managing interpersonal benefits.

As a preliminary approach to a psychology of competency-based intimacy, the author has posited four relationship accomplishments (Weiss, 1978; Weiss and Birchler, 1978) that define general dimensions of relationship achievement. Further, the model orders these accomplishments hierarchically, so that each is dependent upon a prior accomplishment. As defined here, the four relationship accomplishments are Objectification, Support/Understanding, Problem Solving, and Behavior Change.

1. Objectification: Refers to the verbal and nonverbal ways in which a couple accomplishes *denotative* communication. This establishes a relationship rule that says, in effect, there must be agreement on the description of events pertaining to the dyad. Interaction at any other level of communication must stop and revert to this basic "factual" level whenever a partner calls for factual clarification. The pedantic, boring, and restrictive characteristics of such a demand are its saving grace! One cannot accuse the other of not caring, for example, until it has been established that there is agreement about the description of events. Considerable misunderstanding can be eliminated by forcing denotative agreement.

The behavioral technique of pinpointing is used to accomplish this end. Couples learn to speak in a behavioral-object language. Love, appreciation, consideration, and so forth, become behavioral acts that, by mutual agreement, are instances of these desirable abstractions. A partner is inconsiderate when specified behaviors either fail to occur at an acceptable rate or other behaviors occur at a rate deemed too high for comfort, for example, failing to call when late. Pinpointing is action-oriented denotation—in contrast to cataloguing trait descriptors (e.g., lazy, unkind, unappreciative, etc.).

A functional analysis of behavior requires taking *the setting* as well as the topography of the responses into consideration. Objectification includes delineation of the situational control of behavior. Arguments do not simply happen; they happen in a setting. By tracking situational components of a relationship one can objectify the interaction as being under situational control. By correctly labeling the context, a couple may abort an evening of increased argumentativeness, for example, the setting defined by coming together after a hard work day requires both recognizing the other person and using appropriate distancing techniques.

Finally, a couple must objectify benefits they provide one another, and require for themselves. Distressed couples often have failed to keep these kinds of discriminations current.

Various tracking devices have been created to assist couples with objectification requirements, for example, the Spouse Observation Checklist (SOC), which is an inventory of pleasing/displeasing relationship behavioral events.

2. Support/Understanding: Intimacy is not nurtured by objectivity alone. An intimate relationship must provide the partners with support and understanding, whether one chooses to view this as fulfilling dependency needs, defining self-worth, or esteem. Certainly couples turn to communication as a means of providing support and understanding. Here a host of "listening" skills may be relevant (e.g., Guerney, 1977).

3. Problem Solving: The focus here is on outcome, either the conclusion reached by deliberation, or the implementation of an agreed-upon plan of action. There has been a tendency to use this phrase, problem solving, to refer to BMT procedures generally (Jacobson, 1979), but for the modular approach described here (i.e., for tactical reasons) it is best to distinguish that domain of activity from the other aspects of relationship accomplishment.

When objectification moves to a consideration of what to do as a means of accomplishing ends, it becomes problem solving. But problem solving includes more than mere objectification in the sense of pinpointing and developing a denotative-behavioral vocabulary. Bringing behavior under stimulus control—as in the case of agenda sessions, and setting aside administrative times—is essential to this definition of problem solving.

The distinction between support/understanding and problem solving is very important. Too often a partner problem solves when supportive behaviors are called for. A specific technique for helping with this distinction includes discrimination-training, referred to as "modality checking," which determines whether one's spouse wishes to problem solve or to express feelings.

4. Behavior Change: This final accomplishment refers to specific instrumentalities for bringing about relationship change. The use of bilateral contracts (with or without explicit contingency controls) is a common example. It is important to note that specific forms of negotiation training may be accomplished in the previous (problem-solving) module, so that the work of formalized contracting is partly accomplished prior to this point. Also, it is clear that without objectification skills, without increases in goodwill occasioned by increased supportive functions, there would be little chance for behavior change to occur.

The areas of accomplishment just summarized represent the categories of competence requisite for an intimate relationship. Automatic acceptance of these relationship goals is quite another matter, and leads to the question: Why do people resist doing what would be beneficial to them? There are two suggestive answers to this question, the behavioral and the strategic.

The behaviorally based answer suggests that people simply do not track their own interpersonal effectiveness. Bandura (1977) refers to *reciprocal determinism,* the interfaces among the person, behavior, and the environment (p. 9), as a model for incorporating the effects a person has on his/her environment as well as how the environment effects subsequent behaviors, and particularly how the person functions as an active decision maker in the entire process. The latter, it seems, is captured by our proclivity for creating constructs as a means of organizing experience, for example, positing traits, motives, and our sense of choosing alternative actions. We perceive behavior not as discrete events but as organized outcome-relevant (meaningful) events.

The strategically based answer (from a systems perspective) is that intimate relationships are based upon complex negotiations about who has control over which aspects of decision making. The politics of a relationship, as it were, can be expressed metaphorically as the voluntary and involuntary control of transactions. Having agreed to one set of power rules ("You are the one who has the power to make decisions about X") yet expressing dissatisfaction whenever the partner exercises that prerogative ("Oh, I suppose I'll make do if *you* go ahead with X") leads to paradoxical communication and ultimately to relationship distress as seen clinically (Haley, 1963, p. 125). Given this particular model, attempts to intervene at a communication skill level may disrupt the relationship even more than it is since the partners would be unprepared for dealing with the basis of their conflict.

Thus, the answer to our question about the less than enthusiastic acceptance of the four areas of competence has to do with (a) failures to track specific behavioral outcomes, itself a skill deficit, and (b) complex issues of control which define the structure of a given relationship. In the next section we will outline three facets of the cognitive-behavioral interface which are relevant for the larger integration we are proposing in this chapter.

II. TOWARD A MODEL FOR STRATEGIC BMT

In this section we will develop three components of a model for strategic BMT, in order to illustrate how cognitive factors may be incorporated into the practice of BMT. Our use of "strategic" differs from the definition derived from the Haley-Watzlawick axis, in that we propose a much broader set of concepts, and as mentioned above, cognitive restructuring subsumes many of the communications-based applications.

A. Sentiment, Skill, and Choice

Contemporary expression of adult intimacy is found upon voluntary selection of a partner. Each has chosen to become enmeshed in an emergent lifeplan of togetherness. A bargain has been struck that holds promise of considerable benefit to each person. This type of relationship is based largely upon *sentiment,* the love, regard, and fulfilment promised by relatedness; each partner is buoyed by the promise of unconditional positive regard—that one is noncontingently worthwhile in the eyes of the other. Such positive sentiment at the early stages of intimacy is not based upon response-by-response accountability, but rather upon an overriding promise that one's worthwhileness is guaranteed. This sentiment-override makes it possible to provide noncontingently for the other, and to disregard the shortcomings of the other. *Confirmation that such a sentiment is valid does not occur incrementally, but rather cataclysmically.* Validity emerges Phoenix-like from the pool of indiscriminate arousals and doubts, provided principally by the loved other. In our culture, true love requires that one appear stunned or overcome by some affliction that has overtaken an otherwise responsible, cognate person. To suggest to the love-victim that he or she reinstate some empirical response-contingent accountability (e.g., track number of positive favors received) would be tantamount to rejecting the first premise of true love. Universal truths, such as: partners must work at making their relationship succeed, are often ignored in the specific case. This unbridled optimism is likely to reappear with the birth of a first child, the accountability fostered by prenatal classes notwithstanding. The significance of the sentiment-override for relatedness is not to be taken lightly.

In order to accommodate to one another, the partners must not only believe accommodation is an intrinsically desirable goal, but they also must develop skills for accomplishing the objectives of daily living, which include both instrumental outcomes as well as the affectional-communicative aspects of relatedness. The ways in which a couple learns to manage their affection-communication interactions are less open to objective feedback than are the ways in which they learn instrumental skills. To be sure, housekeeping and caretaking skills are not insulated from idiosyncratic values, and couples can weave complicated webs of symbolic meanings around the fact of a sloppy kitchen, but the product (e.g., a clean kitchen) is more readily available to intersubjective scrutiny than are affectional outcomes. The effectiveness of such skills emerges within a particular relationship in which judgments of effectiveness are made by the participants themselves. But it is also true that a couple's ongoing interaction provides a complex environment of reinforcing contingencies that effectively alters interactional behaviors. *The evaluation of interaction patterns is a joint function of sentiment and the outcome of events themselves.* The impact of a behavior may differ from the intent of the person providing that behavior. We know, for example, that attempts to account for daily marital satisfaction with knowledge of specific behaviors exchanged between spouses account for only 25 percent of the satisfaction variance (Wills, Weiss, and Patterson, 1974).

Thus, if there have been no major drawdowns on the sentiment account, attributions of "good intention" will continue; for example, "My partner is well intentioned, but we are having minor difficulties." More likely, after a period of trial and error at accommodating, the control shifts from the positive-sentiment override to a somewhat negative (or at least sentiment-questioning) set of attributions. It is unlikely that "skill deficiency" will be implicated as the "explanation" for difficulties; rather, we suspect attributions about the deliberate choice to withhold or (later) some form of limited malevolence, e.g., a partner is said to be "getting even" for some felt hurt.

Thus, we posit a simple typology, Figure 1, that helps to relate three subjectively held views of partner-behaviors: the quality of sentiment, judgment about requisite skillfulness, and judgment of the other's volition, for example, whether a partner chooses to respond. At this point we focus on the view from the perspective of the spouse, not from that of the therapist.

The examples first can be divided according to the judged quality of sentiment, whether favorable (positive) or unfavorable (negative). (Partner may be seen as caring or not caring, for example.) This division is made by the first and second triads of cases.

Next, a partner may be seen as having or not having requisite skills *independent* of the quality of the sentiment. Since the third (volitional)

Figure 1. Typology combining Sentiment, Skillfulness, and Choice

Situation:	Sentiment	Skillfulness	Choice	
I	+	+	+	
II	+	+	–	Positive Sentiments
III	+	–	0	
IV	–	+	+	
V	–	+	–	Negative Sentiments
VI	–	–	0	

From the perspective of the spouse a partner can be judged to have either positive or negative sentiment, skillfulness, and choice. A + choice indicates that the partner chooses to do behavior X, while – indicates choosing not to do X.

component involves choice of response there is an important asymmetry for skillfulness entries: skill judged to be absent eliminates the possibility of response choice, meaning, a person judged to lack some requisite skill cannot be judged also as having chosen (or not chosen) to make the response controlled by the skill. Thus, whenever skillfulness is judged to be absent (negative signs in the table) the choice component must also be absent (zero). Given these restrictions, the choice component may be judged independently of the sentiment component. Since we never make all the responses we are capable of, the conditions under which we are "willing" to respond become important in marital considerations.

How then can this typology assist our understanding of spouse attributions? Situation I is highly congruent: a spouse is seen as having positive regard, skillfulness, and also chooses to execute the skill-related behaviors. In VI, the situation is somewhat ambiguous, since we do not know whether lack of skill has caused negative sentiment or whether negative sentiment has prevented skill development (in that particular relationship). But, since skillfulness is absent, refusal to comply cannot be attributed to choice. (The same is true for III.)

Situations II and V have the same volitional component (refusal) ("He can, but he won't"), but differ importantly on sentiment, and thus should lead to different outcomes. In situation II, where we find positive sentiment, skillfulness, but withholding the response, the assessment might be that playful cajoling or seductive attempts to persuade will lead to desired (nonwithholding) outcomes, while in situation V there is likely to be an intervening negative judgment ("You bastard!") since situation V conveys the message that the other is not worth making a response for. Such an attribution would lead to coercion, escalation of negative trades, or more simply, withdrawal.

Finally, in situation IV the partner is judged to be willing to make the response but for illicit reasons, that is, reasons based upon factors other than the worthwhileness of the recipient partner. This is a common complaint made to the BMT practitioner—that it is the therapist who is making the response occur, not the true (positive) intention of the spouse.

This same typology, as seen from the perspective of the therapist, indicates that only objective information about skillfulness is possible; sentiment and choice must be inferred. That is to say, the therapist may be able to assess relationship skills within a behavioral model, but the subjectivity of sentiment and choice present unusually difficult problems. We can always assume positive sentiment as a working hypothesis, running the risk of disqualifying the intensity with which the other person holds an opposing view. Similarly, to become embroiled in philosophical problems of why a person chooses or does not choose a certain behavior is beyond the scope of our therapy and may actually lead to an impasse.

B. Cognitions and Competencies

The second facet of the cognitive-behavioral model being proposed here deals with cognitions about competencies within a transactional context. The previous section focused on the phenomenology of sentiment, skillfulness, and choice, and how these provide the basis for particular kinds of *attributions* about the other. The emphasis here is on the dyad itself, impediments to change, and therapist decisions about selecting behavioral applications.

Both behavioral and systems points of view make the same important distinction between linear and circular causality regarding the role of cognitions in behavior. Linear causality holds that cognitions (attitudes, beliefs, etc.), A, lead to changes in behavior, B; this is represented by A → B. Most insight-oriented therapies operate on this assumption. Circular, or nonlinear causality holds that behavior (B) also alters cognitions (A). Diagramatically, this is represented as $\circlearrowright\binom{A}{B}$. In this instance, focusing on behavior change (B) leads to a change in cognitions (A). Although there are obvious limitations on how much a focus on B can bring about a change in A—people would certainly resist any suggestion that they have no say in what they choose to value—changes in behavior do lead to cognitive changes. Clinically, it is not uncommon to observe a marked change in rated daily marital satisfaction brought about through changes in frequency of pleasing behavioral exchanges, although both spouses may still report having attitudinal doubts about the other's motives. The brief time devoted to BMT may be one explanation of the failure of A to catch up with B.

Within his elaboration of cognitive-behavior theory, Bandura (1977) makes an interesting distinction between two types of expectation which he defines as *efficacy* and *outcome* expectations. Efficacy expectations refer to cognitions about whether one can *successfully execute* the behavior required to produce a desired outcome. Performance or outcome expectancies are defined as a person's estimate of the degree to which a *behavior will effectively lead to some desired outcome* (Bandura, 1977, p. 79). This distinction is between estimates of self-efficacy (am I capable of doing such and such) and knowing that certain behaviors lead to particular outcomes in the real world. Thus, a person may acknowledge that paraphrasing and reflecting would be effective in creating a feeling of acceptance, but nevertheless hold the belief that he/she was unable to make such a response. (Thoresen calls these negative self-efficacy statements "belief barriers.") Modifying Bandura's original illustration of these relationships to cover the case of the dyad, we have Figure 2:

Figure 2. Efficacy and Outcome Expectations in BMT

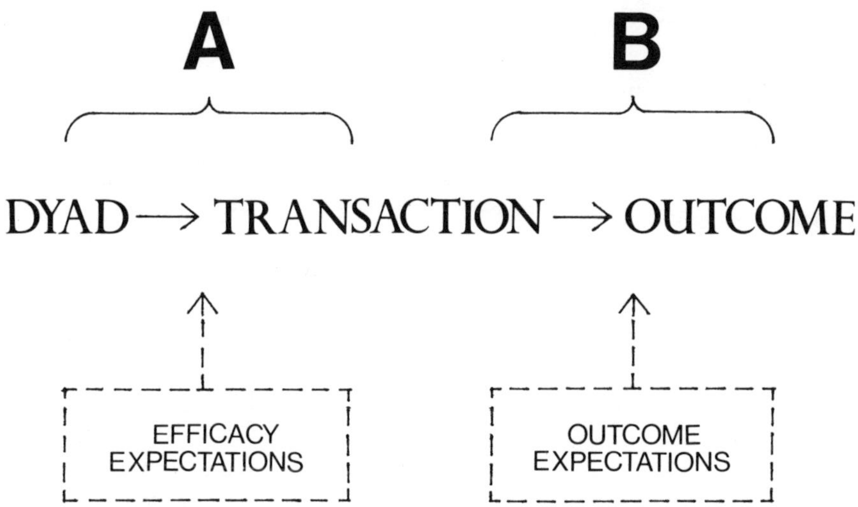

Strategic BMT is concerned with the A Segment of efficacy expectations held by the dyad. Traditional forms of BMT have focused on the B Segment, imputing outcome skills to partners.

Behaviorally oriented therapies often restrict themselves to the B segment of the illustration by providing training in skills (techniques) designed to produce reliable outcomes. For example, assertive "I" statements often facilitate outcomes. Yet, in terms of efficacy expectations, the A segment, it is necessary that persons see themselves as capable of making assertive responses. Typically, the behavioral view holds that once a behavior is changed, the B segment, the cognitive or attitudinal component (A) will catch up, and people will accept themselves as capable of the response.

A strategic decision is required as to whether the focus of intervention should be on the B segment (outcome expectancies) or on the A segment (efficacy expectations). The decision is guided by an assessment of whether behavioral changes *will* provide feedback to cognitive beliefs, or whether "belief barriers" will continue to impede behavioral changes. If the sentiment held by the partners is positive, the situation is best seen as one of response deficits, that is, they need skill training. If the sentiment override is no longer operating, or sentiment is judged to be quite negative, it is necessary to intervene at the level of efficacy expectations. For the intimate dyad, efficacy expectations are not only of the sort "Can we do such and so?" but more complex cognitions forming *a theory of the relationship. Any of the myriad cognitions clients offer as causes for why some outcome is not occurring are efficacy expectations that impede change.*

The particular theory of transactional failure offered by a couple as the explanation of their difficulties is not likely to be useful from the standpoint of initiating change. Typically, active marital therapies do not rely on the heuristic value of such efficacy expectations as do the couples themselves. Intervention at the level of efficacy expectations—the A segment of the diagram—involves some form of *cognitive restructuring,* which in the present usage is a generic term used to encompass insight, strategic, and singularly cognitive therapies. This combination of intervention strategies under the rubric cognitive restructuring is nontraditional and requires further elaboration.

It is easy to recognize that many types of intervention with couples take the form of saying to the couple, "Look, your view of your relationship is getting you both into trouble; you are entertaining the wrong hypotheses about one another's behavior." There are a host of specific tactics for accomplishing these ends, ranging from attempting to develop insights, to milder forms of reframing causal attributions (as with the strategic writers), to rational emotive restructuring of beliefs. When the BMT practitioner engages in these forms of communication with couples, it is usually a preface to a more important message: "And now let's get down to specific training tasks."

In some cases, the strategic goal is to increase markedly the affiliative aspects of the relationship by facilitating the cognition that as partners they depend upon one another for self-evaluative information, they have power to affect each other's moods; in a word, that they have *fate control* for each other. After all, it can be asked, why did they hand over to the other person such power to affect one's sense of well-being? The current level of distress, it is argued, is simply a further manifestation of such fate control, only with the sign reversed from positive to negative. (One cannot be seriously affected by a person for whom one has little regard.) The reasoning continues with such wisdom as: The demands for more time with you, the arguments about being sexually aloof, etc., are all examples of misguided attempts to foster the gratification that was the promise of your togetherness. The problem is not the other person, it is this relationship *thing* which is controlling you.

Once the "problem" is raised beyond the individuals (externalizing the problem?) it may be possible for the couple to join in an attempt to overcome this "thing." These kinds of attributional changes were described in an earlier case presentation (Margolin, Christensen, and Weiss, 1974) and in a study of cognitive-behavioral variations in effecting relationship changes (Margolin and Weiss, 1978).

The above represent fairly direct frontal attacks on the efficacy expectations held about the relationship, and as can be seen readily they apply to those couples who seem to want to make a go of their relationship but for whatever reasons are blocked by their own theories. The next level of complexity is presented by those couples who also seem deadlocked, but for whom cognitive restructuring of the above sort only adds more grist to their cognitive mills. Attempts at reframing only lead to their incorporating the new material into a "yes, but" blocking tactic. Rather than insight or a frontal attack on cognitions, one might consider direct behavior change for the purpose of generating new interactions. At the less complex end of the continuum we have situationally based blocking, as in the example cited by Watzlawick et al. (1974). A couple's markedly reduced frequency of sexual intercourse was remedied by a simple change in context: the couple found themselves in an unusual situation when sleeping in a bed at a friend's house. The husband slept on the side to the wall so that upon getting out of bed during the night he was forced to crawl over his sleeping wife. This initiated amorous behaviors which apparently set off subsequent, more frequent instances of intercourse in their own home setting.

It is worth noting that a couple, as in the example above, may evolve an elaborate "theory" to account for their behavioral difficulties. Both popular dynamic psychology and the current emphasis on sex therapy, make possible ready-made "explanations"; they enable a whole new set of expectations as to what is wrong with one's functioning. A considerable amount of strategic therapy (Haley, 1973; Sluzki, 1978) reduces to clever methods for getting people to interact out of character. Often one person's doing the unexpected throws the other off guard and allows him/her to react out of character. (Techniques of paradox and confusion are particularly effective to this end.) Our point here is that one can effect change without focusing on development of new insights. In one sense, such changes are still at the level of efficacy expectations since what was thought not to be possible of accomplishment is now carried out.

The more difficult cases are those in which the theory of the relationship is both chronic and tenaciously held by two very negative people. These couples usually do not comply with behavioral assignments. Such couples can manage to be just as miserable in a romantic, away-from-home setting as they are at home. It is the patterned aversiveness that makes such couples difficult to work with. Creating new problems for the relationship is often helpful in moving the relationship off dead center. Sluzki (1978) has a number of specific suggestions deriving from the communications model that provide a starting point.

By way of concluding this section, we may note that an important facet of the cognitive-behavior interface is described by what Bandura has labeled efficacy expectations, which for our purposes we have expanded to mean the theory of transaction held by a couple. The efficacy-outcome expectations distinction focuses our attention either on the theory of a transaction as an impediment to change or on skill deficiency as the basis of a marital problem. Attempts to deal with the A portion of the Dyad → Transaction → Outcome model are viewed generically as cognitive restructuring interventions, while those focused on the B portion are described best as competency training. The judgment required by the model is whether one can intervene at the B segment of the chain without also operating at the A segment. The more familiar forms of strategic intervention (use of paradox, reframing, confusion, etc.) operate to unbalance a blocked interaction pattern, thereby bringing about "new" transactions without either concurrent or subsequent training at a skills level. These forms of intervention thus combine the A and B segments, which may foster the view that these techniques rely on art and intuition rather than on explicit principles of behavior change. In the present formulation the impediment to change may be sought in either the A or B segment of the Dyad → Transaction → Outcome chain. In the next section we address the third and final component of the cognitive-behavior interface, the ways in which reciprocal transactions affect both the sentiment-skill-choice complex and their implications for intervention.

C. Reciprocity as Transaction

BMT has relied heavily on notions of behavioral exchange for explaining dysfunctional marriages (e.g., Jacobson, 1979; Jacobson and Martin, 1976; Gottman et al., 1977; Patterson, Weiss, and Hops, 1976). The basic assumptions within exchange theory were taken over directly in work with couples. In one way or another couples were explicitly taught how to increase—usually in a quid pro quo fashion—exchange of positives, or more technically, how to become response contingent in their reinforcing behaviors. Without reviewing all of these technological possibilities for teaching exchange and reciprocity of reinforcing behaviors (Weiss, 1978) we may note the early popularity of contracting methods (Stuart, 1969; Weiss, Birchler, and Vincent, 1974). Contracting, and especially those forms involving an explicit tit-for-tat type of exchange, while often very effective, produced considerable resistance from clients. Gurman (1978) has provided a detailed analysis of the difficulties encountered with the use of external rewards in love relationships.[2] Jacobson (1978) has been critical of the role of contracting in teaching exchange skills, and indeed has found that two popular types of contract ("quid pro quo" and "good-faith") were not differentially effective.

In this section we will review some of the newer developments within BMT regarding reciprocity of exchanges, and also attempt to effect a rapprochement between the A and B components of the Dyad → Transaction → Outcome paradigm within the context of reciprocity. Consistent with the tripartite approach to the cognition-behavior interface already taken in this major section of the chapter, our concern here will be how couples' experiences with reciprocity become a part of their theory of relationship and the extent to which transaction outcomes are affected by the theory or the dynamics of reciprocity.

It will be helpful to recall the point made earlier that relationship transactions often occur quite independently of how they may be cognitively elaborated. A couple may become involved in a coercive loop (exchanging negatives for positives) without as yet having evolved a full-blown theory of their "unsatisfactory" relationship. Daily repetitions of instrumental behaviors may control exchanges without benefit of negative self-statements like "What a bad relationship I have."

From the earlier studies of reciprocity between spouses the data indicated that positive and negative behaviors were exchanged reciprocally within different time frames (Wills et al., 1974). Spouse-reported frequencies of daily Pleases or Displeases could be analyzed over days as *within couple* daily reciprocity, or based upon mean rates taken over a period of time as *between couple* reciprocity. The within couple analysis relies on husband-wife day-to-day covariation in behaviors exchanged; the within couple analysis is based upon the output of each couple taken over some period such as weeks. Reciprocity can be defined as relatively immediate response-contingent exchanges (tit-for-tat) or response contingency on average; one would speak of the exchange of positives or negatives being typical of a given couple on average and relative to the rates for other couples. (The latter is analogous to a given couple's typical couple-exchange rate.) These and other related studies have been reviewed by Weiss (1978) and Jacobson (1979).

Collectively, the research has shown that distressed couples are more responsive to daily variations in exchange of both positive and negative behaviors than nondistressed couples, with some evidence to suggest that negatives are more likely reciprocated in a tit-for-tat manner. This dependency on immediate exchanges can be contrasted to what Gottman et al. (1976) have labeled the "bank account" model of exchange. The bank account metaphor suggests that a couple makes an investment in their relationship by depositing positives (the sentiment override mentioned earlier), and that withdrawals from the account need not be covered (reciprocated) immediately. "Good faith" or "trust" is defined both by the line of credit and by the account balance. We may compare the attempt of two different partners to deal with an overdrawn account: (a) "We need some time for ourselves to enjoy one another; we have been putting out for everyone but us!" or (b) "You never do anything for me! I'm sick and tired of being left alone and stuck with the kids!"

Most of the existing data about reciprocity as a transaction are (a) correlational (although Jacobson and Waldron have made substantial improvements in methodological control), and (b) are based on cross sections of relationships. We simply do not know as yet how the positive sentiment actually erodes within a relationship. The coercive "You never do anything for me, etc." is not likely to be the first response to a withdrawal from the account. Yet, the self-justification ("What do you mean *I* never do anything for you, etc.") can only serve to escalate the perceived estrangement. At this point in a developing relationship it would be far better for the couple to experience directly the benefits of being together than it would to engage in theoretical discussions of intentions. This can be accomplished in one of two ways: (a) engaging in behaviors that bring them together in a comfortable setting, or (b) agreeing upon *a rule* to govern their quality-time together (e.g., "We will reserve the next two Saturdays for ourselves and go to the beach.")

To generalize, we can now suggest that the repetitive, often stereotyped, patterns of marital transactions can be conceptualized in terms of *response*-controlled or *stimulus*-controlled dynamics (Weiss, 1978). A response-controlled transaction is based upon short-term reciprocity. It may involve the escalation of negatives, or it may hold the actors to an immediate accountability. ("I did for you, you must now do for me!") Murstein, Cerreto, and MacDonald (1977) have made a similar argument against the exchange pattern by using an attitude measure of exchange orientation, showing that relative to friendships, intimate couples are more likely to report lower overall marital adjustment concomitant with a higher exchange orientation. Stimulus-controlled transactions range from low level cue control (e.g., the situation itself) to what might be referred to as a higher order list—a family *rule*. Rule control refers to the effectiveness of agreed-upon generalizations for governance of transactions, for example, "Weekends are our time for each other; we have an obligation to be supportive of one another." Both the systems and psychodynamic theories stress that not all rules need be cognitively elaborated into awareness. For the systems-oriented writers (Haley, 1976; Sluzki, 1978) marital interactions are patterned, and such patterning reflects essential family myths that are not to be exposed to the couple. For those working from a psychoanalytic position, developing insight into the patterning of need complementary is not desirable (cf. Gurman's 1978 commentary in this regard). In a somewhat related manner, Stuart (1975) has encouraged measured honesty as a major tenant in good relationships, suggesting that total self-disclosures within a relationship often create severe problems for the partners. Certainly this can be the case in international negotiations where explicit labeling may back other negotiators into a corner, thus forcing them to take even stronger positions.

The advantages of rule-controlled transactions are numerous, including efficiency, predictability, and, perhaps most important for human behavior, the fact that rule-controlled transactions can be cognitively appraised with intellect. When some behavior fails to occur according to a prior, agreed-upon rule one can refer the omission to the rule, acknowledge the good faith of the partner, and simply not respond to the inconvenience caused by the omission. This substitutes for the cognition that "all is now lost!" In the case of tit-for-tat tracking of exchanges, each instance is as important as every other instance. In the bank account model, the balance must decline markedly before the credit line is terminated. In this sense BMT must help couples overcome one troublesome aspect of their cognitive processing of information: the logical fallacy of *pars pro toto*.

While couples are still actively engaged in searching for a "theory" of why their transactions are bothersome, it is not uncommon for them to use single instances as the basis for a relationship generalization. Problems in negotiating limited resources are expressed in the form: "You did that for yourself, therefore I can do this for myself." More serious are those instances in which a couple uses specific sexual response failures to generalize to a clinical syndrome of sexual dysfunctioning. This line of reasoning suggests that some classes of behavior should never be used as the basis for generalizing value, but rather that, for some classes of behavior, rules should be negotiated *independently* of specific instances. To sort out every unfair instance when Husband utilized money for himself (buying a fishing rod that Wife thinks they can ill afford) will lead to further animosity. Rather, to set the task as one for defining rules for resource allocation takes the onus off the spendthrift traits of each person.

Behavior tracking, a stock in trade of the BMT practitioner, thus represents a two-edged sword: On the one hand, it is an excellent device for instructing couples in the kind of discrimination training they lack vis-à-vis their behavioral environments, for example, what pleasing events (describe response topography) occurred today? But, it can also force a moment-to-moment, tit-for-tat transaction rule, which the data at this point suggest is inadvisable for intimates. In fact, any of the behavioral techniques that foster reciprocal exchanges (cf. Azrin et al., 1973), including the widespread use of contracts, run the risk of fostering response-controlled exchanges. Gurman has raised still another spector by suggesting that reward control of behavior may result in the devaluation of the behavior (Gurman, 1978).[2]

III. STRATEGICALLY BASED ASSESSMENT AND INTERVENTION

This final section of the chapter will present our theory for the practice of strategically based BMT. From the preceding discussion of the Dyad → Transaction → Outcome model it was concluded that the cognitive-behavioral interface comprises both efficacy and outcome expectations, and that as marital therapists we must have an adequate assessment of relationship strengths for both sets of expectations. Not only are we concerned with what a couple presents as their theory of their relationship, but we need information about their actual competencies. Our discussion will be organized in two subsections, one on assessment and one on intervention.

A. Strategically Based Assessment

Those familiar with issues in behavioral assessment have long recognized that assessment and intervention are intrinsically related and ongoing (Weiss and Margolin, 1977). The separation imposed here is warranted only for expository reasons. It is well to observe that assessment objectives change with the stage of intervention, such that questions occurring early on with a couple do not occur in the same form later in intervention.

The goals of BMT include (1) assisting couples to decide whether they should maintain or terminate their relationship (Stuart, 1975), and (2) providing couples with relationship skills that can be used by them in the four areas of relationship accomplishment (Weiss, 1978). The presentation for therapy should be taken as an initial desire on their parts to continue the relationship in some form or another. Within our model a couple may decide to stay or stray for the wrong reasons; they may stay together because of efficacy expectations ("It won't be different in any other relationship"), or they may terminate because of overriding negative sentiment derived in large part from their own transactional failures. Stuart (1975) asks his couples to commit themselves to staying together for the course of therapy and to shelve their negative historical reasons for wanting to terminate. By adopting this "as if" stance, the couple should be able to determine whether their new-found skills produce the marital benefits both seek.

Couples' willingness to comply with this therapist request would be an important indication of the therapist's likely control of the process. Indeed, such complying cases may have a far higher statistical chance of continuing to a mutually happy outcome. More typically, the therapist sees a range of relationship problems that outrun the relative simplicity of the dichotomous stay or stray decision. For example, one partner may use the occasion of marital "therapy" to transfer responsibility for his/her dependent spouse to the protection of the therapist, thereby making an early exit from the relationship less painful. Or, a couple may present themselves as hopelessly confused as to what they should accomplish other than how it was their family physician who urged them to "seek counseling." As described elsewhere (Weiss and Birchler, 1978), a variety of somatic complaints can become part of the process of "seeking counseling." Jacobson (1977) has presented data for very distressed couples seen in a private psychiatric outpatient setting, suggesting that, even for individually extreme behaviors, BMT may be useful within a relationship context. However the "misses" with such cases are important to note; both failures to know about outside affairs or markedly disorganized behaviors can prevent the establishment of lasting gains.

There is almost no empirical evidence to help therapists answer the most demanding question: How resistant is this couple likely to be? Signs of compliance with therapist initiated requests are important bits of assessment data. Although the strategic therapies (Haley, Watzlawick) are best known for their tactics in dealing with noncompliance, there has been virtually no empirical research to support or refute these clinical applications. Identifying very early on which couples are likely to be problematic (by defeating intervention attempts presented on a tactical level) is of interest to Frankel, Reilly, and Lert (1978) and our own group at the Oregon Marital Studies Program (OMSP). Frankel and Margolin at the University of Southern California (personal communication) have adopted a strategy similar to our own in providing specific behavioral compliance tests for couples. Frankel et al. (1978) utilized response to a measure of hypnotic susceptibility, similar to the approach reported by Weiss, Ullmann, and Krasner (1960), in the context of assertiveness training. The symposium reported on by Rohrbaugh et al. (1977) includes a model for specifying which type of strategic technique is most suited for which type of resistant client, based largely upon Brehm's reactance theory. Clearly, there is considerable concern on the parts of therapists as to how to identify the client whose presence in therapy is not itself a predictor of successful outcome, yet we must await further research.

During the initial phases of meeting with a couple it is important to test for signs of *positive relationship sentiment*. [A similar point is made by De Shazer (1978) in a model which uses balance theory as a basis for systems focused strategic interventions.] It is quite a different matter to conclude that a couple's difficulty is their inept struggle with relationship skills or whether they have evolved a system that actually prevents them from dealing with intimacy. ("Affection was never displayed in my family nor do I think it is particularly worthwhile.") Any test of whether the couple is "listening" to the therapist is worth considering. Successfully getting beyond the "cassette" the couple brings—the explicit theory of their relationship—often can be tested by judicious use of reframes designed to alter current attributions. A given specific "you don't care because . . . you are the one who doesn't care!" deadlocked interaction may be dealt with (during these early stages) by creating a new problem for the couple: generalizing to an issue they had not considered. [Sluzki (1978) suggests a number of examples for moving to a different level of problem solving in his chapter.] One such example might be for the therapist, as intake worker, to suggest that all relationships have an obligation for mutual support, and "I wonder how you people have solved that within your own relationship?" If a couple fails to respond to such probes—that is, the spouses are unable to give up their cassette long enough to consider these possibilities—one must question whether the point of the contact has more to do with blame assignment than a mutually focused outcome.

The assessment devices used in the Oregon Marital Studies Program (OMSP) are useful in assessing some of the *structural* imbalances for distressed couples. Very low Locke-Wallace score (or Dyadic Adjustment Scale scores), high Marital Status Inventory (MSI) scores—a measure of divorce potential—and high conflict scores from the Areas of Change (cf. Weiss and Margolin, 1977) in the context of self-orientation suggest little hope for building togetherness. It should be noted that it is not necessarily the intensity with which distress is presented, but rather how "interested" a couple appears to be in relationship outcomes.

In assessing a couple's *potential for BMT* (the outcome expectation section) it is helpful to keep in mind the competency-based model of BMT with its four areas of competency. It now becomes necessary to provide the *content* of these four competencies since they will facilitate our answering assessment questions. The model can be illustrated as a $12 \times 4 \times 4$ solid, Figure 3. The twelve interaction categories define cognitively-appealing contents for couple interaction, that is, they represent the affectional, instrumental, and separateness components of intimate relatedness. (At this stage it is less important whether Affection, Sex, and Consideration be combined into a single category). An intimate relationship can be assessed over the front face of the model ($4 \times 12 = 48$) by asking how a couple

Figure 3. Model for Defining Goals of BMT

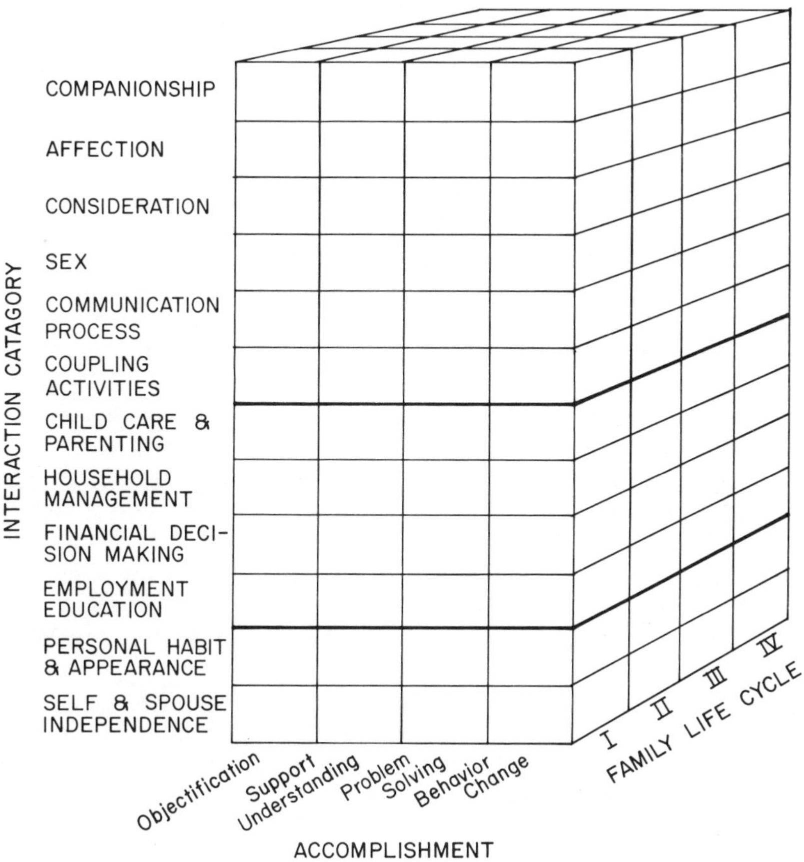

The solid represents the four areas of competency crossed with the 12 content categories of marital interaction. At any given stage in the family life cycle there would be 48 cells for assessing how accomplished a relationship is at that time.

accomplishes in each of the content areas. Clearly, stage of the family life cycle is important since competency requirements will differ with longevity. Vincent and his associates (Vincent, Harris, Ilback-Cook, and Brady, in press) have made an initial effort to sample competencies during the early childbearing years, studying the development of marital adjustment concomitant with having to cope with new offspring. Similarly, one could focus on couples during post-child rearing years and ask competency questions dictated by the 48 cells of the matrix.

Thus, the goals of BMT can be stated in terms of the cells of the Categories × Competency × Stage of Family Life Cycle model. The model provides a template by which initial assessment is organized, and viewed from the other side of the coin, how to define specific intervention strategies. We turn to these next.

B. Strategically Based Intervention

Our recommendations for intervention are strategic in the sense that they are dictated by the particular theory for BMT practice elaborated above. Briefly, we have stressed the importance of the "self-efficacy" vs. skills training aspects of the model, by relating these to behavioral exchanges which are under either response or stimulus control. To do this, it was necessary to consider the basis for relationship attributions (sentiment, skill, and choice interactions). It was noted that behavioral transactions can be cognitively elaborated independently of the topography of the behavior itself. Furthermore, we distinguished between exchanges that seemed to be under short-term control (reinforcing control characterized by quid pro quo exchanges) and those under longer term rule control (characterizing "bank account" exchanges). Available evidence supports the hypothesis that a reliance on reinforcing control appears to be characteristic of distressed relationships.

It is not surprising that couples often use single responses as the basis for generalizing to a relationship rule—clearly an example of cognitively elaborating a molecular transaction. By the same token, a couple may demonstrate a remarkable degree of patterning in some aspect of their transactions that appears to have relatively little cognitive elaboration. Such a couple would express surprise if such regularities of their transactions were pointed out to them. Degree-of-cognitive-elaboration is similar to more traditional designations of awareness (unconscious, outside of awareness, etc.) but is preferred here since we are concerned with the quality of these cognitions as much as whether there has been any elaboration at all.

Attributions are important because they set the reward value of certain classes of behavior within a relationship. All seem to agree that marriage is a relationship designed to affirm the worth of individuals; the market value of commodities exchanged is probably of lesser importance than the manner in which each perceives the intent of the other's offering. Thus, affectional behaviors are highly valued when they are perceived as spontaneous emanations from the other. Companionship and coupling activities are also valued when seen as being spontaneous, although these behaviors require more planning than hugs, kisses, and "I just called to hear your voice." Similarly, certain classes of behaviors suffer from too much cognitive elaboration. Verbalizations about one's affection, or how one *meant* to be considerate, are detractors of such otherwise acceptable rewards.

We can now organize the relationship between these theoretical concepts, degree of cognitive elaboration and response vs. rule control of behavior, into a two-dimensional space which results in an idealized factor analytic representation: we wish to locate the twelve categories of interaction in the two-dimensional space created by the axes defined by degree of cognitive elaboration and response vs. rule control of behavior. This model provides a guide to how we apply specific tactics of intervention. The location of each of the twelve categories in this space provides us with some indication of how a couple would view the behaviors subsumed by the category label as shown in Figure 4.

If affectional behaviors are seen as under rule control (an obligation to provide affection to partner) they will be devalued. (The common complaint, "He is only doing those things because your program makes him!" is a familiar therapy-created example.) Or, responding to a specific personal-habit transgression (leaving dirty clothes lying around) as if the transgression was meant for the other spouse, can lead to overgeneralizations about bad traits. Arguments about ill-advisedly spent money, arguments on a response level, rapidly disintegrate into personal attributions about the other. A couple whose companionship and coupling activities become highly patterned (rule controlled) but are never talked about (low

Figure 4. Theoretical Two-Dimensional Space Relating Type of Control and Degree of Cognitive Elaboration

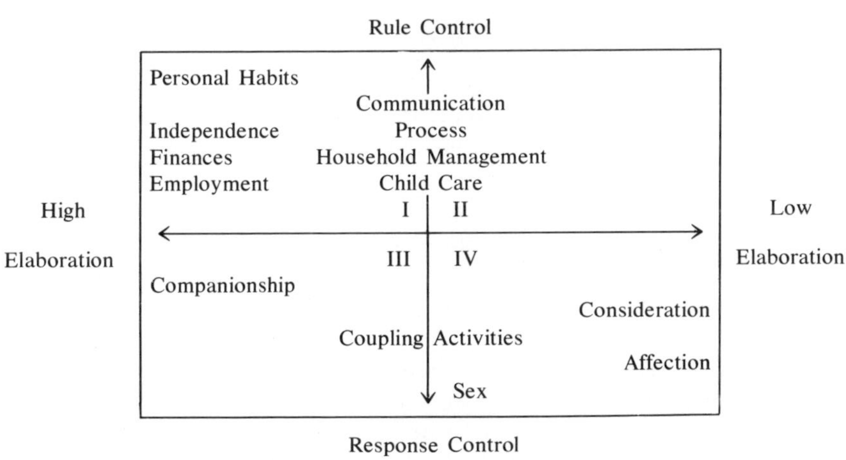

The 12 categories of marital interaction are located in the two-dimensional space created by the distinctions drawn between type of control (response vs. rule) and degree of cognitive elaboration. Quadrants I and III represent a high degree of cognitive elaboration, and Quadrants I and II a high degree of rule control of behavior.

cognitive elaboration) are destined for dull times, or worse, simply taking each other for granted until such time as someone starts acting out their "vague" dissatisfaction.

From these illustrative examples it would seem that intervention should not confuse modus operandi with long-range outcomes—means with ends. That is to say, while it may be necessary to teach some behavioral skills in a tit-for-tat manner (providing practice with the component parts of affectional behavior) it is unwise to encourage continued rule control for certain behaviors. Affectional exchange contracts, according to this analysis, would be most unacceptable to clients. However, it is precisely the inability to offer affection spontaneously that is troublesome to couples.

One can provide a strategic basis for such "training" thereby avoiding entirely the issue of intent. The therapist may decide that the couple should provide data on how well they follow his/her respective directions in providing a richly affectionate day for one another. The issue here is compliance with the therapist's assignment, not whether affection is real or tainted! In this sense the therapist has created a new dyadic problem: Can you people recognize affection when it occurs? Naturally this leads to the next step in intervention, that is, how to help *you* both make the necessary responses. Again, the focus is shifted from the bad intent of one partner and, by implication, the overwhelming capability of the other to accept affectionate behaviors. We combine a skills training problem with an attribution manipulation. Here again reframes are useful tactics to alter cognitive belief barriers.

The placement of the various categories of positive and negative marital interaction in the theoretical factor space also agrees with a clinically relevant prescription from communication theory cited by Stuart (1975): Positive messages are to be communicated both verbally and nonverbally, while negative messages are to be communicated only verbally. Spontaneous messages are more likely to be encoded nonverbally, so that the nonverbal communication of affection would be consistent with the meta message: "This affection is genuine." The more affectional behaviors are cognitively elaborated, the less likely they will appear spontaneous. That is, the more a message is edited, the less its judged spontaneity. Consideration, on the other hand, often increases in impact as a function of how much time and effort a person has expended on behalf of the other. Here a high degree of cognitive elaboration of some gesture is taken as genuine. When negative messages are restricted to verbal (but not nonverbal) channels, as in the upper left-hand quadrant of the figure, a high degree of cognitive elaboration and *rule control* are ensured, both of which tend to defuse the negative emotional impact of the communication. Compare "You lazy S.O.B." with "We have agreed that these housekeeping chores are to be shared." Withdrawal, sulking, or other nonverbal forms of expressing dissatisfaction are only informative in terms of their negative impact, but do little to help the interaction exit from an escalation loop.

The direct intervention approach of the earlier operant applications (Azrin et al., 1973) relied heavily upon interlocking reinforcing contingencies. Affection from husband was made contingent upon affection (or some related behavior) from wife; therapists explicitly formulated reciprocity exchange agreements that operated successfully because of the impact of the reinforcers selected. (The early token exchanges with couples were based on this same logic. See Hickok and Komechak, 1974.) Clients often evolve a new cognition from such response controlled changes, namely, "My spouse cares enough to participate in such a program." Thus, it is probably the case that spouses can bring about changes in one another's behaviors by use of response contingent arrangements (increasing rate of picking up dirty clothes by making laundry contingent upon clothes being in or near washing machine), but for most distressed couples, the overall therapeutic gain comes from the increase in benefits. Strategically, it is necessary to insure that headway is being made on the positive benefit side of the ledger as annoyances are eliminated.

Before categorizing the tactics of BMT within this same two-dimensional space (as a means of explicating therapist options), it will be useful to consider some of the research implications for the Response vs. Rule control distinction we have stressed throughout. Two major findings from the literature are relevant.

The first concerns the fact that couples are likely to be under reponse control for negative or aversive exchanges (Wills, Weiss, and Patterson, 1974; Jacobson and Waldron, 1979; Margolin, 1978). Both in terms of daily exchanges of behaviors (either labeled as Pleases and Displeases, or empirically derived reinforcing events), and in terms of coded interactions in the laboratory setting, there is evidence that negatives are under response contingent control. Clinically, one can see how readily couples escalate their negative exchanges in what starts out as a "discussion."

A second line of evidence deals with the fact that distressed couples "define" daily marital satisfaction in terms of the *absence* of negatives (Jacobson and Waldron, 1979). Wills et al. (1974) had shown earlier that negative behaviors (Displeases) accounted for more of the satisfaction variance than did positive exchanges, but Jacobson and Waldron have further specified the relationship for distressed couples. Clinically, in the Oregon program, we typically graph the relationship between daily satisfaction ratings (DSR) and frequency of Pleases and Displeases (Weiss and Margolin, 1977). There is a clear inverse relationship between DSR and frequency of Displeases, whereas there is no systematic relationship with frequency of Pleases. Distressed couples, it would seem, operate on the principle of "if it doesn't hurt it must be satisfying." Weiss (1978) has shown how such an orientation fits with the kind of aversive control procedures couples acquire; not being nagged, for example, is, for some distressed couples, the best they get.

It is important to note that the negative-going systems couples initially present can be eliminated readily by most direct interventions. Three recent outcome studies dealing with selected aspects of BMT techniques have shown that negative behaviors, measured by both self-report and behavioral techniques, are substantially reduced early on (Jacobson, 1977, 1978; Margolin and Weiss, 1978). In the Margolin and Weiss study, comparing two behavioral and one conjugal form of communication training, all treatment groups showed marked reductions in mean coded negative behaviors, even after a relatively short two session intervention.

Based on this evidence, it is reasonable to assume that couples are often caught up in a response-driven negative exchange paradigm that can be contained by the structure of the counseling itself. Being in marital therapy can provide an umbrella of stimulus control for couples that allows them to reduce the heavy emphasis on aversive control. It is not surprising, therefore, to find what looks like an escalation of problems, or worse, new problems after three or four sessions. Couples benefit from the reduction of negative exchanges but do not as yet have the means for dealing with the demands of intimacy.

Williams (1977) has built on these studies of the exchange of Pleases and Displeases by employing a continuous measure of the quality of a couple's time spent together. Rather than counting specific behavioral exchanges, she asked distressed (therapy) and nondistressed (happy) couples to rate fifteen-minute segments of the day as pleasant, neutral, and unpleasant. Additionally, she asked respondents to indicate what the spouse did that was pleasant, unpleasant, or what could have been done to make a neutral period pleasant. Although her samples were small and variability was often extreme, Williams provided some interesting data pertinent to contingency control of interactions.

While both therapy (distressed) and happy (nondistressed) couples showed interspouse agreement on time spent together, the happy couples showed significantly more agreement on quality of time together. The therapy couples, it would seem, were less in agreement about the transitions from one fifteen-minute interval to the next; one thought a negative period had been resolved, the other did not rate it this way.

The topography of "pleasant" and "unpleasant" behaviors derived from the spouse descriptions was of particular interest. For nondistressed couples pleasant time periods were associated with the *commission of positive* behaviors, whereas for distressed couples it was, once again, *the omission of negative* behaviors. ("For a change she didn't gripe at my coming home late.") The situation was reversed for unpleasant intervals; the happy couples cited omission of positive behaviors ("could have talked more to me and showed affection") while the therapy couple's cited commission of negative behaviors ("He was very rude to one of my friends").

Williams proposes a continuum ranging from Noncontingent Positives through Noncontingent Negatives (as the extremes) and with Contingent Positives and Contingent Negatives as the means. In a *post hoc* inspection of her data, she found that, for the two noncontingent extremes (positive and negative), it was not the behaviors of the spouse but rather the *spouse's presence* that determined the quality rating of the time together. Thus, the mean for ratio of positive to negative intervals for the two noncontingent groups was 104.5 to 1 and 4.5 to 1, respectively. These groups were also characterized by extremes in marital satisfaction ratings, and to be sure, two couples in the noncontingent negative group who sought divorces had ratios where the negatives exceed the positives! In both subgroups a lack of response contingency was noted; the spouses served as discriminative stimuli for either joy or unpleasantness.

The two intermediate groups (contingent positive or negative) showed mean positive to negative time ratios of 69.4 to 1 and 14.8 to 1, respectively. For the contingent positive subgroup, the happy couples cited specific positive events ("he fixed dinner") and the omission of expected positives ("could have shown affection"), while for the contingent negative subgroup, specific negative events triggered retaliation, for example, a wife "accidentally" burned dinner for her late-arriving husband.

From an interventionist point of view, it becomes necessary to increase the spouses' noncontingent positiveness, meaning that the presence of each becomes a discriminative stimulus for good feelings. During the early training stages, the spouses are likely to operate on a contingent negative exchange, but the therapist still has opportunity to reframe such events. A wife recently complained that her husband limited a soothing backrub to five minutes, which was supposed to alert the therapist to what an inadequate pleasure-giver he was. The therapist reframed this by suggesting that she so enjoyed his back-rubbing skills that she wanted much more of it! This was a deliberate attempt to increment positive sentiment by turning an implied criticism into a statement of dependency upon the other's pleasure giving.

We will conclude this section by categorizing the various intervention tactics according to the same two-dimensional space created in Figure 4, above. That is, our modules can be organized according to whether they emphasize response contingency or rule contingency *and* whether there is a high or low degree of cognitive elaboration associated with each.

1. *Objectification.* During early stages of therapy, objectification falls in the lower left quadrant, representing a high degree of elaboration of specific responses. Pinpointing, "I statements," becoming aware of specific pleasing exchanges, etc., all represent training in stimulus discrimination and response differentiation. In one sense it is a conscious effort at vocabulary building. Labeling situations that lead to fighting is another form of objectification, although the fighting cycle itself may be under relatively unelaborated response-contingency control.

2. *Support/Understanding.* Helping a couple learn the rudiments of supportive/understanding behavior (whether by maintaining eye contact, or use of paraphrasing, reflection, etc.) is initially an explicit response-contingent exercise. These functions should be moved toward the implicit side of the continuum in order to insure their authenticity for the couple. After they become somewhat "reflexive" responses, the goal is to create sufficient positive sentiment so that supportive exchanges function as a relatively unelaborated relationship rule. For example, "I am doing this for you because I have an obligation to be nice to you," is less rewarding than doing noncontingently and automatically for the other. Supportive responses that stay within the lower half of the space (Quadrants III & IV) are not as likely to persist as those located in the upper right quadrant.

3. *Problem Solving.* Problem solving reflects a high degree of elaboration and almost exclusive rule control. Couples should be aided in developing a modus operandi for working through choices, allocating resources, and taking action that will be accountable. Negotiated settlements fall into this category as well (the upper left quadrant). Some of the best techniques from the behavioral literature for problem-solving interventions have been described by Jacobson and Margolin (1979) in their treatment guide.

4. *Behavior Change.* The aim of behavior change is to provide a couple with techniques for change based upon positive control procedures. These can run the gamut from positive quid pro quo arrangements to very sophisticated forms of rule control. Jacobson (1978) has recently shown that of the two forms of contracting, "Good Faith" and Quid Pro Quo (Weiss, Birchler, and Vincent, 1974), there seem to be no empirical grounds for choosing one over the other, and, if contracting is to be employed, he favors the Quid Pro Quo arrangement because of its greater

simplicity. However, good faith contracting, especially when done as a bilateral contract (common relationship behavior change) provides very explicit forms of rule control. A couple can refer to their agreement rather than to the bad intentions of each.

Goal attainment scaling can also provide a highly elaborated form of rule control for instituting change. A couple can set goals for themselves and, by judiciously shaping increments of attainment, provide an effective means for positive control.

It is important to view one's intervention options as meeting desired outcomes of lasting competency. The aim in marital therapy is to provide the couple with a means of dealing with conflict and change that extends beyond the alleviation of a specific problem. However, as we have emphasized repeatedly, this means providing them with skills for maintaining the availability of relationship benefits. Couples work and love, and as strategic BMT practitioners, it is important to ensure training in both areas. One can, from this brief outline, select an intervention tactic with the full understanding that the goal is to move to a different quadrant of the control by elaboration space. As an heuristic we have suggested both those classes of behavior that fit better in certain quadrants and tactics to facilitate the reaching of specific goals.

IV. SUMMARY AND CONCLUSIONS

This chapter has presented the basis for a model of strategically oriented Behavioral Marital Therapy (BMT). Starting with the typical difficulties BMT has encountered in dealing with resistant couples, that is, couples who manage to frustrate the efforts of BMT techniques, it was concluded that BMT might become strategic in the sense of developing a theory of practice which incorporates the cognitive belief barriers to change. The main features of a strategic approach, relative to either a technique or tactic dominated approach, are the active role in planning and direction taken by the therapist in focusing outcome objectives and in creating situations which will produce the desired changes. Strategic therapies have become identified with the use of paradox, reframing, confusion, etc., but these represent but one subset of tactics which could be considered strategic in the broader sense employed here.

BMT becomes strategic when the theory of practice actively incorporates the ways in which couples cognitively elaborate their transactions. BMT has been characterized as a response-oriented change technology, one that has assumed that any necessary cognitive changes (changes in attitudes, etc.) would follow from changed behavioral transactions. Bandura's self-efficacy model was suggested here as a convenient way for distinguishing between the phases of the cognitive-behavioral interface descriptive of marital transactions. A modification of the Bandura paradigm was suggested: Dyad → Transaction → Outcome, whereby efficacy expectations refer to dyadic beliefs about the likelihood that some behavior is possible, that is, the Dyad → Transaction link. Outcome expectations modulate the link between Transaction and Outcome, and indicate whether the couple has the necessary skill capability, and whether they are capable of behavior that operates on the environment in a predictable fashion.

One of the major strengths of the BMT model has been its focus on competencies; relationships are built upon specific classes of outcomes or accomplishments. It is necessary for couples to (a) share a language which objectifies their transactions, (b) develop a support/understanding system, (c) be able to problem solve, and (d) effect behavior change in constructive ways. As stated, these outcomes or accomplishments pertain to outcome expectations or performance type skills, but they do not necessarily suggest anything about whether a given couple perceives itself as capable of these outcomes. Efficacy expectations may operate as "belief barriers" which impede acceptance of the behaviorally based skills in therapy.

Efficacy expectations, when applied to couples, can be analyzed in terms of attributions spouses make about causality, that is, why one person has done or failed to do something. They can be analyzed also by conceptualizing resistance to change in systems theory terms—in the notions of the patterning of transactions, and in the tactics of blame assignment which lock couples in power struggles. In terms of the proposed model we are suggesting that intervention at the level of efficacy expectations be thought of generically as cognitive-restructuring, and that strategic approaches (e.g., Haley, Watzlawick, Sluzki) are special cases of cognitive restructuring.

We then focused on the major tenant of BMT, exchange and reciprocity dynamics. An important distinction was drawn between short-term (quid pro quo) reciprocal exchanges, now seen as more characteristic of distressed relationships, and longer-term (bank-account model) exchanges, which seem to characterize non-distressed relationships. These two time-dependent modes can be coordinated with the behavioral distinctions between reinforcing- or stimulus-controlled behaviors. A system operating under reinforcing control is probably based on short-term quid pro quo exchanges, whereas a stimulus-controlled system is analogous to rule-controlled exchanges. It is the differences in how couples cognitively elaborate these two modes of transaction that are important for choice of intervention tactic. Response by response approach to problem solution is likely to foster sentiment about the other which is incompatible with the desired outcome of BMT: spouses will perceive "rewards" as being given because of obligation rather than a favorable evaluation of the spouse's worth. Thus the paradox: The strength of BMT, which lies in reinforcing-contingency control of behavior, flies in the face of cognitions about desirability in an intimate relationship.

A theoretical relationship was suggested between the two dimensions described by response vs. stimulus control and the degree to which a transaction is cognitively-elaborated by the partners. Overgeneralization is in evidence whenever a molecular response is highly elaborated cognitively (i.e., becomes a part of the efficacy expectations). Some classes of behavioral exchange (twelve are suggested as part of our model) are more likely to be accepted by spouses if they are viewed as spontaneous occurrences (e.g., affection). Encouraging verbal elaboration of affectional exchanges will dampen the reward value of such behaviors. On the other hand, the more cognitively a transaction is elaborated, the greater the likelihood that it becomes under rule control. The advantages of rule-controlled transactions are that they allow further cognitive processing to occur and thereby subvert escalating emotional reactions. The model attempts to suggest which kinds of transactions are best dealt with under stimulus- or response-controlled exchanges.

Among the particular implications of this type of integration of cognitive and behavioral aspects of BMT are the following:

1. Cognitive restructuring, as used here, defines those intervention tactics which are designed to alter efficacy expectations. This frontal attack on belief barriers, as it were, is designed in turn to facilitate client acceptance of the skills training that BMT has traditionally provided.
2. Specific techniques from the communications model of strategic therapy are useful to the extent that they define cognitive restructuring tactics. Whereas strategic therapy has been utilized as a means of quickly changing the nature of patterned interactions, its utility in the present model is as an adjunct to subsequent skills-oriented training of couples.
3. Careful assessment is needed to distinguish between those cases in which skill deficits are largely responsible for the difficulties a couple experiences, or whether the problem lies with their efficacy expectations. To be sure, these are not either or judgments in any given case, but rather matters of degree. Many behavioral assignments can be facilitated by judicious use of reframes. But the more serious problem faced by the BMT practitioner is the resistant couple who manages to avoid completing assignments. There are some promising leads as to how we might approach such a behavioral assessment task, that is, how we can identify those cases for whom substantial cognitive re-

structuring will be necessary. Among the early leads in this regard are methods for determining compliance with therapist suggestions, thereby providing a behavioral sample of the kinds of transactions that will be necessary for BMT to be effective.

The contributions of this particular formation are necessarily modest, since we have relatively little data on the effectiveness of cognitive restructuring with couples in combination with BMT. However, it is our judgment that strategically based BMT will be advanced only as we make explicit our theory of practice, setting forth propositions which can be tested empirically. As we attempt to work with cases of increasing difficulty we should expect to revise previously held hypotheses and also to generate exciting new ideas from the clinical endeavor itself. Thus, while this presentation has been excessively theoretical, it is hoped that such an effort will stimulate attempts to find better, empirically sound applications for those who might benefit from our services.

NOTES

1. Remarriage need not result in immediate benefits, nor any greater skillfulness. It does not follow necessarily that trait-like consistencies are responsible for the problems in second marriages.
2. The issue raised by Gurman is a separate technical problem which is beyond the focus of this chapter, but the reader may wish to review the status of this controversy; cf. Bandura, 1977, p. 104.

REFERENCES

Azrin, N., Naster, B., & Jones, R. Reciprocity counseling: A rapid learning-based procedure for marital counseling. *Behavior Research and Therapy,* 1973, *11,* 365–382.

Bandura, A. *Social learning theory*. Englewood Cliffs, N.J.: Prentice Hall, 1977.

Bentler, P. M., & Newcomb, M. D. Longitudinal study of marital success and failure. *Journal of Consulting and Clinical Psychology,* 1978, *46,* 1053–1070.

Bergin, A. E., & Lambert, M. J. The evaluation of therapeutic outcomes. In S. L. Garfield & A. E. Bergin (Eds.), *Handbook of psychotherapy and behavior change: An empirical analysis*. 2nd edition. New York: Wiley, 1978.

Bloom, B. L., Asher, S. J., & White, S. W. Marital disruption as a stressor: A review and analysis. *Psychological Bulletin,* 1978, *85,* 867–894.

DeShazer, S. J. Brief therapy with couples. *International Journal of Family Counseling,* 1978, *6,* 16–30.

Frank, J. D. *Persuasion and healing*. 2nd edition. Baltimore: Johns Hopkins University Press, 1973.

Frankel, A. S., Reilly, S., & Lert, A. A style variable in assertion training. *Cognitive Therapy and Research,* 1978, *2,* 289–292.

Gottman, J., Notarius, C., Gonso, J., & Markham, H. *A couple's guide to communication*. Champaign, Ill.: Research Press, 1976.

Gottman, J., Notarius, C., Markham, H., Bank, S., Yoppi, B., & Rubin, M. E. Behavior exchange theory and marital decision making. *Journal of Personality and Social Psychology,* 1976, *34,* 14–23.

Guerney, B. *Relationship enhancement.* San Francisco: Jossey-Bass, 1977.

Gurman, A. S. Contemporary marital therapies: A critique and comparative analysis of psychoanalytic, behavioral, and systems theory approaches. In T. J. Paolino, Jr. & B. S. McCrady (Eds.), *Marriage and marital therapy: Psychoanalytic, behavioral, and systems theory perspectives.* New York: Brunner/Mazel, 1978.

Gurman, A. S., & Kniskern, D. P. Behavioral marriage therapy: II. Empirical perspective. *Family Process,* 1978, *17,* 139–148. (a)

——— Research on marital and family therapy: Progress, perspective, and prospect. In S. L. Garfield & A. E. Bergin (Eds.), *Handbook of psychotherapy and behavior change: An empirical analysis.* 2nd edition. New York: Wiley, 1978.

Gurman, A. S., & Rice, D. G. (Eds.). *Couples in conflict: New directions in marital therapy.* New York: Aronson, 1975.

Haley, J. *Problem-solving therapy.* San Francisco: Jossey-Bass, 1976.

——— *Uncommon therapy.* New York: Ballantine Books, 1973.

Hickock, J. E., & Komechak, M. C. Behavior modification in marital conflict: A case report. *Family Process,* 1974, *13,* 111–118.

Jackson, D. D. Family rules: Marital quid pro quo. *Archives of General Psychiatry,* 1965, *12,* 589–594.

Jacobson, N. S. A review of research on the effectiveness of marital therapy. In T. J. Paolino, Jr. & B. M. McCrady (Eds.), *Marriage and marital therapy: Psychoanalytic, behavioral, and systems theory perspectives.* New York: Brunner/Mazel, 1978.

——— Behavioral treatments for marital discord: A critical appraisal. In M. Hersen, R. M. Eisler & P. M. Miller (Eds.), *Progress in behavior modification.* New York: Academic Press. In press.

——— Increasing positive behavior in severely distressed marital relationships: The effects of problem-solving training. Paper presented at the annual meeting of the Association for Advancement of Behavior Therapy, Atlanta, December, 1977.

——— Problem solving and contingency contracting in the treatment of marital discord. *Journal of Consulting and Clinical Psychology,* 1977, *45,* 92–100.

——— Specific and nonspecific factors in the effectiveness of a behavioral approach to the treatment of marital discord. *Journal of Consulting and Clinical Psychology,* 1978, *46,* 442–452.

Jacobson, N. S., & Margolin, G. *Marital therapy: Strategies based on social learning and behavioral exchange principles.* New York: Brunner/Mazel, 1979.

Jacobson, N. S., & Martin, B. Behavioral marriage therapy: Current status. *Psychological Bulletin,* 1976, *83,* 540–566.

Jacobson, N. S., & Waldron, H. Topographical and functional differences in the exchange of reinforcement and punishment between distressed and nondistressed couples. Unpublished manuscript, University of Iowa, 1978.

Jacobson, N. S., & Weiss, R. L. Behavioral marriage therapy: III. Critique: The contents of Gurman et al., may be hazardous to our health. *Family Process,* 1978, *17,* 149–163.

Johnson, S. J., & Alevizos, P. N. Strategic therapy: A systematic outline of procedures. Paper presented to the Ninth Annual Conference of the Association for the Advancement of Behavior Therapy, San Francisco, December, 1975.

Lewinsohn, P. M. Behavioral study and treatment of depression. In M. Hersen, R. M. Eisler & P. M. Miller (Eds.), *Progress in behavior modification.* New York: Academic Press, 1975.

Margolin, G. A sequential analysis of dyadic communication. Paper presented at the Association for the Advancement of Behavior Therapy, Atlanta, December, 1977.

Margolin, G., Christensen, A., & Weiss, R. L. Contracts, cognition, and change: A behavioral approach to marriage therapy. *The Counseling Psychologist,* 1975, *5,* 15–26.

Margolin, G., & Weiss, R. L. Comparative evaluation of the therapeutic components associated with behavioral marital treatments. *Journal of Consulting and Clinical Psychology,* 1978, *46,* 1476–1486.

Marks, I. Behavioral psychotherapy of adult neurosis. In S. L. Garfield & A. E. Bergin (Eds.), *Handbook of psychotherapy and behavior change: An empirical analysis.* 2nd edition. New York: Wiley, 1978.

Meissner, W. W. The conceptualization of marriage and family dynamics from a psychoanalytic perspective. In T. J. Paolino, Jr. & B. S. McCrady (Eds.), *Marriage and marital therapy: Psychoanalytic, behavioral, and systems theory perspectives.* New York: Brunner/Mazel, 1978.

Meyer, J. P., & Pepper, S. Need compatibility and marital adjustment in young married couples. *Journal of Personality and Social Psychology,* 1977, *35,* 331–342.

Murray, E. J., & Jacobson, L. I. Cognition and learning in traditional and behavioral psychotherapy. In S. L. Garfield & A. E. Bergin (Eds.), *Handbook of psychotherapy and behavior change: An empirical analysis.* 2nd edition. New York: Wiley, 1978.

Murstein, B. I., Cerreto, M., & MacDonald, M. G. A theory and investigation of the effect of exchange-orientation on marriage and friendship. *Journal of Marriage and the Family,* 1977, *39,* 543–548.

Olson, D. H. Marital and family therapy: Integrative review and critique. *Journal of Marriage and the Family,* 1970, *32,* 501–538.

Paolino, T. J., & McCardy, B. M. (Eds.). *Marriage and marital therapy: Psychoanalytic, behavioral, and systems theory perspectives.* New York: Brunner/Mazel, 1978.

Patterson, G. R., Weiss, R. L., & Hops, H. Training of marital skills: Some problems and concepts. In H. Leitenberg (Ed.), *Handbook of behavior modification and behavior therapy.* Englewood Cliffs, N.J.: Prentice Hall, 1976.

Rohrbaugh, M., Tennen, H., Press, S., White, L., Raskin, P., & Pickering, M. R.; Watzlawick, P. (discussant). Paradoxical strategies in psychotherapy. A symposium presented at the American Psychological Association Meetings, San Francisco, August, 1977.

Rosen, R. C., & Kopel, S. A. Penile plethysmography and biofeedback in the treatment of transvestite-exhibitionist. *Journal of Consulting and Clinical Psychology,* 1977, *45,* 908–916.

Sager, C. J. *Marriage contracts and couple therapy.* New York: Brunner/Mazel, 1976.

Sluzki, C. E. Marital therapy from a systems perspective. In T. J. Paolino, Jr. & B. S. McCrady (Eds.), *Marriage and marital therapy: Psychoanalytic, behavioral, and systems theory perspectives.* New York: Brunner/Mazel, 1978.

Stuart, R. B. An operant interpersonal program for couples. In D. H. L. Olson (Ed.), *Treating relationships.* Lake Mills, Iowa: Graphic Publishing, 1976.

——— Behavioral remedies for marital ills: A guide to the use of operant-interpersonal techniques. In A. S. Gurman & D. G. Rice (Eds.), *Couples in conflict: New directions in marital therapy.* New York: Aronson, 1975.

——— Operant interpersonal treatment for marital discord. *Journal of Consulting and Clinical Psychology,* 1969, *33,* 675–682.

Sundberg, N. D., Snowden, L. R., & Reynolds, W. M. Toward assessment of personal competence and incompetence in life situations. *Annual Review of Psychology,* 1978, *29,* 179–221.

Vincent, J. P., Harris, C. E., Illback-Cook, N., & Brady, C. P. Couples becoming parents: A behavioral-systems analysis of family development. In D. P. Rathjen & Foreyt, J. (Eds.), *Social competence: Interventions for children and adults.* Elmsford, N.Y.: Pergamon Press, forthcoming.

Watzlawick, P., Weakland, J., & Fisch, R. *Change: Principles of problem resolution*. New York: Norton, 1974.

Weiss, R. L. The conceptualization of marriage and marriage disorders from a behavioral perspective. In T. J. Paolino & B. J. McCardy (Eds.), *Marriage and marital therapy: Psychoanalytic, behavioral, and systems theory perspectives*. New York: Brunner/Mazel, 1978.

——— Strategies for couples' therapy. Paper presented to the Tenth Annual Convention of the Association for the Advancement of Behavior Therapy, New York, December, 1976.

Weiss, R. L., & Birchler, G. R. Adults with marital dysfunction. In M. Hersen & A. Bellack (Eds.), *Behavior therapy in the psychiatric setting*. Baltimore: Williams & Wilkins, 1978.

Weiss, R. L., Birchler, G. R., & Vincent, J. P. Contractual models for negotiation training in marital dyads. *Journal of Marriage and the Family*, 1974, *36*, 321–330.

Weiss, R. L., Hops, H., & Patterson, G. R. A framework for conceptualizing marital conflict, a technology for altering it, some data for evaluating it. In F. W. Clark & L. A. Hamerlynck (Eds.), *Critical issues in research and practice: Preceedings of the Fourth Banff International Conference on Behavior Modification*. Champaign, Ill.: Research Press, 1973.

Weiss, R. L., & Margolin, G. Marital conflict and accord. In A. R. Ciminero, K. S. Calhoun & H. E. Adams (Eds.), *Handbook for behavioral assessment*. New York: John Wiley & Sons, Inc., 1977.

Weiss, R. L., Ullmann, L. P., & Krasner, L. On the relationship between hypnotizability and response to verbal operant conditioning. *Psychological Reports*, 1969, *6*, 59–60.

Williams, A. M. The quantity and quality of marital interaction related to marital satisfaction: A behavioral analysis. Paper presented at the Midwestern Association of Behavioral Analysis (MABA) Meeting, Chicago, 1977.

Wills, T. A. Perceptions of clients by professional helpers. *Psychological Bulletin*, 1978, *85*, 968–1000.

Wills, T. A., Weiss, R. L., & Patterson, G. R. A behavioral analysis of the determinants of marital satisfaction. *Journal of Consulting and Clinical Psychology*, 1974, *42*, 802–811.

Research in Community and Mental Health

A Research Annual

Series Editor: **Roberta G. Simmons, Department of Sociology, University of Minnesota.**

The volumes in this annual series will present important original research contributions from leading investigators in the sphere of mental health. Although there will be a heavy sociological input, the contributions will be from a variety of disciplines reflecting the interdisciplinary character of work in this area.

Volume 1. **Published 1979** **Cloth** **Institutions: $ 32.00**
ISBN 0-89232-063-X **386 pages** **Individuals: $ 16.00**

CONTENTS:

Volume 2 continued on following page

Volume 2. **Spring 1980** **Cloth** **Institutions: $32.00**
ISBN 0-89232-152-0 **Ca. 375 pages** **Individuals: $16.00**

TENTATIVE CONTENTS: The Consequences of Teenage Motherhood for Mother, Child and Family, *Sheppard Kellam, Rebecca Adams, Hendricks Brown and Grant Blank.* **Work Experience and Psychological Change in the Transition to Adulthood,** *Jeylan T. Mortimer and Jon Lorence.* **Mattering: Inferred Significance and Self-Esteem,** *Morris Rosenberg and Claire McCullough.* **Toward the Development of a Two-Stage Procedure for Case Identification and Classification in Psychiatric Epidemiology,** *Bruce P. Dohrenwend, Barbara Dohrenwend and Patrick E. Shrout.* **Components of the Sex Difference in Depression: Stress vs. Reactivity,** *Lenore Sawyer Radloff and Donald S. Rae.* **Pubertal Development in Different School Settings: A Longitudinal Analysis of Early Maturers,** *Dale A. Blyth, Roberta G. Simmons, Edward F. Van Cleave, Richard Bulcroft and Diance Mitsch Bush.* **Follow-up Studies on the Families of Hyperactive Children,** *Lily Hechtman and Gabrielle Weiss.* **Adolescents and Violence: An Epidemiological Study of Suicide, Homicide and Accidents,** *Paul C. Holinger and Daniel Offer.* **Mental Health in the Post-Disaster Population of the Flood in Wilkes-Barre, Pennsylvania,** *Mary Evans Melick and James Logue.* **Epidemiologic Significance of Social Support Systems in Depression,** *Alfred Dean and Nan Lin.*